TYR
Myth—Culture—Tradition

TYR

Myth—Culture—Tradition

Edited by
Joshua Buckley and
Michael Moynihan

4

ULTRA
North Augusta, South Carolina
2014

TYR: Myth—Culture—Tradition
Volume 4, 2014
Editors: Joshua Buckley and Michael Moynihan.

Typeset by Joshua Buckley.

Contributors: Carl Abrahamsson, Alain de Benoist, Collin Cleary, Aaron Garland, Joscelyn Godwin, Jon Graham, Anthony Harberton, Steve Harris, Greg Johnson, Claude Lecouteux, James J. O'Meara, Nigel Pennick, Stephen Pollington, Christian Rätsch, Ian Read, Stephen C. Wehmeyer, and Markus Wolff.

Special thanks to Taylor Brode, David Brunner, Liberty Buckley, Edred, Cecilia Esposito, Arrowyn Craban Lauer, Ugnius Lioge, the John Michell Club, Annabel Moynihan, Claudia Müller-Ebeling, the Guerdjieff Foundation of Illinois, Cyndi Smith, Deborah Snyder and Synergetic Press, and Benjamin Vierling.

Note: The reader may notice occasional stylistic inconsistencies between articles, as we have retained conventional British spellings and puntuation at the request of some contributors.

©2014, Ultra Publishing. All rights reserved. Copyrights for individual articles rest with the respective contributors. No part of this journal may be reproduced, transmitted, or utilized in any form or by any means without the express written permission of the publishers and/or authors, with the exception of brief quotations embodied in literary articles or reviews. To contact the publishers or authors, write to the address below.

Additional copies of this volume are available for $25.00 postpaid in the USA or $50.00 postpaid elsewhere from:

Ultra
P.O. Box 6115
North Augusta, SC
29861

www.radicaltraditionalist.com
Email: elecampane@bellsouth.net

ISSN: 1538-9413
ISBN: 09720292-4-9
ISBN 13: 978-0-9720292-4-7

Contents

Editorial Preface...1

What is Religion?..5
by Alain de Benoist

What is Odinism?..61
by Collin Cleary

Traditional Time-Telling in Old England, and Modern........99
by Nigel Pennick

Garden Dwarves and House Spirits..........................123
by Claude Lecouteux

Geiler von Kaiserberg and the Furious Army.....................133
by Claude Lecouteux

On Barbarian Suffering..149
by Steve Harris

Germanic Art in the First Millennium.............................167
by Stephen Pollington

Rockwell Kent's Northern Compass.............................181
by Michael Moynihan

The Mead of Inspiration..219
by Christian Rätsch

The (Nine) Doors of Perception: Ralph Metzner on the Sixties, Psychedelic Shamanism, and the Northern Tradition..237
by Carl Abrahamsson and Joshua Buckley

Finding the Lost Voice of our Germanic Ancestors:
An Interview with Benjamin Bagby..261
by Joshua Buckley

The New Old Ways:
An Interview with Cult of Youth's Sean Ragon.....................287
by Joshua Buckley

Reviews: Music..303

Reviews: Books...329

About the Cover Artist..417

About the Editors and Contributors....................................421

Dedication..428

Editorial Preface

One of the most striking features of the Indo-European tradition is the idea of creation from the sacrifice of a primordial being. Many readers are probably familiar with this motif as it appears in Snorri Sturlason's *Gylfaginninning* and in the *Grímnismál*:

Of Ymir's flesh the earth was shaped
of his blood, the briny sea
of his hair, the trees   the hills of his bones.
out of his skull the sky.[1]

This cosmogony is reflected in the Vedic "Song of Purusa," the Middle Persian *Škend Gumānīg Wizār*, the tale of Atlas's transformation in Ovid's *Metamorphoses*, and in the Roman foundational myth, where the dismemberment of the primordial king Romulus figures prominently. The Indo-European comparative mythologist Bruce Lincoln has written extensively on this theme, and traces its dispersal through nearly three thousand years of written texts.[2] Even after the Christianization of Europe, the idea can be found in such unlikely places as the Old Russian "Discourse of the Three Saints," to Old Frisian and Middle Irish sources. Lincoln and other scholars have even sketched out a rough schematic of the homologies (or *alloforms*) that emerge from a close reading of this material, establishing correspondences such as flesh = earth, bone = mountains, and hair = plants. Even more strikingly, these homologies are interpreted on multiple levels, not the least of which establishes the unity of the human body as microcosm, with the universal, "cosmic man" who encompasses creation on the macrocosmic level. This idea survives in the hermetic tradition, and Antoine Faivre has identified the theory of correspondences (which he traces to Neo-Platonic notions of

---

1. *The Poetic Edda*, trans. Lee M. Hollander (Austin: University of Texas Press, 1962).
2. See Bruce Lincoln, *Myth, Cosmos, and Society*, (London: Cambridge University Press, 1986).

cosmic sympathy) as one of the four intrinsic characteristics of Western esotericism.

Of course, as with any system of correspondences, the relationship between the human body and the cosmic man—whose sacrifice both inaugurates and sustains creation—is a two-way street. This goes a long way towards illuminating the central Indo-European religious institution of sacrifice. As Tacitus tells us in recounting a human sacrifice enacted by the Semnones, sacrifice "celebrates the horrific origins." Much more than just a commemoration (like the Christian Eucharist), however, the ritual dismemberment of a sacrificial victim recapitulates the cosmogonic sacrifice, reaffirming and sustaining the process of creation. In this elegant dialectical interplay, the body itself becomes a powerful nexus in the unfolding of the sacred. Man is an active part of this process, right down to his very bones and blood.

This traditional conception of the body contrasts markedly with the extreme dualism inherent in the monotheistic religions, which have a long history of devaluing the corporeal world in favor of a purely transcendent conception of the holy. With no less catastrophic results, the process of secularization has turned this relationship on its head. Materialism (the dominant philosophy of Western modernity) completes the disjunction between matter and the sacred, but now it is the sacred that is diminished.

As radical traditionalists, we reject both of these alternatives in favor of a pagan holism that recognizes the seamless interconnection between the physical and the spiritual—beginning with the body itself. In many ways, this mirrors the concerns of the National Romantic, *völkisch*, and other counter-cultural movements that arose in the late nineteenth and early twentieth centuries. In both Eastern and Western Europe, and especially in bohemian centers like Ascona, the revival of paganism was closely intertwined with movements devoted to physical culture, natural foods, and *Lebensreform* (life-reform).[3] There was a recognition

---

[3]. On the countercultural atmosphere at Ascona, Switzerland, see Martin Green, *Mountain of Truth: The Counterculture Begins, 1900–1920* (Hanover: University Press of New England, 1986).

that these largely sensual pursuits could have a strongly spiritual component: they could bridge the false divide between matter and the sacred.

Anyone with eyes to see and ears to hear can tell you that the modern world is sick. The solution is neither a solipsistic retreat into an otherworldly mysticism, nor the groundless nihilism of the materialists. The solution is the resacralization of art and culture, of work and play, of the tribe and the community and the family and the home, of food and drink, of sex and the body. The system of correspondences encoded in the language of myth illustrates how the sacral order is mirrored in the terrestrial order, and not the least of all in our own selves. Our task is to take these "human, all too human" things, and to make them sacred once again.

Needless to say, it will not be easy—the delicate filaments uniting *cultus* and culture were severed long ago. Nevertheless, it is our hope that this journal—by promoting both spiritual and cultural reflection, as well as spiritual and cultural *opposition*—can contribute in some small way to making this vision a reality.

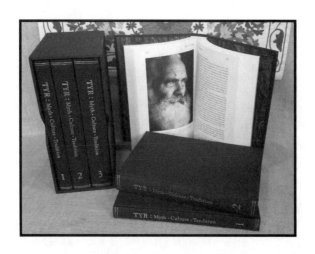

Now Available from ULTRA

The first three volumes of *TYR* are ready to ship in a handbound, burgundy cloth edition with French marbled endpapers. A slipcased set of all three issues is also available in a strictly limited edition of *five copies*. These deluxe editions will not be reprinted and will not be available from stores or other distributors. The slipcased edition is available for $300.00. Individual clothbound editions of *TYR* Volumes 1–3 are available for $85.00 each. Please inquire for availability and shipping rates.

TYR: Volume 2
Edited by Joshua Buckley and Michael Moynihan.
Volume 2, 2003–2004, ISSN 1538-9413, ISBN: 0-9720292-1-4, 6" X 9" perfectbound, illustrated, 432 pages. Contributors include Julius Evola, Alain de Benoist, Collin Cleary, Stephen McNallen, Nigel Pennick, John Matthews, Steve Pollington, Christian Rätsch, Peter Bahn, Markus Wolff, Stephen Flowers, and more. Bonus CD with Blood Axis, Coil, Fire + Ice, and others.
$22.00 ppd. (U.S.A.); $47.00 ppd. (International).

TYR: Volume 3
Edited by Joshua Buckley and Michael Moynihan.
Volume 3, 2007–2008, ISSN 1538-9413, ISBN-13: 0-9720292-3-0, 6" X 9" perfectbound, illustrated, 530 pages. Contributors include Thomas Naylor, Annie LeBrun, Pentti Linkola, Michael O'Meara, Alain de Benoist, Nigel Pennick, Thierry Jolif, Stephen Flowers, Joscelyn Godwin, Ian Read, Geza von Neményi, Gordon Kennedy, Christopher McIntosh, Sveinbjörn Beinteinsson, Vilius Rudra Dundzila, James Reagan, Collin Cleary, and more.
$25.00 ppd. (U.S.A.); $50.00 ppd. (International).

ULTRA - P.O. Box 6115 - North Augusta, South Carolina - 29861

www.radicaltraditionalist.com

What is Religion?

Alain de Benoist

Do we live in the age of the "death of God" or the "return of religion?" Religious beliefs seem to be crumbling, but we keep hearing about the resurgence of "fundamentalism." In fact, in Western Europe at least, there is more talk than ever about religion now that it has lost its grip on so many minds. These two facts are obviously not contradictory, since it is probably the relative decline of religious life that creates the mental distance necessary to study it. By venturing down this path in my turn, my intention is not to pronounce on the intrinsic truth of this or that religious belief, but on the meaning and status of the religious phenomenon itself. In other words: what is one really talking about, when one talks about religion?

Let us admit from the beginning that this approach encounters grave difficulties. To come right down to it, making belief an object of study can seem unbearable to a believer, who is inclined by nature to withdraw everything concerning faith from discussion. Asking about the origin of religion would then amount to adopting an irreligious attitude from the beginning. Here lies an initial dilemma. Can one understand a belief without sharing it? When speaking about a religion without believing in it oneself, is one condemned from the beginning to miss the point? But conversely, if one believes in a religion, what guarantee does one have of speaking about it objectively?

Another difficulty is that speaking about "religious life" or the "religious realm" very quickly falls into anachronism.[1] To isolate religion as a specific realm of social existence—a typically modern approach—contradicts the fact that, in ancient or traditional societies, religion is precisely not a realm separate from the others, but a dimension that cuts across and informs all domains of collective life. Besides, it should be recalled that

---

1. Cf. Jean Delumeau, ed., *Le fait religieux* [The Religious Phenomenon] (Paris: Fayard, 1993).

the majority of ancient languages do not have any specific term for what today we call "religion." As Emile Benveniste writes, "The Indo-Europeans conceived of religion as an omnipresent reality, not a separate institution, so they did not have a word for it."[2] And in many cultures today, the distinction between what is and is not religious remains very problematic. In Hinduism, for example, the idea of religion is expressed by the word *dharma*, which refers at the same time to the guiding foundation of both cosmos and society, and to life in accordance with it.

A religion, finally, is not only a belief, so it is dangerous to separate religion as a social or institutional fact from simple faith, or even from "religious feeling" in Benjamin Constant's sense of the term. Such separation is, however, very widespread today. Marcel Gauchet is not wrong to see this as "the very model of the 'ethnocentrism' of modernity, defining the truth of the phenomenon based on subjective or personal feeling. It is the modern individualistic vision of religion projected on the past."[3] Finally, matters are further complicated because religiosity is very unequally distributed among human beings. It can take quite varied forms, and the same religious practice can be lived very differently, and can even represent different things to those who invoke it.

I

Inquiring minds have to date counted more than eighty different definitions of religion, half of which come before the end of the eighteenth century.[4] Obviously I cannot examine them all here.

---

2. Emile Benveniste, *Le vocabulaire des institutions indo-européennes* [The Vocabulary of Indo-European Institutions], *vol. 2: Pouvoir, droit, religion* [Power, Right, Religion] (Paris: Minuit, 2001), 265; in English: *Indo-European Language and Society*, trans. Jean Lallot (Coral Gables: University of Miami Press, 1973).

3. Marcel Gauchet, *Un monde désenchanté?* (Paris: L'Atelier/Editions Ouvrières, 2004), 74. In English: *The Disenchantment of the World: A Political History of Religion*, trans. Oscar Burge (Princeton: Princeton University Press, 1999).

4. Cf. Michel Despland, *La religion en Occident: Evolution des idées et du vécu* [Religion in the West: The Evolution of Ideas and Experience] (Montreal:

I will merely observe that explanations of the existence of religion are mainly of three types: psychological, sociological, and biological.

Psychological Explanations

Psychological theories, for example, explain religion through man's desire to understand and control natural phenomena. The explanatory power of religion, by giving a supernatural explanation of such phenomena, offers man greater control over his environment, reducing his fear or anxiety. Relieving anguish, religion provides hope or certainty that can compensate for the risks and misfortunes of life, or help one bear them; it renders the idea of death less unbearable; in short, it brings both comfort and consolation. But it does so at the price of an alienation of the spirit, one of the first accounts of which comes from Ludwig Feuerbach. Characterizing religion as both a veil of ignorance and a "dream of the human spirit," Feuerbach asserted, in the early nineteenth century, that God is only an idealized man, apprehended in an illusory manner in an objective form. Religious alienation is man's attribution of his own essence to something else.

For Marx, religious belief is also an alienation of the human spirit. It certainly gives meaning to existence, but by giving men a "false consciousness" of reality. The religious world is a "reflection of the real world,"[5] but a deformed reflection—which makes it possible to describe religion as an ideology. Marx's argument is not on the level of ordinary materialism or atheism, strictly speaking. He does not, moreover, raise the question of God. "Religious misery," he writes, "is on the one hand an expression of real misery and on the other hand a protest against real misery."[6] "Religious misery" is due to the fact that in religion

---

Fides, 1979); Jean-Marc Tetaz et Pierre Giesel, eds., *Théories de la religion* [Theories of Religion] (Geneva: Labor et Fides, 2002).
5. Karl Marx, *Das Kapital*, I, 1, 1.
6. Karl Marx, *Introduction to the Critique of Hegel's Philosophy of Right*, January 1844.

"Vater verzeih' ihnen! Sie wissen nicht, was sie thun" [Father, forgive them, for they know not what they do] by Karl Wilhelm Diefenbach (1887).

man strips away his own qualities and attributes them to God, and convinces himself that his sufferings are in a certain manner justified. In this way, religion is the "opium of the people": it facilitates the oppression of the dominated class by making it accept the fate imposed upon it by the dominant class; it disarms rebellious inclinations by giving man the assurance of an imaginary happiness, specifically, of a consolation in the beyond. But at the same time, religion also expresses a protest and testifies to an aspiration toward a better world. It is thus fundamentally ambivalent. Hence this other formula of Marx: "The abolition of religion as an illusory happiness of the people is the demand for its real happiness."[7]

Freud interprets religion as both the disguised expression of uncontrolled desires that are projected as illusions, that is, as a repressed hallucination, and as a model of "absolute infantile dependence" upon a Father in relation to whom humanity has not yet grown up, or as a form of narcissistic regression of adults towards the emotions of childhood. Before the trials of life, man appeals to an ideal paternal figure who is supposed to give him protection and support. Religion, Freud writes in *Civilization and its Discontents*, is a "collective obsessional neurosis" universally widespread, an illusion born of the necessity in primitive society for moderating certain aggressive and destructive aspects of human nature. The expression of an interior conflict between our conscious aspirations and our unconscious desires, religion is defined above all as a source of guilt and anxiety.

For Nietzsche too, religion is born "from fear and need," which make it impossible to think it contains the smallest truth.[8] Nietzsche's approach is both psychological and genealogical: psychological insofar as it wishes to make psychology the queen of sciences, "which the other sciences have the function of serving and preparing for,"[9] and genealogical in the sense that, for him,

---

7. Let us note that materialism does not necessarily entail metaphysical atheism, but rather agnosticism. Cf. Yvon Quiniou, *Athéisme et matérialisme aujourd'hui* [Atheism and Materialism Today] (Nantes: Pleins Feux, 2004), who argues that materialism pronounces on our relation to Being, but not on Being itself. Engels wrote: "Being is, altogether, an open-ended question starting from the point where our horizon stops" (*Anti-Dühring* [Paris: Editions Sociales, 1973], 27).
8. Cf. Friedrich Nietzsche, *Human, All Too Human*, §110.
9. Nietzsche, *Beyond Good and Evil*, § 23.

bringing to light the origin of a religious belief is equivalent to its refutation. As everyone knows, for Nietzsche, it is Christianity above all that is targeted as a religion whose morals are directly antagonistic to the values of life. Nietzsche judges the Christian religion as pathogenic: it causes a "degeneration" of humanity by leading it to devalue all that concerns "life" on behalf of an imaginary afterworld.

Freud, Marx, and Nietzsche all assert that religion has to disappear. To hasten the end of religious beliefs, Freud once even called for a "dictatorship of reason," by means of which psychoanalysis would allow man to regain control of his unconscious and finally grow up.[10] The communist revolution, according to Marx, will provide man the opportunity to take back what is his own and thus destroy the social need for divine compensation for "real distress." For Nietzsche, finally, a humanity freed from the illusions of the afterworld will discover that the suprasensible world is without causal power, that it "does not grant any life."[11] Thus we are dealing here with a fundamentally hostile attitude toward religion.

Other psychologists, on the contrary, stressed the psychological aid religion can give individuals. William James, in *The Varieties of Religious Experience*, a book that has remained famous since its publication in 1902, makes religion a source of personal well-being, which remedies morbid inclinations and psychological distress.[12] James defines religion above all as a personal experience, which explains why he is interested mainly in the burning and spontaneous enthusiasm of converts. He asserts that religion favors mutual aid and psychological and social support, confers moral comfort, gives meaning to life, and offers emotional

---

10. Freud wrote: "It is our best hope for the future that the intellect—the scientific spirit, reason—will eventually attain a dictatorship over the psychic life of man!" ("*Sur une 'Weltanschauung'*" ["On a 'World-view'"] in *Nouvelles conférences d'introduction à la psychanalyse* [New Introductory Lectures on Psychoanalysis] (Paris: Gallimard, 1984), 228–29.
11. Nietzsche, *Human, All Too Human*, 1, § 133.
12. William James, *The Varieties of Religious Experience* (New York: Longman, 1902). Cf. also Charles Taylor, *Varieties of Religion Today: William James Revisited* (Cambridge: Harvard University Press, 2002).

experiences that can be a source of pleasure and self-esteem.

More recently, the alleviating virtues of religious belief have also been scientifically recognized and studied. One can demonstrate, for example, that prayer, which does nothing to achieve its object, nevertheless soothes the mind, lowers the blood pressure and heart rate, reduces the level of adrenaline, and improves the immune system. If one believes a study published in May of 2000 by Michael McCullough and William Hoyt, believers even enjoy a slightly greater longevity than nonbelievers.[13]

For other researchers, religion has a psychologically positive role because it gives meaning to existence. It answers ultimate questions, thus justifying our presence in the world. This distinction between religion as an aspect of mental well-being and as an answer to the quest for meaning duplicates that drawn by G. W. Allport in 1950 between the "extrinsic" and "intrinsic" value of religion.[14] It is a purely instrumental and utilitarian approach to religion.

In recent years, scientific psychology has taken an interest in religious phenomena. To this end, the most commonly used techniques are measuring cerebral activity by magnetic resonance imaging and studying the effect of certain substances on the brain. One can place in this category all work resulting from progress in the neurosciences, in particular those carried out beginning in the 1990s by Jeffrey L. Saver and John Rabin, which made it possible to determine the cerebral areas most receptive to religious mental activity.[15]

Thus certain researchers, such as anthropologist Alan Fiske,

---

13. In 2002, the psychiatrist David B. Larson, of Duke University in North Carolina, after having assembled 42 medical studies carried out between 1977 and 1999 on nearly 126,000 people, also believed himself able to show that believers live on average 29% longer than unbelievers. He too concluded from this that belief is a remedy against anguish and anxiety.
14. G. W. Allport, *The Individual and His Religion: A Psychological Interpretation* (New York: Macmillan, 1950). Allport's hypothesis was that the extraverted individuals were especially sensitive to religion's "extrinsic" aspect, and the introverted individuals to its "intrinsic" aspect.
15. Cf. Jeffrey L. Saver and John Rabin, "The Neural Substrates of Religious Experience," *Journal of Neuropsychiatry and Clinical Neurosciences* (1997): 498–510.

liken mystical transport to temporal lobe epilepsy (for epileptics are often very religious), or even interpret religious ritual as a benign but systematized form of automatic or repetitive behaviors characteristic of obsessive-compulsive disorder. The latter merely represents a pathological "amplification" of the former. In both cases, failure creates a feeling of guilt or anxiety.

Other specialists, like Eugene D'Aquili and Andrew Newberg, the inventors of the concept of "neurotheology," after having measured the cerebral activity of accomplished meditators—Tibetan Buddhists or Franciscan nuns at prayer—have identified the neuronal bases of mystical transport in our right and left posterior and superior parietal lobes. The "oceanic" feeling of fusion with the world frequently reported by mystics corresponds to a specific state of the brain, characterized by a drop in the activity of the area of the parietal neocortex responsible for spatial orientation. In a famous experiment in cerebral imaging carried out in 2001 by Andrew Newberg of the nuclear medicine clinic of the University of Pennsylvania, the deeper the meditation, the more the zone of the superior parietal cortex situated in the rear part of the upper cranium is deactivated.[16] Visionary mysticism (Theresa of Avila, Hildegard of Bingen, Catherine of Siena) has also been the subject of many psychiatric studies. Trances, altered states of consciousness, and the like have also been studied in the same way.

Other psychological studies concern the distribution of religiosity. It is known, for example, that in all times and places, women believe and practice religion more than men, a difference that remains unchanged in societies where women work. Various hypotheses have been advanced to explain this phenomenon.[17]

---

16. Eugene D'Aquili and Andrew Newberg, *The Mystical Mind* (Minneapolis: Fortress Press, 1999) and *Why God Won't Go Away* (New York: Ballantine Books, 2001). All this work was recently reviewed by Patrick Jean-Baptiste, *La biologie de Dieu: Comment les sciences du cerveau expliquent la religion et la foi* [The Biology of God: How Brain Science Explains Religion and Faith] (Paris: Agnès Viénot, 2003).
17. Cf. Rodney Stark, "Physiology and Faith. Addressing the 'Universal' Gender Difference in Religious Commitment," *Journal for the Scientific Study of Religion* 3 (2002): 495–507; Peter Hills, Leslie J. Francis, Michael Argyle, and

It has also been demonstrated that neurotic personalities (more numerous among women than men) are the most drawn to religiosity, in contrast to psychotic personalities (more numerous among men than women).

A Swedish research team has highlighted the role of certain chemical receptors, called 5HT1A. Situated in a category of neurons known as "serotoninergic," these receptors lower the quantity of serotonin released in the brain. The lower the level of these receptors, the higher the serotonin level, thus the greater the propensity to religiosity. The most religious individuals would thus have a higher serotonin level in the brain.

Twin studies, finally, have also confirmed the strong heritability of the religious temperament.[18]

These explanations of a psychological nature are certainly not without interest, but nevertheless remain rather unsatisfactory. First of all, as one can see, their conclusions are rather contradictory. Undoubtedly religion can in certain cases alleviate anguish or relieve anxiety, but it can just as easily strengthen them, in particular by maintaining a feeling of guilt. The religious universe can also prove terrifying, as witnessed by the title—*Fear*

Chris J. Jackson, "Primary Personality Traits Correlates of Religious Practice and Ortientation," in *Personality and Individual Differences* 36 (2004): 61–73. A neuropsychiatrist like Rhawn Joseph (*The Transmitter to God* [Berkeley: University of California Press, 2001]) does not hesitate to try to explain the greater religiosity of the women by cerebral anatomo-physiological differences: women's amygdalae have more cells, consequently their commissure, which joins together the two cerebral hemispheres, is also thicker. However, this core is mainly responsible for emotions and anxiety. Being more emotive, women would be more inclined than men to seek comfort in religion. Cf. also Jean-Baptiste, *La biologie de Dieu*, 278–79. Other explanations have obviously been offered.

18. Cf. N. G. Waller, B. A. Kojetin, T. J. Bouchard, D. T. Lykken, and A. Tellegen, "Genetic and Environmental Influences on Religious Interests, Attitudes, and Values. A Study of Twins Reared Apart and Together," *Psychological Science* 2 (1990): 138–42; T. J. Bouchard, M. McGue, D. Lykken, and A. Tellegen, "Intrinsic and Extrinsic Religiousness: Genetic and Environmental Influences and Personality Correlates," *Twin Research* 2 (1999): 88–98. The religiosity of twins was also studied by the psychologist Laura Koenig, of the University of Minnesota. The results of the survey, which related to 169 pairs of monozygotic twins, were published in the *Journal of Personality* in 2005.

and Trembling—of a book in which Søren Kierkegaard tried to define the true content of Christian revelation. Moreover, one can show that the correlation between mysticism and happiness is actually negative.[19] As for those who find serenity of soul in the religious life, perhaps they already have a natural predisposition to serenity.

On the political level, religion is no less ambivalent. It can certainly be employed by power to legitimize its control—for example, the idea of "divine right" or the appeal to the values of obedience and submission to disarm social conflicts. But many movements of social revolt—from the Peasants' War to liberation theology—also found a powerful motive for action in religion. This is why Ernst Bloch refused to treat religion as a simple historical "residue" founded on ignorance of the true dynamics of phenomena and, developing another aspect of Marx's thought, was interested above all in religion's power to challenge, the "revolutionary" core of the Messianic promise.

Scientific psychology is only marginally informative. To observe what occurs in a brain of someone who has intense thoughts, and to note that these activate specific neural networks, ultimately tells us very little about the nature of religion.

Sociological Explanations

If psychological explanations deal chiefly with religious feeling, sociological explanations are interested above all in religion as an institution and source of social cohesion. Thus they are systematically more positive toward religion—all while retaining an instrumental viewpoint. Insofar as social cohesion is regarded as good, religion appears likely to contribute to it. Perhaps what it says is false, but it still plays a positive role in the life of human communities. In connection with this idea, it is customary to recall that the word "religion" comes from Latin *re-ligere*, "to reconnect." This etymology, which first appears in the Christian

---

19. Cf. Michael Argyle and P. Hills, "Religious Experiences and Their Relations with Happiness and Personality," *The International Journal for the Psychology of Religions* 10 (2000).

author Lactanius, is in fact quite probably false. Cicero gave the valid derivation, from *re-legere*, "to re-read, to gather," which refers to the ritual role of re-reading formulas and traditional texts, symbolic acts that always amount to founding religious life on what has already been: the emphasis is upon a tradition to which it is advisable to remain faithful ("fidelity" comes from *fides*, as does the word "faith"). However, it is quite true that religion connects, and that it even connects doubly—man to man and society to the divine—starting from a distinction between the visible and the invisible, sacred and profane.

The prototype of sociological explanation was given by Durkheim in his book *The Elementary Forms of Religious Life*, published in 1912. For Durkheim, social reality is never reducible to a sum of individual realities. Thus, according to Durkheim, men maintain society by religious worship, in a quasi-consubstantial relationship with the sacred. At the risk of falling into circular reasoning, Durkheim thus suggests that there is a practical consubstantiality between religion and society. "In religion," he writes, "I see only society, transfigured and thought symbolically."[20] Religion is thus defined at bottom as a kind of hypostasis of the social world, as the symbolic representation of a given social order. Fundamentally structuring social life and politics, religion is only a projection of society, a means of survival.

At first sight, this approach appears more convincing, initially because it highlights the eminently collective dimension of religious activity, and because it can hardly be denied that religion once played a role in framing and structuring society in general. As Jean-Paul Willaime writes, "a religious system produces social bonds, not only by causing specific networks and groupings (institutions, communities), but also by defining a mental universe through which individuals and communities express a certain conception of man and the world in a given society."[21]

---

20. Emile Durkheim, *Les formes élémentaires de la vie religieuse* (Paris: PUF, 1994). In English: *The Elementary Forms of Religious Life*, trans. Joseph Ward Swain (New York: The Free Press, 1965).
21. Jean-Paul Willaime, *"La religion: un lien social articulé au don"* ["Religion: A Social Bond Articulated with the Gift"], *Revue du MAUSS*, no. 22 (2003), 260.

Religion, in other words, above all gives meaning as it creates bonds. Whatever the truth value of its contents, by creating bonds it plays a positive role in the existence of the human society. This is why, whereas many psychologists see religion as a harmful illusion, many sociologists see it instead as a useful fiction. (Let us recall here that an illusion is not the same thing as an error.)

Recently, however, Marcel Gauchet has vehemently protested the idea of the consubstantiality of religion and society. He bases this on the concept of heteronomy. Heteronomy can be summarized as the idea that it is for the sake of the gods, for what is beyond the visible world, that men must be what they are, an idea that consequently limits drastically their political ability to govern themselves. Gauchet defines religion as an "economy of the subjection of men to what is higher than them,"[22] as "man's rejection of his own creative power, the radical denial that the human world, such as it is, matters—the transfer to the invisible world of the reasons governing the organization of the community of the living."[23] Religion, thus defined as "the organization of heteronomy," also becomes a fundamental form of alienation.

This heteronomy, adds Gauchet, results from a voluntary initial choice, which led men to place themselves under the dependence of the gods. Gauchet thus disputes that there is a religious disposition in human nature. Religion, according to him, had a beginning and will most probably have an end. It is not an anthropological dimension constitutive of our species, but just a phase of our history. There is, he writes, "no form of creative necessity at the basis of religion, such that the collective could not exist without it." "The religious," he says, "does not derive from any anthropological facts; it is a matter of convention."[24] Religion is "in the strongest sense of the term, a fact of *institution*, a commitment of human society to heteronomy."[25] It is this that enables him to interpret Western modernity as a vast

---

22. Gauchet, *Un monde désenchanté?*, 183.
23. Marcel Gauchet, *La démocratie contre elle-même* [Democracy Against Itself] (Paris: Gallimard, 2002), 33.
24. Gauchet, *La démocratie contre elle-même*, 30, 33.
25. Luc Ferry and Marcel Gauchet, *Le religieux après la religion* [The Religious after Religion] (Paris: Grasset, 2004), 59.

process of moving from heteronomy, a slow march towards the acquisition of autonomy.

Gauchet's writings are often remarkable, but this thesis strikes me as debatable. First of all, the idea that if a society is more political it is less religious already gives one pause. For Gauchet, in traditional society there is both total submission to the gods and maximum neutralization of politics. All that is given to politics is thus taken from religion. However, this is clearly not true of the Greco-Roman world, as Gauchet himself admits. In European antiquity, one finds an interpenetration of political or state functions and religious functions, both in the exercise of the civil power and in military functions. In Rome, the very exercise of power is of a divine nature. And when the Greeks invented democracy in the fifth century B.C.E., they did not thereby cease to believe in their gods. To Gauchet's view, one could oppose here the opinion of Cornelius Castoriadis who, far from placing all religions on the side of heteronomy, wrote that "there is opposition between the monotheistic tradition as a tradition of heteronomy, and the genuine Greek tradition, or democracy as a tradition of autonomy."[26]

In addition, as we have seen, Gauchet asserts that the "commitment to heteronomy," to which he would reduce religious phenomena, resulted from an arbitrary choice to which men are not bound at all. Thus one wonders how and why, in the past, the same choice was made everywhere. If there is no universal need for religion, how is it that all ancient societies were religious? Doesn't the fact that such a "commitment" was adopted in a systematic way lead one to think instead that it by no means resulted from a choice, but could only be the consequence of a certain anthropological propensity?

Gauchet himself recognizes that "it is quite necessary that there is something like an anthropological substrate from which human experience is capable of being instituted and defined under the sign of religion" and which is a "cardinal phenome-

---

26. Cornelius Castoriadis, *Ce qui fait la Grèce* [What Made Greece], *vol. 1: D'Homère à Héraclite. Séminaires 1982–1983* [From Homer to Heraclitus. Seminars 1982–1983] (Paris: Seuil, 2004), 35.

non."²⁷ He speaks, likewise, of an "anthropological core which has supported religion through the millennia" which is "destined to persist,"²⁸ which somewhat contradicts his thesis. Elsewhere, he defines this "core" as the "bundle of conditions and propensities that allowed the existence of such a religious being, which is in reality a historical creature."²⁹ The last part of the sentence shows that the ambiguity persists, for it is difficult for the same phenomenon to be "anthropological" and "historical" at the same time.

Biological Explanations

This is where the biologists come in. On the principle that any universal human behavior, independent of culture, is likely to have a biological basis connected to the very definition of the species, they advance their own explanations. In recent years, a whole series of works, mostly in English, have proposed to illuminate the "biological basis" of religion.³⁰

In general, this work connects religion to the eminently social character of mankind. Man is a social animal: human beings spontaneously form groups where a certain degree of mutual

---

27. Ferry and Gauchet, *Le religieux après la religion*, 60.
28. Ferry and Gauchet, *Le religieux après la religion*, 109.
29. Gauchet, *Un monde désenchanté?*, 19.
30. Cf. R. D. Alexander, *The Biology of Moral Systems* (New York: Aldine de Gruyter, 1987); Robert Wright, *The Moral Animal: The New Science of Evolutionary Psychology* (New York: Pantheon, 1994); "The God Gene: Does Our Deity Compel Us to Seek a Higher Power?," *Time Magazine*, October 2004 ; "Pourquoi Dieu ne disparaîtra jamais" ["Why God will never Disappear"], *Science et vie* (August 2005): 47–66; Paul Bloom, "Is God an Accident?," *Atlantic Monthly*, December 2005; Jesse M. Bering, "The Cognitive Psychology of Belief in the Supernatural," American Scientist, March–April 2006. The anthropologist Stewart Elliott Guthrie for his part interprets religion as resulting from a systematized anthropomorphic projection, then explains that this anthropomorphism is explained by the fact that people "conceive the world according to their own interests" (Faces in the Clouds: A New Theory of Religion, [New York: Oxford University Press, 1993]). Cf. also Nico M. van Straalen and Jair Stein, "Evolutionary Views on the Biological Basis of Religion," in Willem B. Drees, ed., *Is Nature Ever Evil? Religion, Science and Value* (London: Routledge, 2003), 321–29.

confidence enables them to cooperate with one another, but also to oppose collectively members of other groups. Biology and evolutionary psychology explain the differences and similarities within the human race with hypotheses related to the course of evolution. Certain behaviors, but also certain principles or ideas, would have been selected in the course of evolution because they confer an adaptive advantage on those who adopted them over those who did not. From this point of view, religion would have an "adaptive value" because it rests on principles that pressure the individual to subordinate his own interests to the interests of the group, thus tightening the social bond and supporting the transmission of cultural achievements. The rules of conduct imposed by religion would facilitate the co-operation and the mutual understanding necessary to common life.

The biologist David Sloan Wilson is one of those who adopts this approach. Maintaining that natural selection acts fundamentally upon groups, and not on individuals or their genes (as the "orthodox" Darwinians claim), he describes religions as collective "organizations" that confer on their members advantages in terms of survival and reproduction, in particular by leading individuals to adopt co-operative forms of behavior for the benefit of the groups to which they belong. These behaviors, if not reciprocated, would prove disadvantageous for them. Religion would thus contribute to strengthening altruism, which leads Sloan Wilson to see it as a kind of "mega-adaptation," a "system of complex regulation that links members of a group to each other and make it a functional unity."[31]

Daniel C. Dennett[32] also claims that the emergence of religion corresponds to a natural adaptation that favored the reproductive success of the species, and that religion then evolved, just like language, to ensure its own survival amid ceaseless cultural changes. Thus for him religion is a cultural phenomenon directed by the natural selection processes controlling evolution: it would

---

31. David Sloan Wilson, *Darwin's Cathedral: Evolution, Religion, and the Nature of Society* (Chicago: University of Chicago Press, 2002), 25.
32. Daniel C. Dennett, *Breaking the Spell: Religion as a Natural Phenomenon* (London: Allen Lane/Penguin, 2006).

be "evolutionarily advantageous" to believe.

Other researchers instead stress the tendency of man to adhere to rituals. From an ethological perspective, rituals make it possible to sublimate certain instincts or passions, thus disarming aggressive behaviors. In addition, the rituals have the clear effect of strengthening the bond that exists between those who practice them.

Another more original theory was proposed by the Lacanian philosopher Dany-Robert Dufour. Though describing himself as a convinced atheist, he posits that man is necessarily a "religious being" and claims "to construct a new proof of the very existence of God." "This proof," he writes, "will have to be presented in the form of an *atheistic* proof of the existence of God, the first of this type and the last possible in the order of proofs."[33] Actually, it does not prove the objective existence of God, but his real existence in the human spirit: "I hope to show that the existence of God in the mind of men is a structural necessity"[34] determined by the bio-anthropological specificity of the human phenomenon.

Dufour finds this specificity in the thesis of the *neoteny* of man, a thesis stated by the Dutch anatomist Louis Bolk in the 1920s. The doctrine of neoteny (or "fetalization") conceives of man as a "premature" being, who only reaches his complete development relatively late after his birth, thus preserving through most of his life juvenile characteristics that are only temporary and transitory in other animals. This theory is accepted today by many researchers.

This initial "incompleteness" of man—which goes hand in hand with a considerable lengthening of the period of mothering, a long period of sexual latency, and slow rate of growth—means that man, throughout his existence, lacks most of the internal rules of behavior that other species have. His instincts not being programmed with knowledge of their objects, his existence is

---

33. Dany-Robert Dufour, *On achève bien les hommes: De quelques conséquences actuelles et futures de la mort de Dieu* [They Shoot Men too, Don't They?: On Some Current and Future Consequences of the Death of God] (Paris: Denoël, 2005), 12.
34. Dufour, *On achève bien les hommes*, 15.

more problematic: "All the animals are equipped by nature, man is without equipment."[35]

To guide themselves and actualize themselves, men must invent a "new nature," which can be made legitimate only by supposing the existence of a higher invisible being. A great symbolic figure thus controls his imagination, fictional perhaps, but nevertheless vital for him: "God is the necessary supposition of the human neonate."[36] Therefore man is the only animal who has a genuinely symbolic imagination.

The problem, consequently, is knowing what range of real autonomy can profit a man who, in himself, "killed God": "Does the death of God, liberating man from all his inhibitions, not set in motion the Promethean project to the point of bringing about his own death?"[37] In Lacanian terms, we would have to say that God "is absent in his place"—that he is present in his absence, that he is there to the very extent that he is not there.

Thus, as with most of the sociological explanations, religion is credited with some virtue. Some biologists, however, do not share this viewpoint.

Steven Pinker, for example, while accepting the idea that religions could once have had an adaptive value for individuals or groups, thinks that this value disappeared with the emergence of critical reason and the growth of scientific knowledge. He adds that the thesis according to which religion would have appeared in human society because it would be useful for the cohesion of groups or would give moral comfort to individuals, does not explain why the human spirit should invent supernatural entities to comfort itself, or why the belief in invisible divinities would be, biologically speaking, a better means of ensuring the cohesion of the communities or groups than confidence, friendship, honesty, and solidarity.[38]

Another well-known researcher, Richard Dawkins, who is a

---

35. Dufour, *On achève bien les hommes*, 23.
36. Dufour, *On achève bien les hommes*, 89.
37. Dufour, *On achève bien les hommes*, 342.
38. Cf. Steven Pinker, "The Evolutionary Psychology of Religion," annual lecture of the Freedom from Religion Foundation, Madison, Wisconsin, October 29, 2004.

virulent propagandist of atheism as well as the inventor of the concept of the "selfish gene," holds that religions today have lost all usefulness, because whatever good they have done can henceforth be assured by other means. He goes further, since he does not hesitate to see in religion a true mental pathology, resulting from a dysfunction of the human brain. Dawkins speaks of "memetic" diseases, cognitive distortions altering the processing of external data that the brain normally accomplishes through its symbolic, logical, and linguistic capacities. Religious beliefs would be "mental viruses" living, like their biological counterparts, at the expense of the cerebral cells that lodge them and transmitting themselves from generation to generation by means of psychological, social, and cultural indoctrination. This is also the opinion of James Watson, who was one of the "discoverers" of the structure of DNA.

Pascal Boyer, in a recent book, expresses a rather similar opinion. Refusing to consider that religion ever conferred by itself an adaptive advantage during evolution, he instead makes it a side effect or by-product of certain cognitive characteristics selected instead of others by evolution. The general idea is that the explanation of religious beliefs and behaviors is to be sought in the way in which the human mind functions. That is not to say that the human brain is naturally or spontaneously religious, but that it is structured such that it allows one to acquire a religion.

Boyer's thesis is that "our systems of inferences produce intuitions ordered by relevance, i.e., by the wealth of the inferences that can be drawn from a specific premise."[39] More specifically, beliefs come from the activation of innate mental modules that drive man to attribute hidden intentions to natural phenomena. Thus religion is reduced to a simple collection of mental representations that our brain judges more credible than others, and that can appear effective in certain contexts, either because they confer an adaptive advantage on those who believe them, or

---

39. Pascal Boyer, *Et l'homme créa ses dieux: Comment expliquer la religion* [And Man Created his Gods: How to Explain Religion] (Paris: Laffont, 2001), 458; in English: *The Evolutionary Origins of Religious Thought* (New York: Basic Books, 2001).

because, while being unverifiable, they are sufficiently plausible to be retained by the human mind: "The religious concepts that persist are those that succeeded in maintaining themselves at the expense of many others."[40] Systems of inference activated by their relative pertinence, by-products of cognitive functions present in both believers and unbelievers, religious concepts "mobilize the resources of mental systems which would be there [in any case], religion or not."[41] In other words, religion is "only one *side effect* of the operation of our brain."[42]

Boyer adds that "If religious concepts and behaviors have persisted for millennia—and even longer, no doubt—if they present the same themes the world over, it is simply because they are optimal in the sense that they activate various systems in a way that favors their transmission."[43] Religion would thus find its origin in the selection of a certain number of propositions and concepts. Some religious concepts would be more powerful than others, in the sense that they propagate themselves better than others, which would better enable them to live as parasites upon our mental activities. "To explain religion," Boyer writes, "is to explain a particular type of mental epidemic."[44] Religion would be one of the prices to be paid for our mental architecture, while being a vestige destined to disappear.

II

This brief overview shows the extreme diversity of possible explanations of the religious phenomenon. It also shows they are somewhat unsatisfactory. Admittedly, a certain number quite likely contain some measure of truth. This is particularly true of the sociological explanations, since the psychological ones, in addition to having the disadvantage of separating religion from faith, very often consist of mere hypotheses. But one is right to

---

40. Boyer, *Et l'homme créa ses dieux*, 50.
41. Boyer, *Et l'homme créa ses dieux*, 468.
42. Boyer, *Et l'homme créa ses dieux*, 380.
43. Boyer, *Et l'homme créa ses dieux*, 478.
44. Boyer, *Et l'homme créa ses dieux*, 71.

doubt the overall explanatory power of all of them. There are several reasons for this.

First, these various theories seldom depart from a certain ethnocentrism. Claiming to speak about religion in general, they are actually deeply conditioned by a paradigm dominant within Western civilization: in fact, the Christian or Judeo-Christian paradigm. This paradigm is then taken as universal model of all religious phenomena, which makes it possible to extrapolate it to any other faith, by neglecting the differences, however considerable, that exist between the religions.

One notes, for example, that a great number of these explanations are based on the idea that religion is above all normative, a dispenser of moral rules. It is enough, then, to ask about the utility (for the individual or the group) of these moral rules to think that one has elucidated the nature or purpose of religion. But the idea that religion is a belief "in which any credible moral source implies God" (Charles Taylor) is quite simply untenable. Regardless of the fact, confirmed by daily experience, that from the moral point of view believers do not behave better than unbelievers, and sometimes behave even worse,[45] religion and morality are not necessarily synonymous.

A religion like old European paganism, to cite only one, is clearly not a moral religion. Obviously that does not mean pagans had no morals, but that they drew on other sources besides religion: the mores or values honored by society—the word "moral," let us recall, comes from the Latin *mores*, "manners," just as "ethics" comes from the Greek *ethos*, "place of residence, habit"—or the philosophical reflections of thinkers like Aristotle, Seneca, Cicero, and so many others. The pagans, in other words, did not need God to tell them that courage is worth more than cowardice, generosity worth more than selfishness, sincerity worth more than lying, and nobility of heart worth more than

---

45. In the United States, 52% of Americans of Asian origin, 68% of Whites, 72% of Hispanics, and 89% of African-Americans answered in the affirmative the question: "Is your religious faith important for you?" The statistics concerning criminality reveal exactly the opposite hierarchy: among Americans of Asian origin it is the least; in African-Americans it is the greatest (cf. *National Review*, December 14, 2005).

self-debasement. Contrary to the proverb that "if God does not exist all is permitted," there are societies without God, but there are none where all is permitted.[46]

This ethnocentrism naturally tends to legitimate a unitary approach to religion. The most common approach consists in noting that all ancient societies had a religious dimension, then to conclude from it that "religion" must be definable by characteristics that all these beliefs have in common. But where to find this common element? In morality? Certainly not, as we have just seen. In belief in one or more gods? But there exist religions without God, like Hinayana Buddhism or the Brahmanism of the Upanishads. In divine transcendence? But there is an enormous difference between a religion that defines the divine as a personal being, ontologically distinct from the world, and a religion that assimilates it to cosmic harmony.[47]

Such an approach does not make it possible either to understand why certain religions have only one God whereas others have several, why some are dualistic and others not, why some rest on the idea of salvation whereas others by no means aim at the liberation of the soul and are hardly concerned with the beyond, why some adhere to a linear vision of temporality and others to a cyclical vision, why some tend to exclude from the sphere of truth all beliefs which they denounce as "idolatry," whereas others easily admit that each people has its own gods, why some, like polytheism, lead to a pluralist and democratic vision of social life, whereas others, like those derived from monotheism, so often legitimate intolerance and despotism.[48]

---

46. Pascal Boyer advances the hypothesis that, far from religion commanding and supporting morality, it is instead "our intuitive moral reflection [that] makes certain religious concepts easy to acquire, preserve, and communicate" (*Et l'homme créa ses dieux*, 291).
47. Cf. François Cavallier, ed., *La religion* [Religion] (Paris: Ellipses, 2000), 4–5, 33, 48. Cf. Jan Assmann, *Moïse l'Egyptien: Un essai d'histoire de la mémoire* (Paris: Aubier, 2001). In English: *Moses the Egyptian: The Memory of Egypt in Western Monotheism* (Cambridge: Harvard University Press, 1997).
48. On the question of violence, one regularly finds two opposite interpretations: according to the one, the violence of "God's madmen" is the direct consequence of their belief; fundamentalism is then nothing but an exacerbated form of religious conviction. According to the other, religious extremism on

In paganism, the gods constitute models, archetypal figures, but they do not require, promise, or demand anything. They testify to the presence of Being, of the invisible dimension of the world, not of another world that is supposed to have an ontological perfection that this world lacks. These gods are not only multiple; they oppose one another and are not even eternal. The divine presence in the world is thus immanent, and does not express an absolute transcendence. Sacrifice tends to found and maintain on earth an order corresponding to the cosmic order. Worship is inseparable from collective existence, and more particularly from civic life. One does not practice a religion to secure one's salvation. One does not seek to convert. Religion knows neither dogmas, nor orthodoxy, nor heresies. In this, paganism

---

the contrary does not have anything to do with religion, of which it is nothing but a caricature; it simply arises from the psychology of extremists, whom one finds everywhere. These two interpretations are frequently opposed today in connection with Islam, both sides citing Koranic texts to support their views. In some circumstances, they are not mutually exclusive. Certainly violence is initially in the man, and religion is just one more occasion for it to manifest itself in its own proper form. "If fundamentalism were only an extreme form of religious conviction," writes Pascal Boyer, "that would not inform us about the reasons that push certain people, in certain circumstances, to adopt this specific version of their religious tradition" (*Et l'homme créa ses dieux*, 424). It is granted, nevertheless, that universalistic religions by nature are more inclined to be violent (which does not mean that they are always so). Belief in a single God and the conviction that it is at the same time possible and necessary to convert all of humanity to what one considers the only true religion, are obviously at risk of drifting towards fanatic intolerance and violence. Paganism, on the contrary, tends in the direction of the "polytheism of values" discussed by Max Weber; it recognizes the legitimacy of pluralism in systems of values, references, or convictions. "The belief in the absolute entails violence. The relation to the other is potentially violent. Religion, as the union of these two factors, increases the risk of violence," observes Luc Pareydt ("Croyance en l'absolu, violence entre les hommes") ["Belief in the Absolute, Violence between Men"], *Projet* 281 (2004), 7). Indeed, the absolute prohibits all compromise, does not authorize any restriction, does not tolerate any discussion or contradiction. The absolute is what exists independently of anything other than itself. One finds here the ambivalence of religious life, which, on the one hand, gathers together those who share the same faith, and on the other, accentuates the division between the community of believers and the rest of humanity.

is radically different from the universalistic revealed religions, directed to the pursuit of individual salvation and founded on the system of error and sin.[49]

But monotheism itself is not a unity—to the point that it is no exaggeration to say, contrary to a somewhat naive "ecumenism," that Christians, Jews, and Moslems do not worship the same God. That Judaism is a "religion," in the classical sense of the term, has often been questioned. It is first of all the religion of a people, but in the sense that this people made itself the object of its own belief, since it is by the Covenant (*Brith*) that God himself is supposed to be revealed. Here universalism joins with ethnocentrism, of which it constitutes, if not the projection, at least the justification. It is also a religion which, quite contrary to others, privileges the here and now to the detriment of the beyond: it is in this world that Messianic prophecies must be achieved, and it is also this world that must be reshaped to prepare it for the arrival of the Messiah. In line with Moses Mendelssohn's contention that "Judaism does not know revealed religion," philosopher J. M. Salanskis could assert that there is no "Jewish religion." Judaism, according to him, is not based on belief in God, but on the ceaseless reinterpretation of a foundational text. The core of "Jewish life" is not God, but the Torah.[50]

In addition, from the point of view of orthodox Judaism, the truly monotheist character of the Christian religion is doubtful. It is a question of whether the divinity of Jesus is compatible with the monotheist idea. If not, Christianity would be mere "idolatry."

Finally, even though the majority of the Christian theologians place Islam among the revealed religions because of its belief in a single God, and not among the "natural religions," that is, the pagan religions, this thesis has also been disputed.[51]

---

49. Even in ancient Judaism, the observance of the Law (the achievement of the 613 *mitsvot*) implies more than the sacrificial rituals (cf. Hosea 6:6).
50. J. M. Salanskis, *Extermination, Loi, Israel: Ethanalyse du fait juif* [Extermination, Law, Israel. Ethoanalysis of the Jewish Phenomenon] (Paris: Belles Lettres, 2003).
51. Alain Besançon thinks Islam can be regarded as "the natural religion of revealed God" ("L'islam," *Commentaire* (2004): 589–96). He stresses the

If one sticks just to Christianity, what remarkable differences exist between primitive Christianity, medieval Christianity, the Christianity of the Counter-Reformation, and modern Christianity! What a difference between Protestantism, which makes faith prevail over religion at the risk to falling into literalism or an abstract theism, and Catholicism which, not recognizing the text as the *ultima ratio*, pushes in the opposite direction at the risk of falling into the sacralization of institutions!

The truth is that the various religions do not themselves understand religious life in the same way. Let us not forget that, in the Roman empire, Christians were long regarded as atheists because they did not recognize the existence of the gods, and that Saint Paul, addressing the Athenians, almost reproached them for being too religious (Acts, 17:22). Far from the study of religions revealing a convergence, it instead reveals differences. Indeed, the spectacle of these differences can lead one to doubt the very

---

absence in Islam of the idea of progressive revelation, the completely different status of the Bible (the "inspired" word) and the Koran (the "increate" word), the nonanthropomorphic character of the God of the Moslems ("this One God, who demands submission, is a separate God. To call him Father is an anthropomorphic sacrilege"), the indifference of Islam to history. He then stresses what makes it possible to assimilate Islam to paganism: "The object of faith is not God, but the oneness of God. As for the Greeks and Romans, it is enough to contemplate the cosmos, creation, to be certain before any reasoning that God (or the divine) is, such that not to believe in it is a sign of insanity that excludes the unbeliever from human nature. This is not the view of Christian theology, according to which reason can accept the existence of God only by means of investigation and reasoning. . . . The law of Islam is a law external to man, which excludes any idea of imitation of God as it is proposed in the Bible. . . . From this point of view, it is unsurprising to find in it some of the same norms as in pagan ethics. Asceticism is foreign to the spirit of Islam. Islamic civilization is a civilization of the *bona vita*. It offers varied pleasures and license in the realm of the senses. There is a Moslem *carpe diem*, a Moslem happiness that often fascinated Christians, just as they had nostalgia for the ancient world. Predestination, as Islam understands it, is not far away from the ancient feeling of destiny. . . . No original sin, no eternal hell for the believer" (593). Salman Rushdie, for his part, remarks, in his novel *Furie*, that the poles of the ethical universe of Islam are honor and shame, whereas those of the Christian world are sin and redemption. In *The Antichrist*, Nietzsche already opposed the licitness of pleasure in Islam to the contempt of the body in Christianity.

validity of a general concept of "religion," and the unitary character of this category.[52]

But there is another reason, undoubtedly more fundamental still, that leads me to doubt the value of the majority of the explanations discussed above. It is that they are almost always explanations of the functionalist type. To explain what religion is, they think it sufficient to identify the need it answers or the function it performs. The basic idea of functionalism is the reduction of essence to function or utility: everything has a function and its essence is reduced to the functional role it supposedly plays. To say what religion *is* would thus be to say *for what* it is useful. This functionalist or "desubstantialist" approach, already denounced in his time by Benjamin Constant,[53] is the most widespread today, because it claims to be more scientific and especially because it corresponds to the profoundly utilitarian spirit of our time, which is characterized by the increasing functionalization of society—a society where man himself becomes little by little a functional object.[54]

---

52. Régis Debray also tends to reject the term "religion," in which he sees "a terrible blanket term which it would be best to get rid of as much as possible" (Régis Debray and Claude Geffré, *Avec ou sans Dieu: Le philosophe et le théologien* [With or without God: The Philosopher and the Theologian] [Paris: Bayard, 2006], 33). Cf. also Régis Debray, *Les communions humaines: Pour en finir avec « la religion »* [The Human Communions: Towards an End to "Religion"] (Paris: Fayard, 2005).
53. "The defenders of religion often think they can particularly impress us representing it as useful. What would they say if they were shown that they render the worst possible service to religion? By seeking in all the beauties of nature a positive goal, an immediate use, an application for everyday life, one bleaches away all the charm of this magnificent whole. Likewise, by incessantly attributing a vulgar utility to religion, one makes it dependent on this utility. It no longer has anything more than a secondary rank; it appears to be nothing but a means, and consequently it is degraded" (Benjamin Constant, *Principes de politique applicables à tous les gouvernements* [Principles of Politics Applicable to All Governments], the version of 1806–1810 [Paris: Hachette-Littérature, 2006), ch. 8: "De la religion considérée comme utile" ["On Religion Considered as Useful," 52).
54. Cf. J. M. Yinger, *The Scientific Study of Religion* (London: Macmillan, 1970). On this point, cf. also Shmuel Trigano, *Qu'est-ce que la religion? La transcendance des sociologues* [What is Religion? The Transcendence of the Sociologists]

But to note that religion has, for example, a certain psychological or social function by no means signifies that this function suffices to explain its existence. It is one thing to claim that religion makes it possible (in certain cases) to cure fear, another thing to say that fear gave birth to it. Also, when this step is taken, there is a great risk of adopting simple *ad hoc* explanations. As Pascal Boyer himself recognizes, "it is not because one believes one knows the reasons why people have certain ideas that one can actually explain why they have them."[55] Indeed, one of the errors of functionalism is failing to see that, for a religious value to be transferred to a social fact, it must already have been recognized as a value before this transfer.[56]

Biological explanations are also typically functionalist, because they are always supported by reasoning of an economic-utilitarian type: social reality being explained from the start in terms of investments and benefits, religion supposedly makes it possible to maximize the benefit that the individual draws from social relations. Religion is treated as a biological organ, and one asks what function it plays in the organism. But belief cannot be explained only in terms of benefits, because many times it is prejudicial to those who profess it. The functionalist explanation, as a causal explanation, is in fact necessarily indifferent to the specific contents of religious belief. It is in addition eminently reductionistic, since it implies that one can reduce a symbolic system to its functionality, whereas religion by definition exceeds any functionality.[57] As Jean-Paul Willaime writes,

> ... religion is undoubtedly what exceeds any functionality by managing gaps, uncertainty, otherness.... Religion is a symbolic activity that has its own consistency, so to speak,

---

(Paris: Flammarion, 2001).
55. Boyer, *Extermination, Loi, Israel: Ethanalyse du fait juif*, 137.
56. Cf. Leszek Kolakowski, "La revanche du sacré dans la culture profane" ["The Revenge of the Sacred in Profane Culture"] in *Le besoin religieux: Rencontres internationales de Genève, 1973* [The Religious Need: International Meetings in Geneva, 1973] (Neuchâtel: La Baconnière, 1974), 16–17.
57. Pascal Boyer goes so far as to write that "religion is above all practical" (Boyer, *Extermination, Loi, Israel: Ethanalyse du fait juif*, 196).

though it may be entirely socially determined—and it is in a thousand ways—it enjoys a relative autonomy compared to all these determinations. It is precisely because religions constitute cultures, i.e., complex worlds of signs and meanings that fall into history and are transmitted from generation to generation, that they enjoy a relative autonomy compared to all the social determinations that inform them.[58]

Finally, the functionalist approach inevitably leads to a theory of the religion substitute. If religion is defined solely by its function, one is indeed immediately led to wonder about the way in which this function could be performed differently. The idea that the end of religion is at hand is often based on this very idea: religion will disappear because its functions will be taken over by means that will fulfill them in a more credible or effective way. "Functionalism," notes Jacques Dewitte, "inevitably results in admitting that a substitute can serve just as well as the original, that one can replace something with any of its functional equivalents that are in principle interchangeable." It is this mistake, for example, that is committed by Marcel Gauchet when he writes that religion is a "secondary system whose old functions can be socially filled and replaced by something entirely different."[59]

The theory of the substitute is not in itself absurd. It can encourage fruitful reflection on the "religious" character of phenomena that are not defined as such. One can then speak about "secular religions," "substitute religions," and so on. This step is not in itself illegitimate, but it nonetheless rests on an ambiguity neatly exposed by Hannah Arendt in a polemic against Jules Monnerot in the early 1950s. In his *Sociology of Communism*,

---

58. Willaime, 253, 258.
59. Gauchet, *La démocratie contre elle-même*, 30. Régis Debray appears also to surrender to functionalism when he states: "For me, the meaning resides in the function," adding that it is precisely the "religious function" that seems to him an anthropological invariant (Debray and Geffré, *Avec ou sans Dieu*, 36–37). And further: "It is the belief, at bottom, that interests my approach: what is belief and what is its use? How does it function?" (41), and: "For me the sacred is not a reality in itself, but rather a function" (58).

the latter noted that the great modern ideologies, in particular Soviet Communism, took on a certain number of typically religious features and could play the same role in human society, which entitles us to regard them as "secular religions." Likewise, ideological wars took the place of religious wars, which have the same implacable character. Ideology and religion, far from being mutually exclusive, in this respect have an obvious continuity, because they have "common formal characteristics." The fact appears undeniable.

However, Hannah Arendt quite subtly pointed out that this functionalist reasoning (ideology has the same *function* as religion), actually makes it impossible to know how religion differs from ideology. If everything that fulfills the same function can receive the same name, what then is the distinct mark of religion? How can religion be distinguished from the nonreligious ideology supposed to replace it? "I can only define what is distinct," wrote Arendt, "and arrive at definitions, so far as that is possible, by making distinctions." "For my part, of course," she added, "I do not believe that everything has a function, or that function and essence are the same thing."[60]

The idea, inherited from the philosophy of the Enlightenment and nineteenth-century positivism, that religion will disappear when the functions that it fills are assumed by more credible procedures, is in fact doubtful. Admittedly, from the rationalist point of view, religion rests on certain assertions that violate our intuitive expectations and for which no empirical verification is possible. So the procedure with belief has usually consisted in excluding it from the field of rationality. From such a viewpoint, religion constitutes an "irrational" or "obscurantist" answer to legitimate questions that can be satisfied more rationally. Thus religion is perceived as a pre-scientific mode of knowledge destined to be dethroned by science. From this it is inferred that

60. Hannah Arendt, "Religion and Politics," *Confluence* 2/3 (September 1953). This critique gave rise to a polemical exchange between the two authors that is not without interest (*Confluence*, December 1953 and September 1954). Around the same time, Hannah Arendt notices that "our rediscovery of the functional utility of religion will produce a substitute for religion" (*La crise de la culture* [The Crisis of Culture] [Paris: Gallimard-ideas 1972], 137).

the more science develops, the more religion will dwindle.

This conclusion has already been contradicted by the facts, and indeed it is rather scientism itself that appears as an act of faith. It is certainly correct that, in general, in scientific circles unbelief is most widespread,[61] but it is no less obvious that, generally speaking, modern societies are no more "rational" than those that preceded them. The United States, which has long canonized the scientific spirit, is also the Western country where the most various beliefs continue with the most force (only 5% of Americans describe themselves as without religion). Also let us recall that Islamic "fundamentalism" is not a matter of the illiterate and ignorant, but often of perfectly well-educated people, particularly engineers and scientific researchers.

Pascal already said that God is not merely an explanatory principle. It is not because we know today that, when lightning flashes across the sky, it is not because Zeus is angry, that certain traditionalist groups ceased interpreting great natural disasters, *inter alia*, as invisible "signs" or divine "punishments." And in fact sometimes the progress of science even nourishes new beliefs, either because of the complexity of its statements, or because of the fact that, by definition, the greater the extent of positive knowledge, the greater the extent of what remains unknown. A survey published in England in 2004 even revealed that nearly a third of avowed atheists also admit that they pray from time to time!

---

61. In 1914, the American psychologist James H. Leuba carried out a pioneering survey of the 1000 greatest American researchers (selected according to the importance of their work). He discovered that 73.6% of scientists denied or doubted the existence of God (Leuba, *The Belief in God and Immortality: A Psychological, Anthropological and Statistical Study* [Boston: Sherman French & Co., 1916]). Leuba repeated his survey nineteen years later, which allowed him to observe that the proportion of unbelievers in this milieu had exceeded 85% (*Harper's Magazine*, 1934, 291–300). In 1996, Leuba's survey was given again by Edward J. Larson and Larry Witham to members of the American National Academy of Sciences (NAS). The two researchers found a rate of unbelief of 93%, which reached 94.5% among the biologists (but fell to 85.7% in the mathematicians). The results were published in the magazine *Nature*, 1997, 435–36. Cf. also Benjamin Beit-Hallahmi and Michael Argyle, *The Psychology of Religious Behaviour, Belief and Experience* (London: Routledge, 1997).

The explanatory power of science is, moreover, limited. Science can, by nature, only remain mute on the ultimate questions, like the meaning of our presence in the world. It ascertains facts that can only yield their meaning to interpretation, which does not itself come from science. Heidegger says that science "does not think, because its procedure and its auxiliary means are such that it cannot think—i.e., think in the manner of thinkers."[62] At the same time, science rests on a belief that is proper to it, the primacy of method (in the sense of Descartes) over knowledge, the mathematical project of a nature technically dominable because rationally knowable—in Heideggerian terms, of the "increasing domination of nature through the scientific interpretation of the *thing* as *object*" (Jean Beaufret).

Let us note, finally, that the age-old conflict of science and faith—which obscured the fact that the rise of science was initially made possible by the desacralization of the world caused by Christianity—persists today only on the margins of opinion, for example, with the "creationist" sects. "Concordism" is no longer the goal of theologians, and religion has renounced venturing on the terrain of positive knowledge, where it is obviously not competitive. Schopenhauer already said: "Knowledge is made of tougher stuff than faith, so that, if they collide, it is faith that breaks."[63] A kind of implicit agreement occurred, science admitting that it does not have anything to say about God, and religion renouncing the search for scientific confirmation of its beliefs. Today, many think that the two spheres are mutually incapable of refutation, because they deal with fields that do not overlap. The most common (but debatable) opinion is that science deals with facts, while religion treats values and norms—the distinction between what is and what ought to be—or that science investigates "how" while religion wonders about "why."

The functionalist approach, by deconstructing the object that it claims to study, leads in fact to its dissolution. Indifferent to the

---

62. Martin Heidegger, "Que veut dire 'penser'?," in *Essais et conférences* (Paris: Gallimard-Tel, 1952), 157. In English: *What is Called Thinking?*, trans. J. Glenn Gray (New York: Harper & Row, 1968).
63. Arthur Schopenhauer, *On Religion*, §175.

specific contents of belief, the theories it inspires always explain religion by something other than religion: the usefulness of the social bond, fear, the need for illusion, the requirements of politics, domination, and frustration. From such a viewpoint, religion no longer exists in itself, but only depending on something other that itself. It says something, but it is always something different from what it wants or claims to say. To understand its discourse we must translate it into a different language that is supposed to be more accessible, more transparent, or more true. Religion, in other words, is always something other than what it claims to be. With the result that ultimately, one still does not know what belief is or why religion exists.

In reality, religious beliefs relate much more to ideas than facts or deeds, meaning that they are more subject to reasons than to causes. If one wants to reject functionalism, it is thus necessary to start by admitting that religion presupposes thought contents, existential attitudes that are not substitutable, and one must give these thought contents priority if one wants to know what religion is:

> In other words, religion or the sacred must be understood as an "originary phenomenon," as a creation of meaning that cannot be derived from something else and which can only be known from itself. Thus, it is impossible to derive it from its functional uses, the various manners in which it was "put in service" of certain interests, for the good reason that these functional uses, which are undeniable, presuppose precisely this creation of meaning or this preexistent value from which they will draw.[64]

It is necessary, in other words, to return to a substantive (or substantial) definition of religious phenomena.

A substantive (or substantial) definition of religion has as its primary characteristic not emptying belief of its contents, of

---

64. Jacques Dewitte, "Croire ce que l'on croit. Réflexions sur la religion et les sciences socials" ["To believe what one believes: Reflections on Religion and the Social Sciences"], *Revue du MAUSS* 22 (2nd sem. 2003), 74.

not regarding these contents as pretense, projection, derivation, metaphor, and transposition. It privileges the contents of religion, that is, the very object of its discourse. Thus it goes back to the source of the phenomenon; it respects its specific mode of givenness. It asks about the thing itself, for itself, and from itself; about its essence, its substance, its intrinsic ends; about what explains why, even before one asked about it, this thing and not some other was already there. It begins with the assumption that people who claim to believe something really believe what they claim to believe, instead of claiming that the basis of their belief is something other than what they believe. That does not mean that what they believe is true, but that it is true that they believe what they say they believe. It means ultimately that religion does not have any other object than what is expressly professed by the believers.

Cicero gave a simple definition of religion: "concerning oneself with a certain higher nature that one calls divine and rendering it worship" (*De inventione*). This definition is not so bad, because the religious state obviously refers to human society's relation to what exceeds its own existence. Roger Caillois, for his part, saw the opposition of sacred and profane as the most essential foundation of religion.[65] Furthermore, religion also concerns a system of gifts and counter-gifts: gifts that the gods make to men, gifts that men make to the gods, gifts that men give one another on the basis of shared belief, including of course the gift of oneself.

Thus for my part, I will say, with much diffidence, that a religion is a form of human association founded on a set of beliefs and practices, symbols and values, related to the distinction between the visible and the invisible, the empirical and the super-empirical, the profane and the sacred, and, at the same time, a socially established worship which structures individual and collective existence by placing it in a universe of meaning, in a symbolic universe governed by an intangible reality.

---

65. Roger Caillois, *L'homme et le sacré* [Man and the Sacred] (Paris: Gallimard-Idées, 1950), 17.

III

Where are we today? What is the situation of religion today? To find out, we can of course consult the surveys that inform us periodically about the state of beliefs and practices. These surveys, in general, testify to a continuous decrease of religious feeling, a drying up of religious observance, and a crisis of vocations.[66] But one would be wrong to cling to these sorts of indications, first, because they are purely cyclical matters, second, because the problem must obviously be approached from a broader point of view, and, finally, because concepts like the distinction between believers and practitioners, and even between believers and unbelievers, have already largely lost their relevance to current developments. How then to characterize these developments? Three essential phenomena are to be taken into account.

The first corresponds to what Gauchet, in a whole series of works published since 1985, calls the "departure from religion." What does he mean by this expression? Quite simply that the societies of Western Europe today are emancipated from any religious norms, that they constitute a world no longer organized around religion. This "departure from religion" by no means implies that nobody believes in a God any more, or

---

66. In 1999, only 37% of the French regarded religion as "very" or "rather important" in their lives (*Futuribles* 260, [January 2001]). A CSA survey for *Le Monde* and *La Vie*, which was published in April 2003, shows that today 62% of the French (40% of the 18–24 year olds) are professed "Catholics" (against 71% in 1981), but that the existence of God is not "certain" or "probable" for 58% of them. Religious practice is constantly declining: approximately 50% are baptized (against 95% in 1970), 7% regularly attend mass or religious services (against 37% in 1948). The religious vocations fare no better: today there are only 13,500 priests in France, against more than 45,000 in 1960, and their average age is almost 70 (it will reach 73 in 2015). A survey of 21,000 people from 21 different countries appeared in the European edition of the *Wall Street Journal* on December 10, 2004. It indicates that 25% of West Europeans define themselves as atheists (49% in the Czech Republic, 41% in the Netherlands, 37% in Germany and Denmark, 36% in Belgium). Only 18% of Spaniards declared themselves practicing Catholics today, against 98% 50 years ago. According to another survey carried out in January 2004 on behalf of the BBC, only 31% of the English believe in God.

that the number of the believers is necessarily doomed always to decrease. It means only that, for the first time in history, we live in a society where religion no longer structures social and political space, provides essential values, or furnishes the encompassing norms of collective existence. It marks "the transition to a world where religions continue to exist, but within a political form and a collective order that they no longer determine."[67] Thus a society that has departed from religion may well contain a vast majority of believers (as in the United States today); what counts is the social status that it gives to religious fact. Gauchet writes:

> God did not die, he simply ceased mixing with the political affairs of men. He moved away. He drew back into an 'elsewhere' where each believer can reach him individually, but where he does not connect with the order and the rules that link men collectively. Religion does not disappear, but we leave behind the religious organization of society, the religious comprehension of the universe in which we developed.[68]

In a society that has "departed from religion," where there is no longer a guarantor above society, everyone is free to gather in churches, chapels, in Christian, Buddhist, pagan, or other sects. But these options do not have any general importance for society. Thus belief becomes one opinion among others. Faith changes "from a standard of reference encompassing the community to a particular choice of the citizen." The Churches reorganize as one among many components of a civil society that is organized on the basis of the voluntary adherence of its members. Except for certain minority traditionalist groups, hardly representative of the mass of believers, the very idea of a religious society loses its

---

67. Marcel Gauchet, *La religion dans la démocratie: Parcours de la laïcité* [Religion in Democracy: The Path toward Secularity] (Paris: Gallimard, 1998), 11.
68. Marcel Gauchet, "Croyances religieuses, croyances politiques" ["Religious Beliefs, Political Beliefs"], *Le Débat* (May–July 2001), 9.

meaning. "Belief," continues Gauchet, "became at this point an individual faith, changing its meaning." The bond between religious belief and social order is undone. Faith as such has nothing to say about social and political organization. Its object is of another kind. The most fervent believer no longer has the idea of proclaiming a Christian order or *a fortiori* a politics of God."[69]

This situation represents the culmination of a long process of secularization, a process of a complex and ambiguous nature, with very old roots. Indeed, one cannot understand it without taking into account the distinction between created and uncreated being postulated by Christian theology. In Christianity, the creator God does not merge in any way with the world he created, thus the world cannot in any way be regarded as an intrinsically sacred place. God is not ontologically related to any place. The result is the desacralization of the cosmos that technoscience then continues at an accelerated pace.[70]

In this "disenchanted" world, the individual achieves his own salvation. The inmost self takes precedence over membership in the city, just as spiritual membership, sanctioned by baptism, takes the place of family relationships (cf. Luke 14:26). The emphasis placed on the inmost self, on consciousness as the seat of the soul and place privileged by the encounter with God—in connection with the revalorization of what Aristotle called "ordinary life" (in opposition to the "good life")—already separates the believer from public life.

If God is ontologically distinct from this world, it is by detaching oneself from the world that one can best join with him, by apprehending him inside oneself. As Gauchet writes, "to live for one's salvation, is something different from living according to the rules of this world."[71] Moreover, convinced that the Second Coming was at hand, the first Christians affirmed themselves as "renouncers" of the world. Wanting first to be citizens of heaven, they emphasized that it was necessary to die to the world to live

---

69. Gauchet, *Un monde désenchanté?*, 160.
70. Cf. Mircea Eliade, *The Sacred and the Profane: The Nature of Religion*, trans. Willard R. Trask (New York: Harcourt Brace Jovanovich, 1987).
71. Gauchet, *La démocratie contre elle-même*, 59.

in God. "To them, any foreign land is a fatherland and any fatherland a foreign land," one reads in the *Epistle to Diognetus*, the first apology for Christianity dated to the second century, whose author is unknown. In the third century, Tertullian still states that, "nothing is more foreign to us than public affairs." "The freedom that Christianity introduced into the world," observes Hannah Arendt, "was freedom *from* politics."[72]

To the theological distinction between created and uncreated being, unknown to paganism, Christianity adds another, just as new: the distinction between spiritual and temporal power, which is also the distinction between the supernatural good and the spiritual common good. Each of the two spheres is proclaimed competent only in its domain, but it is a wholly relative distinction, since it falls under a strictly hierarchical perspective, founded on the subordination of the temporal to the spiritual: positive law cannot go against "natural law." Thus posed, the duality very quickly showed itself to be problematic. How can these two orders, each sovereign in its sphere, but nevertheless one subordinate to the other, work themselves out? "In Christianity," notes Gauchet, "the articulation between heaven and earth is fundamentally *problematic*; it bequeathed this to post-Christian society, which continues to be agitated by it."[73]

Secularization initially took the form of the sacralization of politics and a religious transfiguration of sovereignty. From the end of the Middle Ages, the state is constituted as a veritable spiritual power. To better establish its legitimacy and authority, it created a relationship with religion that was simultaneously imitative and rivalrous, by asserting that it too had a metaphysical dimension.

This process led to absolute monarchy. The France of the Old

---

72. Hannah Arendt also stresses that secularization does not mean that nobody believes in God any longer, but that religion loses its political role, that is, its power to organize and provide norms for society as a whole: "Religious institutions do not have constraining authority on the public level and ... reciprocally, political life does not have a religious sanction" ("Religion et politique" ["Religion and Politics"], in *La nature du totalitarisme* [The Origins of Totalitarianism] [Paris: Payot, 1990], 145).

73. Gauchet, *Un monde désenchanté?*, 156.

Regime was simultaneously a denominational state—in the sense that Catholicism had a privileged, even exclusive, position, and the power of the king was known as divine right—and a "secular" state, in the sense that the king did not control the church while the church did not control the monarchy.

In a second stage, which came after the Revolution, the nation, in the modern sense of the term, became "the horizon of the intrinsic completeness of a political arena containing its entire justification within itself."[74] Politics was increasingly defined as self-sufficient from a metaphysical and ontological point of view, but nevertheless without losing its religious character. Temporal power initiates

> a revolutionary reorientation of its features and its ends. Instead of embodying here below the fundamental reality of the beyond, it would slowly endow the body politic with ontological sufficiency and plenitude. Against the sacrality of the ultimate ends which the church imposed upon individual pursuits, it exalts the collective sacrality of the terrestrial achievement.[75]

That will not happen without a severe struggle for influence, as the history of "secularism" shows. As everyone knows, this fight was finally won by political authority, which did not cease to free itself from the subordination in which the representatives of spiritual power had held it for so long. But we should not lose sight of the dialectical dimension of this struggle. Political power emancipates itself from religion, but it emancipates itself by borrowing religion's forms. It distances itself from it, paradoxically, by imitating it.

There is thus a dialectic of secularization that prohibits interpreting it simply as a unilateral process of laicization or of a deterioration of beliefs and religion. The idea that religion and modernity are mutually exclusive, such that every gain by one

---

74. Gauchet, *Un monde désenchanté?*, 113.
75. Gauchet, *La démocratie contre elle-même*, 62.

comes at the expense of the other, is not sustainable.[76] Actually, modernity transforms the status of religion without making it disappear. Today it is admitted that Christianity has itself largely contributed to modernization, or at least that modernity could be established only by employing themes of Christian origin. Likewise, the Calvinist Reformation played a well-known role in the advent of capitalism. Secularization is less a movement of marginalization of religion than a movement of laicization (or profane retransposition) of certain Christian values. It is, of course, a "heretical" movement from a traditional Christian point of view, but its Christian filiation is no less obvious. This dialectical aspect of the process of secularization was stressed by Gauchet, who rejects the misleading idea "of a simple emancipation of lay or secular space compared to the religious field." Gauchet writes:

> One is dealing with a completely different process. It is nothing like a zero-sum game, in which one camp gains what the other loses. It is a profound transformation that will transfer the old articulations of religious order to the "emancipated" profane order, in a light and orientation so opposed to what they were in the past that we may not recognize them. It functions in modernity as an authentic replacement for religion.[77]

Religion has, kicking and screaming, and without of course being able to recognize itself, created in the field of modernity political and social orders that bear its mark. One already sees it in the Revolution of 1789, which overthrows the power of divine right and absolute monarchy, then immediately transfers their prerogatives to the nation. Fundamentally anticlerical, it also promotes the worship of the "supreme Being" and incorporates

---

76. Cf. Anne Fortin, "L'exclusion réciproque de la modernité et de la religion chez des penseurs contemporains. Jürgen Habermas et Marcel Gauchet" ["The Mutual Exclusion of Modernity and Religion among Contemporary Thinkers: Jürgen Habermas and Marcel Gauchet"], *Concilium* 244 (1992), 79–91.
77. Gauchet, *Un monde désenchanté?*, 124.

many religious elements in its discourse.[78] Political belief thus takes over from religious belief. As Carl Schmitt shows, all of the great modern political concepts are old religious concepts brought down to the profane sphere—this is the whole theme of "political theology."[79] The omnipotence of God serves as a model of the legislator or the sovereign. The political decision is modeled on the *potentia absoluta* [absolute power] of God whose will precedes any reference to mere reason. The ideology of human rights secularizes biblical morals (the system of *dignity* in opposition to the system of *honor*). The ideology of progress, by secularizing eschatological expectation, constitutes a profane version of the belief in the inescapable advent of a better world.

---

78. Dale K. Van Kley, *Les origines religieuses de la Révolution française, 1560–1791* [Religious Origins of the French Revolution, 1560–1791] (Paris: Seuil, 2002), sees the revolutionary events as the fruit of a long process of secularization of the Jansenist quarrel, itself connected to the wars of religion. The Jansenist spirit, heir to medieval "conciliarism" and parliamentary constitutionalism became the main progenitor of the "patriotic party." For a radically opposed point of view, cf. Catherine Maire, *"Aux sources politiques et religieuses de la Révolution française: Deux modèles de discussion"* ["On the Political and Religious Sources of the French Revolution: Two Models of Discussion"], *Le Débat* (May–August, 2004): 133–53. Van Kley has replied: *"Sur les sources religieuses et politiques de la Révolution française"* ["On the Religious and Political Sources of the French Revolution"], *Commentaire* (Winter 2004–2005): 893–914.
79. It is well-known that Schmitt's thesis on secularization ("All the fertile concepts of the modern theory of the State are secularized theological concepts," in *Théologie politique* [Political Theology] [Paris: Gallimard, 1988], 46) agrees with the "secularization theorem" stated by Karl Löwith. In English: *Political Theology: Four Chapters on the Concept of Sovereignty*, trans. George Schwab (Cambridge: MIT Press, 1985). On the other hand, Schmitt was harshly criticized by Hans Blumenberg (*La légitimité des temps modernes* [The Legitimacy of the Modern Age, 1966], [Paris: Gallimard, 1999]), who offers a "functionalist" critique: according to him, in political theology, there is more an identity or transfer of functions than an identity or transfer of contents. Schmitt replied to Blumenberg in his second *Political Theology* (1970), while reproaching him for having discussed the legality of modernity and not its legitimacy. On the Schmitt-Blumenberg debate, cf. Olivier Tschannen, *Les théories de la secularization* [Theories of Secularization] (Geneva: Droz, 1992); Jean-Claude Monod, *La querelle de la sécularisation, de Hegel à Blumenberg* [The Quarrel of Secularization, Hegel to Blumenberg] (Paris: J. Vrin, 2002).

The golden age (the lost paradise) being transferred to the end of history instead of being placed at its beginning, the future takes the place of the beyond, happiness replaces salvation, faith and hope are brought down to terrestrial affairs, and so forth. The secular model of society is thus really a contradictory mixture. The great ideologies of the nineteenth and twentieth centuries presented themselves as alternatives to religion, from which they borrowed many characteristics, first by purporting to be complete systems of meaning and explanation regarding social life, the history of the world, and the ends of humanity, then by requiring a quasi-sacerdotal commitment from their members.[80] Another contradiction: on the one hand, society emancipates itself from tradition and begins to represent itself as capable of producing or generating itself; on the other, it professes that there is a meaning to history, a historical necessity that constitutes an objective limitation on the freedom and autonomy it claims for itself. From such a perspective, taking into account secularized theological contents is thus essential to the intelligibility of political modernity. The rupture with religion occurs upon a backdrop of deep continuity.

It is this political society, which is secular but deeply marked by religion, that collapsed in late modernity. Traditional society was a heteronomous society in the sense that there the general ordering of the world, and thus also of society, was conceived of as given and imposed by an authority inherited from the past, exceeding any human capacity to dispose of oneself. This conception affected the form of the social bond, which was

---

80. Gauchet stresses that modern ideologies are haunted by the loss of social unity characteristic of past society and that they aim very often to restore this unity in other ways. From then on, unity is no longer seen as a legacy of the past, but posited as a future prospect: "The form of Unity, resulting from the age of heteronomy, will be connected to the most radical versions of autonomy. The promise *par excellence* for the future is the restoration or introduction of collective unity. . . . The driving question of ideologies, from this point of view, is summarized in the following way: how to produce the collective Unity produced by religion by other than religious means?" ("*Croyances religieuses, croyances politiques,*" 10). But the rise of individualism will prevent this, because it leads to the disintegration of collective ideals and the dissolution of the social bond.

fundamentally "holist," as well as the form of political power, which incarnated in one or more people the principle of order that came both from the past and from on high. In modern societies, this "archaic" externality of the foundation disappears, but heteronomy is maintained while changing its meaning. With the ideology of progress, from now on it is the future not the past that orders historical necessity, while the great ideologies express themselves as so many secular religions. Postmodernity corresponds to the moment when this second form of heteronomy is erased in its turn. It is erased because we live in the moment of the "profound dissociation of religious and political belief."[81] While religious belief increasingly ceases being political (except for some traditionalist groups, Catholics themselves no longer believe in the possibility of returning to a "Christian society"), political belief empties itself of the sacral components inherited from theology. On the one side, God loses any imaginable social figuration; on the other, "the commonweal no longer asserts its higher dignity compared to private things,"[82] showing that politics has lost all sacrality and that the emancipation of the political sphere from religion is completed. The profane collective ideals disappear at the same time. The "departure from religion" has run its course.

IV

The second fundamental fact, which results directly from the former, is the increasing individualization of religious life. As mentioned above: religion as sociological or institutional membership is increasingly disconnected from belief as personal conviction. As the churches no longer have the power to normalize society overall, only those who have personal reasons to believe continue to do so. Religion is nothing more than a matter of personal choice and conviction. The crisis of belief or vocations does not result from a specific event—Vatican II, for example, as Christian traditionalists generally believe—but from

---

81. Marcel Gauchet, *"Croyances religieuses, croyances politiques,"* 4.
82. Marcel Gauchet, *Un monde désenchanté?*, 185.

a much more general, fundamental movement.

This individualization of belief, which initially went hand in hand with its privatization, is, significantly, regarded by many as supporting a more "authentic" faith because it is inscribed in one's heart of hearts, thus being assimilated to a pure individual spiritual experience. A sociologist like Danièle Hervieu-Leger speaks here of a "minimal creed," of "belief without membership," of "wandering believers," of "religiosity reduced to feelings" that "reduces the relation with transcendence to emotional and personalized proximity with the divine being."[83] As Jacques Dewitte writes:

> Everything happens as if, for the contemporary believer in the regime of radical individualism, "believing" were not only cut off from any institutional and public existence, but also cut off, so to speak, from every external content or object seen and recognized as distinct from inner feeling.[84]

The result of this tendency to search for an "intimate" authenticity is the spiritual eclecticism and dilettantism that one so often observes today.[85] Spirituality functions on the self-service principle, each person making up a religion à la carte in an eclectic and opportunist manner. This explains some surprising facts revealed by the surveys: the fact, for example, that a certain number of professed Christians no longer believe in hell or the virgin birth of Christ, or resurrection after death, while others who call themselves "rationalists" say that they are certain of

---

83. Danièle Hervieu-Léger, *Le pèlerin et le converti: La religion en mouvement* [The Pilgrim and the Convert: Religion in Motion] (Paris: Flammarion, 2001).
84. "Croire ce que l'on croit," 79.
85. "Everyone becomes in his way a dilettante ready to handle and manipulate ideas and beliefs," writes Daryush Shayegan ("La renaissance des religions" ["Rebirth of Religions"] in Thierry Fabre, ed., *Dieu: Les monothéismes et le désenchantement du monde* [God: Monotheism and the Disenchantment of the World] [Marseille: Parenthèses, 2005,] 109).

the existence of God.⁸⁶ "Nothing is more oppressive than a belief without any well-defined form," said Victor Hugo. This is exactly where we have arrived today: the remodeling of religious convictions according to individual preferences, the syncretism of sources, the borrowings from Buddhism or the Kabbala, the influence of the New Age, and the vogue of paranormal beliefs.⁸⁷

We must note—as one of its most important characteristics—that this spiritual dilettantism and eclecticism is perfectly in conformity with the present Westernized world—the exploding, fractal, rhizomatic world—and with the spirit of our time, insofar as the demand for meaning takes on an essentially utilitarian and hedonistic character. One expects the same thing from belief that one expects from psychoanalysis or hydrotherapy: it helps one to "feel good," to "think positive," to be "more comfortable with oneself." As Gilles Lipovetsky writes, "from a religion centered on salvation in the beyond, Christianity changed into a religion in service of worldly happiness, stressing the values of solidarity and love, of harmony, inner peace, the total realization of the person."⁸⁸ To describe this "hedonism of faith," it would be necessary to speak of "spiritual materialism," of a recourse to the spiritual solely from the point of view of a greater personal comfort, which obviously amounts to forgetting what belief once entailed: asceticism, effort, discipline, renunciation, and sometimes suffering.

Generally, as Patrick Michel writes, "the individual no

---

86. A Louis Harris poll in January 2003 shows that in the United States, 8% of Christians do not believe in the survival of the soul after death and that 18% refuse to accept the existence of hell. However, the same survey reveals that 26% of professed non-Christians believe in the resurrection of Christ. In France, only 12% of Catholic practitioners believe in the resurrection of body; 7% doubt that Jesus is really the son of God; yet 42% of those who define themselves as "rationalist" also say they are sure of God's existence.
87. The belief in paranormal phenomena is positively correlated to religious belief, but negatively correlated with religious practice. Cf. A. Orenstein, "Religion and Paranormal Belief," in *Journal for the Scientific Study of Religion* (2002): 301–311.
88. Gilles Lipovetsky, "La société d'hyperconsommation" ["The Society of Hyper-Consumerism"], *Le Débat* (March–April 2003), 94.

longer accepts a normative answer to his quest for meaning."[89] In addition to the reigning hyper-individualism, the progressive disappearance of what is sometimes called "inherited beliefs" leads, here as everywhere, to the questioning of authority and institutions. Religion is no longer a "particular manner of believing whose distinctive characteristic was to appeal to the legitimating authority of a tradition."[90] Also significant is the fact that, in Christian milieus, Jesus, perceived as the big brother of all mankind, takes the place of God the Father, who is judged to be too remote and too demanding.[91] We have left the (hierarchical) world of the fathers for the (egalitarian) world of the brothers. The individual of today may well believe; what he finds hard is admitting that belief entails an obligation to obey. The pope is more applauded than obeyed. Even when he is admired, his warnings are ignored when they touch upon private morals. Equally significant is the rise of sects—be they evangelical, Buddhist, "neopagan," or purely whimsical—which attests to the way in which the individualization of belief goes hand in hand with the flowering of small groups able to provide more or less comfortable "communitarian niches" on the basis of shared conviction.[92]

The questioning of authority and tradition goes hand in hand with a disqualification of the concept of absolutes, regarded as synonymous with intransigence, even intolerance. No longer is any absolute value regarded as able to be normative for global society. Liberal theory, moreover, obliges the state to remain "neutral" and not to choose between different conceptions of

---

89. Patrick Michel, *"La 'religion,' objet sociologique pertinent?"* ["'Religion,' Pertinent Object of Sociology?"] *Revue du MAUSS* 22 (2003), 159.

90. Danièle Hervieu-Léger, *La religion pour mémoire* [Religion for Memory] (Paris: Cerf, 1993), 121.

91. Cf. Régis Debray, "Christ parricide" ["Christ Parricide"] in *Dieu, un itinéraire: Matériaux pour l'histoire de l'Eternel en Occident* [God, an Itinerary: Materials for the History of the Eternal in the West] (Paris: Odile Jacob, 2003), 295–324.

92. "The more belief is individualized, the more it is homogenized; the more it is homogenized, the more the believers circulate; the more individual believers circulate, the more they need 'community niches'" (Patrick Michel, *La 'religion,'* 167).

the "good life" expressed within society. The concept of absolute evil, however, still has meaning, but it is generally political not metaphysical. But the idea of absolute good is systematically rejected. Whoever claims to militate for the absolute good is readily seen as a fanatic ("fool of God"), so much so that faith as it has been expressed for centuries, as a mindset that suffers no compromises, becomes entirely incomprehensible to minds that live entirely in a relative and floating world. The disenchantment of the world leads to a relativism that, paradoxically, makes the relative into an absolute.

The third and last phenomenon, particular to Western Europe, is due to the way in which religions today find a new kind of visibility in the public sphere. This phenomenon seems to contradict the other two but actually does not. Indeed since politics and religion have completely separated, since the emancipation of the political arena with respect to religion has run its course, nothing now prevents public authorities from giving beliefs hitherto confined to the private sphere a new social visibility which henceforth no longer threatens them. Such is the case, for example, when the state secures the advice of this or that "moral authority" who takes part in collective discussion of certain social matters, to accompany it in its reflection, or when it legally recognizes this or that religious community. But one must not be deceived here, for it is not by any means a return to the *statu quo ante*. Religion no longer has its former social position. It returns to the public sphere only as one component of civil society among others, as one of the components that henceforth claims public visibility and recognition, but by no means claims to provide norms for society as a whole. Private belief recovers a public status without, for all that, religion recovering its former role.

If there is any innovation here, it resides above all in a new articulation of private and public. The private accedes to public space without ceasing to be private. It is precisely as private, on account of its private opinions, that it wishes to be publicly recognized. The State, for its part, more and more renounces being the incarnation of the common interest of all citizens regardless of their respective characteristics, but, on the contrary, aspires to reflect the diversity of the components of civil society at the risk of being unable to take the point of view of the general interest or common good, that is, to give a meaning to living together.

> No authority exists any longer—no church, no state—that is entitled to speak on the meaning of common existence: it is only individual consciences that can grasp this fundamental question and give their own personal response. Civil society is thus founded in order to appear in a fully autonomous way, in all the diversity of its components.[93]

Based on its "neutrality," the liberal state guarantees all group identities, beginning with religious identities, the possibility of expressing themselves in the public sphere and being recognized in the role of components of public space, while the citizen, who was once defined as an individual able to identify himself with the point of view of all, or the General Will, becomes someone who can assert his particularity before a global society whose point of view he is no longer required to share or approve. Within an irremediably pluralistic society, citizenship no longer prohibits the assertion of a particular identity, the state being nothing more than the referee of coexistence. Marcel Gauchet writes:

> The reversal is of importance. One was defined [yesterday] by abstraction from his memberships and his private singularities, beginning with his religious convictions. . . . One is defined, henceforth, by the subjective appropriation of one's memberships and singularities, the stake being public recognition of one's private identity.[94]

Is this situation, whose contours I have described, destined to continue? Some refuse to believe it, like Régis Debray, who insists

---

93. Danièle Hervieu-Léger, "Sortie de la religion et recours à la transcendance" ["Exit from Religion and Recourse to Transcendence"], in *French Politics, Culture & Society* 20:3 (Autumn 2002), 128.
94. Gauchet, *Un monde désenchanté?*, 199.

on the permanence of religion, which he sees as a true invariant, a fundamental symbolic aspect of social existence, an elementary condition of group living.[95] Those who share this opinion and dispute the idea that our society has definitively "exited" religion, usually argue instead that it has been transferred (the sacred has merely been displaced toward other authorities or locales), or that it has just been inhibited (the more forcibly religion has been eclipsed, the stronger will be its return). In this view, one periodically announces the "return of religion" or the "return of the sacred"; one repeats the apocryphal saying of Malraux that the twenty-first century "will be religious or it will not be," and one cites willy-nilly, in support of this prediction, the renewal of the "spiritual need" one observes nowadays, the development of the phenomenon of sects, the vitality of religious beliefs in the United States, without of course forgetting Islam's return in force and the convulsive rise of "fundamentalism."

These arguments, let us immediately state, are not very convincing. Admittedly, in the long run, human history is by definition always open. But as regards the foreseeable future, I personally tend to share Gauchet's opinion that nothing allows us to foresee a "return of religion" in the phenomena most commonly alleged today as heralding such a possibility.

We already saw the confused and heterogeneous character of the "spiritual need" that is expressed nowadays. The multiplication of sects testifies rather to a pathology of individualism that, by compensation, requires the formation of "niche" communities comparable to "tribes" among others. As for the United States, if it is correct that religion played a leading role there from the beginning (and continues to play it today),[96] the reason, already

---

95. Cf. Régis Debray, *Le feu sacré: Fonctions du religieux* [The Sacred Fire: Functions of Religion] (Paris: Fayard, 2003). Régis Debray defends the *homo religiosus* thesis which was also shared by, *inter alia*, Rudolf Otto, Gergadus van der Leeuw, and Mircea Eliade.
96. According to recent surveys, 69% of Americans claim to have an unfailing faith in God, against only 20% of the French. Two thirds of Americans belong to a church or temple; 96% claim to believe in a God; 40% are regular practitioners; 72% state that it is important for them that the President of the United States express strong religious convictions.

correctly observed by Tocqueville,[97] is purely historical. Whereas in Europe, political freedom and democracy were born from a reaction against the intimate relation of state power and established religion, in the United States, democratic modernity was constituted on the basis of religious spirit. This is why America always regards itself as a chosen nation and religious convictions always serve political arguments,[98] while at the same time

---

[97]. "Most of English America was populated by men who, after throwing off the authority of the pope, never submitted themselves to any religious domination; they thus introduced into the New World a Christianity that could best be characterized as democratic or republican: it would particularly favor the establishment of the Republic and of democracy in public affairs. From the beginning, politics and religion were in agreement and have remained so since" (Alexis de Tocqueville, *De la démocratie en Amérique* [Democracy in America], vol. 1, [Paris: Gallimard, 1961], 301).

[98]. The founding fathers, who seldom described themselves as Christians, instead believed in an impersonal Enlightenment form of deism. The Puritan ideology secularizes the ideals of the Reformation by endorsing a system of shared morals. In 1823, James Monroe placed his famous doctrines of foreign policy under the sign of Providence. The United States will never cease being "One nation under God." It is even written on the dollar: "In God we trust." Political discourse refers openly to God: prayer vigils at the White House, collective baptisms in the army, and political interventions in the form of homilies. In 1898, the U.S. president William McKinley claimed to have spoken with God in the corridors of the White House, and to have received from him the order to continue to occupy the Philippines "to civilize" the inhabitants. After the attacks of September 2001, George W. Bush did not hesitate to lead a "crusade" and to state that he made war in the name of God. The American political regime is in fact based on a civil religion, whose creed is expressed in the Declaration of Independence. This civil religion, which is not related to any specific denomination ("Our government makes no sense," said President Eisenhower, "unless it is founded on a deeply held religious belief—and I don't care what it is."), is at the heart of political life in the United States. It "expresses the essence of the American way of life characterized by respect for the Constitution and the form of government which it incarnates, egalitarianism balanced by the spirit of commerce, optimism and idealism, and finally a whole series of rituals related to the celebration of the American regime" (Daniel Tanguay, "Néoconservatisme et religion démocratique" ["Neoconservatism and Democratic Religion"], *Commentaire* 114 (2006): 319–20). It is certain that in recent years, it [this civil religion] has only gained in magnitude. Jacques Julliard notes: "We can see the development in the United States, under the influence of George W. Bush himself, a new civil religion—patriotic, moralistic, and Messianic—of which the Pres-

secularization has advanced there to the same degree as in other Western countries. The separation of church and state is just as real there, but it does not have the same meaning: in Europe, it means that the state must be free of the influence of the churches, while in the United States it means that the churches must be free of the influence of the state.

The present revival of Islamism, about which there is so much talk today, was initially a political phenomenon, a political "product" cast in religious terminology, as the demands of its adherents testify. A consequence of the historical failure of secular nationalist movements in the Arab world—a failure that was strongly promoted by the United States during the Cold War—it is above all sustained by unsolved political problems, and for this reason calls for a political solution.

More generally, Islamic fundamentalism testifies less to a hostility towards modernity than a frustration born of the difficulty of entering it. It is a violent answer to the overall challenge posed by the appropriation of the instruments of modernity, which very often amounts to modernizing under the guise of combating modernization. Of Wahhabite or Salafist inspiration, fundamentalist Moslems claim to follow a tradition that they are in fact forced to reconstruct or reinvent, the true motive of their action being, here as elsewhere, personal conviction. "Contrary to their own intention," says Marcel Gauchet, "the fundamentalists work at the exit from religion whose reign they hopelessly strive to restore."[99]

---

ident is somehow the high priest. Its objective is to make the United States the epicenter of the whole world" ("Le Dieu américain" ["The American God"], *Le Nouvel Observateur* 28 [October 2004]). "For the majority of Americans," writes Sebastien Fath, "the Star-Spangled Banner and the lifestyle it represents replaced Jesus Christ as the eschatological figure of a millennium of happiness.... Formerly the strong arm of the Christian Messiah, Uncle Sam has become the Messiah himself" (*Dieu bénisse l'Amérique: La religion de la Maison-Blanche* [God Bless America: The Religion of the White House] [Paris: Seuil, 2004]). The Americans, the new chosen people, have come to worship themselves.

99. Gauchet, *Un monde désenchanté?*, 162. For a serious analysis of the "Islamist revival," cf. in particular François Burgat, *L'islamisme au Maghreb* [Islamism in the Maghreb] (Paris: Karthala, 1988); "La génération Al-Qaeda. Les courants

As for the "Islam of the suburbs," present in most large European cities, it is only one symptom among others of the identity crisis that characterizes our time. Also a consequence of an eminently personal choice, above all it plays the role of an identity marker for populations that do not manage to find their place in society. Still, one should not be mistaken: it is not so much religion *qua* religion that makes its return, but the desire for identity taking on religious trappings, less out of a desire to secede or band together, as it is believed too often, than in the hope to be recognized as a full member of overall society.

Clearly these considerations need to be qualified. One could wonder, for example, if certain political subjects are not still regarded as sacred, if the ideology of human rights does not constitute the last of the secular religions to date,[100] and if the idea of the infinite has not been brought down to the economic and technoscientific domain, with the headlong rush into perpetual growth and development, the quest for an ever expanding, ever tightening enthrallment of the world, and the flight into boundless commodities. However, even taking all that into account, we remain quite far from the "return of religion" that some think they can predict.

V

Ernest Renan, in an article on "The Religious Future of Modern Societies" published in 1860, said that Christianity is "susceptible to infinite transformations." It is quite possible, and one

---

islamistes entre 'dénominateur commun identitaire' et internationalisation de la résistance 'islamique'" ["The Al-Qaeda Generation: Islamist currents between the 'identitarian common denominator' and internationalization of 'Islamic' resistance"] *Mouvements* (November–December 2004): 77–87; Bruno Etienne, "L'islamisme comme idéologie et comme force politique" ["Islamism as ideology and political force"], *Cités* 14 (2003): 45–55.

100. Following many others, Luc Ferry himself recognized, "in a certain way, the Declaration of the Rights of Man—in a completely different fashion and on a completely different level—is quite often nothing more than secularized or rationalized Christianity" (Ferry and Gauchet, *Le religieux après la religion*, 32).

What is Religion?

"Du sollst nicht töten" [Thou shalt not kill]
by Karl Wilhelm Deifenbach, 1902.

should not forget that today Christians still represent one third of the world population (versus 19% for Islam) and also that the trade unions and political parties are, all told, even worse off than the Churches. But the fact remains that Christianity generated, in spite of itself, a society that can now leave it behind—a unique case in the history of humanity—and one cannot exclude the possibility that by doing this, it has completed its historical course, fulfilled its time.

Marcel Gauchet asserts that we have to think two phenomena simultaneously: on the one hand, the "departure from religion understood as departure from the power of religion to structure politics and society," and on the other "the permanence of religion on the level of the ultimate convictions of individuals."[101] He also says that the motives that gave rise to religion from the collective point of view have disappeared, but that those that give rise to it from the point of view of individual experience remain.[102] The whole question is whether the one can continue without the other. What indeed would a "pure religion" be that no longer has a dimension of organizing society, where religious life would be purely and simply reduced to individual belief? Can religion really become a purely personal phenomenon, concerned only with "religious feeling," even though there has never been a religious phenomenon that was not socially established? And to what tradition can we refer, when the authority of the past is rejected everywhere, and the main threat that weighs on the Churches is less the argued criticism of their dogmas or principles than the generalization of indifferentism and practical materialism?

For his part, Gauchet sees current society as proof of the "perfect viability of human existence, personal as well as social, without the gods": "If God is dead, *nothing* happens. Nobody notices it. Nothing new is prohibited or permitted. No one is better or worse off."[103] One might be tempted to grant his argument, when one sees how so many of our contemporaries, whose spirit is shaped solely by the consumerist imagination, seem to adapt to this situation.

---

101. Ferry and Gauchet, *Le religieux après la religion*, 55.
102. Gauchet, *Un monde désenchanté?*, 129.
103. Gauchet, *La démocratie contre elle-même*, 85–86.

This is also why the question of the language allowing one to talk about God in the present day is a difficulty of the first magnitude for theologians.[104] But a glass half full is also half empty. The dissolution of social bonds, the feeling of the absurdity of existence, rising anxiety, increasing numbers of suicides, the proliferation of drugs, the distress born of individualism and "the lonely crowd," with all that it implies about the need for "meaning" and "points of reference"—all this shows that Freud's "civilization and its discontents" is obviously not an illusion.

The apparently irreversible character of the phenomenon of secularization actually forces the reappearance, with even greater force, of questions that one is tempted to call eternal. Is it conceivable that human social existence can persist without being ordered by a collective meaning? Can human cultures do without a horizon of meaning? Can society continue to exist without referring to something other than itself? Confronted with his personal finitude, can man form a unity with his fellows without adhering or opening himself to something that exceeds him or transcends him infinitely? Without having common values and shared beliefs? Without giving a meaning to his existence and thus justifying his presence in the world? Without "creating the ideal"?[105] And if this is the case, isn't this precisely where contemporary nihilism resides, where spiritual dereliction merges with the oblivion of Being?[106] Whether one wants it or

---

104. "Many theologians," writes Anne Fortin, "will tell you that God exists for those who take the trouble to take it into account in their language. This movement of negative theology explains, in the domain of theology, why people publish more on Meister Eckhart than Hegel, on Saint John of the Cross than Thomas Aquinas" ("Identités religieuses et changement de paradigme: L'impossible historicisme religieux au fondement de la théorie morale de Charles Taylor" ["Religious Identities and Paradigm Shifts: the Impossible Religious Historicism in the Foundation of the Moral Theory of Charles Taylor"], in Guy Laforest and Philippe de Lara, eds., *Charles Taylor et l'interprétation de l'identité moderne* [Charles Taylor and the Interpretation of Modern Identity] (Paris: Cerf/Presses de l'Université Laval, Québec, 1998, 272).
105. Emile Durkheim, "Jugement de valeur et jugement de réalité" ["Judgment of Value and Judgment of Reality"], in *Sociologie et philosophie* [Sociology and Philosophy] (Paris: Alcan, 1924).
106. Cf. André Grjebine, *Le défi de l'incroyance: Une société peut-elle survivre*

not, doesn't religion enter the moment that one asks whether there are values higher than the strictly material life? But if there is a religious dimension of man, can it remain without collective outlet? And can political action, whatever its form, be maintained durably without ever wondering about its foundation or its ends? Without ever being able to justify social obligation other than by fear of the gendarme or respect for the law? Without ever conceiving a civilizational project? Without ever saying anything concretely about the man whose "rights" we proclaim?

All these questions may well amount to wondering whether the society in which we are living can remain livable—if collective existence can live perpetually—in a regime of weightlessness or lack of principles. There is obviously no ready answer to these questions.

In any case, in the immediate future, we are quite far from the old gods. "Today," said Jean Beaufret, "we are all atheistic. Not in the sense that atheism is an option because of the decline of faith or scientific progress that can compete victoriously with it. But in the sense of Oedipus according to the Greek myth, i.e., deserted by the divine and the gods."[107] "Deserted" is the appropriate word. In ancient paganism, the gods expressed and incarnated the presence of a world. Not of a *revealed* world, but of a *manifested* world. But the divine has withdrawn from our world, which seems devoted to nomadism and tribulation, a world where one exploits the Earth, no longer knowing how to honor it. The divine has migrated to a place whose contours we do not know. The oblivion of Being will end only when nihilism has run its course. In a famous interview granted to *Der Spiegel* in 1966, but published only ten years later, a few weeks after his death, Heidegger said: "Only a God can save us." This enigmatic formula has given rise to many commentaries. I will go no further.

(Translated by Greg Johnson)

---

sans référence surnaturelle? [The Challenge of Unbelief: Can a Society Survive without Reference to the Supernatural?] (Paris: Table ronde, 2003).
107. "L'athéisme et la question de l'Etre" ["Atheism and the Question of Being"], in *Dialogue avec Heidegger* [Dialogues with Heidegger], vol. 4: *Approche de Heidegger* [Approaches to Heidegger] (Paris: Minuit, 1974), 102.

This essay originally appeared in Alain de Benoist, "Qu'est-ce qu'une religion?," in his *Jésus et ses frères, et autre écrits sur le christianisme, le paganisme, et la religion* (Paris: Association des Amis d'Alain de Benoist, 2006), 153–99. The translator wishes to thank Alain de Benoist for permission to translate and publish this essay and for checking the translation. He also wishes to thank F. Roger Devlin for checking the translation.

ARKTOS

Alain de Benoist

Arktos is proud to announce the publication of the first three volumes in an ongoing series of English translations of the work of Alain de Benoist, the founder of the French 'New Right'.

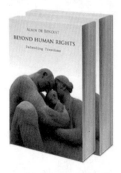

BEYOND HUMAN RIGHTS

Alain de Benoist traces the history of the concept of human rights from Antiquity to the present day, showing how the relationship between rights and belonging to a community has gradually been replaced by the idea of a sovereign individual who exists independently of any communal identity or responsibility. **120 PAGES.**

Softcover: $20 | Hardcover: $36

THE PROBLEM OF DEMOCRACY

The Problem of Democracy is the first of Alain de Benoist's book-length political works to appear in English. It presents the complexity and depth which underlies all of de Benoist's work and which is often neglected by those who seek to dismiss him by oversimplifying or distorting his arguments. **106 PAGES.**

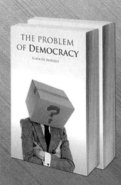

Softcover: $18 | Hardcover: $35

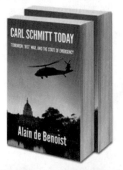

CARL SCHMITT TODAY

Alain de Benoist critiques those who claim Carl Schmitt as an inspiration behind the American 'neoconservative' movement that held sway during the administration of President George W. Bush, showing that the politics of the 'war on terror' do not actually reflect Schmitt's ideas. Benoist demonstrates that Schmitt was therefore a much greater visionary than the American neoconservatives, who failed to understand the geopolitical forces at work today. **110 PAGES.**

Softcover: $18 | Hardcover: $35

WWW.ARKTOS.COM

What is Odinism?[1]

Collin Cleary

1. Odin the Philosopher

Edred Thorsson has stated that Odinism[2] is not the path of one who worships Odin, but who strives to *become* him:

> [The] active Odian does not so much seek to worship an external god-form of Óðhinn as he does him-*Self* to embody and to develop the Self-concept and consciousness given by *the god*. Whereas other religious cults turn outward to the objective manifestation of the particular god, the cult of Óðhinn turns inward and seeks a deification of the Self. The Odian does not worship his god—he becomes his god.[3]

So the Odinist emulates Odin, but in what respect? Obviously not in all. Odin is a multifaceted figure, as indicated by the countless names applied to him in the literature (Allfather, Delight of Frigg, Lord of the Æsir, Enemy of the Wolf, Worker of Evil, Lord of the Undead, Concealer, Wanderer, etc.).

To learn what it means to be an Odinist, we must identify Odin's essential features—those that not only make him unique,

---

1. This essay is dedicated to Edred Thorsson.
2. Edred Thorsson prefers the terms "Odianism" and "Odian" to "Odinism" and "Odinist." The reason for this is that "Odinism" has long been used as a synonym simply for Ásatrú. However, by "Odianism" Thorsson means a particular path to which not all Ásatrúar will be called. (Also, certain academics have made a spurious distinction between "Odinism" and "Ásatrú," claiming that the former is somehow politicized, whereas the latter is not.) I prefer the less cumbersome "Odinism" to "Odianism," so I will simply stipulate that in this essay my use of "Odinism" is identical to what Thorsson means by "Odianism."
3. Edred Thorsson, *Runelore: A Handbook of Esoteric Runology* (York Beach: Samuel Weiser, 1987), 179. I will discuss the concept of "the Self" at length in Section Four.

but that explain or unify (in one fashion or other) all of his myriad characteristics. Quite simply, Odin's key feature is his ceaseless quest for knowledge. Closely connected with this is his striving for power. But these are so tightly linked they are almost corollaries of each other. Greater knowledge—increased insight into the nature of the universe and its secrets—brings with it an increase in the ability to manipulate and to control all manner of things. So that, as the saying goes, knowledge *is* power. (Wagner was very perceptive in making the pursuit of knowledge and power the central feature of his Wotan.[4])

A number of the legends concerning Odin depict his attempts to uncover the secrets of the universe, and thus attain wisdom. First, I must mention Odin's relation to the god Mímir. Rudolf Simek notes that "Mímir probably means 'the rememberer, the wise one' and is etymologically related to Latin *memor* [remembering, unforgetting]."[5] Mímir, along with the god Hœnir, was given to the Vanir as a hostage. Though Hœnir was renowned for his wisdom, the Vanir discovered that he had nothing to say unless advised by Mímir. Enraged, they decapitated Mímir and returned his head to Odin, who kept the severed head alive through magic and acquired "hidden lore" from it.[6] This story raises interesting philosophical questions about the relationship between wisdom and memory. As Plato recognized, the attainment of wisdom involves *recollection* of eternal forms, patterns, or laws in nature. For Plato, these are present innately in the mind of the knower and must be "recollected," in the sense of brought to conscious awareness. But we can also speak of the "recollection" of eternal truths simply in the sense of the recovery or return to them.

Mímir's Well (Mímisbrunnr) lies underneath one of the roots of the world tree Yggdrasill. Whoever drinks from its waters gains wisdom, but before Odin is allowed to drink he must sacrifice one

4. See my essay "Wagner's Place in the Germanic Tradition" in Greg Johnson, ed., *Our Wagner: The North American New Right Bicentennial Symposium* (San Francisco: Counter-Currents, forthcoming).
5. Rudolf Simek, *Dictionary of Northern Mythology* (Rochester, NY: Brewer), 216.
6. See Edred Thorsson's account in *Runelore*, 180.

What is Odinism?

ANTON VAN ROOY (1870–1932) AS WOTAN IN WAGNER'S "DER RING DAS NIBELUNGEN." PHOTO BY AIMÉ DUPONT.

of his eyes. (Later I will discuss the significance of Odin's sacrifice, and the problem it creates for Odin—and for ourselves.) Mention must also be made of the fact that Odin sought special powers and insights through the practice of *seiðr* (a form of sorcery) even though, for reasons that remain obscure, it was considered *ergi*, unmanly. Further, we must consider Odin's theft of the poetic mead from the etins (giants). The mead itself was brewed from the blood of Kvasir, who was created by the combined saliva of the Æsir and the Vanir. Like Mímir, Kvasir was reputed to be extremely wise, but unfortunately (or, perhaps, fortunately) he ran afoul of some dwarfs who killed him and brewed mead from his blood, only to have the precious substance—the source of poetic inspiration—fall into the hands of the etins. To make a long story short, Odin transformed himself into a serpent and slithered into the mountain in which the mead was concealed. He then gulped down all of the mead, which was held in three vessels, and flew back to Asgard as an eagle, where he regurgitated it for the use of the Æsir (and mankind—since it is said that some of the mead dribbled onto the earth during Odin's flight).

Again and again we find Odin searching for wisdom and power in one way or another. And he is willing to do so at all costs, recklessly breaking all the bonds of convention and prudence. He tears one of his eyes from his own head. He is willing to engage in "unmanly" practices to acquire the powers of sorcery. And, as Thorsson points out, he gains access to the mountain that conceals the mead of poetic inspiration via "cunning and oath-breaking," in his guise as Bölverkr (Worker of Evil).[7]

But surely the most significant and dramatic of all the stories recounting Odin's quest for wisdom is the tale in *Hávamál* of how he won the runes:

> I know that I hung on a windy tree
> nine long nights,
> wounded with a spear, dedicated to Odin,
> myself to myself,
> on that tree of which no man knows
> from where its roots run.
>
> No bread did they give me nor a drink from a horn,
> downwards I peered;
> I took up the runes, screaming I took them,
> then I fell back from there.[8]

Odin hangs himself on Yggdrasill for nine nights, wounded by a spear, starving, sacrificing *myself to myself*—so the text states enigmatically. And he is rewarded for his suffering by the discovery of the runes. It is not surprising that many have seen in this

---

7. Thorsson, *Runelore*, 193.
8. *The Poetic Edda*, trans. Carolyne Larrington (Oxford: Oxford University Press, 1996), 34.

a shamanic vision quest.[9] It would seem that Odin's thirst for wisdom knows no bounds at all.

We tend, nevertheless, to take these familiar stories of the god for granted, without reflecting on how genuinely surprising they are. Odin, after all, is the chief god of the Æsir. He is the Allfather, who created the known universe out of the corpse of Ymir, shaping things according to his own design. *And yet he does not know.* Nor is he all-powerful. He must work to discover the secrets of the universe he helped give form to. And he is vulnerable. The figure of Odin stands in sharp contrast to other "chief gods" of divine pantheons. He is a far cry from Zeus, for example, whose knowledge and power are seemingly unlimited. In the Germanic system, it is Hermes/Mercury who is the chief god. This is actually quite extraordinary.

It is extraordinary that the chief god of the Germanic peoples is characterized principally by his ceaseless striving for wisdom. Odin, in fact, is a philosopher in the literal sense—a lover of wisdom. Odin is a god, but he is definitely not *God*: he is neither omniscient nor omnipotent. Indeed, one way to understand Odin and what motivates him is to say that he is striving to become God.

And so now we have arrived at a more concrete understanding of exactly what it means to be an Odinist. As Thorsson says, the Odinist (or Odian) strives to become Odin. And that means, essentially, to strive to know: to make the search for wisdom the ruling passion of one's life. To become as "divinely mad" as Odin was in his quest to unlock the secrets of the universe, at any price.

But we now know something else as well: to follow Odin means, in effect, to strive to become "God": supreme, all-knowing, and all-powerful (what I will describe later on, following Thorsson and others, as "the Self"). And if we seriously undertake this challenge and reject the idea, as Odin clearly did, that there need be any limits to our quest for wisdom, then we must realize that in principle *our goal is to surpass Odin himself*. Odin is our guide, our

---

9. On Odin as shaman see, for example, Mircea Eliade, *Shamanism: Archaic Techniques of Ecstasy*, trans. Willard R. Trask (Princeton: Princeton University Press, 1974), 379–87.

guru. But the pupil may surpass the master. To set our sights any lower is, in fact, to fail to be true Odinists.

No, we most definitely do not worship Odin.

Gustav Meyrink writes (in passages excerpted in Julius Evola's *Introduction to Magic*):

> The only truly immortal being is the *awakened* man. Stars and gods disappear; he alone endures and can achieve anything he wants. There is no God above him. It is not without reason that our way has been called a *pagan way*. That which a religious man believes about God is nothing but a *state* that he himself could achieve, if he could only believe in himself. But he obtusely sets up obstacles over which he dares not jump. He creates an image of worship, instead of transforming himself into it. If you want to pray, pray to your invisible Self: it is the only God who can answer your prayers.[10]

And somewhere Meister Eckhart states that "Man's last and highest leave-taking is leaving God for God." I will amend this as follows: the Odinist must leave god for "God." Not to worship God, of course, but to *become* him—for this is the goal of the Odian quest.[11] Our goal, like Odin's, must be divinization. We must be like Wagner's Siegfried, who shatters the old man's spear and ends his reign, crying:

> Ha, rapturous glow!

---

10. Julius Evola and the UR Group, *Introduction to Magic*, trans. Guido Stucco (Rochester, VT: Inner Traditions, 2001), 40.

11. In speaking of "God" I am not drawing upon any particular religious tradition. Still less am I saying that Odinists should be monotheists—for again, I am not saying that we must *worship* this God. I would assert, however, that the idea of a supreme, all-powerful being is perennial, and that the human mind is so constituted as to conceive of it. It appears not just in monotheistic traditions but in polytheistic traditions as well. For example, in the Vedanta of the ancient Aryans we find the idea of a supreme power that is greater than the gods, of which the gods may be mere inflections. And further this supreme power is said to be identical to our innermost selves. We also find the latter point in the medieval German mystics.

Radiant gleam!
The pathway lies open,
Shining before me.
To bathe in the fire!
To find the bride in the flames![12]

Do you see this as hubris? As sacrilege? As impiety? Then the Odinist path is not for you. On this path, the very first thing that must be left behind is piety.

2. The Allfather

The idea that the Odinist must strive not just to become Odin but to surpass him—to seek to realize an ideal of perfect knowledge and supremacy—is obviously a very provocative one. And my readers will want to know exactly how this path is followed. But first, I want to further explore the curious fact named above: that the Allfather, the chief god of the Germanic peoples, is a seeker of wisdom. What we will find is that this gives us a key that can unlock three things: the nature and purpose of the cosmos itself, the nature of the Germanic peoples, and the cosmic role or mission of the Odinist. The first and third of these issues will be explored in this section. The second will be discussed in the section that follows.

Let us briefly review the Germanic creation story, as it has come down to us in Snorri's *Prose Edda*. It can be divided into three ages or stages: the elemental age, the age of the Titans (drawing this term, of course, from a parallel stage in the Greek creation myth), and the age of the gods.

In the beginning, all that existed were two elemental realms: Muspelheim in the south, filled with fire, and Niflheim in the north, an ice realm. These two elements, fire and ice, are impersonal and unconscious. Snorri tells us that there are inhabitants of these realms, but apparently they are not conscious beings.

---

12. Siegfried, Act 3, Scene 2. The translation is in *Wagner's Ring of the Nibelung: A Companion*, ed. Stewart Spencer and Barry Millington, libretti translated by Stewart Spencer (New York: Thames and Hudson, 1993), 264.

The fire giant Surtr lives in Muspelheim, but arguably the chief characteristic of the giants is their lack of consciousness. In Niflheim, all that is to be found are countless venomous serpents. Between these two realms is Ginnungagap, a void whose name has been interpreted as "yawning gap," but—more interestingly—as a "space filled with magical powers."[13] The icy rivers of Niflheim (filled with the "yeasty venom" of the serpents) flow into Ginnungagap, where the ice is struck by fiery sparks from Muspelheim.

The result of this interaction between opposites is the coming into being of the Titans of Germanic mythology: the monstrous, unconscious, haphazardly produced beings that precede the gods. The frost giant Ymir—father of the other frost giants—is first to be created. He survives by drinking the milk of Audumla the cow (who also somehow or other appears on the scene). From under Ymir's left arm grow a "man and a woman," and one of his feet begets a son with the other. Audumla draws sustenance from licking a salty ice block. But as she licks away the ice, the block forms into "a man" called Búri, "handsome and tall and strong." As I note in my essay "The Ninefold," it is extremely important that *humanoid* forms—so far, Ymir, the Frost Giants, and Búri—keep appearing haphazardly, without any intelligence seeming to guide the process.[14] It is very much as if the human is the inexorable *telos* (the end or goal) of creation.

Búri gives rise to a son, Borr, who weds Bestla, daughter of a giant. They are the parents of the brothers Odin, Vili, and Vé. And it is with them that humanoid consciousness first appears, along with humanoid form.[15] Now the stage is set for the end of the age of the Titans, and its disordered production of monstrosities and abortive humanoids. Odin, Vili, and Vé slay Ymir, drag

---

13. See Jan De Vries, *Altnordisches etymologisches Wörterbuch* (Leiden: Brill, 1977), 167.
14. By "humanoid" I mean having human-like shape or approximating to the human. Ymir, the Frost Giants, and Búri are humanoid, not human. See my essay "The Ninefold" in *What is a Rune? And Other Essays* (San Francisco: Counter-Currents, forthcoming).
15. I have discussed the character of the three brothers extensively in my essay "The Gifts of Óðhinn and his Brothers," in *What is a Rune? And Other Essays*.

his body into the center of Ginnungagap, and from his dismembered remains they construct a cosmos, where before there had been little more than chaos. (Greek *kosmos* means "orderly arrangement," related to the verb *kosmein*, "to arrange or put in order," or "to establish a regime.") In the center of everything the gods build Midgard, a realm for the human beings who they create out of two trees, Ask and Embla. And the gods also build a world for themselves in the heavens: Asgard. Bifröst, the rainbow bridge, links the realm of the gods to the earth.

There is more to the account, of course, but the foregoing is all that need be told for the purposes of the present essay. It is important to note that Odin and his brothers (who Thorsson argues may actually be aspects of Odin[16]) do not create everything; this is no creation *ex nihilo*. Not only does Odin not create the *matter* out of which he forms the universe—Ymir's corpse—there are entities in the universe that he does not form at all (some of which pre-exist him, and continue to exist after his seizure of power, such as the Frost Giants). The most significant feature of the universe that is not created by Odin is Yggdrasill. There is no mention in any of the sources of Yggdrasill having been created by him.[17] And it does not make sense to think that Odin created the three Norns (Urd, Verdandi, and Skuld) who weave his destiny, as they do the destiny of all other beings. It also makes little sense to think that he created the Völva (the Seeress) whom he consults in *Völuspá*. If he created her, why does he need to seek her counsel? Why wouldn't he know what she knows? (Her words, in fact, imply that she remembers the time prior to the coming of Odin and the other gods.) And if he had created Mímir and Mímir's Well, why would he need to ask after their wisdom? Why would he need to give up an eye to gain wisdom from something that he himself had conceived and fashioned? The Allfather is, in truth, not literally father of all. And

---

16. *Runelore*, 179.
17. The *Prose Edda* does mention that trees were created from Ymir's hair. But there is no specific mention of Yggdrasill having been created thus. Given the significance of the World Tree, if it had been created out of Ymir's remains one would think that Snorri would have mentioned this.

a pattern has now emerged: in general Odin seeks wisdom from primeval sources he did not himself create.

But let us now step back and consider this account as a whole, and try to discern the *worldview* that it conveys in mythic form. Unlike some "creator gods," Odin does not pre-exist the natural world. Instead, he *arises out of* the natural world. Though he himself is fully conscious, with a consciously directed will (indeed, he is the first being to possess these characteristics) he and everything that precedes him arises as a result of purely unconscious, undirected natural forces. And having come into being, he turns upon nature and says a gigantic "No!" to it, slaying the primal first being and re-fashioning the natural world according to his own consciously chosen and willed design. In short, through a series of events that happen by purely natural necessity, not choice, nature gives rise to a being who *negates* nature. Odin's actions, on the other hand, are not necessitated. They are chosen with full consciousness—a consciousness that simply did not exist prior to him.

Looking at the process of creation as a whole, from its beginning in fire and ice to the slaying of Ymir, it would appear that the *telos* of the natural world is the coming into being of an *unnatural* being who negates nature as-it-is and re-fashions it according to his own ideas of law and order. And who then seemingly devotes his existence to wresting nature's secrets from her.

The irresistible conclusion that suggests itself is that the coming into being of Odin and his refashioning of the cosmos—*and his search for wisdom*—is part of the unfolding "plan" of existence itself. (That there is such a "plan" is revealed in the prophecy of the Völva.)

Nature gives rise to a conscious being who, as a free agent, is a vehicle of the further unfolding and development of nature itself. The monstrous age of the Titans—an age with few laws and no consciousness—is canceled and, through the agency of Odin, the universe proliferates according to consciously-conceived ideals and laws. Odin imposes his order not just one time—but in his continual governance of things, decreeing of laws, and manipulation of events (as we see, for example, in the *Völsungasaga*). In doing so, he searches for wisdom that would guide him. This search is itself part of the "plan" of nature—an intrinsic element in the development of the cosmos.

Now, at this point one is tempted to draw an obvious conclusion: Odin actually represents humanity. We are, after all, the being who arises out of nature, yet negates the nature that we find, in order to refashion it according to our plans and ideals. But it is not just power over nature that human beings seek, but knowledge and wisdom as well. We seek knowledge that would help us improve our lot in life—but like Odin, we also seek it, and seek it passionately, *for its own sake*. We may then argue—again, taking Odin to represent the human spirit—that the coming into being of humanity is a part of nature's process of self-completion. Nature is transformed and re-organized through man's labor, and the plans and ideals we put into it. Further—and this point is absolutely crucial—through the production of a species that yearns (like Odin) to know everything in heaven and on earth, nature achieves consciousness of itself. In other words, nature reveals itself as a process, an unfolding of myriad forms, which issues in a very special sort of natural-supernatural being (man) who, through his relentless quest for knowledge and self-knowledge, holds up a mirror to nature itself.

The foregoing, again, is an attempt to discern the import of the Germanic mythic material—to express its underlying "philosophy." It cannot be emphasized enough that what is so unusual about this mythology is that it makes the highest being in the universe—nature's highest, most exalted production, as it were—a being who seeks wisdom. What is this telling us about the Germanic *Weltanschauung*? It is saying that the universe achieves consummation and completion through *being comprehended*. Thorsson writes: "*Wōdhanaz* [Odin] should be clear enough by now as that which integrates the many into a conscious whole *and describes this entire process*."[18]

We are all Odin, it seems. Or at least those of us who are lovers of wisdom. And thus we can now see that Odinism is much more than one path among others. Odinism—the search for

18. Thorsson, *Runelore*, 196. My italics.

wisdom—is the path of divinization. It is the highest of all the forms in the universe, and the one that comprehends all others. Anyone who pursues wisdom ceaselessly, fearlessly, and uncompromisingly, forsaking all else (including piety, reputation, and personal safety), is an Odinist, whether he realizes it or not. *And it is to give rise to such men that the universe exists at all.*

The above account is certainly an exalted one. But it is incomplete in one crucial respect, as I will explain in the next section.

3. The Odinic and the Faustian

Let us return to the story of Mímir's Well, and Odin's sacrifice of an eye. What does this loss signify? As Wagner recognized, it means that while Odin gains wisdom, he also becomes half blind.[19] On a literal level, this is obvious. But what is it that he becomes blind to, and what is it he is able now to "see," once he drinks from Mímir's Well? Very simply, the drink opens Odin's eye to eternal truths—hidden truths—that are not available through ordinary, sensory experience.

Of course, it is in fact his *mind's eye* that is opened to these truths. The "vision" that the drink gives him turns him *inward*, toward the things that can only be known by the mind. But the loss of one of his literal eyes signifies that in the process he loses half of his *outward* vision: his vision of the world at his own feet, so to speak. His consciousness is now divided between an enthralling world of eternal verities—with which Odin, the seeker of wisdom, desires to thoroughly involve himself—and the "external" world of finite particulars, which he now perceives with about half the acuity that he had before he took his famous sip from the well.

Now, what does this story have to teach us? The turn

---

19. Thorsson gives a "positive" interpretation to the loss of the eye, whereas my interpretation (and Wagner's) is more "negative." Thorsson writes: "Óðhinn 'hides' his eye down in the column of vertical consciousness, down in the depths. There his eye remains active, always able to see, to 'drink in,' the wisdom of all the worlds. Thus, Óðhinn always has two visions—one over 'this world' (from Hlidhskjálf) and one in the 'other worlds' (from the Well of Mímir)." *Runelore*, 192.

"inward," the opening of the eyes of the mind to the realm of truths that only the mind can know, is the source of much that is great. It is the source of scientific and philosophical speculation. But it is bought at the price of the partial disconnection from the world. The lover of wisdom is always in danger of failing to see much that is plainly in front of him. There is always the danger, for example, that he may be misled by theories or ideals that are divorced from reality. For example, instead of acting as the steward of nature, he may be seized by delusions masquerading as grand ideals, which lead him to pervert or violate nature. (This lesson is absolutely crucial to Wagner's interpretation of Wotan/Odin.[20]) He may become bewitched by implausible theories about the perfectibility of man, and set about trying to radically change human nature, and society.

Now we begin to see that what the figure of Odin really represents is not so much man per se but Western man, more specifically Northern European man—with all his great virtues, and his great faults. This is who we are, like it or not. Oswald Spengler's understanding of Northern European man as "Faustian" (which I have discussed in a number of other essays) is quite useful here—both for illuminating the nature of Odin, and our own nature (which comes to the same thing).

In his two-volume work *The Decline of the West* (1918–1923) Spengler argues that each civilization is characterized by a distinctively different spirit. According to Spengler, the prime symbol that reveals the soul of Faustian man is "pure and limitless space":

> Far apart as may seem the Christian hymnology of the south and the Eddas of the still heathen north, they are alike in the implicit space-endlessness of prosody, rhythmic syntax and imagery. Read the *Dies Irae* together

---

20. See my essay "Wagner's Place in the Germanic Tradition." I argue that Wagner should be viewed as a major interpreter and continuer of the Germanic mythological tradition, and that *Der Ring des Nibelungen* should take its place alongside such texts as the *Nibelungenlied* and *Völsungasaga* as a canonical source for Odinists and Ásatrúar.

with the Völuspá, which is little earlier; there is the same adamantine will to overcome and break all resistances of the visible.[21]

Further, he states that "the Faustian is an existence which *is led* with a deep consciousness and introspection of the ego, and a resolutely personal culture evidenced in memoirs, reflections, retrospects and prospects and conscience."[22] What characterizes the Faustian soul, then, is a kind of duality. On the one hand it is given to solemn inwardness; to looking within, and finding the answers within our own individual conscience (Odin's "inward vision"). But this goes together with an outward-striving will that, in multiple forms, yearns for the infinite.

One commentator (John Farrenkopf) expounds upon Spengler's conception of the Faustian as follows:

> The architecture of the Gothic cathedral expresses the Faustian will to conquer the heavens; Western symphonic music conveys the Faustian urge to conjure up a dynamic, transcendent, infinite space of sound; Western perspective painting mirrors the Faustian will to infinite distance; and the Western novel responds to the Faustian imperative to explore the inner depths of the human personality while extending outward with a comprehensive view.[23]

In sum, Spengler holds that European man is animated by the will not just to master all of nature, but to transcend the limits of the physical world itself.

Spengler writes

> What is Valhalla? . . . [It] is something beyond all sensible actualities floating in remote, dim, Faustian regions.

---

21. Oswald Spengler, *The Decline of the West*, trans. Charles Francis Atkinson (New York: Knopf, 1926), Vol. I, 183, 185–186.
22. Spengler, *Decline*, 183.
23. Quoted in Ricardo Duchesne, *The Uniqueness of Western Civilization* (Leiden and Boston: Brill, 2011), 335.

PORTRAIT OF OSWALD SPENGLER, CIRCA 1935.

Olympus rests on the homely Greek soil, the Paradise of the Fathers is a magic garden somewhere in the universe, but Valhalla is nowhere. Lost in the limitless, it appears with its inharmonious gods and heroes the supreme symbol of solitude. Siegfried, Parzeval, Tristan, Hamlet, Faust are the loneliest heroes in all the cultures. Read the wondrous awakening of the inner life in Wolfram's Parzeval. The longing for the woods, the mysterious compassion, the ineffable sense of forsakenness—it is all Faustian and only Faustian. Every one of us knows it. The motive returns with all its profundity in the Easter scene of [Goethe's] *Faust* I.

"A longing pure and not to be described
drove me to wander over woods and fields,
and in a mist of hot abundant tears
I felt a world arise and live for me."

Of this world-experience neither Apollinian [Greco-Roman] nor Magian [Middle Eastern] man, neither Homer nor the Gospels, knows anything whatever.[24]

It is rather obvious, in fact, that the Faustian is equivalent to the Odinic. Wagner clearly saw this, and modeled the Wotan-Loge relationship in *Das Rheingold* on the relationship of Faust to Mephistopheles.[25] To the examples Spengler gives concerning architecture, music, and painting must surely be added the intellectual tradition of Northern Europe: philosophy, science, theology, and mysticism. Here we truly see the Odinic, in our insatiable desire to bring everything into our ken; to find ourselves in everything. Thorsson writes: "By his very nature Óðhinn *synthesizes* everything around him. He makes all things his own and uses them according to his *will*, while remaining in an

---

24. Spengler, *Decline*, 185–186.
25. See my essay "Wagner's Place in the Germanic Tradition." See also Deryck Cooke, *I Saw the World End: A Study of Wagner's Ring* (Oxford: Oxford University Press, 1991), 131.

essential way *apart* from outside things."[26] The entire Northern European intellectual tradition is Faustian, or Odinic. And we should speak specifically of "Northern European." Because although there is a European character that we can see in both the Greeks, for example, and the Germans, there are significant differences. These differences are very revealing, and I will offer a brief sketch of some of them.

For the Greek thinkers the soul is potentially all; whereas the Germanic tendency is to think that it is *actually* all. Contrast Aristotle with Leibniz (or Hegel). For Aristotle the mind has the potential to become one with its object by taking on the object's intelligible form. Further, the mind has the potential (never fully actualized) to take on the intelligible forms of *all things*—the potential, in other words, to contain the entire universe. But Aristotle tells us in *De Anima* that it has this ability in virtue of having no form itself; in virtue of being *nothing*. Leibniz's philosophy of mind is essentially the complete inversion of Aristotle's. Mind does not potentially contain the entire universe, it *actually* does. Mind is not open to a world "out there," for the world is already "in here." Minds (monads) are "windowless," Leibniz declares: we do not peer from our interior at a boundless "out there." Instead, it is our interiority that is boundless. And mind is not "nothing"; in fact, it is everything. Leibniz's position is Odinic or Faustian: we find truth in the all, but we find the all in ourselves.

For the Greeks, the soul is passive; for the Germans it is active. For Aristotle, the intellect (*nous*) is merely an empty receptacle for the intelligible ideas. For the German Idealists—Leibniz, Kant, Fichte, Schelling, Hegel, *et al.*—the soul is active. It constructs the world we experience, in part or in whole. For Fichte, it is the vocation of man to impose his will upon the natural world and to re-shape it, bringing the real into accord with the ideal—*our* ideal. (Fichte is arguably the most Odinic of all the German philosophers.)

Further, the Greek tendency, which we find in Orphism, Pythagoreanism, Parmenides, Plato, and Hellenistic Gnosticism,

---

26. Thorsson, *Runelore*, 179.

is to devalue nature and the body; to declare that they are unreal, or at least an impediment to the attainment of wisdom. The Germanic tendency has been more "this-worldly"—seeking truth in the body and in the world around us. This is evident, of course, in the spirit of the mythic sources, and in the idealism of Schelling and Hegel, which is the highpoint in the development of the Germanic speculative impulse. For Schelling and Hegel, we find ourselves in nature. In knowing the world around us, we know ourselves. The "speculative impulse" is just the Odinic spirit: seeking itself in all things, and all things in itself.

Here is how Hegel characterizes the soul of European man:

> The principle of the European mind is . . . self-conscious Reason, which is confident that for it there can be no insuperable barrier and which therefore takes an interest in everything in order to become present to itself therein. The European mind opposes the world to itself, makes itself free of it, but in turn annuls this opposition, takes its other, the manifold, back into itself, into its unitary nature. In Europe, therefore, there prevails this infinite thirst for knowledge which is alien to other races. The European is interested in the world, he wants to know it, to make this other confronting him his own, to bring to view the genus, law, universal, thought, the inner rationality, in the particular forms of the world. As in the theoretical, so too in the practical sphere, the European mind strives to make manifest the unity between itself and the outer world.[27]

Consider how Odinic-Faustian this account is. The European mind "takes an interest in everything," "confident that there can be no insuperable barrier" to its knowledge. This is exactly what I characterized in Section One as the true spirit of the Odinist. The European mind "makes itself free" from nature, "opposes itself" to it, but then "annuls this opposition . . . to make manifest the unity between itself and the outer world." Compare this to

---

27. *Hegel's Philosophy of Mind*, trans. William Wallace and A. V. Miller (Oxford: Clarendon, 1971), 45.

what Thorsson has to say about the Odinic spirit:

> Óðhinn's being teaches the way of the "whole-I," the "all-self"... It can mingle with the natural, organic cosmos. It can mingle with the non-natural, numinous realms. It does so, however, in order that it may further its willed aims. It is the essence of the way of the true seeker, never resting, always searching in darkness and in light, high and low, in life and in death.[28]

And Hegel's conclusion to the above passage is decidedly Odinic-Faustian: the European mind "subdues the outer world to its ends with an energy which has ensured for it the mastery of the world."[29]

What we have in Hegel's philosophy is simply the self-understanding of European man. But that self-understanding is already there centuries earlier, in mythic form, in the figure of Odin. It is important to note, however, that the self-assessment of European man encoded in our myths is far more nuanced and pessimistic than Hegel's account, which was influenced by Enlightenment ideals. The figure of Odin is deeply ambivalent. On the one hand he is a heroic figure, bravely seeking wisdom and power. On the other hand, however, he is clearly a tragic figure. I have already noted the significance of his partial blindness. And his lust for power, and intervention in the lives of others, often has destructive consequences. Again, of all the bards who have retold and amplified the legends of Odin, it is Wagner who most clearly and powerfully brings out the tragic nature of the god. And since Odin represents us, I have already noted the sobering conclusions we must draw, when we reflect upon his character.

What more have we now learned about the path of the Odinist? We have learned, first of all, that it is a Western path. In following it, we Westerners are realizing in the flesh what Jung referred to as the "Wotan archetype," which is planted deep in the

---

28. Thorsson, *Runelore*, 198.
29. *Hegel's Philosophy of Mind*, 45.

European—especially, of course, Northern European—soul.[30] In following the Odinic archetype, furthermore, we Westerners really do make a kind of Faustian bargain. In our ceaseless pursuit of knowledge and power—in stretching ourselves out towards the infinite—we risk losing much more than an eye. We risk losing our souls.

Spengler saw the Faustian West as characterized by a sublime will to totality and transcendence, but he saw it ultimately issuing in the West's undoing. With the advent of the Industrial Revolution and capitalism, Spengler believed, the Faustian will to infinite, outward expansion took on a rootless economic and technological character. He predicted, with remarkable prescience, that eventually the West would exhaust itself in hedonism, declining birth rates, and globalist entanglements. He also expected the West to decline in material terms as well, as its technology spread to Asia, which he believed would eventually become a formidable rival.[31]

Is there hope for the Odinic-Faustian West? This is the most important question of the present age—the most important question for *us*. But there is a deeper philosophical question that lies behind this one: is the Odinic spirit necessarily tragic? Does it doom us? To this question the Odinic answer can only be: *we will not accept this*. This is certainly the only answer I can give, for the Odinic spirit is my own—it is my ancestral spirit. It is impressed upon my soul, and cannot be effaced. I cannot, therefore, shake the conviction that *only* the Odinic spirit is capable of

---

30. C. G. Jung writes that "the god of the Germans is Wotan and not the Christian God." Wotan, Jung says, is "a fundamental attribute of the German people" and "a Germanic datum of first importance, the truest expression and unsurpassed personification of a fundamental quality that is particularly characteristic of the Germans." Although a good deal of Jung's essay—written in 1936—deals with modern Germany, we must understand him in these passages to be speaking broadly of the Germanic peoples. See C. G. Jung, "Wotan," in *Civilization in Transition*, trans. Gerhard Adler and R. F. C. Hull, *The Collected Works of C. G. Jung*, Vol. 10 (Princeton: Princeton University Press, 1970), 191, 186.

31. See Duchesne, *The Uniqueness of Western Civilization*, 336. See Spengler, *Man and Technics: A Contribution to a Philosophy of Life*, trans. Charles Francis Atkinson (London: European Books Society, 1992).

solving the problems that it has created. Only the pursuit of more knowledge—no, of *wisdom*—can give us the power to correct our course. Is this merely the archetypal Odinic blindness speaking? Perhaps. Or perhaps it is Odinic wisdom speaking.

We have seen Hegel claiming that the Western spirit holds that there can be no "insuperable barrier" to its knowledge. This is certainly an expression of the Odinic spirit. But while we may not accept barriers to what we can *know*, wisdom may involve coming to understand that *what we are* is delimited in certain ways—that, in fact, *to be* is to be determined or delimited. (For example, I stated above that I am determined to believe, true to my Odinic blood, that there can be no "insuperable barrier" to my knowledge.) I have argued elsewhere that the next phase of the West's self-knowledge will involve the recognition of the futility and destructiveness of denying the unchosen conditions—biological, cultural, historical, social—that make us who we are. We will choose instead to affirm those conditions. Paradoxically, this affirmation of limits is the action of a *fully* self-aware, free, and autonomous being.[32]

Affirming the unchosen conditions for our freedom doesn't mean the same thing as "settling down." We Westerners are dyed-in-the-wool Faustians: determined to strive, restlessly. It is this fact about ourselves that we must make peace with, and affirm.[33] And so we will go on striving, but this time with full consciousness of who we are. Will this lead us again into misadventures? Almost certainly. But they will make glorious material for sagas, songs, and tragedies. And, ultimately, this is perhaps the

---

32. See the final section of my review of Duchesne's *The Uniqueness of Western Civilization* in *North American New Right*, vol. 2, ed. Greg Johnson (San Francisco: Counter-Currents, forthcoming).

33. I know self-proclaimed Odinists/Odians and Ásatrúar who take what amounts to an anti-intellectual position, insisting that the root of modern ills is precisely our ceaseless quest for knowledge and power. Apparently, they think that we can simply "stop"—that we can change our nature, and dam up the "infinite thirst for knowledge" that Hegel held to be our chief feature as a people. This is not only highly unrealistic, it is contrary to the spirit of Odinism and Ásatrú. And those who profess such beliefs lack self-knowledge. We are all Odinists, for better or worse. We cannot get that eye back, try as we might, or pretend that we never hung on Yggdrasill.

most satisfying thing that can be said about the life of a man, or of a people. (Again, the Odinic spirit speaking.)

4. Odinism as an Esoteric Path

So far, I have essentially argued that to be an Odinist is to be a lover of wisdom—one who puts nothing before this love, including piety towards Odin. Odinism is the path of divinization—the Odinist seeks to become "God" (supreme, all-powerful, all-knowing), just as Odin did. I then went on to make a striking cosmological claim: that the universe exists *in order to be known*, and that the Odinist is the vehicle of the universe's self-knowledge. Further, I have argued that Odin is the archetype that expresses the Northern European identity, and that Odinism is fundamentally a Western path. This path, however, is fraught with dangers. It is the source of all that is great about us, and all that is terrible; of all the tremendous achievements of our past, and the terrible problems of our present. What the *Katha Upanishad* says about the path it teaches is also quite applicable to our own: "Arise, awake, and learn by approaching the exalted ones, for that path is sharp as a razor's edge, and hard to go by, say the wise."

The foregoing account, however, may not fully satisfy some of my readers—a very special, select group of readers. What I have argued thus far is that we Westerners are, in a sense, *all* on the Odinic path, very broadly construed. I stated near the end of Section Two that it is possible to be on the Odinic path—to embody the archetype of Odin—unconsciously. Such men as Paracelsus, Fichte, Hegel, Wagner, Nietzsche, and Heidegger were, arguably, "unconscious Odinists." But what of the *conscious* Odinists among us? I mean those of my readers who wish to consciously and deliberately follow this path, and who are steeped in the lore of our ancestors. They will want something more than just the exhortation to "pursue wisdom."

This is where we must enter into a discussion of what I will call "esoteric Odinism." But it must begin with a reconsideration of the "cosmological" argument of Section Two, and approach these matters on a deeper level. This will lead, in the end, to a discussion of the *practice* of Odinism.

In the foregoing I have argued for the thesis that it is man that brings the whole (the universe) to completion through his quest for knowledge of the whole. Through man, in other words, the universe achieves knowledge of itself: it holds a mirror up to itself. In order to fully understand why this is the case, one must keep squarely in mind that man arises out of nature; he is a natural being, though of a peculiar sort.

As Aristotle saw (and later Hegel, following Aristotle) man recapitulates within himself the rest of nature, in possessing the appetitive and nutritive functions (plant nature), and the sensory and locomotive (animal nature).[34] Biologically, we comprise the whole—in a sense we combine all creatures within ourselves; we are all things. We are the microcosm that reflects the macrocosm. But we step beyond all other creatures at the same time, in being capable of achieving self-knowledge.[35] Thus, in striving to know ourselves—which always necessarily involves, as Hegel makes clear, finding ourselves in the world around us, taking an interest in all—we are the whole knowing itself. Man occupies a privileged position in nature, reigning over all as the highest terrestrial being—in virtue both of his knowledge, and his power. Man is part beast, part god (as Aristotle recognized).

The above only puts the argument of Section Two in a slightly different way. The next step is to recognize that man's knowledge or consciousness of the whole (which is simultaneously his self-consciousness, in the most profound sense) is purely impersonal. Each man is, to one degree or another, the "carrier" of this consciousness, but it is something radically distinct from my consciousness of myself as an individual. To achieve knowledge of the whole, I must go beyond the personal ego and its attachments, and identify myself with a "higher self" that strives to

---

34. It can also easily be argued that we possess "mineral nature" as well, in that most of the elements found in the earth's crust are also found in the human body. The "mineral" aspect of the human body is most readily apparent in bone.

35. Aristotle expressed this point by saying that man, and only man, possesses a "rational soul," in addition to a "vegetable soul" and "animal soul."

embrace all. In other words, *I must sacrifice myself to myself.*

A different way to put the same point is to say that I must shift my sense of identification from the personal self to what I will call, following Thorsson, the Self. Thorsson writes,

> The "birth" of Ódhinn and the World-Tree sacrifice are essentially simultaneous—without it Ódhinn is not Ódhinn. In this process Ódhinn gives his self to him-Self while hanging on Yggdrasill (the steed of Yggr [= Odin], or the yew column). The subject has turned upon itself and has successfully made itself the object of its own work.[36]

The Self is equivalent to what is sometimes referred to as "cosmic consciousness" (though this term has certain unfortunate associations with New Age authors). The Self is, again, the whole's consciousness of itself. And it is my *true Being*—who I *really* am. But it is not reducible to me, since it is not the same thing as my personal ego (my small "s" self). Again, each man—insofar as he realizes the Odinic ideal—is the carrier of this Self. It lives through us—but it does not die when we die. Thorsson writes, further, "Ódhinn's being teaches the way of the 'whole-I,' the 'all-self,' as well as the 'higher self.' This higher self is a supraconscious entity, the 'holy self' or the magical ego of the runemaster."[37]

The Self is therefore a being distinct from us, though, as I have said, it is realized in the world through us alone. To draw a philosophical analogy, it is similar to the Aristotelian understanding of form as actuality. The form or being of an object is not reducible to the object (since other, similar objects share the same form), but it is realized in the world through the objects that actualize or exemplify it. Similarly the Self is something distinct from me, but it is possible—by disengaging myself from identification with the finite me—to realize my fundamental identity with it. (Just as Odin does in the sacrifice on Yggdrasill.) When this occurs, the Self is "actualized" in the world *and the world itself*

---

36. Thorsson, *Runelore*, 191.
37. Thorsson, *Runelore*, 198.

is actualized, since, as I have argued, the *telos* of the whole is its consciousness of itself.

The Self is thus not just my Being—it is the Being of all things. Everything comes to be out of the universe's drive for manifestation. Of course, it is not as if the universe is a "thing" that manifests itself. Rather, the universe *is* this manifestation. If we ask *what* is doing the manifesting, the answer is the Self. This may at first seem like an odd answer, since what I have said earlier seems to imply that the Self is realized *later* in the process of creation, through human beings who, in their pursuit of knowledge, constitute the universe's self-awareness. But it is vital to understand that the Self is there from the beginning, prior to manifestation—logically, but not temporally prior, as the Being or essence of the universe itself, which is only fully actualized through human knowledge. The picture that emerges is that the entire world is an infinite Self coming to consciousness of itself, and that each and every being in the universe plays a role in the manifestation of the Self to itself. But the crucial role is played by the one being who is capable of self-awareness and of knowledge of the whole: man.

There is thus a great "World I" that my own "I" is but a reflection of. And I have a fundamental choice that is not faced by any other being. I can behave as if my personal I exists for its own sake, abiding in perfect aloneness, detached from the whole. This is the path of foolish "attachment" to things that do not last. It is the path of egoism and self-aggrandizement; it is the path, in fact, of non-being. My other choice is to shift my sense of identity from that petty, personal I to the World I—the ideal aim being to realize that World I in myself; to make myself the Self. To sacrifice my self to my Self. Thorsson writes, "The Odian does not seek 'union' with Odin but seeks union only with that with which Odin sought union—the Self."[38]

The left-hand path *cannot* mean the exaltation of the limited, imperfect ego. It cannot mean, for example, that *that* ego attains "special powers." That is the dream of an adolescent, or of a petty egoist. The left-hand path must mean the transmutation and

---

38. Thorsson, *Runelore*, 198.

perfection of the ego; it is not the aggrandizement of the self, but the identification with the Self. It is not an "annihilation" of the self and an absorption into the Absolute (this is the "mystical path," what Evola calls the "wet way"). The left-hand path (the "dry way") means that here, now, in this world I become the Self. It is a path of self-mastery and divinization that is lived within time and in engagement with the world.

But how do we do this? There are two ways, which are not mutually exclusive, indeed they should accompany each other: the way of theory, and the way of practice. "Theory" derives from the Greek verb *theorein*, "to see, or behold." A theory is therefore a "seeing," or better "a beholding." The way of theory involves, first of all, seeing the world in the manner I have described above: the purpose of existence itself as our quest for wisdom. The way of theory thus, in part, amounts to adhering to a certain philosophical outlook. But it is not enough simply to accept these ideas: one must actively be a seeker; one who searches for wisdom as Odin did. One must, in other words, *theorize*—strive to understand, or to behold more and more.

The way of theory is extraordinarily liberating. If we can learn to find ourselves in the world by realizing that that world is there *for us*, and for our seeking, then we recognize that nothing matters save that seeking. And if we can free ourselves from everything that would hold that seeking back or confine it, then we become the freest of men.

But theory and theorizing are not all. There is also practice. I am using that term in the sense in which it is used in esoteric, initiatory traditions. Is there a spiritual practice of Odinism?

The key to this question is to be found in the story of Odin's self-sacrifice on Yggdrasill. I have dealt with this matter in another essay.[39] Here I will approach the same material in a different and much simpler way.

A student of that most Odinic of philosophers, J. G. Fichte, left behind the following remarkable account of one of the great man's lectures, delivered in the winter semester of 1798/1799 at Jena:

---

39. See "What God Did Odin Worship?" in *Summoning the Gods: Essays on Paganism in a God-forsaken World* (San Francisco: Counter-Currents, 2011).

I cannot deny that I was awed by my first glimpse of this short, stocky man with a sharp, commanding tongue. Even his manner of speaking was sharp and cutting. Well aware of his listeners' weaknesses, he tried in every way to make himself understood by them. He made every effort to provide proofs for everything he said; but his speech still seemed commanding, as if he wanted to dispel any possible doubts by means of an unconditional order. "Gentlemen," he would say, "collect your thoughts and enter into yourselves. We are not at all concerned now with anything external, but only with ourselves." And, just as he requested, his listeners really seemed to be concentrating upon themselves. Some of them shifted their position and sat up straight, while others slumped with downcast eyes. But it was obvious that they were all waiting with great suspense for what was supposed to come next. Then Fichte would continue: "Gentlemen, think the wall!" And as I saw, they really did think about the wall, and everyone seemed able to do so with success. "Have you thought about the wall?" Fichte would ask. "Now, gentlemen, think him who thinks the wall." The obvious confusion and embarrassment provoked by this request was extraordinary. In fact, many of the listeners seemed quite unable to discover anywhere whoever it was that had thought about the wall. I now understood how young men who had stumbled in such a memorable manner over their first attempt at speculation might have fallen into a very dangerous frame of mind as a result of their further efforts in this direction.[40]

What Fichte was asking his astonished students to do was to shift their attention from the objects around them to attention itself: to remember the self that attends to the world. In our daily lives

---

40. From the memoirs of Hendrik Steffens, quoted and translated in J. G. Fichte, *Introductions to the Wissenschaftslehre and Other Writings*, trans. Daniel Breazeale (Indianapolis: Hackett, 1994), 111. I have amended the translation slightly.

we are always occupied with this object or that. The object may be a physical something, such as the keyboard in front of me, or it may be an idea, an expectation, a hope, a fear—anything that, for whatever reason, presents itself to us and "catches" our attention. (Even absence may present itself to us and preoccupy us, as when—to use the sort of example Sartre would have used—we arrive at the café at the appointed time expecting to see Pierre, but register only his absence.) The self always has some object or other. But there is, in addition, "another self" that can step back from one's attachment and reflect upon it. A self that is aware of the self that is aware. It remains detached and observant, whereas the characteristic of the mundane self is that it is always "attached" in one way or another.

The key to the Odinist "practice" is the identification with this detached self. Just *how* to do this is hard to describe. We could say that we must "shift" our identification from the mundane, attached self to the detached, observing self. But what does the shifting? It might be better to say that we must simply *become* this self, though this hardly sounds like giving instructions at all. In practice, one will find that one can simply *do* this—though how we do it is mysterious. And the practitioner will find at first—and for a long time—that shifting to the perspective of this detached self is hard to sustain for very long. Something will always come along to "grab" us and suddenly we find ourselves attached again, and identified with the mundane self.

The teaching I am describing here is perennial, and one finds traces of it in many different sources. In the UR material edited by Julius Evola (and published as *Introduction to Magic*), "Abraxas" writes that

> the secret . . . consists in creating in yourself a dual being. You must generate—first by imagining and then by realizing it—a superior principle confronting everything you usually are (e.g., an instinctive life, thoughts, feelings). This principle must be able to control, contemplate, and measure what you are, in a clear knowledge, moment by moment. There will be two of you: yourself standing

before "the other.". . . All in all, the work consists of a "reversal": you have to turn the "other" into "me" and the "me" into the "other."[41]

Abraxas goes on to comment upon "you have to turn the 'other' into 'me' and the 'me' into the 'other'" as follows, and his words are worth quoting at length: "Depending upon which of the two principles the person focuses on, you will have the *Dry Way* or the *Humid Way*, the magical method or the mystical method." In the mystical method, "the mind creates an 'other' that still remains 'other.'" One loves or yearns after this "other." Abraxas refers to this standpoint as "feminine," "negative," and "dependent" ("it has the character of *need*"). He states "To turn [this standpoint] into the purely affirmative, central, and self-sufficient solar nature requires a qualitative leap and a daring that is very difficult for a mystic to achieve, considering the contrary nature of the previous mortification."[42]

This "daring leap" is, of course, what is required of the Odinist. Abraxas continues:

> In the magical, dry, or solar way, you will create a duality in your being not in an unconscious and passive manner (as the mystic does), but consciously and willingly; you will shift directly on the higher part and *identify* yourself with that superior and subsistent principle . . . Slowly but gradually, you will strengthen this 'other' (which is yourself [i.e., your Self]) and create for it a supremacy, until it knows how to dominate all the powers of the [lower] natural part and master them totally. What is required of you is a discipline of firmness and sobriety until an equilibrium is created, namely the quality of a life that owns itself and is free with regard to itself, cleansed from instinct and from the obscure appetite of the natural being, in both flesh and mind.[43]

---

41. Evola and the UR Group, *Introduction to Magic*, 48.
42. Evola and the UR Group, *Introduction to Magic*, 49.
43. Evola and the UR Group, *Introduction to Magic*, 50–51. Abraxas's entire

In sum, the first step of the work consists in dividing consciousness into an active, watching self, and a passive, experiencing self. The aim of the Odinist is to identify with the superior, detached, watching self.

Now, very simply, this superior self *just is* the Self discussed earlier. It is not *you*. It is an *infinite consciousness* in the sense that it is not finitized through attachment or absorption in this object or that. It is the "World I" gazing at itself: the consciousness of existence itself, born through you. In these moments in which we achieve identity with this detached, observing consciousness, the Self is "actualized" in the world and—as I argued earlier—the world itself is actualized, since the purpose of the whole is its consciousness of itself. In these moments of identification with the Self, *you are the whole knowing itself*.

And you are Odin—or, more specifically, you reach the Odinic goal. Just like Odin, you have arisen from nature, from the all, and brought consciousness of the all into being. But before Odin could do this, he had to "negate" the nature from which he had arisen. In order to achieve the Odinic consciousness, you must do the equivalent: you must sever your consciousness from finite attachment, and infinitize it.

As I have noted, remaining identified with the Self is extraordinarily difficult. There are a number of different sources which contain hints about how to go about achieving this. These include the works of Edred Thorsson and Julius Evola (though they offer only hints; both writers know more than they are willing to say openly). There is, in addition, a great deal of practical information to be found in works dealing with the so-called "Fourth Way" teaching of the Greek-Armenian mystic G. I. Gurdjieff (1866–1949), a decidedly Odinic figure.[44] For all intents and purposes, Gurdjieff's "self-remembering" is identical to the practice I have described here.

essay—and the volume itself—handsomely repays multiple readings.
44. Stephen E. Flowers writes, "If we were to measure the magnitude of 'occult leaders' by the greatness achieved by those whom they taught or in some positive way influenced, then certainly the greatest such teacher of the twentieth century would be George Ivanovitch Gurdjieff." See Flowers, *Lords of the Left-Hand Path* (Rochester, VT: Inner Traditions, 2012), 272.

GEORGE IVANOVICH GURDJIEFF. PHOTO COURTESY OF THE GURDJIEFF FOUNDATION OF ILLINOIS.

The Fourth Way is practiced in the world, not in separation from it. Gurdjieff contrasts it to three other paths: the way of the fakir (who works to master the body), the way of the monk (who masters the emotions), and the way of the yogi (who masters the mind or intellect). These paths not only tend to involve the isolation of the practitioner from the world, they lead, so Gurdjieff believed, to one-sided development. The Fourth Way works on mastering all aspects of the self and, again, it requires that this self-mastery be sought while the practitioner is fully engaged with life. And we must take special note of the fact that Gurdjieff offered his teaching as a mystical path *for the West*. It is also easy to see that the Fourth Way belongs to the left-hand path.[45] It

---

45. Flowers writes, "From a structural and methodological standpoint, the Fourth Way generally presents a picture in complete harmony with those of the left-hand path. It is only in the lack of recognition of the historical and archetypal analogs of the system with Satanic symbolism that the Fourth Way

uses the distractions and pressures of modern life as a means to mastering the self. For just this reason, it is obvious that this path is well-suited to the present time: the Wolf Age, Iron Age, or Kali Yuga. Finally, it is a *tough* way: there is nothing "touchy-feely" about it (which is why many New Age types tend to be put off by Gurdjieff).

The Gurdjieffian way is not without its pitfalls (and my discussion of it here does not in any sense constitute an "endorsement"). So-called "Gurdjieff groups" are often uncomfortably cultish, and sometimes—in their efforts to "remember the self"—members develop a cold, emotionless quality (ironic, given Gurdjieff's insistence that his teaching was about overcoming the "robot" in all of us). The Fourth Way has probably harmed about as many people as it has helped, and driven some people quite mad. This is undeniably part of its allure (at least for the dauntless Odinist). It must also be noted that Gurdjieff's initiatory teaching of self-mastery is coupled with cosmological speculations that strain credulity.[46] In my eyes, these are more objectionable, in fact, than his claim that the Fourth Way is "esoteric Christianity." (The simple reason being that "esoteric [i.e., mystical] Christianity" in certain ways bears a passing resemblance to Odinism, especially in the hands of the classical German mystics.)

Nevertheless, the Fourth Way has much to teach us about the practice of Odinism; first and foremost, the technique of identification with the Self. But Gurdjieff's followers are also notoriously guarded about the actual methods of what they call "the Work," insisting that it can only be imparted through "group." To an

---

may fall short of the criteria of being a school of the left-hand path, but this is practically a matter of aesthetics. Fourth Way teachings, and even its methodology, are often antinomian. There is a constant 'going against the grain' of nature, of God, of the mechanism of the universe. Its aim is the attainment of an awakened, independently existing intellect and relative immortality (self-deification). This is individualistic, it comes in initiatic stages . . . and its chief technology is doing: the use of the will to cause the mechanism to conform to its volition (i.e., 'magic')." Flowers, *Lords of the Left-Hand Path*, 292–93.

46. Flowers gives a concise and accurate summary of Gurdjieff's theories in *Lords of the Left-Hand Path*, 272–93.

Odinist, this is nothing more than a gauntlet thrown down, for we are not "joiners." One must therefore "read around" quite a bit in Fourth Way literature and connect many dots in order to uncover what the actual practice consists in.[47]

I can summarize the basics of it as follows.

What is required, first of all, is the simple act of "self-observation." In this act, the self—as described above—bifurcates into an active, watching self, and a self that is watched. (This watching self and the Self, I have argued, are metaphysically identical.) Just what do we observe? Begin with the practice of grounding yourself in the present moment. Focus on bodily sensations: on the experience of touch, sight, sound, smell. Thoughts will come to you about what you are touching, seeing, etc. Observe this, and

---

47. Perhaps the best book with which to begin is *Self Observation: The Awakening of Conscience*, by Robert Moore, writing under the pen name Red Hawk (Prescott: Hohm Press, 2009). There is some off-putting mushiness in this book, but it is filled with practical instructions and reveals far more than most Fourth Way texts. Also of great value are the posthumously published notes of Gurdjieff's chief disciple, Jeanne de Salzmann, published as *The Reality of Being* (Boston: Shambhala, 2011). The book with which curious readers most often begin is P. D. Ouspensky's *In Search of the Miraculous* (New York: Harcourt Brace Jovanovich, 1949). This contains valuable information, but the reader must be patient with Ouspensky's fixation on some of the more incredible aspects of Gurdjieff's theories. Ouspensky's *The Fourth Way* (New York: Random House, 1957) is also helpful, though extremely dry. The writings of Gurdjieff himself are not the place to begin. I find his magnum opus, *Beelzebub's Tales to His Grandson*, to be completely unreadable. There is more than a little Loki in Gurdjieff, along with the Odinic element. He was a grand trickster, as were many figures in the occult and esoteric traditions. I am sure there is a teaching in *Beelzebub*, but Gurdjieff did his best to bury it under material that would make the average reader dismiss him as a madman. More accessible is Gurdjieff's *Views from the Real World* (New York: Dutton, 1975). And his *Meetings with Remarkable Men* (London: Penguin, 1985) is quite interesting as autobiography, though it strains credulity. (This book was made into a film in 1979, directed by Peter Brook, and is worth seeing despite its flaws.) Finally, a great deal can be gleaned from a source that is not technically part of the Fourth Way, but is most definitely aligned with it: Julius Evola's *Introduction to Magic*, which is cited above. The reader would gain a great deal by reading this latter text alongside any of those mentioned above. Also quite useful is Evola's *The Hermetic Tradition* (Rochester, VT: Inner Traditions, 1995).

then gently draw yourself back to the experience of the sensations themselves. Properly practiced, this will give rise to a very special sort of realization which, if put into words, would simply say "I am." It should be obvious that what is involved in self-observation is a very special form of attention or awareness in which you become intensely present to Being. This almost inevitably leads to the experience I have described elsewhere as *Ekstasis*—wonder in the face of Being, in the sheer fact that things *are*—which I have argued is equivalent to *óðr* of which Odin is the personification.[48]

When you practice self-observation you will note such things as tension in the body. Most of the time, you will find that this tension is unnecessary, given the circumstances you are actually in. You may also notice emotions that are not appropriate to those circumstances. But what you will notice especially is unnecessary thoughts: the constant chatter of the mind. Self-observation is extraordinarily frustrating at first, because as soon as one has achieved a state of observing without attachment, some stray thought will come along and suddenly one will find oneself "absent" from the present, and thinking about some petty concern. The particular danger for the lover of wisdom is that the experience of self-observation will give rise immediately to "insights," and the attention will then shift from observation to theorizing. Theorize later. But make no mistake, self-observation deepens theorizing—and vice versa.

It should be obvious by now that this practice requires extraordinary patience. It is a constant struggle between finite and infinite attention; between attachment and detachment; between the ordinary, mundane self or I and the World I or Self. But, with practice, it gets easier.[49]

---

48. See my essays "The Gifts of Óðhinn and His Brothers" and "The Stones Cry Out: Cave Art and the Origin of the Human Spirit," in *What is a Rune? And Other Essays*.
49. It should also be obvious at this point that what I am describing is a kind of "active meditation." The exact same principles apply to meditation practice. In my view, both the active, Fourth Way meditation and the classical "sitting still, doing nothing" meditation should be practiced. The former is practiced throughout the day. The latter is reserved for a specific time of the day, for a

One must also resist the temptation to *change* what is observed, for then one loses the perspective of the detached observer and becomes involved. So if, for example, there is tension in the body, merely observe this. What you will find, oddly enough, is that this very act of observation releases the tension. The simple reason is that in observing it, one is not identifying with it. One is saying, in effect, "that is not me." And the tension often simply melts away. It is equally important not to *judge* what one observes for then one gets caught up in judging rather than observing. But according to the Gurdjieff teaching—and this is one of the most profound insights it has to impart—the simple act of self-observation will, in time, change one's undesirable or unhealthy features. The reason, again, is that the act of observation detaches one from these features; one ceases to identify with them. Performed repeatedly, therefore, self-observation has the power to weaken the hold that these features have over us. This leads us to the obvious conclusion that self-observation is a path to freedom and to power—over oneself and circumstances (for without self-mastery, no other mastery is possible). (Again, the Odinic nature of this practice is obvious.)

Further, one must be totally, ruthlessly honest with oneself. There may be no blind spots in self-observation. This leads to what is called in Gurdjieff's teaching "voluntary suffering," because inevitably much that one observes about oneself is negative. But one must always keep in mind that the Odinist path is the love of wisdom—and that it is simultaneously the quest for knowledge of the whole, and for self-knowledge. The Self that we strive to identify with or to actualize is, again, an infinite openness: it sees all, and attaches itself to nothing. Because it *is* all. Thus, if we close ourselves to any aspects of reality, no matter how painful, then we remain identified with the finite self. (The Gurdjieff teaching also cautions us, however, that we have erected many "buffers" that prevent us from seeing the truth—and if too many of these are removed too quickly, the result can be traumatic.)

---

delimited period of time. I prefer to meditate upon awakening each day, for thirty minutes or more.

It should be obvious from all the foregoing why the mind resists self-observation. Not only is it difficult, it leads to pain and, ultimately, the radical transformation—or overcoming—of the self. But the self (the ordinary, mundane self) does not want to be overcome. The self is to the Self as nature is to Odin. Nature issues Odin; it gives rise to its own overcoming. But the Titans do not want to be overthrown. Ymir does not want to be killed and dismembered. Yet, this primeval murder is, as I argued much earlier, all part of nature's actualization as a cosmos—as an ordered arrangement—through the arising of Odin. Similarly, on the level of the individual Odinist, our mundane, finite self must be "killed," and dragged to the void that is the infinite, observing Self, which is nothing and all. And it must be taken apart, it must undergo "voluntary suffering," and be rebuilt. But we resist this. We hide from ourselves, just as nature conceals itself from us, forces us to dig deeper, always holding something back. ("Nature loves to hide," Heraclitus said.)

It is inevitable that there will be resistance to self-observation, but the Fourth Way teaches that in fact there is no progress without this. And the more truths about yourself that you awaken to, the fiercer the resistance will become. Then you will feel an extremely strong temptation to give up. This must be resisted at all costs. For the Odinist path is the path of the awakened being; we cannot settle for a return to sleep. This is the path of Self-realization, and it is extraordinarily hard. But it is the only path to true freedom and awakening. It is the perfection of the human individual—and, as I have argued, simultaneously the perfection of the world itself.

Clearly, the Odinist path is not an easy one—nor is it without its dangers. I will conclude with a warning from "Abraxas" in Evola's *Introduction to Magic*:

> If you want to approach our Art, be aware that this is a painful struggle and somewhat like walking on a razor's edge. You may win or lose, and two things lead to certain disaster: to be afraid and to interrupt the operation. Once you have begun, you must go all the way, since an inter-

ruption leads to a dreadful reaction, with the opposite result. You can easily understand why: at every step you take, an increasingly higher quantity of swirling energy is arrested and pushed upstream; having been excited and provoked, it is filled with tension. As soon as you give up, it will come crashing down upon you and sweep you away. . . . One does not have to embark [on this path], but once you have done so, there are only two alternatives: succeed or perish.[50]

---

50. Evola and the Ur Group, *Introduction to Magic*, 20, 78.

BESTSELLING TITLES FROM AN AUTHORITY OF RUNOLOGY, EDRED THORSSON

AVAILABLE WHEREVER BOOKS AND EBOOKS ARE SOLD.

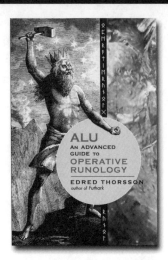

ALU, An Advanced Guide to Operative Runology
978-1-57863-526-9
Paperback · $24.95

Futhark
A Handbook of Rune Magic
978-0-87728-548-9
Paperback · $16.95

Runecaster's Handbook
978-1-57863-136-0
Paperback · $16.95

Runelore
The Magic, History, and Hidden Codes of the Runes
978-0-87728-667-7
Paperback · $18.95

Weiser Books
www.redwheelweiser.com • 800.423.7087
orders@rwwbooks.com

Traditional Time-Telling in Old England, and Modern

Nigel Pennick

We are so used to counting in tens, using decimal coinage and metric measurements, that it is difficult sometimes to realize that ten is an arbitrary number, derived from the number of digits on each hand. The traditional way of dividing things up is not in tens, for this is not the natural way of doing things. The basic way to divide things up is to cut them in half, then in half again, and so on. This means of division is thus twofold, fourfold, eightfold, sixteenfold, and so on. It requires no measurement against a stick or tape with units. "Cut a round of bread;" wrote Alfred Watkins, "it is too large a slice and it is halved; if too large these are halved, and if necessary halved again. No one ever divides the slices into fifths or tenths."[1] And in 1985 in *Natural Measure* I wrote, "This eightfold division of weight, distance and capacity is related to the geometrical properties of the square rather than to intellectually later concepts such as number."[2]

Traditional weights, measures, and money as well as time were based wholly or partly upon an eightfold system, and contemporary pagans punctuate their yearly cycle with eight festivals. The compass rose is the most common extant example of this method of dividing space by repeated halving, having thirty-two basic divisions. Although it has been driven down by the decimalization of commerce, the octaval system is still valid because it is derived from our natural perception of the world. In agricultural and seagoing societies, people are always aware of the horizon visible from where they are, both for the observation of the apparent motions of the sun, moon and stars, and to be in harmony with the qualities and virtues inherent in the shape of the landscape.

---

1. Watkins, "Must We Trade in Tenths?" 3.
2. Pennick, *Natural Measure*, 1.

Octaval Old England

In the Germanic North, the basic layout of the land was visualized according to natural measure by the division of the circle into its four quarters by conceptual lines that run north–south and east–west. Between these lines, the horizon is further subdivided by conceptual lines running to the intercardinal directions. This produces the eightfold geometrical division one needs to lay out a square or rectangular building or enclosure whose sides face the four quarters of the heavens. The southern quarter is thus the quadrant between southwest and southeast; the eastern quarter is between southeast and northeast; the northern sector is between northeast and northwest; and finally, the western quadrant is between northwest and southwest. The four cardinal directions are thus at the midpoints of the four quarters.

These eight directions come from the physical structure of the world we live upon: the north-south polar axis and the east-west one at right angles to it, the plane of the Earth's rotation. From these the fixed directions inherent in the structure of our planet come the others between them by geometrical division. In Old Norse, these eight directions were called *ættir*: in Scotland and northeastern England they are called the *airts*, and across the Pennines in the northwest they are known as the *haevers*.[3] The Old Norse word more generally means direction, as, for example in the verb *átta*, "to orientate oneself." *Ætt* also means a "family, a clan, a lineage," or a "house" in the sense of a noble ancestral line. This is of course related to the place where the line originated and lived. The *ættir* of the horizon correspond with the eight periods of time called *eyktir*, a word that Otto Sigfrid Reuter linked with the English word *yoke* and the German *jochand*.[4] Each group of eight runes in a rune-row is also an *ætt*. Alexander Warrack notes that in Scots dialect, *airt* means "a quarter of the heavens; point of the compass; the direction of the wind" as well as being connected with transitive movements in a direction such as "to point out the way to a place; to direct; to turn in a certain

---

3. Harland and Wilkinson, *Lancashire Folk-Lore*, 149.
4. Reuter, *Skylore of the North*, 7.

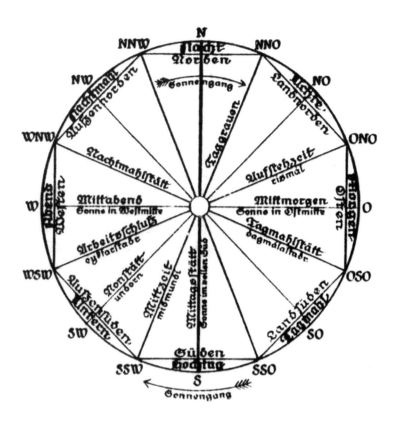

THE AIRTS, AFTER OTTO SIGFRID REUTER.

direction . . . to aim at."[5] In modern Gaeilge (Irish), *aird* means a direction or a point of the compass. All of these northern words are related to "the astronomical directions as a clock face."[6]

Because of the considerable differences in day length during the year in northern Europe, the awareness of the directions was more highly developed and widespread than in many other parts of the world, for it was a necessary part of survival. Hence the incompatible difference in time-telling between the Egyptian Christian hours called *temporal hours* and those of the octaval northern tradition. The knowledge and lore of the *airts* was an integral part of the knowledge of farmers, builders, millers, drovers, pedlars, hunters and seafarers. This awareness of direc-

---

5. Warrack, *The Scots Dialect Dictionary*, 4.
6. Reuter, *Skylore of the North*, 6.

tions has subtle ramifications in all manner of areas, unsuspected by those who have never encountered a traditional landscape.

The eight *airts* come directly from the fixed directions inherent in the structure of our planet. But in addition to these physical directions, there are variable directions with a cyclic nature. These are defined by the apparent motions of the heavenly bodies, in relation to the fixed ones. Depending on the latitude we live at, the visible position of the rising and setting sun at the solstices—the longest and shortest days of the year—and at other times of the year marked by sacred festivals, are at different places on the horizon from the intercardinal directions that mark the *airts*. Furthermore, the height of the horizon above or below our viewing-point will alter the apparent rising and setting positions of the sun, moon, and stars. Also, unless the viewing-place has a horizon of equal height all around it, we will not see the celestial bodies rising and setting symmetrically with relation to the cardinal directions. On a level horizon, there is an annual solar geometry in which the midsummer solstice sunrise appears diametrically opposite midwinter sunset, and the winter solstice sunrise is correspondingly directly opposite the midsummer sunset. The apparent motion of the moon behaves quite differently from the sun, in a far more complex cycle.

How long daylight lasts varies with the season. In northern Europe, the difference between the length of daylight at midwinter and midsummer is considerable. The range between the height of the sun at noon on midwinter and noon on midsummer is also notable. Between the southernmost rising of the sun at midwinter, and the most southerly sunrise at midsummer, the sun rises due east at the equinoxes, crossing the east-west line in an apparently southerly movement in winter and northwards in summer. This defines the two halves of the year, the dark half and the light half. At its maximum northerly position is the summer solstice, and at its maximum southerly position, the winter solstice. These positions are a function of the viewer's geographical latitude. They also define the two parts of the year, the first half of the sun's increase, from the winter solstice to the summer one, and then the second half of the sun's decrease, from the summer to the

Traditional Time-Telling in Old England

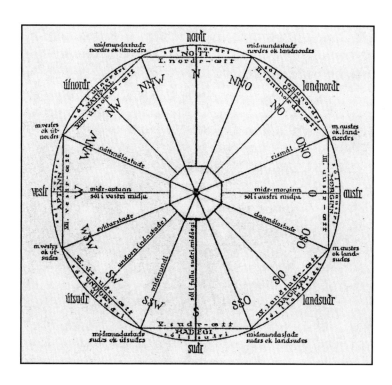

ICELANDIC WHEEL OF TIME, EARLY TWENTIETH CENTURY.

winter solstices.

The traditional agricultural landscapes of northern Europe embed some of these mark-points in the placement and layout of settlements. Viewed from farmsteads or sacred places, these rising, setting, and standing points of the sun were indicated either by natural features, or by artificial markers such as standing stones, tall posts, specially planted mark-trees or cairns. Reuter notes that from the earliest times houses were orientated to the cardinal directions so that "whoever stepped out of the south door had before them the true south, true west to the right, true east to the left. If for any reason the house did not face the cardinal points, and if moreover the horizon lacked natural high spots to act as *eykt* markers, then artificial markers were erected to show the directions. In front of every old Icelandic house, in fact before the door, lay the "'house stone,'" onto which the observer had to step in order to tell the correct time from the position of the sun, moon, or appropriate star."[7] He further points out, "The time marker *eykt* point (west-south-west) was permanently fixed and recognizable for every farmstead by a landmark on the horizon."[8] Where natural features mark these important *airts*, it is clear that the location from which they are viewed was chosen with regard to the *airts* related to the natural configuration of the horizon.

In addition to the location of sunrise at notable times of year, these markers also indicate the time of day (or night) when the sun and other celestial bodies stand over them. When the sun rises due east at the equinoxes, that is 6:00 hours in the modern reckoning of time, and when it sets due west, it is 18:00. When the sun stands due south at any time of year, it is 12 noon, but the sun at midsummer stands much higher in the sky—the highest it will ever reach at that latitude. At winter solstice noon, it is at its lowest point. In his work on northern European astronomy and time-telling, Reuter noted: "Among all peoples the time of day has been told by the position of the sun, moon or stars above fixed landmarks such as mountains, trees and other high spots on the horizon."[9] At any time of year when the sun is above the horizon, it will always be above the same horizon marker at the same time of day.

The word *day* is used to denote two different things. The period of daylight between sunrise and sunset is called day, as opposed to night. But a day is also the period defined now as twenty-four hours, and in the ancient Germanic understanding, the period between one sunset and the next was deemed a day. Traditional festivities to this day have an abundance of "eves," where the celebration begins at sunset on the calendar day before—New Year's Eve, May Eve, All Hallow's Eve (Hallowe'en) and Christmas Eve are the four best known of a larger number. But also, in Old England, time-telling of individual days began at the point of *Dæg-Mæl*, 7:30 a.m. in modern reckoning. Depending on whether one was keeping up the day; keeping the time of day, as did the *tidsceaware*, the person who served to announce the time;

---

7. Reuter, *Skylore of the North*, 7.
8. Reuter, *Skylore of the North*, 8.
9. Reuter, *Skylore of the North*, 6.

or whether the day was deemed to begin at first light, the day had three different perceptions, depending on the required function of time-definition. Added to this, the incompatibility between local tradition and the ecclesiastical system of time-reckoning brought confusion among the priests when the Christian religion was introduced.

The Christian division of time was developed by the early monastic communities in Egypt to govern the times of their daily prayer-cycle. Their "temporal hour" system of time-telling divided the day, that is the individual period of daylight, into twelve equal divisions called hours. There was not a significant variation between the length of the day in summer and winter at Egyptian latitudes around thirty degrees, so the differences did not concern the monks. But in northern Europe, between twenty and thirty-five degrees further north, the length difference between summer days and winter days is extreme. Otto Sigfrid Reuter wrote that "since the nights in winter are longer than the days, but in summer shorter, the hours are unequal: the daylight hours are shorter in winter than in summer. In Mediterranean latitudes the difference was acceptable; in Iceland, however, where the day (from sunrise to sunset) lasted twenty-one of our hours in summer but only three hours in winter, the corresponding hours by the church's method had the length in summer of one and three-quarters hours and in winter of a quarter of an hour by our modern reckoning. The uselessness of the medieval 'temporal hour' system inevitably roused resistance soon after its introduction into the North, having led to great confusion there." He continues, "Our twenty-four hours of equal length did not become customary until the fourteenth century, following the introduction of striking clocks."[10]

In the octaval system of northern Europe, the Tides of the Day are not at all related to the length of daylight, but a whole cycle of light and darkness. The octaval system divides the modern twenty-four hour period into eight equal divisions called Tides. They are viewed as beginning and ending at 7:30 a.m. in modern reckoning. These Tides have no relation to the

---

10. Reuter, *Skylore of the North*, 6.

identically named tides that ebb and flow in the seas and oceans. The markers of the time Tides are taken from where the sun is in its apparent course, and so they are always the same. So it works on an entirely different principle from the monkish temporal hours that divide equally the period of daylight, regardless of how long its actual duration is. In the octaval system, the position of sunrise and sunset does not determine the division; like the modern twenty-four hour system, sunrises and sunsets vary between the Tides, depending on the time of year. In winter, a certain point in a Tide will be in darkness, when in summer, at the same point it will be light.

Described according to the twenty-four hour clock system, the eight Tides of the day as observed in Old England are:[11]

>   *Morgen,* from 4:30 to 7:30
>   *Dæg-Mael,* 7:30 to 10:30. This is the first Tide of the Day.
>   *Mid-Dæg,* 10:30 to 13:30
>   *Ofanverth Dæg,* 13:30 to 16:30
>   *Mid-Aften,* 16:30 to 19:30
>   *Ondverth Nott,* 19:30 to 21:30
>   *Mid-Niht,* 21:30 to 1:30
>   *Ofanverth Nott,* 1:30 to 4:30

In England and Scotland are a number of extant ancient sundials marked for the traditional Germanic octaval time-telling by Tides. As the beginning of the day on some Old English sundials, the point of *Daeg-Mael* (7:30 a.m.) is specially marked by a cross, *Dæg* rune, or swastika incised on the line. In England, a classic octaval dial exists at Warnford in Hampshire. The church of the Holy Cross at Daglingworth in Gloucestershire has a similar Anglo-Saxon dial carved on a square, perhaps cubic, stone. It is a double circle divided horizontally by a line. The upper half is plain, and the lower half divided by four lines, three with cross-lines and the fourth, which is the *Daeg-Mael* point, is plain. Kirkdale Priory in north Yorkshire has a sundial using this system. It dates from between the years 1056 to 1066. Carved

11. Based on Green, *Sundials,* 23.

around it is the Old English text *Þis is dæges solmerca æt ilcum tide* (This is the day's sun-marker at every tide). Other inscriptions record the makers Hawarth and Brand, priests, and Orm, son of Gamal, who reconstructed the church after it had fallen into ruins. At Escombe, County Durham, there is another octaval dial dating from the second half of the seventh century.

Other Old English dials exist at Old Byland and Weaverthorpe in Yorkshire and at Edston, the latter bearing an inscription telling us that it is the time-teller of travellers. Some dials attempt to reconcile the octaval system with the Temporal Hours of the church. Of course these church hours cannot be represented on a sundial because they vary in length according to the duration of daylight. A dial divided for the Tides of the Day and the twelve-hour system is carved on the Northumbrian rune-inscribed stone cross at Bewcastle, Scotland, dating from around the year 675. A sundial at St Michael's church in Winchester has the western quarter divided into duodecimal parts, while the eastern is a sixteen-fold division.[12]

Vernacular Time-Telling

Knowing the directions and the height of the sun at particular times of day played an integral part in traditional ways of life. It was achieved by means of common objects, the human body, and local knowledge. "From pre-Christian times there comes a popular method for announcing an agreed time to stop work, or any other time," Reuter wrote, "by using the height of the sun instead of its direction." For instance, the law defined the "shaft height of the sun." This occurred in the afternoon when "the lower edge of the sun appears to rest on the point of a spear set up nine feet from the observer." The law expressly provides that this shall be the observer's own spear, and that he shall set up the spear so that he can still reach comfortably with a "shaft hand" (that is, a thumb held out from the fist) up to the socket of the iron spear head, in other words, that in all circumstances, "the

---

12. Pennick, *Beginnings*, 180–82.

same sighting angle shall be ensured."[13] (This technique removes the necessity to observe the horizon, using a common weapon as the instrument of measurement.

Another related technique of time-telling with the body is the hand-dial, effectively making the human hand into a sundial. The hand is held out from the body at head height, palm upwards, and a small straight stick is held in the crook of the thumb at the angle of the latitude. This forms a gnomon. Before noon, the stick is held in the left hand, orientated towards the west; after noon, it is in the right hand, pointed to the east. The shadow cast by the stick shows the time by the position of its shadow against the joints and fingertips.

Turf dials or Shepherds' Dials continued in use in rural southern England until the early part of the twentieth century. By that time, they were being made only by shepherds in the counties of Kent, Surrey, Sussex and Essex. It seems people stopped making them around the time of World War I. Traditionally, English shepherds used the dials to determine the time to begin the drove from the pasture back to the fold before sundown. To make the simplest form of Shepherd's Dial, one cuts in the turf a circle about eighteen inches in diameter and thrusts a straight stick about a foot long into the ground vertically at its centre. A stick, with notches to mark the hours, is laid east–west inside the circle to the north of the centre stick, with each end touching the circle at right angles to a north–south line.

The north–south line comes from one's local knowledge of the landscape, using a distant landmark. The centre-stick serves as the gnomon and the time is read off where the shadow touches the notches. In the absence of a notched stick, small ridges were made as markers. An alternative version makes the same circle, but a shorter stick is put into the centre. Another stick, about a foot long, is put in the ground on the circle, due south of the centre-stick. Other sticks are placed on the circumference at appropriate distances for the hours or tides to either side of the meridional one. It is customary to use seven. These sticks serve as gnomons, and the shorter one at the centre as the marker of

---

13. Reuter, *Skylore of the North*, 8.

the hours; it is the reverse of the other kind of dial.[14] The traditional methods of reckoning solar time were used in northern Europe until the arrival of cheap clocks and the imposition of standardized time in time zones, first by railway companies, then by governments. This created the concept of legal time, where the official mean time or "daylight saving time" determined by central governments was considered the reality, and the natural real time of the sun was thereafter deemed wrong and ignored. After that, ancient and traditional methods continued to be used by only a very few people, for now real time was out of kilter with official clock time.

The Days of the Week

The seven-day week is first recorded in the fifth century B.C.E. among the Hebrews.[15] The week is quite a different form of time-division, artificially overriding all other fixed divisions of the year such as the months, the equinoxes and solstices. Essentially a religious construct, it took the day later dedicated to Saturn as the sacred day of rest, beginning it and ending it, like all the other weekdays, at sunset. The days of the week were known by numbers under Judaism, except for Friday, which was the eve of the Sabbath, and Saturday, the Sabbath itself. The Christian religion, once it split from Judaism, took over the idea of the Sabbath, but soon began to celebrate it one day later than Jews did. It has been suggested that this change originated in Asia Minor, where the Mithraists had celebrated Sunday as their holy day, "The Lord's Day of the Lord," long before the arrival of the new religion and its adoption of Sunday as its Sabbath.[16]

The early Roman week, the *nundinum*, was octaval, but the Emperor Augustus, when he reformed Roman paganism, adopted the seven-day week in its stead, taking in the Chaldean interpretation ascribing each day to one of the non-fixed celes-

14. Gossett, *Shepherds of Britain*, passim.
15. Nöldeke, "Die Namen der Wochentage bei den Semiten," 161; Wartburg, *Von Sprache und Mensch*, 46.
16. Laing, *Survivals of Roman Religion*, 149.

PLAQUE WITH THE SWABIAN GODDESS ZISA AT AUGSBURG.

tial bodies. Naturally, the planetary deities thus ascribed were named according to the *interpretatio Romana*, and so the days were named for Saturnus, Sol, Luna, Mars, Mercurius, Jupiter and Venus.[17] Images of the planetary deities exist on Gallo-Roman bases of Jupiter Columns dating from the first to the fourth centuries c.e., with several notable examples in Baden-Württemberg, Germany.[18] Thus it appears that the seven-day

---

17. Gundermann, "Die Namen der Wochentage bei den Römern," 175–80.
18. Bauchhenss, *Jupitergigantensäule*, 22–23, 67; Filtzinger, *Hic saxa loquuntur: Hier reden die Steine*, 87–88.

week as a basis for the sequential worship of the seven planetary gods was spread northwards via the Celtic regions of the Roman Empire into Germany. There, the *interpretatio Germana* came into play, and the Germanic equivalent names took over the days.

There was always a conflict between the pagan day-names and the sensibilities of the more fundamentalist of the Christians. There was no attempt to abolish the seven-day week, because the Jewish system of a seventh day of rest and worship was and is integral to the religion. But some Christian interpretations of the days abolished the god-names, and the occurrence of these elisions may indicate those places where the worship of particular deities was most persistent. In these places, it seems that the Church considered it impossible to abolish the worship of the gods without also eliminating their names completely. Hence in England we have *Wednesday*, the day of Woden, but in Germany, Wotan is abolished and the descriptor *Mittwoch*, the day at the middle of the week, is used. In the area around Augsburg in Bavaria, where the worship of the goddess Zisa was centred, Tuesday was renamed *Aftermontag* from *Zîstag* to remove associations with the Swabian goddess. There are other instances in mainland Europe. But in English-speaking lands, we have the full panoply of the old gods—Sun, Moon, Tîw, Woden, Thunor, Frigga and Saturn.

The Seasons and Stations of the Year

The monastic chroniclers detested the rites and ceremonies of the pagan country people around them; in fervent faith they felt obliged to obliterate local ancestral traditions and to impose the Christian religion upon them by force. Yet in their attempts to discredit the Elder Faith, they recorded enough to preserve the knowledge of what our spiritual ancestors did, so that we can understand the meaning of their rites and ceremonies. The ordering of the year in all traditional societies cannot be separated from both the aspects of life and work at each time of year, and the sacred festivals that celebrate them. "Keeping up the day," as it is known in Cambridgeshire, is an essential part of the

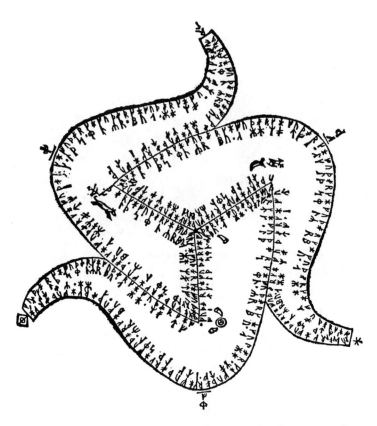

RUNIC CALENDAR FROM OLAF RUDBECK'S "ATLANTICA."

annual cycle of life, celebrating particular days in the year that link the individual, the family and the community to the work on the land through its spiritual dimension. The church could not change the cold and darkness of winter or the long hot days of summer; it did not alter the ways of cultivating field and orchard; Christianity had nothing to say about the ways of beekeeping, animal husbandry, hunting or fishing. Neither did it affect the techniques and needs of craftspeople. So while the rural way of life lasted, the significant days of the working year were kept up. Fragments and survivals of this way of life have formed the basis for contemporary manifestations of traditional religion.

The Angles divided the year into two halves, defined by the solstices. These are thus two equal periods of increasing light and decreasing light: increasing from the winter solstice, Geola

(Yule), to the summer solstice, Litha, then decreasing from Litha to Geola. By the time Bede wrote about them in the seventh century, the two halves of the year had been subdivided by standardized lunar cycles into six months each. In earlier times, it appears that a year of thirteen twenty-eight-day months had been in use. Reuter quotes the Faeroese rhyme:

> I know a tree
> On top of the hill
> With thirteen boughs.[19]

Bede's descriptions of the months are partly his historical understanding of what they were before his time, when the Angles were still in Angeln, and what they had become in England by his time. So there is some confusion over the year's reckoning. In addition, the systems used by individuals and in separate communities doubtless varied from place to place. Whatever was functional to those who needed a calendar was used, for there was no central authority to impose a standardized system.

The Anglo-Saxon year as it has come down to us can be equated with the twelve-month year. Each solstice is bracketed by two of these months: in the winter before the solstice comes the month of *Ærra Geola*— (Before Yule), and after the solstice *Æftera Geola* (—After Yule). In the summer, two months bracket the summer solstice—: *Ærra Liða* comes before Midsummer, and *Æftera Liða* after it. Some have seen these double months as single sixty-day months, and ascribed a sixfold division to the year, as in the much later Danish runic calendar shown here. Philippson suggests that these Anglo-Saxon double months began on November 11, January 13, March 17, May 12, July 12 and September 17.[20] Paralleling the twelve Anglo-Saxon month-names with modern ones, January is *Æftera Geola*, and February is *Sol-monaþ*. In his *De Temporum Ratione*, Bede described the latter month's name as signifying cakes offered to the gods (in contemporary tradition, Soul-Cakes), but it is also interpreted as

---

19. Reuter, *Skylore of the North*, 14.
20. Philippson, *Germanisches Heidentum bei den Angelsachsen*, 205.

meaning the "mud-month."[21]

March is *Hreðmonath*, when offerings were made to the goddess Hreð.[22] It has the non-religious title *Hlydmonath*, referring to the March winds, an instance of the imposition of new names on time that was the policy of the Church, Charlemagne's reign in mainland Europe being the most extreme instance of this. The Old English *Eostre-monaþ* is April, which was reckoned as the first month of spring. The Anglo-Saxon goddess of the dawn and of the springtime is Eostre, and it is from her that the Christian festival of Easter is named, though Easter's date is reckoned according to a modified version of the ancient Jewish lunar definition of the feast of Passover that guarantees that the Christian and Jewish festivals cannot coincide. May is called *Þri-milce*, "three milkings": the month of such abundance that the cows produce freely. *Ærra Liða* parallels the modern month of June, and July, which began on the other side of the solstice, is *Æftera Liða*. August is *Weodmonaþ*, the month of weeds, and September is *Halig-monaþ*, the "holy month," the time when the harvest festival was celebrated. At some point, the festival of the first loaf, Lammas, the first of August, became the key festival marking the harvest.

Halig-monaþ was far too heathen for the Church, so the new month-name *Hærfest-monaþ*, Harvest Month, was invented. Winter begins with the month called *Wynterfylleþ*, October, whilst November is *Blot-monaþ*, "sacrifice month," when the farmers who were slaughtering livestock that could not be over-wintered dedicated them as sacrifices to the gods and ate them in ceremonial feasts. The Christian feast of Martinmas, November 11, is possibly a Christianization of the main festival of *Blot-monaþ*.[23] Finally, December is equivalent to *Ærra Geola*.

The Contemporary Pagan Eightfold Year

Contemporary pagans in Britain use an eightfold division of the

---

21. Bede, *De Temporum Ratione*, chap. 15.
22. Bede, *De Temporum Ratione*, chap. 15.
23. Chaney, *The Cult of Kingship in Anglo-Saxon England*, 58.

year, which is in keeping with the tradition of octaval division, though this has not been proven historically and is a matter of serious contention as to its authenticity, especially in a sacred context. As Prudence Jones notes, "Eight is often more a 'working number' than a sacred number," and she suggests that it appears as a sacred number in the pagan North only in conjunction with nine.[24] This eminently practical nature of the octaval system had been championed earlier, in 1919, by Alfred Watkins in a tract entitled "Must We Trade in Tenths?" Watkins—who has been called "a twentieth century edition of [William] Cobbett—a Radical Traditionalist"[25]—wrote: "Octaves are as right in commerce as they are in music, science and wavelengths. We try to use them all the time, but are baffled by unsuitable notation."[26] Jones notes the example of the festival held every ninth year at Uppsala, that is, at the end of eight full years, or perhaps ninety-nine lunar months. It lasted eight days, on each of which nine males of every creature were sacrificed to whatever cause was uppermost on the national mind at the time.[27] Similarly, before the tenth century, the Danish national festival was held at Yuletide at Lejre "after every eight full years."[28] But both of these festivals culminated an eight-year period, not an eightfold year.

The contemporary pagan calendar is a synthesis of the Anglo-Saxon two-period year, subdivided by the equinoxes into four, then again subdivided by adding the *cross-quarter days* of February, May, August and November. These are assumed to be Celtic in origin, and are known alliteratively as The Four Fire Festivals.[29] Contemporary pagans in the early twenty-first century give these four festivals names derived from Celtic languages: Imbolc or Oimelc, Beltane, Lughnassadh and Samhain. The festivals of February and November are current Roman Catholic feasts, Candlemas and All Saints' Day. Of course, their placement in the year makes an unequal division, for these festivals fall around

24. Jones, *Eight and Nine*, 1.
25. Allen Watkins, *Alfred Watkins of Hereford*, 3.
26. Alfred Watkins, "Must We Trade in Tenths?" 6.
27. Jones, *Eight and Nine*, 1, 5.
28. Reuter, *Skylore of the North*, 16.
29. Cf. McLean, *The Four Fire Festivals*.

forty days after the preceding solar marker-days and fifty days before the subsequent ones. Ronald Hutton states that these four festivals have little evidence of being systematic or widespread in antiquity, for they were noted in a systematic analysis of old Irish texts by Charles Vallancey in the eighteenth century and assumed by the nineteenth to have been observed in ancient Britain as well.[30] Hutton notes that Charles Hardwick believed that the fire ceremonies of Beltane were carried out on all four dates, and hence the concept of the fire festivals arose.[31] Thus, for instance, Alexander Warrack in 1911 states that the name Beltane was also applied to the festival of midsummer, "a festival formerly kept by shepherds and young people on May 1 and June 21."[32]

The eightfold year emerged among British Wiccans in the second half of the twentieth century, and was an integral part of pagan observance by the 1960s.[33] In 1969, June Johns, reporting on the usage of the covens of Alex Sanders, the "King of the Witches," refers to the festivals of 20 December; Candlemas, on 1 February; Beltane, or May Eve Sabbath, on 30 April; Midsummer night festival, on 21 June; August Eve or Lammas on 31 July; the Autumn Equinox, on 20 September; and Hallowe'en, on 31 October. The Celtic year as perceived today starts at sunset on Samhain, October 31 in the Gregorian calendar. While some pagans take this as the year's beginning, Hutton states categorically that there is absolutely no firm evidence from the written record that the year opened on November 1.[34] This date is All Hallows' Eve, better known as Hallowe'en (Hallowmass Even). This is the contemporary pagan festival called Samhain, which more specifically is the day of Lá Samhna, for Samhain also means the month of November, and in Ireland Hallowe'en is called Oíche Shamhna.

The next of the eight festivals is the winter solstice, Yule, to which no Celtic name is given. On either the first or second of

---

30. Hutton, *The Stations of the Sun*, 408.
31. Cf. Hardwick, *Traditions, Superstitions, and Folk-Lore*, 30–40.
32. Warrack, *The Scots Dialect Dictionary*, 27.
33. Johns, *King of the Witches*, 142–44.
34. Hutton, *The Stations of the Sun*, 410.

February, the festival of Imbolc or Oimelc is the patronal day of Brigid of Kildare (452–525 C.E.), a Christian saint who bears the same name as a Celtic goddess. Hutton notes that this festival was observed in Ireland but not kept anywhere in Great Britain.[35] Beltane is the first of May, traditionally celebrated with maypoles in England and Wales and fires in Scotland. Lammas, from the Old English *hlæf-messe*, the festival of the first loaf of the new harvest, is usually called by pagans its Gaelic name Lughnassadh, though in Ireland the name Lúnasa refers to the month of August.

McLean associates the solar marker-days with male gods: the winter solstice with Christmas; Easter as the vernal equinox; the summer solstice with St John the Baptist; and the autumnal equinox with Michaelmas, the Archangel Michael.[36] Less convincingly, he ascribes the fire festivals to female deities: Samhain to the Old Moon Goddess, Hecate; Imbolc as Brigantia to the Goddess Bride or Brigit; Beltane to the earthly May Queen who represents the Goddess; and Lammas, though it is named for the Irish god of light and artisanry, Lugh, to the god's mother, Tailtiu.[37]

The influence of the Wiccan perception of festivals and the naming of the four cross-quarter days as Fire Festivals continues to resonate in contemporary British paganism, having become a common way of ordering the sacred year.[38] The historical genesis of this calendar after 1950 does not invalidate it as a working system or it would not have been adopted so widely, but projections back upon the past that it was actually observed *in toto* in ancient days do not stand up to scrutiny. Just like time-telling during the day and night, inevitably the festivals of the year historically varied from place to place, tribe to tribe, from clan to clan, family to family, from trade to trade. Nineteenth-century nationalist ideas, both the pan-Celtic and pan-Germanic causes, led to a search for coherent cultural observances in antiquity, and helped

---

35. Hutton, *The Stations of the Sun*, 411.
36. McLean, *The Four Fire Festivals*, 7.
37. McLean, *The Four Fire Festivals*, 7–8.
38. Cf., e.g., Pennick, *Labyrinths*, 8; *Practical Magic in the Northern Tradition*, 33–40; *The Pagan Source Book*, 14–20.

to create new ones. And religions always undergo reformations and re-empowerments at times when this is needed. In the pagan historical sphere, one may note the Emperor Augustus's reformation of Roman paganism in 17 B.C.E.,[39] the establishment of Old Prussia as a theocratic pagan state in the sixth century C.E.,[40] and King Mindaugas, who reformed and established Lithuanian polytheism as the state religion in the thirteenth century C.E.[41]

The re-emergence of the four festivals and their placement within the stations of the sun led inevitably to the modern eightfold year. But historically, this has tended to produce an overview that is a simplification and generalization of what is a multiple, pluralistic and essentially unrecoverable palimpsest of transient observances, changing over time as circumstances changed. But as a usable system, with a coherent relationship to the seasons, the emergence of the eightfold pagan year in the latter part of the twentieth century is another instance of the coming-together of the multiple threads of the Web of Wyrd into a new form appropriate for the needs of these times, whilst acknowledging our ancestral octaval division of time.

---

39. Jones and Pennick, *A History of Pagan Europe*, 54.
40. Trinkūnas, ed., *Of Gods and Holidays*, 148.
41. Jones and Pennick, *A History of Pagan Europe*, 171.

Bibliography

Amos, G. S. *The Scratch Dials of Norfolk*. South Walsham, n.d.

Bauchhenss, Gerhard. *Jupitergigantensäulen*. Aalen: Limesmuseum Aalen, 1976.

Bede. *De Temporum Ratione*. Trans. Charles W. Jones. Cambridge, Mass.: Medieval Academy of America, 1943.

Cheney, William A. *The Cult of Kingship in Anglo-Saxon England*. Manchester: Manchester University Press, 1970.

Dennis, Andrew, Peter Foote, and Richard Perkins. *Grágás I: Laws of Iceland*. Winnipeg: University of Manitoba Press, 1980.

Drinkwater, Peter I. *The Art of Sundial Construction*. Shipston-on-Stour: privately published, 1996.

Durdin-Robinson, Lawrence. *Juno Covella: Perpetual Calendar of the Fellowship of Isis*. Enniscorthy: Cesara, 1982.

Filtzinger, Phillip. *Hic saxa loquuntur: Hier reden die Steine*. Aalen: Limesmuseum Aalen, 1980.

Gossett, A. L. J. *Shepherds of Britain, Past and Present. From the Best Authorities*. London: Constable, 1911.

Green, Arthur Robert. *Sundials: Incised Dials or Mass-Clocks*. Reprint edition, London: Society for Promoting Christian Knowledge, 1978 [1926].

Green, D. H. *Language and History in the Early Germanic World*. Cambridge: Cambridge University Press, 1998.

Gundermann, G. "Die Namen der Wochentage bei den Römern." *Zeitschrift für deutsche Wortforschung I* (1901): 175–80.

Haigh, D. H. "Yorkshire Dials." *Yorkshire Archaeological Journal* (1896): 134–222.

Hardwick, Charles. *Traditions, Superstitions, and Folk-Lore*. Manchester: Ireland & Co., 1872.

Harland, John, and Wilkinson, T. T. *Lancashire Folk-Lore*. London: Frederick Warne and Co., and New York: Scribner and Co., 1867.

Hutton, Ronald. *The Stations of the Sun*. Oxford: Oxford University Press, 1996.

Johns, June. *King of the Witches: The World of Alex Sanders*. London: Davies, 1969.

Jones, Prudence. *Eight and Nine: Sacred Numbers of Sun and Moon in the Pagan North.* Fenris-Wolf Pagan Paper No. 2. Bar Hill, U.K.: Fenris-Wolf, 1982.

———. *Northern Myths of the Constellations.* Bar Hill, U.K.: Fenris-Wolf, 1991.

———. *A 'House' System from Viking Europe.* Bar Hill, U.K.: Fenris-Wolf, 1991.

———, and Nigel Pennick. *A History of Pagan Europe.* London: Routledge, 1995.

Laing, Gordon J. *Survivals of Roman Religion.* London: Harrap, 1931.

McLean, Adam. *The Four Fire Festivals.* Edinburgh: Megalithic Research Publications, 1979.

Nöldeke, Theodor. "Die Namen der Wochentage bei den Semiten." *Zeitschrift für deutsche Wortforschung I* (1901): 161–63.

Pennick, Nigel. *Ogham and Runic: Magical Writing of Old Britain and Northern Europe.* Bar Hill, U.K.: Fenris-Wolf, 1978.

———. *Labyrinths—their geomancy and symbolism.* Bar Hill, U.K.: Runestaff, 1984.

———. *Natural Measure.* Bar Hill, U.K.: Runestaff, 1985.

———. *The Cosmic Axis.* Bar Hill, U.K.: Runestaff, 1985.

———. *Practical Magic in the Northern Tradition.* Wellingborough, U.K.: Thorsons, 1989.

———. *The Pagan Source Book: A guide to festivals, traditions and symbols of the year.* London: Rider, 1992.

———. *Beginnings: Geomancy, Builders' Rites and Electional Astrology in the European Tradition.* Chieveley: Capall Bann, 1999.

Philippson, E. A. *Germanisches Heidentum bei den Angelsachsen.* Leipzig: Tauchnitz, 1929.

Reuter, Otto Sigfrid. *Skylore of the North.* Trans. Michael Behrend. Bar Hill, U.K.: Earthlore Institute, 1987.

Trinkūnas, Jonas, ed. *Of Gods and Holidays.* Vilnius: Tvermē, 1999.

Warrack, Alexander: *The Scots Dialect Dictionary* (1911). Poole, U.K.: New Orchard Editions, 1988.

Wartburg, Walther von: *Von Sprache und Mensch.* Bern: Francke, 1956.

Watkins, Alfred. "Must We Trade in Tenths? A plea against Decimal and for Octaval coinage as more exactly fitting the wants and usage of all who make, buy, sell, or grow things." Reprinted as Fenris-Wolf Pagan Paper No. 4. Bar Hill, U.K.: Fenris-Wolf, 1983 [1919].

Watkins, Allen. *Alfred Watkins of Hereford*. London: Garnstone Press, 1972.

Featuring Vinyl, CDs, Shirts and More from
Blood Axis, Changes, Darkwood, Der Blutharsch,
Derniere Volonte, Fire+Ice, Of The Wand & The Moon and
Other Industrial/Folk/Experimental Artists from Around the World

TESCO DISTRIBUTION USA
PO Box 286530 New York NY 10128
www.tesco-distro.com / tescousa@gmail.com

Garden Dwarves and House Spirits

Claude Lecouteux

The impression that we have of dwarves from fairy tales is essentially based upon nineteenth-century folk literature. In fact, once upon a time they were a fantastical people that lived in wild and uncultivated regions, some of whom entered into the service of lords or heroes.

According to the *Poetic Edda*, dwarves were originally born out of the decomposing body of Ymir, the primordial giant, although the traditional accounts are hardly unanimous. These children of Ymir who created a race in their image were named Móðsognir and Durinn. They were not the only ones, however, since the gods took Ymir's skull to use as the celestial vault, set it atop four columns, under each of which they placed a dwarf. These dwarves bear the names of the four cardinal points: Norðri, Suðri, Austri, Vestri.

In the tenth century, the various Germanic terms for a dwarf—such as Old High German *zwerc*, Old Norse *dvergr*, and Old English *dweorg*—were portmanteau words that concealed all manner of figures from folk mythology. The names designate elves as well as nightmares, howlers, fauns, satyrs, ogres, goblins, and brownies. The dwarf's own image suffers as a result of this, and a number of its actions can only be explained in the light of such conflations.

The first dwarf turns up in medieval German literature between 1023 and 1050, but other non-literary evidence exists to show that dwarves were present long before this. As a result, it becomes apparent that the medieval romances drew upon folk traditions, among other things.

In this same geographical region, the *Heldenbuch* (Book of Heroes), printed in Strassburg around 1483, puts a Christian spin on the earlier mythological material when it relates how God peopled the earth that he had just created. God first made dwarves to develop the earth; afterward he created the giants whose duty it was to protect the dwarves against the then-

KOBOLDS AT WORK. WOODCUT FROM OLAUS MAGNUS, "HISTORIA DE GENTIBUS SEPTENTRIONALIBUS," SIXTEENTH CENTURY.

teeming population of dragons. But the giants turned treacherous and began oppressing the dwarves, at which point God created heroes to restore and keep secure His order. Another very old text, the thirteenth-century Middle High German translation of the *Magnificat*, says: "God distributed the demons among the entire earth. In the waters and mountains lived the Nixies and the Dwarves, in the forests and swamps the Elves, the Thurses, and other spirits." We should note that an Icelandic tale collected in the nineteenth century, *Huldumanna genesis* (The Origin of the Hidden Men), made dwarves the children of Eve. Because they were unwashed, Eve hid them from the eyes of God, who then decreed: "Whatever should be hid from my sight should also be hid from that of men." These children were therefore invisible: they dwelt in the hills and mountains, in holes, and among the rocks.

The Dwarf Proper

There are three major types of dwarves in the Germanic regions. The first is the old, bearded figure, who is somewhat rare but whose existence is attested to by the figure of Alberich in the *Nibelungenlied*; this type of dwarf is ubiquitous in folktales and, much later, in European gardens. Next, there is the extremely

"The Elves and the Shoemaker." Nineteenth-century illustration by George Cruikshank for the Brothers Grimm fairy tale.

beautiful child, a type for which the sole evidence is found in the thirteenth-century epic romance *Ortnit*, but this depiction actually corresponds with that of an elf. Finally, there is the figure of the dwarf knight, which appears quite frequently and is a diminutive version of a human hero.

Dwarves reside in hollow mountains, have hierarchical systems and families, and their society is similarly structured to that of humans. Like human beings, dwarves fall prey to their passions, wage war, become jealous, and so on.

Originally, the dwarf had no set size, but rather could transform at will to whatever size he desired. Furthermore, we constantly come across expressions in the Middle Ages like "little dwarf" or "miniscule dwarf," as if it was necessary to indicate that a given dwarf was a small or tiny figure. The small size of the dwarf undoubtedly stems from the influence of the scholarly tradition regarding the pygmies, which were called *Trispithames* because they measured three *spithames*, in other words, around three feet tall. Generally speaking, dwarves measured between two to four feet in height.

The dwarf possessed the strength of twelve to twenty men, which is sometimes explained by their ownership of magic objects such as a belt, a helmet, or a ring.

As a cave dweller and a subterranean inhabitant of wild and rocky places, the dwarf knew all the secrets of nature: the virtues of plants, waters, and minerals. For this reason, he is an excellent smith, although the weapons that he manufactures under coercion—often after having been captured—turn out to be malevolent in nature. He can go wherever he pleases in the blink of an eye, knows the future, is the keeper of great wealth, and sometimes kidnaps women to be his brides. His hereditary enemies are dragons and giants. In Germanic mythology, dwarves and giants often bear the same name, and giants have dwarves for sons. A figure like Regin, the smith who took in the young Siegfried, was even described as a giant with the size of a dwarf. Again it becomes apparent that "dwarf" and "giant" do not connote the size of the creatures they designate; these are the generic names of mythological races.

Names That Speak

Thanks to the names of dwarves, we are able to see that these creatures are regularly confused with elves—one is named Gandálfr, for example, which literally means "Elf with the magic wand." Elves are typically craftsmen and more especially smiths, and we find dwarves with names like Sindri ("Spark Sprayer"), or even simply Brokkr ("Blacksmith"). The harmful nature of dwarves is evident from names like Alþjófr ("Master Thief"), Ginnar ("Deceiver"), Þráinn ("Threatener"), Dori ("Damager"),

Freya in the cave of the dwarves. Illustration by "H. L. M.," "Asgard Stories," 1901.

Eitri ("Poisonous One"), or Mjǫðvitnir ("Mead Wolf"). They know magic, as is evident in such names as Galarr ("Enchanter") or Finnr, Fiðr ("Finn," i.e., Sámi or Laplander, a people who were regarded as sorcerers). Their physical nature is displayed in such names as Dúfr ("Twisted"), Bǫmburr ("Fatty"), Hárr ("Hoary"), and Blindi ("Blind"). This last name refers to a very specific characteristic of dwarves: the sun blinds and petrifies them. Undoubtedly even more interesting are the names that clearly show that dwarves represent a mythical vision of the dead, or, at the very least, that they have a very close bond with the dead. Here are several of them: Dáinn ("Died"), Nár and Náinn (both meaning "Corpse"), Frosti ("Cold"), Funinn ("Decomposed"), Dvalinn ("Torpid"), Hornbori ("Pierced by a Horn"), Haugspori ("The One Who Enters the Burial Mound") and Búinn ("Ready-for-Departure," i.e., for burial). To this list we can also add Nýi ("Dark") and Niði ("New Moon"), since this planetary body is

A BOISTEROUS HOUSE SPIRIT. POSTCARD ILLUSTRATION, FIRST HALF OF THE TWENTIETH CENTURY.

that of the deceased, and Ái ("Ancestor"), which clearly indicates the transformation of the dead into dwarves. Furthermore, the natural habitat of the dwarves is the lithic realm, which is of course that of the deceased. We should note that the malevolent dead (those who experienced a premature, violent, or unusual death) become dwarves and revenants. The good dead, as I have shown in another study, *Fantômes et Revenants au Moyen Âge*, become elves. One final detail is that whoever follows a dwarf into his kingdom never returns, as is related in the legend of the Scandinavian king, Sveigdir, and, with a subtle difference, in the legend of King Herla in England, the leader of the Infernal Hunt, which is also known under the name of *Mesnie Hellequin*.

Dwarves are fabulous artisans who forged various instruments and objects owned by the gods: Thor's hammer, Odin's spear, Njord's boat, the ring Draupnir, and Freyr's boar. All of these items are magical. But it was dwarves, too, who crafted the grate that seals off the underworld, Hel, and the chain that shackles the wicked Loki. When they forge things for men, their wickedness comes to the fore: the weapon is baleful. As for their treasures, whoever makes off with them will die, the best example being the cursed gold in the legend of Siegfried. In short, what is predominant among the "true dwarves" is their sly and ill-scheming nature, a quality that reappears in the romance literature. It is this character attribute that distinguishes them from elves.

Household Deities

Garden dwarves have adopted some of their traits from goblins and from spirits of the mines: their red caps come from the former and their lanterns from the latter. The beard is an old attribute intended to represent their great age and therefore their erudition and wisdom. The pipe is an element that was apparently added to this figure during the nineteenth century. But the garden dwarf has another, much more profound meaning, in that it actually represents the household deity: a creature that oversaw the proper functioning of the house and the well-being of its inhabitants on the condition that they granted it their respect, gave it regular offerings of food (broth or dairy products), and made sure never to set foot in the territory reserved for it, such as a corner in the attic. There is a spirit that lives in the main house, and others reside in the outlying farm buildings. All of these spirits have various names in the Germanic countries and are characterized by their physical aspect. Names referring to objects are not uncommon, such as "Piece of Wood" (*Poppele*) or "Block" (*Butz*); these beings were originally amorphous and gradually were given human features. In earlier times they were certainly idols. Their generic names may also refer to anthropomorphic features., such as *Junge* ("Youngster"), *Kerlchen* ("Little Fellow"), *Männchen* ("Little Man"), or, in the case of *Grieske and Schrättli,* connote the idea of deformation. They can refer to their color (which may be gray, white, or red), or a distinctive feature of their dress, such as *Hödeken* ("Little Hood"), *Blauhösler* ("Blue Pants"), or *Stiefel* ("Boots"); or simply their vague and indefinite nature such as *Umg'hyri* ("Disturbing Monster") or *Spuk* ("Phantom").

The majority of these spirits are of male gender and their names, which are quite often diminutives, suggest the notion of their small size as well as that of familiarity and affection.

Beyond the aforementioned sorts of names, we come across those that simultaneously designate spirits, deities, and the dead who are predisposed to smoothly running households.

A house can have one or more spirits. When they are numerous, a family of spirits may be involved, although this notion seems due to a contamination with the dwarves. A Frisian account relates how a poor peasant finally managed to finish building his house thanks to the gifts from his neighbor. To ensure his good fortune, he invited the *Puke* [spirits] to live with him. They soon arrived to inspect the new house, and danced about it until one of them, about three inches high, decided to stay there and chose a hole in the beam for his home.

Typically, each individual building of a homestead is inhabited by its own spirit. This explains the multiplicity of names that we find for these spirits in a single geographic area.

These spirits that we see today, frozen in our gardens and reduced to the status of simple decorations, are the misunderstood vestiges of a former time when they were vitally alive and participated in the lives of men. They have lost their names and are now little more than generic dwarves. Since men no longer believe in them, and because our habitat has profoundly changed, they have abandoned us—they no longer perform any domestic duties, and, with their disappearance, part of a dream has vanished.

(Translated by Jon Graham)

A version of this article originally appeared in *La Grande Oreille* 35 (2008): 52–55. For publication in English, it has been slightly expanded in collaboration with the author.

Selected Works by Claude Lecouteux on This Theme:

Claude Lecouteux. *Nos bons voisins. Nains, elfes, lutins, gnomes, kobolds et compagnie, textes réunis, présentés et annotés.* Paris: Corti, 2010.
———. *Les nains et les elfes au Moyen Âge.* 3rd edition. Paris, Imago, 2004.
———. *Eine Welt im Abseits. Studien zur niederen Mythologie und Glaubenswelt des Mittelalters.* Dettelbach: Röll, 2001.
———. "Zwerge und Verwandte." *Euphorion* 75 (1981): 366–78.

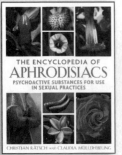

The Encyclopedia of Aphrodisiacs

Psychoactive Substances for Use in Sexual Practices

CHRISTIAN RÄTSCH and CLAUDIA MÜLLER-EBELING

The culmination of more than 30 years of cultural, anthropological, and scientific research, this encyclo-pedia examines the botany, pharmacology, history, preparation, dosage, and practical use of more than 500 erotically stimulating substances from antiquity to the present day.

$125.00, hardcover, 736 pages, 8.5 x 11, Full-color throughout
ISBN 978-1-59477-169-9

The Encyclopedia of Psychoactive Plants

Ethnopharmacology and Its Applications

CHRISTIAN RÄTSCH
Foreword by Albert Hofmann

In the traditions of every culture, psychoactive plants—those known to transport the mind to other dimensions of consciousness—have been regarded as sacred. This book details the history, botany, and use of psychoactive plants and is lavishly illustrated with color photographs of the people, ceremonies, and art related to the ritual use of the world's sacred psychoactive plants.

$125.00, hardcover, 944 pages, 8.5 x 11, 797 color photographs and 645 b&w illustrations, ISBN 978-0-89281-978-2

The Tradition of Household Spirits

Ancestral Lore and Practices

CLAUDE LECOUTEUX

Why do we hang horseshoes for good luck or place wreaths on our doors? Why does the groom carry his new bride over the threshold? These customs come from a time when people had a sacred relationship with their homes and the spirits who lived there with them. This book draws on studies and classic literature from old Europe to explain the pagan roots behind these traditions.

$16.95, paper, 248 pages, 6 x 9, Includes 8-page color insert and 21 b&w illustrations, ISBN 978-1-62055-105-9

Shamanism and Tantra in the Himalayas

CHRISTIAN RÄTSCH, CLAUDIA MÜLLER-EBELING, and SURENDRA BAHADUR SHAHI

The result of eighteen years of field research, this book presents for the first time, a comprehensive overview of shamanism that is based on the knowledge and experience of the different tribes from the Himalayan kingdom of Nepal.

$49.95, hardcover, 320 pages, 8.5 x 11, 605 color and b&w illustrations
ISBN 978-0-89281-913-3

The Book of Grimoires

The Secret Grammar of Magic

CLAUDE LECOUTEUX

Grimoires began simply as quick-reference "grammar books" for sorcerers and magicians, but over time many of the abbreviations were misinterpreted and magical words misspelled, rendering them ineffective. In The Book of Grimoires Professor Lecouteux provides exact reproductions of various secret alphabets, symbols, and glyphs with instructions for their correct use.

$19.95, paper, 272 pages, 6 x 9
45 b&w illustrations, ISBN 978-1-62055-187-5

The High Magic of Talismans and Amulets

Tradition and Craft

CLAUDE LECOUTEUX

Professor Lecouteux reveals the chains of sympathy, astrological geography, and invocations used since ancient times to activate the powers of amulets and talismans. He examines many different kinds of talismans, such as the rabbit's foot, horseshoe, and gris-gris bag, revealing the principles and symbology behind each object, and showing that their use is as widespread today as at any time in the past.

$24.95, hardcover, 256 pages, 6 x 9
38 b&w illustrations, ISBN 978-1-62055-279-7

Rochester, Vermont • www.InnerTraditions.com • 800-246-8648

Geiler von Kaiserberg and the Furious Army

Claude Lecouteux

Und es war die Zeit des Vollmonds
In der Nacht vor Sankt Johannis
Wo der Spuk der Wilden Jagd
Umzieht durch den Geisterhohlweg

(And it was the time of the full moon,
In the night before Saint John's,
When the apparition of the Wild Hunt
Moved through the haunted hollow.)
—Heinrich Heine, *Atta Troll*, XVIII

For more than two thousand years, legends have been circulating that tell of the passage of a troop of the dead, either by land or through the air, on certain dates of the year.[1] Depending on the form of the narratives, the country, or region, this phenomenon has been referred to as the *Wütendes Heer* (Furious Army), the *Mesnie Hellequin* (Retinue of Hellequin), or the *Chasse Artus* (Arthur's Hunt), among others. For more than a century, scholars and researchers—following the lead of Jacob Grimm and Elard Hugo Meyer—have asserted that Wotan/Odin was the leader of this dead host, but Lutz Röhrich, bringing clarity to the matter, quite rightly notes that "In no instance is the equivalence of Wode (the Low German name of the wild huntsman)—and Wotan certain."[2] Leander Petzoldt correctly distinguishes between

---

1. Hans Plischke, *Die Sage vom Wilden Heer im deutschen Volk*, Dissertation, Leipzig, 1914; Alfred Endter, *Die Sage vom Wilden Jäger und von der Wilden Jagd*, Dissertation, Frankfurt, 1933; Michael John Petry, *Herne the Hunter, a Berkshire Legend* (Reading: William Smith, 1972). My own subsequent book-length study of this topic is Lecouteux, *Chasses fantastiques et cohorts de la nuit au Moyen Âge* (Paris: Imago, 1999); English edition: *Phantom Armies of the Night: The Wild Hunt and the Ghostly Processions of the Undead*, trans. Jon Graham (Rochester, VT: Inner Traditions, 2011).
2. "Nicht einmal gesichert ist die Gleichung Wode–Wotan." Lütz Röhrich, *Sage*, 2nd ed. (Stuttgart: Metzler, 1971), 24.

the Wild Hunt and the Cursed Huntsman in his *Dictionary of Demons and Elementary Spirits*.[3] The confusion between the two legends is based on a body of beliefs maintaining that the dead can come back, which has then been coupled with a Christian interpretation of the facts: these dead are sinners who are going through purgatory as members of this host, or they are, quite simply, the damned. These beliefs took the form of legends that cross-contaminated one another to form, at the turn of the fifteenth to sixteenth century, a complex web whose various threads can be delineated as follows:

1. The belief in nocturnal hosts led by Diana, Hecate, or Herodias, and the belief in revenants.

2. The belief that the *spiritus*, or psyche, remained near the body for thirty days immediately following death.

3. The belief that death only entailed an exile to the grave or to another world, during which time the deceased person retained all faculties, kept watch over the activities of friends and family, and intervened in human affairs, either *in corpore* or *in spiritu* (as is the case with dreams).[4]

This type of belief concerning death, which went hand in hand with ancestor worship and specific funerary rites, was too deeply anchored in people's minds to disappear when they were converted to Christianity. The Church had to make do with it and divert these beliefs for its own benefit. As a result, a compound legend arose that concerned the damned who wander the earth on certain dates,[5] and the notion of impiety punished (which is

---

3. Leander Petzoldt, *Kleines Lexikon der Dämonen und Elementargeister* (Munich: Beck 1990), 186–90.
4. Cf. Claude Lecouteux, *Geschichte der Gespenster und Wiedergänger im Mittelalter* (Cologne and Vienna: Böhlau, 1987); Claude Lecouteux and Phillipe Marcq, *Les Esprits et les Morts, Croyances médiévales* (Paris: Honore Champion, 1990).
5. During the Ember Days, Christmas, the three final Thursdays of Advent, Saint Sylvester's Day, Saint John's Day, Saint Martin's Day, Saint Walpurgis's

the source of numerous legends, including those of the Cursed Huntsman and of the Man in the Moon).

The two variants of pagan folklore that had been Christianized continued to influence each other and, because they provided an open narrative structure, receptively incorporated motifs from other legends relating to death and to the beyond (for example, the legends of Mount Venus and of "Loyal Eckhart"). The Christian texts are starkly didactic and deliver a clear message: there is no prayer of posthumous salvation for those who have not respected the commandments of God and his Church. They fall into the category of "pedagogy through fear," similarly to the literature of revelations (incidentally, the last example of the latter genre, and a humorous one at that, is Alphonse Daudet's *Le Curé de Curcugnan*).

In order to rediscover the primary meaning of the Furious Army (I will use this name here to avoid any confusion), a distinction must be drawn between the original content of the legend and the later accretions. For example, we must avoid blending—as was so often the case until now[6]—this theme with that of the Cursed Huntsman who succumbed to his passion for hunting on a day sacred to the Lord, or who unwittingly swore an oath committing him to this activity for eternity. If I must venture a simple definition of the Furious Army, I would say that it was originally a group of revenants which had the right to leave the Other World for a limited time, as was the case with the ancient Greek festival of Anthesteria (February 11–13). The last day of this festival (*chytroi*) was dedicated to propitiating the dead and their leader, Hermes Chthonios. In ancient Rome, the festival of Lemuria on May 9, 11, and 13 was an occasion for the dead to burst into homes.

We can refine this definition in accordance with its historical evolution. While in the Greek festival all the dead were involved, in Rome the revenants were recruited exclusively from the ranks of those who had died prematurely—including

---

Day, Saint Peter's Day, Pentecost, etc.
6. Cf., for example, Gustav Neckel, *Sagen aus dem germanischen Altertum* (Leipzig: Philip Reclam, 1935), 21–56.

"Die wilde Jagd." Oil painting by Franz Stuck, 1899.

suicides and the victims of violent death—and those who had not received a ritual burial.[7] In the Middle Ages, the members of the Furious Army were sinners first and foremost. In contrast with the "normal" dead who appeared during Anthesteria or Lemuria, medieval revenants could surge out on any date, but this occurred individually and not as a group. I believe that a shift between the regular dead and revenants took place here, with the latter collected together to form a troop, perhaps under the influence of other beliefs, traces of which can be found in the Germano-Scandinavian world. Here, the dead who are unhappy with their fate and are moved by feelings of vengeance gather together under the leadership of the first to die. This can mainly be seen with occurrences relating to epidemics, as we find in the *Eyrbyggja Saga*.

In short, whether in Greece, Rome, or the Germanic countries, we encounter the essential elements of something that can be condensed into a narrative of purportedly true events. The first detectable amalgam is that of the *immaturi* (*aori, biothanati*) with the common dead leaving the Other World in February or May. Here, the Church first adopted characteristic elements from this narrative—it retained the notion of the troop, essentially a nocturnal host—but made the members of this troop into the damned or the inhabitants of Purgatory.[8] If they made an appearance, it was to reveal their torment and beseech the living for suffrages so that they might find redemption and be freed. In his *Liber visionum*,[9] written between 1060 and 1067, Otloh of Saint-Emmeram reported what he called a memorable *exemplum*: two brothers spied a large host in the sky; evoking protection with the sign of the cross, they requested that these people tell who they were. One of them, their father, informed them of the sin

---

7. Cf. Claude Lecouteux, *Fantômes et Revenants au Moyen Âge* (Paris: Imago 1986), translated into English as *The Return of the Dead* (Rochester, VT: Inner Traditions, 2009); and Lecouteux, "Fantômes et Revenants," in Denis Menjot and Benoît Cursente, eds., *Démons et Merveilles au Moyen Âge* (Nice: Université de Nice-Sophia Antipolis, 1990), 267–82.
8. Jacques Le Goff, *La naissance du purgatoire*, Paris, Gallimard, 1981.
9. Paul Gerhard Schmidt, ed., *Liber visionum* (Weimar: Böhlau, 1989), 67ff.

for which he was being punished.[10] He had stolen the property of a monastery and would only be redeemed when that property had been returned. In Orderic Vitalis's work[11] (circa 1092), a certain Robert, son of Ralph the Fair-Haired, told the priest Gauchelin (or Walchelin): "In addition, I have been allowed to appear to you and show you how wretched I am" (*Mihi quoque permissum est tibi apparere, meumque miserum esse tibi manifestare*). He owed his torment "to his sins" (*pro pecatis*) but had "hopes for deliverance" (*anno relaxationem ab hoc onere fiducialiter exspecto*). Another one of the dead had a similar desire—"Exactly a year after Palm Sunday I hope I will be saved" (*a Pascha florum usque ad unum annum spero salvari*)—and added that Gauchelin should also seek atonement: "You should truly worry about yourself, and correct your life wisely" (*Tu vero sollicitus esto de te, vitamque tuam prudenter corrige*). Ekkehard, the Abbot of Aura, reported that a member of the Furious Army who appeared near Worms in 1123 said: "We are not ghosts (*phantasmata*) . . . but the souls of recently slain knights (*animae militun non longe antehac interfectorum*)."[12] The arms they bore were responsible for making them sin (*instrumenta peccandi*) and are therefore a torture for them (*material tormenti*). The chronicler adds that Count Emicho (died 1117) was said to have appeared with such a troop and declared that he would be delivered from his torments by prayers and alms (*ab hac pena orationibus et elemosinus se posse redimi docuisse*).

Starting at the onset of the eleventh century, several types of tales coexisted with the sort attested by Orderic Vitalis and Ekkehard. These include: the legend of King Herla; legends of demoniacal hunters (whose appearance is confirmed by the

---

10. Jean-Claude Schmitt, *Les Revenants, les Vivants et les Morts dans la Société médiévales* (Paris: Gallimard, 1994), makes a mistake and reverses the meaning in the text (p. 63) when he says a "knight came out of the this troop and asked them on the part of their father. . . ." The text says: *Ego pater vester rogo*. . . .

11. Orderic Vitalis, *Historia ecclesiastica*, ed. Auguste Le Prévost, (Paris: J. Renouard, 1838–1855), vol. III, 367–77.

12. Franz Josef Schmale and Irene Schmale-Ott, eds., *Frutolfs und Ekkehards Chroniken und die anonyme Kaiesrchronik* (Darmstadt: Wissenschaftliche Buchgesellschaft, 1972), 362.

Anglo-Saxon Chronicle for the year 1127[13] and by *The Chronicle of Hugh Candidus* for the same date[14]); legends of friends who have sworn a mutual oath that if one dies, he will return and tell the surviving friend about the fate he has experienced after his death (this is the theme of the *Reuner Relation*[15] written between 1185 and 1200, as well as of a passage by Hélinand de Froidmont [1150–1221/29]); and legends of armies that continue waging their battles after death.[16]

An important motif emerges from the Christian legends: one of the members of the Furious Army speaks up to explain his fate. In the *Reuner Relation*, the dead individual appears on a mountain where his still-living friend had arranged their meeting. The friend "heard the mingled voices of a throng like a host hastening to some siege. Shortly he saw a large multitude which appeared to be riding and they were all armed" (*audit cuiusdam multitudinis voces confuses quasi exercitus ad aliquam obsidionem festinantes. Videt post modicum quasi equitum grandem multitudinem et hii omnes armigeri*). Two hosts emerge, followed by a third made up of the *principes et rectores tenebrarum* (princes and leaders of darkness). But the motif of the "revealer" broke away from the theme of the Furious Army. In the work by Pierre le Chantre (died 1197), master Silo (Siger of Brabant) beseeches one of his students to come visit him after his death to relate the situation in which he found himself; soon afterward, the other appeared and shared news of his torment.[17] Hélinand de Froidmont provides a good glimpse of how the legendary traditions spread their influence. In the eleventh chapter of *De cognitione sui*, transmitted by Vincent de Beauvais in the *Speculum historiale* XXIX, 118, he records the

---

13. Charles Plummer, ed., *Two of the Anglo-Saxon Chronicles Parallel* (Oxford: Clarendon, 1892), vol. I, 258.
14. W. T. Mellows, ed., *The Chronicle of Hugh Candidus* (Oxford: Oxford University Press, 1949), 76ff.
15. Hans Gröchenig, *Die Vorauer Novelle und die Reuner Relation* (Göppingen: Kümmerle, 1981), 29ff.
16. Vincent de Beauvais, *Speculum historiale*, XXX, 200, (Douai, 1624), 1225ff.
17. Jacobus de Voragine, *Légende dorée* (The golden legend), trans. J. B. M. Roze, (Paris: Garnier-Flammarion, 1967), vol. II, 326.

story that Henri of Orleans, Bishop of Beauvais, heard from the mouth of the canon, Jean. The first part of this chapter is similar to the *Relation de Reun* and can most likely be traced back to the same source: the two friends swear that the first to die will come visit the other within thirty days, if he is able (*intra XXX dies, si posset, ad socium suum rediret*). In his conversation with the deceased Natalis (Noel), the living friend, Burchard, asks, "But I beseech that you would tell me if you are deputies in that army called the Hellequins?" Natalis responds "No," because the phenomenon stopped once his period of penitence was over. This indicates that the *militia Hellequini* is a wandering Purgatory.[18]

This long preamble is necessary if we truly wish to grasp what Geiler von Kaiserberg (1445–1510) recorded at the beginning of the sixteenth century. Born in Schaffhausen, Geiler left behind a significant body of work: speeches, translations of Jean Gerson's sermons, and most importantly *Das buoch von der Omeissen* (known as the *Emeis*), a collection of sermons published in 1515 by the Strasbourg printer Johann Grüniger and republished in 1517. In 1856, August Ströber, well known for his interest in Alsatian legend, extracted everything from these sermons relating to folk belief that was condemned as superstitions, believing this comprised a good description of persistent mental attitudes that were closer to paganism than Christianity.[19] The very long full title of the *Emeis* further points in this direction: *Gibt vnderweisung von den Vnholden oder Hexen vnd von gespenst der geist vnd von dem Wütenden heer wunderbarlich vnd nützlich ze wissen was man davon glauben vnd halten soll*. . . (Provides education about the Demons or Witches and about spirit ghosts and the Furious Army, extraordinary and useful for knowing what to believe about them and how one should deal with them. . .).

---

18. Phillipe Walter, *Mythologie chrétienne* (Paris: Imago 1992), cf. index 285. Translated into English as *Christianity: The Origins of a Pagan Religion* (Rochester, VT: Inner Traditions, 2006).
19. Cf. August Stöber, *Die Sagen des Elsasses* (St. Gallen: Scheitlin and Zellikofer, 1852) and August Stöber, *Zur Geschichte des Volksaberglaubens im Anfange des XVI. Jahrhunderts. Aus Dr. Joh. Geilers von Kaisersberg Emeis* (Basel: Schweighauser, 1856). The text can also be found in Karl Meisen, *Die Sagen vom Wütenden Heer und Wilden Jäger* (Münster i.W.: Aschendorf, 1935), 96ff.

"Der wilde Jäger." Oil painting by Johann Wilhelm Cordes, circa 1864–1869.

We will examine here what Geiler said of the Furious Army, which will allow us to raise the question of the transmission of so-called folk beliefs, with the understanding that a belief is never set in stone, but rather evolves over time.

In 1508, Geiler gave a sermon on the Thursday following Reminiscere (the second Sunday of Lent), in which he stated: "You ask, 'What shall you tell us about the Wild Army?' But I cannot tell you very much, as you know much more of it than I." Such a formula is a standard classic in preaching and can often be found coming out of the mouth of Bertold of Regensburg:[20] the preacher sets himself apart from his audience, emphasizing the gap that separates him from the unfounded beliefs that smack of paganism. In a nutshell, he announces that what he is about to say is merely an echo of widespread rumors, but we shall see what kind of credence we can give him. Geiler immediately adds, "This is what the common man says: Those who die before the time God has fixed for them, those who leave on a journey and are stabbed, hung, or drowned, must wander after death until the date that God has set for them arrives. Then God will do for them what is in accordance with His divine will." This belief is

---

20. Cf. Claude Lecouteux and Phillippe Marcq, *Berthold de Ratisbonne, Péchés et Vertus. Scènes de la Vie au XIIIe siècle* (Paris: Desjonquères, 1991).

extremely old and can be seen in ancient Rome where premature deaths produced revenants. It made its way into the Medieval West by way of Tertullian (*De anima* 56): "They say those souls which are taken away by a premature death wander about hither and thither until they have completed the residue of the years which they would have lived through, had it not been for their untimely fate" (*Aiunt et immature morte praeventas eo usque vagori istic donec reliquatio compleatur aetatum quacum pervixissent, si non intempestive obissent*).

It would take too long to follow its meandering course through the ages, so we satisfy ourselves with the testimony of William of Auvergne, whose *De universo* was written between 1231 and 1236. William knew of the existence of the *Mesnie Hellequin* (*De Universo* III, 12), which had been brought out of the shadows by Orderic Vitalis at the end of the eleventh century and enjoyed a much larger impact than what is claimed by Jean-Claude Schmitt, who, ignoring many accounts, has a tendency to restrict the legend to Normandy. William says (III, 14):

> On the point that these [knights] appear in the shape of men, I say: of dead men, and those most often slain by iron, we can undoubtedly, based on the advice of Plato, consider that the souls of men thus slain continue to be active the number of days or the entire time it was given them to living in their bodies, if they had not been expelled by force. (*De hoc autem, quod in similitudine hominum apparent, hominum dico mortuorum et maximo gladio interfectorum, videatur forsitan alicui iuxta sententiam Platonis, quod agere viderentur numeros dierum vel temporum debitorum animae mortuorum huiusmodi, temporum dico, quibus in corporibus victurae erant, eas nisi mortis huiusmodi violentia expulisset.*)[21]

There is nothing "folkloric" about this notion because the men of this time had other explanations, a glimpse of which is provided above. Geiler goes on to say that the Furious Army made its

---

21. William of Auvergne, *Opera Omnia* (Paris, 1674), vol. I, 1074.

appearance during the Ember Days and especially at Christmas, which is entirely in keeping with the beliefs of the time. Christmas, and more specifically the Twelve Days (*Rauhnächte*), is a period when the Other World is open, which is to say that a free passageway has been established between the realm of the dead and that of the living. Geiler next states: "And each proceeds in the dress of their status: a peasant in peasant garb, a knight as a knight, and they race therefore bound to the same rope. One is holding a cross in front of him, the other a head in his hand." Here our preacher follows Hélinand de Froidmont or Vincent de Beauvais, in any case a written source from clerical literature. In Vincent de Beauvais's book (*Speculum historiale*, XXIX, 118), which borrows a passage from Hélinand's *De cognitione sui*, we read:

> But this false opinion . . . that souls of the deceased, lamenting punishments of their sins, are in the habit of appearing to the masses in the style of dress in which they had formerly lived: that is to say, country folk in rustic clothing, soldiers in military dress, just as the masses are wont to claim about the family of Hellequin. (*Haec autem falsitas opinio . . . quod animae defunctorum suorum peccatorum poenas lugentes multis apparere solent in eo habitu, in quo prius vixerant: id est rustici in rusticano, milites in militari, sicut vulgus asserere solet de familia Hellequini. . . .*)

Here again, the blending of popular and scholarly assumptions is clearly apparent. Ancient Scandinavian literature, which is our best witness of things relating to revenants, indicates on numerous occasions that the dead return in the same appearance as they had at the time of their death.[22] In Germany, the testimonies are much rarer (which in no way means that this vision

---

22. Claude Lecouteux, "Fantômes et Revenants germaniques, Essai de Présentation," *Études Germaniques* 39 (1984): 227–50; 40 (1985): 141–60; and Lecouteux, "Altgermanische Gespenster und Wiedergänger: Bemerkungen zu einem vernachlässigten Forschungsfeld der Altgermanistik," *Euphorion* 80 (1986): 219–31.

did not exist), but fraught with significance. In a charm from the fourteenth or fifteenth century, the speaker requests God's protection from:

Wutanes her und alle sine man,
Dy di reder und dy wit tragen,
Geradebrech und irhangin...[23]

(the Furious Host and all its men,
who carry wheels and fetters,
broken apart and hung)

The members of the Furious Army appear here bearing the instruments of their torment. The *Zimmern Chronicle* describes one of the members of this procession in this fashion: "His head had been split in two down to the neck" (*Dem ist das haupt in zwai thail biß an hals gespalten gewesen*)."[24]

The only motif yet to be explained by scholars is the rope mentioned by Geiler. This could be a recollection from Lucian of Samosata (*Discourses*, Hercules 1–7), who depicts the god Ogmios, an infernal psychopomp, pulling along "a large number of men attached by the ears with bonds of tiny gold and amber chains that resembled beautiful necklaces." It so happens that in Albrecht Durer's *Kunstbuch* of 1514, he depicted the allegory of eloquence as the god Hermes pulled humans by chains that connected his tongue to the ears of his captives.[25] I offer the hypothesis for what it's worth, but these parallels merit pointing out.

"One came before the rest," added Geiler, shouting: "'Get out of the road so that God may spare your life!' This is what the

---

23. Johannes Franck, "Geschichte des Wortes Hexe," in Joseph Hansen, *Quellen und Untersuchungen zur Geschichte des Hexenwahns* (Hildesheim: Olms, 1963), 614–70, here at 639ff.
24. Karl August Barack, ed., *Das Zimmersche Chronik*, 2nd. ed. (Freiburg and Tübingen: Mohr, 1881–1882), vol. IV, 122–27.
25. Cf. Friedrich Winkler, *Die Zeichnungen Albrechts Dürers*, vol. III, 79. This matter is discussed, with a bibliography, in Françoise Le Roux, "Le Dieu celtique aux Liens," *Ogam* XII (1960): 212–18.

common man says." This new motif of the figure sounding the alarm comes directly from Orderic Vitalis's narrative in which the priest Gauchelin saw the *Mesnie Hellequin*. Here, a giant man holding a club broke from the host and approached him saying: "Stay where you are. Do not come closer!" (*Sta, nec progrediarius ultra*). The figure delivering a warning quickly became quite popular; Jacob Trausch (died 1610), the author of the *Strasbourg Chronicle*, borrowed this figure and had him shout: "Get back, back, so that nothing happens to anyone!"[26] In this instance, however, the legend is re-contextualized into the polemic between Catholics and reformers: such deceptions and superstitions have ceased ever since Dr. Martin Luther attacked Papism. The motif can also be found in the work of Johannes Agricola, this time with the addition of a novel element: the warning figure is named the Loyal Eckhard (*der treüwe Eckart*).[27] This latter example attests to the contamination of the Furious Army by the Venusberg legend (*Tannhäuser*).[28]

To illustrate his point, Geiler did as all good preachers do: he repeated a story—an *exemplum* or *historiola*. In this case, he borrowed it from Hélinand de Froidmont, undoubtedly by way of the *Speculum historiale* by Vincent de Beauvais. His text follows the source so closely it could be called a literal translation, as the end of the story shall prove.

[Geiler:] *Bist du auch in dem wütischen her gelaufen, von dem man sagt? Er sprach: Nein, Karolus Quintus hat sein penitens erfült, un hat daz wütisch heer vff gehört.* ("Are you also proceeding in the Furious Army that men talk about?" He spoke: "No, Karolus Quintus has fulfilled his penitence

---

26. The reader may also refer to Johannes Geffken, *Der Bildercatechismus des fünfzehnten Jahrhunderts und die catechetischen Hauptstücke in dieser Zeit bis auf Luther. I: Die Zehn Gebote* (Leipzig: T. O. Weigel, 1855), 37ff.
27. Text in Karl Meisen, *Die Sagen vom Wütenden Heer*, 98ff. It will be noted that this individual has become a figure of legend; cf. Lütz Röhrich, *Das große Lexikon der sprichwörtlichen Redensarten* (Freiburg im Bresgau, Basel, and Vienna: Herder, 1991–1992), vol. I, 350ff.
28. Cf. J. M. Clifton-Everest, *The Tragedy of Knighthood: The Origin of the Tannhäuser-Legend* (Oxford: Oxford University Press, 1979).

and has ended the Furious Army.")

[Hélinand:] *sed obsecro ut dicatis mihi, si vos estis deputati in illa militia quam dicunt Hellequini. Et ille: Non, domine. Illa militia jam non vadit, sed nuper ire desiit, quia poenitentiam suam peregit.* ("But I beg that you would tell me if you are deputies in that army they call the Hellequins?" "No, sir. That army does not advance now, but recently ceased marching because it fulfilled its penitence.")

The sole modification—*Karolus Quintus* for *militia Hellequinus*—stems from the fact that Geiler was using a gloss by Vincent or Hélinand, which stated: "Corruptly, however, 'Hellequinus' is said by the common people instead of 'Karlequintus'" ("*Corrupte autem dictus est a vulgo Hellequinus pro Karlequintus*").

In light of the preceding information, it is easy to see how clerics worked and, more importantly, the omnipresence of the scholarly and bookish tradition. Thus, when a belief or legend is encountered in the religious texts of the late Middle Ages, it is necessary to be very prudent before asserting that the author was faithfully echoing reality. The sole reality is that men believed the dead returned on certain dates. Recontextualized by the Church, the belief was incorporated into the great cycle of the punishment of sin.

What is the case with the other folk traditions recorded by Geiler? Comparative analysis allows us to see that the preacher always worked in the same way: he took a "superstition," then reduced and destroyed it with the help of the clerical literature. But did the object of his efforts correspond to a local reality? In the case of the werewolf,[29] this is subject to doubt. In the case of witchcraft, the answer can be in the affirmative if we recognize that the Church contributed greatly to forging the belief—but we can only confirm the latter and not take the descriptions at face value. Researchers have indeed provided evidence that the

---

29. Cf. August Stöber: *Zur Geschichte des Volksaberglaubens*, 31 ("werewolf"); 11ff.; 12; 17ff., 33ff. ("witch"). Regarding the werewolf, however, Geiler was inspired by Vincent de Beauvais, Valère Maxime, and William of Auvergne.

catalogs of beliefs were accumulated bit by bit over time and that they were recapitulations of everything lurking in the writs of councils and synods, in the penitentials, and in the treatises on the Decalogue.[30] This was how the various *Mirrors of Sin* were born, such as the one by Martin von Amberg,[31] as well as the great fifteenth-century collections of "superstitions." Narrative literature followed this same evolution, as is evident from the works of Michel Behaim[32] and Hans Vintler.[33] On the other hand, all these texts document the enduring nature of beliefs and practices—an enduring nature encouraged by the preachers who never stopped talking about them and therefore giving credence to those things they took to be errors, sins, and idolatry. The *exempla* with which they embellished their sermons then came into the public domain and gave birth to new narrative traditions. When Geiler speaks of a haunted house in the Mainz bishopric, in his sermon "Am mitwoch nach Occuli," his inspiration is *The Golden Legend* of Jacobus de Voragine,[34] and when he mentions "the wax that runs from the manes of horses," he

---

30. Cf. the fine studies in Marianne Rumpf, *Perchten: Populäre Glaubensgestalten zwischen Mythos und Katechese* (Würzburg: Königshausen & Neumann, 1991) and Karin Baumann, *Aberglaube für Laien. Zur Programmatik und Überlieferung mittelalterlicher Superstitionenkritik* (Würzburg: Königshausen & Neumann, 1989).
31. Stanley N. Werbow, ed., *Martin von Amberg. Der Gewissensspiegel* (Berlin: Schmidt, 1958).
32. Cf. Ernst-Dietrich Güting, "Michel Behaims Gedicht gegen den Aberglauben und seine lateinische Vorlage. Zur Tradierung des Volksglaubens im Spätmittelalters," in Dietz-Rüdiger Moser, ed., *Glaube im Abseits* (Darmstadt: Wissenschaftliche Buchgellschaft, 1992), 310–67.
33. Cf. Max Bartels and Oskar Ebermann: "Zur Aberglaubensliste in Vintlers Pluemen der tugent," *Zeitschrift des Vereins für Volkskunde* 23 (1913): 1–18; 113–36. Cf. also the article by Anton E. Schönbach, "Zeugnisse zur deutschen Volkskunde des Mittelalters," *Zeitschrift des Vereins für Volkskunde* 12 (1902): 1–16. On the list of superstitions in the work of Thomas de Haselbach, see Franz-Josef Schweitzer, *Tugend und Laster in illustrierten didaktischen Dichtungen des Spätmittelalters* (Hildesheim: Olms, 1993), 180–84.
34. Who drew his material from the Chronicle of Sigebert de Gembloux for the year 858, cf. J. C. Migne, ed., *Patrologia Latina* 160, col. 163. This information can also be found in Vincent de Beauvais (*Speculum historiale* XXIV, 37) and in the works of many other authors.

is following a passage from William of Auvergne's *De Universo*. In order to establish the difference between local traditions and scholarly traditions, it is necessary to work diachronically, which is the only means for avoiding errors.

(Translated by Jon Graham)

This article originally appeared in French in the journal *Études Germaniques* 50 (1995): 367–76. The translation here is published by kind permission of the author.

On Barbarian Suffering

Steve Harris

Eall is earfoðlice eorþan rice, "All is difficult on earth." So says the Anglo-Saxon Wanderer, describing his long suffering in a famous tenth-century poem. To suffer is to experience a privation of some good. Suffering is thereby implicitly tied to one's understanding of the good life. When we read ancient Germanic poetry, and see in it suffering, we are invited into an ancient Germanic anticipation of the good life. We are also invited to imagine how Anglo-Saxons understood suffering. *Beowulf*, written over a thousand years ago, seems to be in part a poem that asks its readers to think carefully and deeply about suffering. It offers no certain answers, but poses the questions well. In the end, the poem (and the ancient Germanic traditions on which it's based) invites us to consider the close relationship between suffering and divinity. At the heart of this relationship between the mystical forces of the world and one's own fate is a moral code. That moral code is capacious, all-encompassing, and links an individual and his community to the heavens. When the Catholic Church absorbed the religions of Britain, that ancient link did not disappear. It has yet to disappear. Pagans and Christians, dissimilar in so many ways, nevertheless share a sense of *Beowulf* that postmodern secularists do not: the inescapable effect of the invisible, mystical forces of the world on the individual life.

Beowulf is a masterfully crafted poem. Even through its structure, the poet indicates something of his (or her) view of the cosmos. The poem's grand structure is mirrored in the poem's small events: macrocosm in microcosm. The poem begins and ends with a funeral over water: the coming of the king, and the leaving of the king. And in each scene there is approach and withdrawal, coming and going, tradition and variation. In each half of the poem, the central plot device is an attack on a human habitation by a monster—in the first half, a monster of water, in the second, a monster of fire. And in each scene, the monstrous threatens the established order, even if the monstrous is found within the human. Through both halves flows a fateful inevitability that cannot be overcome, only mastered. Wyrd, or Fate, is the dominant force under heavens ruled by God, and it hovers over each scene and compels the individual to withstand. *Wyrd oft nereð unfægne eorl, þonne his ellen deah*—"Fate often saves a man if his courage holds." Most importantly, those attacks by monsters speak to traditional worldviews: they raise a fundamental question about the integral bond between the self and the world. Does some failing of Hroðgar's bring on the demon Grendel? If not, then why is he forced to suffer (*þolian*) sorrow for thegns (*þegnsorge*)? Clearly, since he does not suffer randomly, then this king must somehow be connected to the health of his kingdom. But how?

Perhaps it is not the king's fault: perhaps one of Hroðgar's retinue is at fault—possibly Unferth, who killed his own kin. But this raises even more questions. What effect does a man's moral failing have on the security of his neighbor? Can the suffering of a community really be the result of an individual's moral failure, of disloyalty or dishonor or cowardice? *Beowulf* asks us to imagine a world where each person has an effect on the unseen forces that bring wealth or disaster. Moreover, those unseen forces flow between members of a community. When those forces are unleashed, they are unleashed not on the offending individual, but on his or her entire community. They do not destroy a foreign or alien group. A Danish fault brings a Danish fall, but not to the Swedes. This effect implies that there is something integral or supernatural about the bonds of a community. The Danes suffer for the moral failings of Unferð or Hroðgar, and are therefore tied to the moral reckoning of each member. So, what moral responsibility does the individual owe to his or her community?

The question to start with is this: Why did Grendel attack the hall? Some say that he was angry. Grendel heard mirth—*dream gehyrde*—and being unhappy (*wonsælig*), he killed the joyful men. But that's hardly enough to motivate the poem. The poet himself (or herself—we don't know who wrote the poem) says that God is involved. There's a bigger picture. Grendel bears God's ire, and is the Wrath of God. Importantly, the poet never says whether this is the Christian God or Woden. And the poet does a magnificent job of walking the line between Christianity and paganism. A pagan reader could read *Beowulf* and think it a perfectly pagan poem; a Christian reader could read it and think it a perfectly Christian poem. And in both worlds, pagan and Christian, the question is still the same: did the hall dwellers do something to *deserve* the attacks? In other words, is the All-Father causing the violence?

A responsible reader of *Beowulf* must entertain the assumption that certain large-scale, real-world effects (like fires, war, disease, and flood) have a direct relation to individual action. If we ask about the moral cause of the attack on Heorot, we ask after the ethical culpability of the individual characters. This question requires us to understand the attack not as a pathological whim of an angry monster, but as a consequence of an ethical failure. This link is common coin: we recognize it not only the attacks by Grendel on the great hall of Heorot, but also the wars between Swedes and Geats, the creation of the ring of power in *The Lord of the Rings* and the dissolution of the fellowship of the ring, and so on. All of these calamities occur because of the moral failures of some characters. And the calamities affect far more than the individuals with moral failings: they affect an entire community. Communal culpability is an ancient assumption of the English legal tradition. In the earliest English and Germanic laws, an individual's perfidy was compensated by his or her family. Conversely, innocence was proved by an oath of friends or family members. It was King Edmund of England (939–946) who first made a criminal personally responsible for murder, rather than putting the responsibility on the family. Even today, associations or corporations can be found responsible for the actions of their individual members, for example.

Western ideas of justice have long included a belief in the moral cause of suffering. This is not the wheel of fortune, *fortuna rota*, which is blind to the moral nature of her victims. Instead, it is Santa Claus: the good are rewarded, and the sinful suffer. One of the more powerful examples comes in a very ancient

Hebrew text, the Book of Job. There, Job's friend Bildad sees Job suffer and says, "If thou wert pure and upright; surely now He would awake for thee, and make the habitation of thy righteousness prosperous" (Job 8:6). Bildad says that Job's suffering is an *effect* of his own sin. But God tells the reader that Bildad is mistaken: Job *is* righteous. Since the Jewish or Christian reader must believe God in this story, he must conclude that Job is not punished for his sins. So why does Job suffer?

One apparent lesson of the Book of Job is that God does not distribute even-handed retribution. Sins are not punished by pain, and good deeds are not rewarded by wealth. The lesson is a central tenet in Judeo-Christian thought. But, a dominant strain of ancient Western tradition refuses to see the meting out of justice to a community in that way. Instead, the moral causation of communal suffering, what we might call Bildad's equation, is as ancient as it is ubiquitous. Plagues, floods, fires, and invasion have long been considered the results of human iniquity–from Adam and Eve's expulsion from Eden, to the destruction of Sodom, to the barbarian invasions, to the American Civil War, even to the present day. It cannot be explained to someone who lives in a mental world without mystical powers and a governing divinity (or divinities). But to those who do live in that world, the moral causation of human suffering is a very ancient way to think about one's place in the world.

Scourges

For millennia, disease, war, famine, and flood were all considered part of a divine calculus to mete out justice. One tool of this justice was the scourge: barbarian Vikings, Huns, Avars, and Visigoths, among others. The awesome violence and terror these tribes brought was seen as a direct consequence of a moral decay in Western civilization. To take one example, in the second week of August of the year 991, a Viking fleet attacked English troops near the town of Maldon in eastern England. Afterwards, the victorious Vikings, weighed down with loot and slaves, terrorized Britain's eastern shore. Some years later, an Anglo-Saxon monk

BARBARIAN HORDES AS THE SCOURGE OF GOD. "LA INVASIÓN DE LOS BÁRBAROS," OIL PAINTING BY ULPIANO FERNÁNDEZ-CHECA Y SAIZ, 1887.

at the English monastery of Ramsey, perhaps not fully versed in Christian theology, wrote:

> A threat was once issued to the Jews, similar to what our people, then and now, were and are enduring. For the prophet Jeremiah said, reproachfully, "Because (said the Lord) you have not heard my words, behold I will send and take all the kindreds of the North, and I will bring them against this land, and against the inhabitants thereof, and against all the nations that are round about it, and I will destroy them."[1]

To this very traditional thinker, the destruction wrought by the Vikings was caused by English sin. At about the same time Wulfstan, Archbishop of York, wrote a sermon in which he said,

---

1. "Talis enim olim comminatio Iudeis promissa est, quam nostrates tunc et nunc sustinebant et sustinent. Dicet enim comminans propheta: 'Pro eo quod non audistis verba mea, ecce ego mittam et assumam uniuersas cognationes aquilonis (ait Dominus) et adducam eas super terram istam, et super habitatores eius, et super omnes nationes que in circuitu eius sunt, et interficiam illos.'" Michael Lapidge, "The Life of St Oswald," in Donald Scragg, ed., *The Battle of Maldon, AD 991* (Oxford: Blackwell, 1991), 54; Lapidge's translation.

For it is evident and plain in all our lives that we have previously sinned more often than we have improved, and therefore much is attacking this people. Things have not prospered now for a long time at home or beyond our land, but there has been warfare and famine, burning and bloodshed in every district time and again, and theft and murder, plague and pestilence, murrain and disease, malice and hate and the plundering of robbers have harmed us very severely . . . and bad weather has very often caused bad harvests; because in this country there has been, as it may seem, for many years now many crimes and unstable loyalties everywhere among men.[2]

Wulfstan was a proponent of a Christianity that was mixed heavily with pagan elements. His sermon concludes with a plea to Englishmen to reorder their lives and submit themselves to the binding force of a common law: "And let us order our words and deeds rightly and earnestly cleanse our thoughts, and carefully honor oath and pledge . . . ."[3] For Wulfstan, bad weather is caused by crime and a lack of loyalty. In this cause we see a very ancient pagan tradition brought into a Christian setting.

Bad weather was widely considered a manifestation of God's anger. That anger was effected through magical beings, no longer called elves or wraiths, but demons. St. Jerome, the Venerable Bede, and other early medieval writers allowed that there were demons in the air. Thomas Aquinas wrote in his *Summa Theologica*, "Rains and winds, and whatsoever occurs by local impulse alone, can be caused by demons." In the late fifteenth century, Pope Urban V gave the Emperor of Byzantium three cakes of wax thought capable of dispelling storms and pestilence. Seventeenth-century writers in Salem, Massachusetts claimed that witches could be "weather makers." One characteristic of bad weather, lightning, was widely considered an especially clear form of God's displeasure. In 1752, Benjamin Franklin invented

---

2. Wulfstan, "Sermon of the Wolf to the English," *The Anglo-Saxon World*, ed. Kevin Crossley-Holland (Oxford: Oxford University Press, 1999), 295.
3. Wulfstan, "Sermon of the Wolf," 299.

A 1778 ALLEGORICAL PORTRAYAL OF BENJAMIN FRANKLIN AS A HEAVENLY DEITY. DRAWN BY FRAGONARD AND ETCHED BY MARGUERITE GÉRARD, THE PRINTED IMAGE CARRIED THE TITLE "ERIPUIT COELO FULMEN SCEPTRUMQUE TIRANNIS" (HE SEIZED LIGHTNING FROM THE HEAVENS AND THE SCEPTER FROM TYRANTS) WITH A DEDICATION "TO THE GENIUS OF FRANKLIN."

the lightning rod, which saved innumerable churches and homes all over the world from fire. Three years later, Massachusetts suffered a devastating earthquake. Thomas Prince, pastor of Old South Church in Boston, claimed in a sermon that the earthquake had been caused by Franklin's device: the lightning rod had unnaturally perverted the natural course of God's justice.

This traditional connection between crime and the chastisement of the heavens governed ancient and medieval thinking about the causes of large-scale disaster. St. Augustine of Hippo in North Africa thought that the barbarian invasions of the fourth century were caused by Roman crimes. Gildas, historian of the early medieval Britons, thought the invasions of England by the Romans under Caesar and, later, by the Continental Angles and Saxons were caused by British crimes. Parisians, too, believed that the destruction of Paris by Vikings in the ninth century was caused by Parisian crimes. In fact, a three-day feast was developed in Gaul to assuage the anger of God. It was known as Rogationtide.[4] The rituals were celebrated in hopes that they act as a supplication to God and appease Him. So appeased, He would lessen the burdens of the prayerful community.[5] The feast was based on an old pagan festival that took place in Rome. There, the god of blight would be given supplication that he might keep his hand from the crops. In *Beowulf*, we see the Danes pray to heathen gods in a similar attempt to supplicate them.[6] But Grendel still attacks. Grendel, we come to learn, is a scourge of God: the poet tells us that Grendel *Godes yrre bær*, "bore God' wrath."[7] Prayer will not be enough to make up for the crime.

Our deep connection to *Beowulf* and its traditional thinking is neither anachronistic nor easily dismissed as folk beliefs. On March 4, 1865, President Abraham Lincoln spoke in his second inaugural address of the "sin of slavery," claiming it was that sin that had brought on the American Civil War.[8] Lincoln reduced

---

4. Joyce Hill, "The *Litania maiores* and *minores* in Rome, Francia, and Anglo-Saxon England: terminology, texts, and traditions," *Early Medieval Europe* 9 (2000): 211–46. See also Amalarius of Metz, *De ecclesiasticis officiis*, Patrologia Latina 105: 985, 1067C.

5. Ælfric, an eleventh-century Anglo-Saxon monk of Eynsham, makes the point in his sermon, *De oratione Moysi*, lines 36–37, "*ac we ne scelon swaðeah geswican þære bene / oðþæt se mild-heorta god us mildelice ahredde*" ("but nevertheless we should not desist from that prayer / until the compassionate God mercifully deliver us"). *Ælfric's Lives of the Saints*, ed. and trans. Walter Skeat (London: Early English Texts Society, 1966), vol. 1, 286.

6. *Beowulf*, ll. 175–80.

7. *Beowulf*, l. 711b.

8. "The Almighty has His own purposes. 'Woe unto the world because of offenses; for it must needs be that offenses come, but woe to that man by whom the offense cometh.' If we shall suppose that American slavery is one of those offenses which, in the providence of God, must needs come, but which, having continued through His appointed time, He now wills to remove, and that He gives to both North and South this terrible war as the woe due to

the many causes of the war, including profound differences about states' rights, to the single cause of slavery. And he presented large-scale disaster as a function of a single moral cause. His claim was adopted by the people, and has stood the test of time in the public imagination. No matter how clinical the secular, scientific mind attempts to be, the traditional, unseen, magical connection between man and his world is too powerful to ignore. It is not uncommon after a natural disaster to hear affected people ask, "What did we do to deserve this?"

Perhaps one of the more famous American inquiries into the complexity of just suffering is a sermon by the puritan minister Cotton Mather. In *The Voice of the Glorious God in the Thunder*, Mather tries to combine traditional thinking (or what we called Bildad's equation) with Job's Judeo-Christian thinking. The sermon was preached in Boston on September 12, 1694, during a thunderstorm. Mather took as his text Psalm 29:3, "The Voice of the Lord is upon the Waters, the God of Glory Thundereth." Mather acknowledges Bildad's equation by allowing that "Whatever the witch-advocates may make of it, it is a Scriptural and Rational Assertion, *that in the Thunder there is oftentimes, by the permission of God, the Agency of the Devil.*"[9] The mystical powers of the air are renamed Satan. Dividing the voice of thunder into the psalm's seven parts (he calls them the seven voices of thunder), he explains the many lessons one ought to draw from thunder. Mather's fifth voice declares that thunder, by which one is to understand physical suffering, is not always the result of collective guilt. Sometimes physical suffering results from a personal

---

those by whom the offense came, shall we discern therein any departure from those divine attributes which the believers in a living God always ascribe to Him? Fondly do we hope, fervently do we pray, that this mighty scourge of war may speedily pass away." —Abraham Lincoln, "Second Inaugural Address," (Western Standard Publishing Company, 1998), n.p. The view is based on the fact that that both North and South had permitted slavery. By 1789, Massachusetts alone had outlawed slavery. Forty-one percent of New York state residents in the Colonial era held slaves, a greater proportion than any state in the South during that period.

9. Cotton Mather, *The Voice of the Glorious God in the Thunder* (London: John Astwood, 1695), 15. His emphasis.

failing. It says, "Let this Thunder convict you of what you may justly reckon your own iniquity."[10] Mather is vague here: on one hand, he seems to say that thunder is merely a symbol to remind you to reflect on your inner life; on the other hand, he seems to allow a mystical connection between physical pain and moral failure.

So, we might ask returning to Anglo-Saxon England, what is the significance of the hall attacks and the dragon fire in *Beowulf*? Are they a sign of human failure and of divine displeasure? Or are they a symbol? Before attempting an answer to that question, one might reasonably complain: don't we need to accept the existence of a divinity in order to accept this question? In fact, we do not. The same relation between suffering and external forces, strangely enough, exists in post-modern secular thinking, as well. It is as if the connection forged by tradition is stronger than the novelty that seeks to undermine that tradition.

The connection between weather, violence, suffering, and sin has a secular counterpart. Just as the same phenomenon might be seen in two ways, so the same behavior might be seen in two ways. An act of greed is a phenomenon which can be categorized religiously as a sin, or more secularly as improper behavior. A secular version of Bildad's equation sees a contravention of public values causing large-scale retribution. In a rough homology, the causative hand of God disappears, and the causative hand of Society takes its place. National tragedy can thus be described as the inevitable result of *social* injustice. For example, an intemperate desire for power condemns a community to its deserved suffering. After the bombings of 7/7, certain segments of British society considered their own moral culpability in the violence. When British newspapers and public commentators called for an increase in social justice, namely in diversity and tolerance, they relied on a causal connection between violence and public values.

If one takes the view that British society is responsible for the creation of the ethos of each of its members, then "society" bears responsibility for its own suffering. In turn, such responsibility depends upon a notion of society as a community presumably

---

10. Mather, *Voice*, p. 12.

acting as a single, morally interconnected unit, as "a supposed sphere of causal and moral self-sufficiency lying between the political and the personal."[11] If we apply a secular version of Bildad's equation, we might conclude that the suffering of indiscriminate members of a society indicates that society's culpability. But there is an intriguing assumption here about the organic nature of a society. The bombers of 7/7 apparently imagined themselves to be bombing Britons first, and individuals second, if at all. This metaphor implies an almost medical connection between the larger organism and its unthinking, diseased parts. "Society" is an eighteenth-century invention—a metonym for processes, institutions, and individuals—but it has come to be personified as a single force or body, greater than the sum of its components. As a personified, quasi-human entity, it takes on human characteristics such as *the ability to oppress*, or *to liberate*, or *to suffer* (which logically belong to individuals, but only metaphorically to concepts). The traditional, mystical body has adopted a scientific sheen.

But the scientific sheen wears away when one is forced to consider formal causation. In other words, on what basis is injustice (and justice) determined? Any reasonable connection between random meteorological events and human behavior has no observable, scientific basis. In a religious community, as I hope to have illustrated, understanding the moral causes of storms and violence depends upon the assumption that in pleasing God or gods, a community is granted peace. A community like that in *Beowulf* fears displeasing the All-Father because he is the lawmaker. Good behavior is directly, if inversely, tied to divine retribution. But a secular community depends on no such controlling mechanism. Its harmony depends on ubiquitous legal behavior. Generally speaking, illegal behavior has no demonstrable connection to natural disasters, for example. In *Beowulf*, this means that a religious reading (pagan or Christian)

---

11. Geoffrey Hawthorn, "Society," in *The Oxford Companion to Philosophy*, ed. Ted Honderich (Oxford: Oxford University Press, 1995), 836. There is strong debate about whether society, rather than the individual, can be the grounds of moral judgment.

sees the monsters as a divinely sanctioned threat to immoral men. But those who posit the independent ethical and legal authority of each community can allow that the monsters have their own community, their own ethics and law. Why shouldn't Grendel's mother revenge her son? Why shouldn't the dragon seek revenge for the theft? Is the dragon ethically justified in causing suffering? Legally justified? According to whose legal or ethical codes?[12]

Society stands in for God in the secular calculus of suffering and retribution. The abstraction is treated in the language of sociology as the creator and legislator of human behavior.[13] The social production of an ethos is a tenet of cultural materialism, which in part proposes that each individual is chiefly the product of social forces acting upon him or her. Institutions, folk practices, language, government policy—all these are thought to shape or *construct* each one of us out of the gray mud of our mechanical brains. The individual is conceived of as a product of social forces, but not as an independent, self-governing entity

---

12. Here we might distinguish between shared law and a shared moral code. Acting sinfully and acting illegally are not always the same thing. Adultery, for example, is not illegal in every state. So, while there is an obvious moral link between an increase in adulterous behavior and widespread sinful behavior (as Wulfstan illustrated), there is no obvious legal link between increasing crime rates and decreasing marriage rates. In other words, there is nothing in the legal constitution of marriage that would suggest that its dissolution leads to criminal behavior. And to speak about the ethics of adultery is not the same as speaking about the legality or illegality of adultery. While the law is common to all members of a secular society (and all are expected to act legally), no ethos is necessarily held in common (so all cannot be expected to act ethically—whatever that might mean in a secular society).

13. Auguste Comte in *The System of Positive Polity* wrote that science "replaces theology in the Religion of Humanity." See Richard G. Olson, *Science and Religion, 1450–1900* (Westport, CT: Greenwood, 2004), 159. Comte saw all societies moving through three stages: the theological, the scientific, and the positive. In the latter, "one moves to a purer form of understanding, where one confines explanations to the expression of verifiable and measurable correlations between phenomena." Michael Ruse, "Comte," in *The Oxford Companion to Philosophy*, 145. Here, he anticipates Marxist thought, which in turn draws on similar formulations by Hegel.

ontologically *prior* to those forces.[14] Even one's sense of independence is a socially constructed and socially determined notion. Those who fail to understand are alienated from themselves, operating under a "false consciousness."[15] Accordingly, in this view, responsibility for individual violence is ultimately society's, not an individual's. This is because the individual is, more than anything else, an envoy of social forces. There is no real rupture here between the modern and the ancient. Grendel, for example, would be created by his alienation from men. The ultimate *cause* of violence and injustice in the world of the poem is therefore the society that makes an individual. Aberrant men, or monsters, are in this view the results of an aberrant social system. In short, the demons of the air have been given technical names.

Cause

God and Society are two similar ways of answering the question, "What did we do to cause this awful thing?" But to be a little more precise, one should define "cause."[16] Aristotle in his *Posterior Analytics* divided causation into four types. A *material* cause is that out of which another comes. An acorn causes a tree; an athlete, the smell of sweat. A *formal* cause is an archetype

---

14. The Marxist notion, derived ultimately from Fichte, is that each individual contains within himself Humanity. Thus, self-realization can be compelled by a state apparatus that claims to have understood this Humanity. One is *free*—one is truly an individual—when one complies with the dictates of Humanity as proposed by an "enlightened" oligarchy. Freedom is conceived as submission to the state. Fichte is thought to have given birth to totalitarian utopianism.

15. For Marx and Engels, humans are determined by the material conditions of life. Both followed Hegel in this point; Hegel writes, "It is not consciousness that determines life, but life that determines consciousness." Thus, it seems, consciousness depends on social conditions. Those whose thought differs from the "true" thought of the enlightened Party merely fail to understand the nature of social conditions, and are *alienated* from their true, social selves. See Leszek Kolakowski, *Main Currents of Marxism* (New York: Norton, 2005), 128–30.

16. Much of this section is taken from Mortimer J. Adler and William Gorman, *The Great Ideas: A Synopticon of Great Books of the Western World* (Chicago: Encyclopedia Britannica, 1952), s.v. "Cause."

or plan, as a blueprint is the cause of a house, or an epic poem the cause of its imitation. An *efficient* cause is that which causes a change, as a bowler causes a ball to roll or fire causes water to boil. And a *final* cause is "that for the sake of which a thing is done." Good health causes exercise, a need to protect one's wealth causes banks to exist. In terms of suffering, the material cause is the nervous system of the human body. The formal cause is the cultural and psychological manner of experiencing suffering. The efficient causes are the physical and psychological phenomena that literally touch upon the suffering individual. And the final cause is the matter of debate.

So, the attack on Heorot was caused by Grendel—that was its efficient cause. But what was its final cause? And what details of plot and character lead us to understand why, as a final cause, the attack occurred? As a result of the larger philosophical and theological questions it raises, final cause is largely a speculative matter, incapable of physical confirmation. When ancient poets ask about the causes of human suffering, what kind of answers should today's reader pursue? Social answers? Social answers are in vogue in today's academy. In fact, it is not uncommon in schools and universities to treat literary characters today as social metonyms. It seems that the individual is becoming lost in his or her signifying role. A woman in a poem is not seen primarily as an individual, but as all-women: Queen Wealhtheow becomes all women in Anglo-Saxon society, from milkmaids to housewives to warrior queens. The relation of an individual to his or her final cause is in today's critical environment less metaphysical and more physical, more social. And so literary critics seek for the cause of suffering in a world below the clouds.

The French novelist Stéphane Audeguy writes about a moment in the eighteenth century, after the full force of the Enlightenment had been felt, when men all over the world looked up at the clouds, suddenly seeing only clouds and not Heaven. In 1867 the English poet Matthew Arnold wrote in "Dover Beach":

The Sea of Faith
Was once, too, at the full, and round earth's shore

Lay like the folds of a bright girdle furled;
But now I only hear
Its melancholy long withdrawing roar,
Retreating, to the breath
Of the night-wind, down the vast edges drear
And naked shingles of the world.

For Arnold, faith provided freedom from the isolation and unthinking brutality of the physical world. It was a brutal world "red in tooth and claw," as Tennyson had written. Arnold could not understand how men might find their final end in "the great mundane movement" of "the life of the world."[17] For Germanic peoples, the fields of the world were never as green as the fields of the afterlife, the great open plains where men took their ease. It was there that life found its reward, its final cause. Today, the final cause of human life has become an object of *scientific* inquiry, something that can blind us to the traditional, metaphysical inquiry of Western literary tradition.

Finally, how do these considerations bear upon the purpose of suffering? When we consider the final cause of retribution as a physical phenomenon, we implicate our larger beliefs in the final cause of human life. And when we ask after retribution and the causes of natural calamities, we build upon a series of assumptions about the relation of human society to its final purpose. I would suppose that this is because those without a sense of the divine, of the magical, of the unseen forces of the spirits of the air, have to limit human life to its component role in a larger biological or social system, a system whose final cause is its own perpetuation. Considered in this mundane light, the purpose of retribution is found only its material and efficient causes, its biological purpose. But, if we keep the question of final cause distinct from questions of efficient cause, then we should avoid seeking the cause of hurricanes in the daily behavior of men. While human behavior does have its efficient and material causes, only in the realms of religion and myth are its final cause most fully explicable. That is to say, scientific explanations can

---

17. Preface to *Essays in Criticism*, 1st series (London, 1865).

reasonably offer only observations on the properties and material conditions of human behavior. When an ancient tale like *Beowulf* asks us to contemplate the final cause of human suffering, we would do well to look away from the cogs and levers of society to the realms of myth for our answers. There, we might conclude that the cries of women that mixed with the smoke of Beowulf's pyre lamented not just the death of the hero, but of the dragon, their last conduit to the unseen justice of the All-Father.

DOMINION
special offers for *TYR* readers

BOOKS

The Golden Thread: The Timeless Wisdom of the Western Mystery Traditions
by Joscelyn Godwin
Special clothbound edition, limited to 200 copies signed and numbered by the author. A clear and engaging overview of esoteric philosophies and movements in the West from antiquity to the present. See review in this issue of *TYR*.
$30 postpaid in the USA / $40 airmail postpaid to the rest of the world.

Confessions of a Radical Traditionalist
by John Michell
Selected and introduced by Joscelyn Godwin, this book features 108 biting and brilliant essays on cultural, religious, and historical topics ranging from the hellish to the heavenly. Clothbound edition with full-color dustjacket, textured endsheets, etc.
$25 postpaid in the USA / $40 airmail postpaid to the rest of the world.

The Details of Time: Conversations with Ernst Jünger
by Julien Hervier
Wide-ranging interviews with Ernst Jünger, one of the most remarkable German writers of the last century, as he entered the ninth decade of his life. Hardcover edition with dustjacket, out of print.
$30 postpaid in the USA / $40 airmail postpaid to the rest of the world.

The Secret King: Karl Maria Wiligut, Himmler's Lord of the Runes
Translated and introduced by Stephen E. Flowers
A collection of original texts and documents relating to the strange case of Karl Maria Wiligut, the self-proclaimed "Secret king of Germany" and a high-ranking advisor on esoteric and occult matters to Heinrich Himmler. Limited clothbound printing. Last copies available.
$75 postpaid in the USA / $90 airmail postpaid to the rest of the world.

The Secret King: The Myth and Reality of Nazi Occultism (revised and expanded second edition)
by Stephen E. Flowers and Michael Moynihan
Contains additional historical analysis and newly translated material. Paperback only; co-release with Feral House.
$10 postpaid in the USA / $22 airmail postpaid to the rest of the world.

Juice of Life: The Symbolic and Magical Significance of Blood
by Piero Camporesi
A fascinating sanguinolent study from a great Italian historian, anthropologist, and folklorist. Hardcover edition with dustjacket, out of print.
$40 postpaid in the USA / $50 airmail postpaid to the rest of the world.

MUSIC

Blood Axis—*Born Again*
Epic studio album on CD featuring Michael Moynihan, Annabel Lee, Robert Ferbrache, Bobby BeauSoleil and others, with songs in English, Old English, and ancient and modern German. Deluxe presentation with gatefold cover, complete lyrics, translations, photos.
$12 postpaid in the USA / $20 airmail postpaid to the rest of the world.

Changes—*Fire of Life*
Retrospective CD of vintage recordings (1969–1974) by the psychedelic folk duo of Robert N. Taylor and Nicholas Tesluk. Music that is mythical, pagan, and captivating. Includes booklet with liner notes, complete lyrics, photos & artwork. Original 1996 pressing, only a few copies remain.
$25 postpaid in the USA / $32 airmail postpaid to the rest of the world.

Some items in limited supply; reservations are accepted by email: <dominionpress@comcast.net>.
Send name and address with list of desired items, plus check or money order payable to Dominion to:

Dominion, Post Office Box 129, Waterbury Center, VT 05677-0129
www.dominionpress.net

Forthcoming in winter 2014–15:
Wotan's Awakening—The Life and Times of Guido von List, the Runemaster of fin-de-siècle *Vienna*

Anglo-Saxon Books

See our website for details of titles and prices
Many of our titles can be supplied to the US at the English price,
which is less than the US cover price.
www.asbooks.co.uk

First Steps in Old English
Stephen Pollington

The Elder Gods
The Otherworld of Early England
Stephen Pollington

Anglo-Saxon Tools
Dennis Riley

Leechcraft
Early English Charms Plantlore and Healing
Stephen Pollington

The Meadhall
Stephen Pollington

English Martial Arts
Terry Brown

Germanic Art in the First Millennium

Stephen Pollington

There can be few who have dipped into the culture of the early Germanic folk who have not wondered about the convoluted and complex art that characterises their cultures. While "Celtic art"—meaning principally the more developed forms of La Tène—has many admirers today and is firmly absorbed into modern concepts of "tribal art," the Germanic material is less well known. Yet the majority of popular books offering "Celtic" designs include a significant amount of Germanic material, be it drawn from the Vendel culture of the northern Baltic or the Anglo-Saxon material from Sutton Hoo. With the recent find of a large hoard of decorated metalwork near Lichfield—the so-called Staffordshire Hoard—it seems likely that even more Anglo-Saxon designs will be disseminated and adopted.

It is appropriate to ask what purpose all of this endeavour served, what the art meant and how it developed. At the risk of asking too many questions, the purpose of Germanic art is clearly symbolic display, but what qualities is the art meant to convey to the observer? What is the purpose of this display? What does it say about the person displaying it? Questions of this sort are difficult to answer given the chronological distance that exists between us and the original users of the art. However, it seems reasonable to deduce that the "display" was not an end in itself. It served some wider purpose.

In a pre-literate society, symbolic uses of significant motifs and patterns can be an important conveyor of social information. The displayed message could relate to identity in terms of sex, age, social status, wealth, family background, ethnic group or religion. A hierarchy of Germanic Iron Age ornament has been proposed, with the highest male rank (king) bearing a thick gold arm-ring; male and female members of the king's kindred and men of "leader" (*þegn, ealdor*) rank wore heavy arm-rings with snake-headed terminals; affiliated chieftains wore finger-rings with raven-headed terminals; below them, noblewomen, warriors and freemen marked their status with plain rings of gold or other metals. While this strict ranking may seem rather contrived to us, it is not unlikely that some such hierarchy of display existed, and that a casual observer could deduce several significant facts about a person from a cursory examination of his dress and accessories.

Display from Iron Age or Migration period culture is most evident to us when undisturbed accompanied inhumation graves are excavated, since the nature and arrangement of the grave-goods can be studied. Cremations lack the opportunity for ritual placement of significant artefacts, but do offer the important alternative message of the stamps and decorations on the urn holding the ashes, both in terms of the types of decoration and the arrangements of motifs.

It seems a safe assumption that information about the deceased was encoded within the burial rite. No less was it true that the person's artefacts, costume and belongings conveyed messages about social status, ethnicity or religious adherence. It is important to remember that grave-goods should not be taken at face value: they are a coded message, and the presence of a spear and shield in a grave does not mean simply "this is a warrior."

It is notable that Berhard Salin's classification of Style I art occurred in certain areas of Germanic Europe (Scandinavia, Thuringia, Lombardic Italy, eastern England) where societies were in the process of transformation from late antique "tribal" societies to a more clearly-ranked, pyramidal, proto-kingdom structure. Equally, some areas where Style I is absent—central and southern Francia, the lower end of the Jutland peninsula—apparently had a different social dynamic. In the former case, the power structures were essentially Late Roman in nature, while, for example, in Lower Saxony there is evidence that "kings" were absent as late as circa 780 C.E. in the testimony of the missionary, Lebuin. Presumably, Continental Saxon society functioned without kings and kingship, as a federacy of chiefdoms, a commonwealth. The Saxon cemetery of Issendorf had no weapon burial rite among its graves until the very latest heathen phase, when a Thuringian infiltration of the area took

SALIN STYLE I: SWORD HILT FROM SNARTEMO, NORWAY, CIRCA EARLY SIXTH CENTURY. ILLUSTRATION BY LINDSAY KERR.

place. It is likely, then, that adoption of the weapon-burial rite (as part of a cultural package that included Style I decoration) was a badge of adoption of an early mediaeval style of leadership (or "kingship"). By contrast, Style II art was to some extent a collateral competitor and may have expressed an alternative model of kingship—perhaps influenced by Christianity and other factors. In England, at least, Style II only began to achieve widespread adoption once the Christian missions were at work, whether the users of this art were themselves converts or not.

One problem we face in dealing with the worship and belief of the Anglo-Saxon and Scandinavian peoples before they were exposed to monotheistic religious systems is that the world of the gods was not some ethereal, inaccessible realm, but was attainable for mortal men who knew the way and had the courage to take it. Religious observances, rites and customs, were part of everyday life; so were competition, violence and warfare, which likewise formed part of the backdrop to daily existence.

The exact nature of Anglo-Saxon pre-Christian religion cannot be determined directly; we lack even a talented poet and storyteller (such as the Icelander Snorri Sturluson) to offer an interpretation of the cultural and religious world of the Anglo-

Saxons. We may surmise that animism, totemism, and various other "constructs" of comparative anthropology were present, and that a world of many gods existed side-by-side with the world of men. The interaction between the human and animal worlds is a fruitful area for investigation in this context. The link between the spirit in animal form on the one hand, and the figure of the man becoming an animal on the other, invites speculation as to the meaning of this design when it is encountered in Germanic Style I art. The conclusion that the man-become-beast must be a visual expression of the spirit-traveller or shaman seems inescapable.

The shaman inherits the assistance and goodwill of one or more "spirits," which may be in animal or human form; these spirits attach themselves to groups and families, and are connected by strong bonds to the shaman's spirit-self or soul. Guardian spirits are always zoomorphic, and the form they take relates to the functions they perform: a large quadruped usually protects, a bird watches and takes the soul to heaven, a fish or snake shows the way into the underworld.

It would be easy to overplay the shamanic qualities in Germanic material culture—to see every depiction of a wolf, boar, or eagle as necessarily a guardian spirit. However, the correspondences between northern European cultures and those of the circumpolar regions are too striking to dismiss. Clearly, certain animals played a crucial role in the cultural and ritual life of the Germanic peoples, and continued in use among neighbours in areas such as Finland and the eastern Baltic until contact with Christianity brought about ideological suppression or subversion of these concepts. Christian orthodoxy did not admit of the possibility of the soul leaving the body except at death, and regarded the world and everything in it as having been made for exploitation by humanity. On this basis, the essential communality between a person and an animal was not acceptable, and could be viewed as unorthodox, heretical or "pagan," to use a Christian term. Germanic animal styles were still present in the earliest English Christian manuscripts, but they were soon transformed into "harmless ornament" without significance or meaning.

The transformation of a human into an animal—or more properly, of a human soul into an animal spirit—forms part of the typical shamanic cultural complex, insofar as there is such a thing, and is a reasonable interpretation of some of the motifs found repeatedly in Germanic art.

Display involves a hierarchy of terms and conventions, a coded series of messages that can be used in meaningful combinations. The larger an item is, or the more reflective or highly coloured, then the greater its visibility. Indeed, this notion applies to all early Anglo-Saxon works of art, where the most easily visible level is the object itself. On closer inspection, the individual fields and something of their contents can be discerned. At very close range, the individual elements of the design are accessible and can be interpreted, if the viewer has the appropriate key, the correct background knowledge. The most important messages are encoded at the maximal level, in order to broadcast them to the widest possible audience—for example, the difference between a circular brooch and a bow brooch. This can further be interpreted in the context of post-Roman Britain, in the process of conversion from Romano-British to Germanic societies, as the display of "belonging," of ethnicity and group or cultural identity. Belonging to a group is partly an expression of difference from other groups with which there is contact, and to this extent it is a matter of perception. Yet, because a group's identity is also a product of the group's history, it is inherently conservative, especially where group members feel threatened or exposed. Therefore, in times of danger, instability and stress, the sense of group solidarity will be emphasised, and one method of achieving this emphasis is through outward display of coded messages in costume and dress accessories.

As a corollary, in times of stress, secret or magical information might be encoded in hidden messages, of which decoration and inscriptions on the reverse of an item would seem to be obvious examples. Such messages were present and invoked by the wearer, but not in a manner available to the casual viewer. One example is the Nordendorf fibula, a seventh-century Alemannic brooch from Germany with a curious runic inscription on the reverse:

logaþore
wodan
wigiþonar
awaleubwini (written upside down)

This possibly constitutes an invocation of the gods known in their Norse forms as Lóðurr, Óðinn and Þórr, with "[from] Awa, [for] Leubwini" as a dedicatory inscription. However, the text has invited a great deal of speculative reading and the temptation to see *Loki* or the word *logeþere*, "schemer, wizard," in the first inscription has been great. It seems safe to say that the names of the old gods were not for public display in the religious climate of the seventh century. Brooches in Scandinavian Germanic societies (of which the *Anglii* were one) could be viewed as "texts or patterns of meaning" whereby "both form and ornamentation once delivered a message," dependant on "the status, sex and social position of the person making use of the item in question, how the object was worn and under what circumstances."[1] Therefore, while the smiths and jewellers added symbolic elements to the decoration of their products, the individuals and the groups to which they belonged gave meaning to these symbols and derived information from them.

As far back as 1926, Shetelig had foreseen such ideas, stating that "[i]t is even probable that much of the decoration appeared to the initiated as figure subjects representing myths, which are hardly accessible to modern students."[2] Nevertheless, he felt that in some cases a tentative identification could be suggested: for example, some brooches with multiple zoomorphs could be viewed as "a man struggling with a crowd of ferocious monsters." In spite of the extremely schematic handling of the human and animal form, he understood that "they are something more than pure and meaningless decoration: they were in fact regarded as living forms, handled by intelligent masters." He added that "the task here is something like deciphering a lost language; much

---

1. Magnus, "Monsters and Birds of Prey," 161.
2. This and the following four quotations are from Shetelig, "The Origin of the Scandinavian Style of Ornament," 2–3.

SALIN STYLE II: PATTERN ON A BRONZE DIE FROM ICKLINGHAM, ENGLAND, SIXTH TO SEVENTH CENTURY. ILLUSTRATION BY LINDSAY KERR.

formal work has to be done in establishing the meaning of sounds and the rules of grammar, before we may proceed to examine the contents and value of the texts. In the study of Migration [Period] ornament we are still at the stage of mere formal investigation, and long training is required to eliminate the first impression of stereotyped profusion." It is fair to say that, since this article was written, the study has proceeded at a faltering pace and we are only slowly coming nearer to decoding the hidden messages within the designs.

Discussing the possible amuletic quality of equal arm brooches, Bruns stated: "It is hardly possible to decide how far we can go in deciding which item was an object that indicated social status and what was an amulet for protection."[3] It is not clear that these two functions—social status and supernatural protection—would be mutually exclusive. (Today, people wear large crosses, crucifixes and other religious tokens as an outward sign of devout faith, but with a collateral implication of wealth and status alongside piety.) Objects as complex as some of those the Anglo-Saxons used were certainly capable of conveying a range of meanings according to context. For example, bracteates were symbols of power within the societies that produced and used them. The mixture of Roman visual allusions (e.g., the imperial diadem) and Germanic culture (e.g., the warrior's long hair worn in a plait) proved irresistible. There have even been

---

3. Bruns, *Germanic Equal Arm Brooches*, 47.

attempts to link the "interlace" visual structure to the "interlaced" verbal motifs used in Old English poetry.[4] The dense and intriguing patterns of both physical design and verbal art offer suggestive parallels.

The purpose of most Germanic material culture in the Migration Period was largely to display both rank and ethnicity (a level of identity above the individual, kindred and region). Ethnicity can be shared between peoples living hundreds of miles apart who feel bound together by it, especially in times of migration and upheaval, but it may equally exclude people who are close neighbours. Ethnicity is to some extent an accident of birth and is not normally mutable, but in some circumstances certain people may be encouraged to display adherence to a new group rather than their original one: such is the case when a bride enters her host community. Hinton noted the role of brides in introducing new fashions to communities, and suggested that exchanges of women, even at the lower social levels, could easily involve movements of fifty miles or so.[5]

Mediaeval thought considered ethnicity in terms of certain key characteristics, being mainly based around language, laws, weaponry, customs and descent; at certain times, when it has offered advantages, descent has been stressed above all others. Changes in ethnicity are usually motivated by some perceived advantage deriving from a new identity. However, the accomplishment of such a change is contingent on the person wishing to transfer being accepted by the existing members of the community into which he or she wishes to be absorbed. It has been argued that mediaeval identities were primarily exclusive, but that the advent of the universalist religion, Christianity, may have changed this over time.

A person's ethnicity was displayed through "ethnic markers," which are critical badges of membership of a specific ethnic group. These may include specific behavioural traits—customs, laws, traditions and the like—as well as physical markers such as dress styles, art styles, building techniques, hairstyles and so

---

4. Leyerle, "The Interlace Structure of Beowulf."
5. Hinton, *Gold and Gilt, Pots and Pins*, 28.

on. These markers are subdivided into *emblematic styles*, which convey information about the group, and *assertive styles* that deal with the individual; emblematic style can relate to groups based on ethnicity, but also to sex, age, and status. As a general rule, early mediaeval art and costume could convey both vertical status (rank within the social order) and horizontal status (overall ethnicity, specific settlement or kindred group) within a region. Archaeological remains are often a poor guide to ethnicity through costume because they are, at best, no more than partial and can be misleading.[6]

In general, ethnicity is a created category, given prominence at certain times—such as competition between ethnic groups—but downplayed when it is expedient to do so, for example, after a military conquest.[7] The markers of ethnicity are also mutable, and could be critically important as badges of solidarity when new hierarchies were being established. Ultimately, ethnicity is not based solely on biology nor on politics, although both feature in its composition, but rather on the desire or need to distinguish one group from another: it is a mark of exclusivity, of belonging, of one group's consciousness of its differences from others.[8] In this regard, we may recall that Sidonius Apollinaris commented on the Frankish warband of the royal nobleman, Sigismer, who all carried similar shields with a white rim and a red-yellow board, and Hydatius remarked that Visigoths in the fifth century assembled for a formal meeting with spears of different colours. This common design must have marked these troops off from all others, and have created a single group identity for the band.

Høilund Nielsen looked at the meaning of Salin's Style II art and its use as a military and political badge of allegiance.[9] Her study focused on the complete animal, present in Scandinavian art of many periods and recognizable wherever it occurs. In conjunction with weapon burial—itself a statement of social identity—the Style II animal was a powerful marker of affiliation. It is

---

6. Owen-Crocker, *Dress in Anglo-Saxon England*; "Gold in the Ground or Just Rust in the Dust," 15–18.
7. For more on such dynamics, see Pohl, "Telling the Difference," especially 17–19.
8. Halsall, *Early Medieval Cemeteries*, 56–61.
9. Høilund Nielsen, "Retainers of the Scandinavian Kings."

notable that such displays can evolve: for example, Polychrome Style (mainly geometric designs executed in garnets, coloured glass and gold) emerged in eastern Europe as part of the Hun identity adopted by Goths, Gepids and others. It was adopted by the Franks as a badge of military power, used to decorate swordhilts and other weaponry. In time it spread to belt buckles and brooches, where it remained as a statement of Frankish identity long after it had ceased to be used on weapons. A similar trajectory was followed by Salin's Style II among the Austrasians. Hines noted the importance of a traditional, "national" costume as part of the ethnic identity of Anglian England.[10]

Ethnicity also tends to be a more important factor among the higher tiers of the hierarchy; as the leaders of the group in political, military, and religious matters, the élite have a greater interest in the political success of the ethnic group than those lower down the scale, while also having greater power to influence the details of the display. Effros believes that it was relatively easy for one group to adopt the outward appearance of another,[11] but this is questionable: if Hunnish or Gothic or Frankish ethnicity conferred privileges on its bearers, then it is unlikely that they would have made the trappings of their status available to all who wanted them, because to do so would only devalue their identity and finally render it meaningless. In some early mediaeval societies, a claim was made to legitimacy by evoking the Roman past and claiming continuity of tradition from the days of the Empire. There seems to have been no mechanism by which Franks could be denied fictive Roman ethnicity, but the converse does not seem to have been true and Frankish identity was guarded and preserved.

In the case of Anglo-Saxon England, the deployment of new technologies based on Continental Germanic rather than Iron Age British or Romano-British precedents is interesting. In tandem with the new expressions of ethnicity—at this stage primarily tribal—expressed through costume and language, these developments suggest that states and identities were in the process of

---

10. Hines, *Clasps—Hektespenner—Agraffen*, 92–93.
11. Effros, *Merovingian Mortuary Archaeology*, 109–110.

Germanic Art in the First Millennium

QUOIT BROOCH STYLE PENANNAULAR, FOUND IN A GRAVE AT ALFRISTON, ENGLAND, FIFTH CENTURY. ILLUSTRATION BY LINDSAY KERR.

formation in the British Isles—British, Irish and Germanic. It seems to be a reasonable inference that the mixing of migrating North Sea peoples produced new "Insular Germanic" identities and with them, new techniques for displaying these identities in costume and language.

Status in pre-capitalist societies was not necessarily based on social class, in the modern sense, but rather on membership of a closed group that could be based on birth or membership in a specific social order. Such a group identified itself through badges and markers of a "heraldic" nature.[12] These functioned as insignia and conveyed information about prestige and access to both resources and secret knowledge. In the context of early Anglo-Saxon England, such badges were constituted by art styles such as Style I, Style II and Quoit Brooch Style. Since automatic membership (through birth into a kindred) gave access to

---

12. Parker Pearson, *The Archaeology of Death and Burial*, 83–85.

membership of the closed social group, the system was inherently more stable than one whereby prestige had always to be earned. However, the great emphasis placed on visible burials such as grave mounds might mark the transition from a kin-based society towards one where land-based wealth was dominant; however, since many Anglo-Saxon barrows were re-used Bronze Age structures, it seems likely that such monuments were appropriated in order to show political mastery of the physical landscape and the Otherworld.

Probably the safest initial assumption in interpreting Germanic art is that prominent use of high-quality artistic decoration was a display of *weorð* or "worth." *Weorð* is a concept much discussed yet difficult to define. It corresponds in some senses to the idea of "honour" and "reputation," but without the sometimes egocentric and vain notions surrounding those modern terms. *Weorð* has perhaps a greater sense of "usefulness to the community" than is present in the notion of personal honour or individual reputation. *Weorð* is "worth" only in the sense of "value" in the context of human society; it is one's "standing" within the community.

A note of caution is appropriate, however, when attempting to decode meaning from systems we do not understand: it is misleading and methodologically incorrect to assume that any single motif *always* meant the same thing. The boar displayed prominently in the round on the crest of the Benty Grange helm may not have conveyed the same message as the flat boar's heads forming the ends of the eyebrows on the Sutton Hoo helmet. Still less might a serpent on the Sutton Hoo buckle represent the same thing as one on a bracteate, or on a drinking horn mount. Symbols can have several tiers of overlapping meanings, all at the same time: a public versus a private one, or a decorative versus a cultic one. For example, the nominally Christian symbol of the cross is among the most popular stamps on heathen funerary urns, where its Christian meaning is automatically excluded; cremation was forbidden for Christians. The *formal* sign is the same, but the content and symbolism is very different. Likewise, the popular Germanic figure group of a rider, armed with helmet and spear, riding down a serpent appears to have cult significance in Germanic culture, but probably derives from the sculptural art of Roman military tombstones. Context is everything in reading these motifs.

This essay is based on the research that was undertaken for *Wayland's Work: Anglo-Saxon Art, Myth & Material Culture from the 4th to the 7th Century* by Stephen Pollington, Lindsay Kerr, and Brett Hammond (Swaffam, UK: Anglo-Saxon Books, 2010). The illustrations from that work which accompany the present essay are reproduced by kind permission of the artist.

Bibliography

Bork, Robert, ed., *De Re Metallica: The Uses of Metal in the Middle Ages.* Aldershot, UK: Ashgate, 2005.

Bruns, Dorothee. *Germanic Equal Arm Brooches of the Migration Period.* Oxford: Archaeopress, 2003.

Effros, Bonnie. *Merovingian Mortuary Archaeology and the Making of the Early Middle Ages* Berkeley: University of California Press, 2003.

Halsall, Guy. *Early Medieval Cemeteries: An Introduction to Burial Archaeology in the Post-Roman West.* Glasgow: Cruithne, 1995.

Hines, John. *Clasps—Hektespenner—Agraffen. Anglo-Scandinavian Clasps of Classes A-C of the 3rd to 6th centuries A.D. Typology, Diffusion and Function.* Stockholm: Almqvist & Wiksell, 1993.

———, ed. *The Anglo-Saxons From the Migration Period to the Eighth Century: An Ethnographic Perspective.* Woodbridge, UK: Boydell, 1997.

Hinton, David A. *Gold and Gilt, Pots and Pins: Possessions and People in Medieval Britain.* Oxford: Oxford University Press, 2005.

Høilund Nielsen, Karen. "Retainers of the Scandinavian Kings: An Alternative Interpretation of Salin's Style II (Sixth–Seventh Centuries AD)." *Journal of European Archaeology* 5:1 (1997): 151–69.

Leyerle, John. "The Interlace Structure of Beowulf," *University of Toronto Quarterly*, vol. 37, no. 1 (Oct., 1967): 1–17.

Magnus, Bente. "Monsters and Birds of Prey. Some Reflections on Form and Style of the Migration Period." In T. Dickinson and D. Griffiths, eds., *The Making of Kingdoms: Papers from the the Forty-seventh Sachsensymposium, September 1996*. Oxford: Oxford University Press, 1999.

Owen-Crocker, Gale R. *Dress in Anglo-Saxon England*, Woodbridge, UK: Boydell, 2004

———. "Gold in the Ground or Just Rust in the Dust: Measuring Wealth by Metalwork in Anglo-Saxon Graves." In Bork, ed., *De Re Metallica*.

Parker Pearson, Michael. *The Archaeology of Death and Burial*. College Station: Texas A&M University Press, 1999.

Pohl, Walter. "Ethnic Names and Identities in the British Isles: A Comparative Perspective." In Hines, ed., *The Anglo-Saxons From the Migration Period to the Eighth Century*.

———. "Telling the Difference: Signs of Ethnic Identity." In Walter Pohl, ed., with Helmut Reimetz, *Strategies of Distinction: The Construction of the Ethnic Communities, 300–800*. Leiden: Brill, 1998.

Shetelig, Haakon. "The Origin of the Scandinavian Style of Ornament During the Migration Period." *Archaeologia* 76 (1926): 107–20.

Rockwell Kent's Northern Compass

Michael Moynihan

> Beyond the North, beyond the ice, beyond death,
> is *our* life, *our* happiness . . .
> —Nietzsche[1]

For centuries, the Far North has exerted a magnetic pull not only upon explorers, but also on writers and mystics, cartographers and mythographers. Such northern fascinations represent a desire for escape from the comfortable and the commonplace. They may center around the exploration of unknown and little-visited geographical places or the allure of exotic, far-off cultures which successfully subsist—and even thrive—in extreme climates. They might also draw inspiration from the mystique of the various pagan and animistic religions, real or imagined, that have their roots in the Arctic and sub-Arctic realms.

In the twentieth century, exploration and adventure were the hallmark of most northern pursuits by those who traveled there from the lower latitudes. The Norwegian Fridtjof Nansen is primarily known for his feats of polar exploration and survival, although he was also a popular writer as well as a scientist, diplomat, artist, and photographer. Knud Rasmussen, a Dane, became legendary for his "Thule expeditions" across Greenland and Alaska, where he engaged in cultural and linguistic studies among the native Inuit and Eskimo groups. Others, such as Robert Peary and Frederick Cook, are remembered for their controversial claims to have been the first to reach the North Pole.

In the case of the American artist Rockwell Kent (1882–1971), his achievements are weighted much more toward the creative realm: he was a painter, writer, illustrator, and visitor-explorer whose work was consistently and almost magnetically oriented toward the North. His paintings and illustrations were intimately

---

1. "Jenseits des Nordens, des Eises, des Todes—*unser* Leben, *unser* Glück . . ." (*Der Antichrist*, §1).

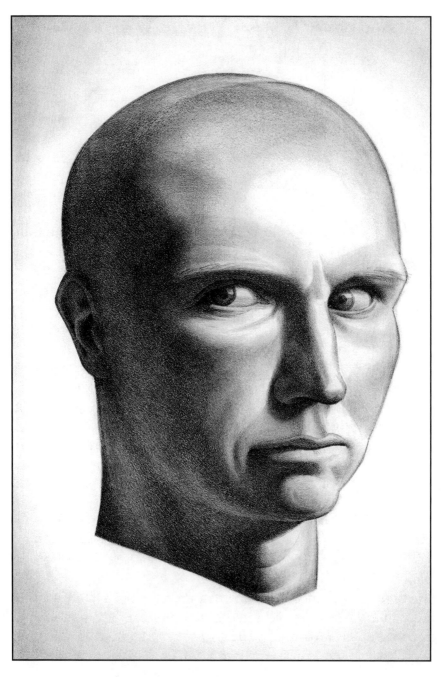

"Das Ding an sich" (The Thing In Itself), self-portrait, 1934. Rockwell Kent Collection.

"Northern Night," wood engraving, 1930. Rockwell Kent Collection.

combined with his writings, which were typically journals of his experiences in Alaska, Greenland, and elsewhere. Alongside his work as a commercial illustrator, these more personal pursuits served to establish his reputation and importance.

Kent was drawn to the North both physically and artistically. His visits and explorations gave him the opportunity not just to paint and draw, but also to write and to contemplate. The lives and the narratives of two populations whose roots lay in the North—the Vikings and the Greenlanders—were of deep interest to Kent and surface time and again throughout his art and writings. In the following survey I will attempt to delineate the key points in the artist's lifelong engagement with northern themes, examining how they found expression in his creative works. In addition to discussing his early influences I will also consider his relevant illustrative work and certain defining elements in his personal life. It is not my intention to recount Kent's biography in any comprehensive way, nor will I analyze the course of his actual journeys to Alaska or Greenland—for this has already been done in detail by Kent himself, as well as by many who have written about him.[2] Instead, this essay serves to collate some revealing incidents, thoughts, and comments regarding the attraction of the North (and some of its literature) as an inspirational force to a major artist of the twentieth century. In the process, essential aspects of Kent's personality will hopefully be revealed as well, allowing for a better understanding of the role the Far North played in his mind and his artistic endeavors.

Early Years and Decisive Influences

For someone whose artistic enterprises as a landscape painter would be crucially dependent on the sun and its natural light, it seems fitting that Rockwell Kent was born at the summer solstice, on 21 June 1882, in New York State. He was the first of three children born to Sara Holgate Banker and Rockwell Kent, Sr. When the younger Kent was only five years old, his father died of typhoid fever. The children were then raised by their mother, with whom Rockwell Jr. always shared a strong bond.

As a youth in the 1890s, Kent attended modest private schools in Connecticut and Manhattan, but he also absorbed many influences from the Old World. In 1895 he took a four-month trip to Europe with his aunt, Josephine Holgate, during which they visited England, Germany, and the Netherlands. Kent felt an affinity with the German language and culture from a young age. This was surely nurtured by his parents in light of their own backgrounds. His grandfather on his mother's side was an Austrian from Vienna; his father, an American of English descent, had lived in Germany and obtained a degree in Freiburg before returning to the United States to study law.[3] An Austrian nanny named Rosa, who was hired to help look after the Kent

---

2. Besides Kent's own voluminously detailed memoirs, *This Is My Own* (1940) and *It's Me O Lord* (1955), biographical details can be found in David Traxel, *An American Saga*; Wien, *Rockwell Kent*; and the essays by Kent's friends Fridolf Johnson and Dan Burne Jones in Richard V. West, *"An Enkindled Eye."* Gretel Ehrlich reflects on Kent's Greenland experience and describes her visits to some of his haunts there in *This Cold Heaven*; see in particular the chapter "N by E: Illorsuit, July 1996," 75–117.
3. Kent, *It's Me O Lord*, 4.

children, also made a deep impression. In his autobiography Kent tells of the bedtime prayers he would recite, stating, "It was always in German, of course, that with Rosa I prayed, and German—long before I knew a word of English—that I spoke."[4] During his youth Kent mentions his appreciation of Wagner's operas, but most especially of *Lieder* (songs for voice and piano by German classical composers), which he himself was known to occasionally sing in public. He asserted: "German having been my childhood tongue, I thought in German, felt in German, and loved the feel of German on my tongue and lips."[5] Kent's appreciation for the German language and German culture would never wane, despite the occasional difficulties it would cause for him as a result of the anti-German sentiments that arose in the wake of the two world wars.

Kent demonstrated an interest and facility in the visual arts from a young age, and upon graduating from high school he attended the summer school of art on Long Island run by William Merritt Chase (1848–1916). Here he was trained in approaches to painting that would serve as the foundation upon which to develop his own style. In Kent's words, "Chase was an exponent of the *plein air* school. He went to nature, stood before nature, and painted it as his eyes beheld it.... More interested in *impressions* of the subject than in deeper and more labored probing... [a]nd valuing facility or fluency of brush work, he favored large canvasses."[6] In a like manner, Kent's primary impulse in nearly all of his own paintings was the depiction of nature in a realistic but impressionistic style that privileged dramatic, distanced views of majestic and stark environments. He also favored large canvasses (typically about four feet wide) upon which to execute these scenes, often carrying them to remote locations where he could paint for long periods in solitude.

In 1900, under family pressures and concerned with his future prospects, Kent entered Columbia University to study architecture. He could only maintain his interest for a time and decided

---

4. Kent, *It's Me O Lord*, 21.
5. Kent, *It's Me O Lord*, 188–89.
6. Kent, *It's Me O Lord*, 76.

to quit in his senior year, opting instead to study oil painting under Robert Henri (1865–1929) and Kenneth Hayes Hiller (1876–1952) at the New York School of Art. He had previously been awarded a scholarship to the school, and had already taken night classes while studying architecture at Columbia by day. But for Kent the subject of architecture—based on *expressing* an artistic vision to be imposed on wood, brick, or concrete—was far less inspiring than the visions that might *impress* themselves upon a sensitive painter, and which the painter could then attempt to convey to a secondary viewer via a canvas. Kent would later explain:

> The belief that I had chosen well rested primarily upon my growing and sharpening perception of the beauty of the world around me . . . so poignant that the responsive adolescent heart could hardly bear it. . . . The Hudson River and the hills and palisades beyond, all bathed in early morning light; the city as its ships, towers, domes, theaters and temples all lay bright and glistening in the smokeless air.[7]

Kent thrived under his new mentors, working in a stimulating environment that included George Bellows (1882–1925) and Edward Hopper (1882–1967) as fellow students. And as a vocal progressive and "man of the people," Robert Henri's influence extended beyond art and left a mark on Kent's developing political ideals. These would soon develop into a life-long commitment to socialism.

Kent was, however, anything but a slavish disciple to his teachers. By temperament he was rebellious and possessed of a combative spirit that would never abate during his lifetime. Kent's rebellion was a means to define himself as a sovereign individual. "[S]eeing my teachers as the embodiment of arbitrary authority," he explained, "I was in constant arms against them, for that very warfare against odds fostered—however little it may have been justified—such self-reliance as, by the isolation it implies, breeds

---

7. Kent, *It's Me O Lord*, 75–76.

in its turn integrity."[8]

It was not long before Kent's rebelliousness led to a rejection of the Christian religion in which he was raised. He later recalled: "Ever since, as a little boy, it dawned upon me to question the concept of a being, God, as the originator and ruler of mankind, his world and universe, I had felt a vague, critical dissatisfaction with the accepted answers." These nagging questions about the nature of the universe did not sit well with Kent's restless mind: "relegated . . . to the plane of the unconscious, they smoldered, gathering heat that needed but the match's touch to set aflame."[9] Kent was thus ripe for the same sorts of revelations that many of his iconoclastic contemporaries had already been proclaiming in the latter half of the nineteenth century.

The catalyst for a conscious rejection of specifically Christian dogma came in the form of a book: Charles Darwin's 1859 work *On the Origin of Species*. Kent recalled of his encounter:

> To assert that I read the book painstakingly from cover to cover, only to be at last convinced, would be to attribute to myself the nature and character proper to a scholar or a scientist. And I am neither. I've used the symbol of a match: I was as tinder to that match; as tinder heated to near combustion point. A touch of the flame, and I exploded. . . . "Of course!" I cried; for suddenly it was as though a great light, a new sun, has risen on a world of darkness.[10]

With God now removed from the larger equation, Kent could dedicate himself wholeheartedly to discovering and depicting the most powerful aspects that emanated to him from the natural world.

---

8. Kent, *It's Me O Lord*, 75.
9. Kent, *It's Me O Lord*, 90.
10. Kent, *It's Me O Lord*, 91.

Gateways to the North

In 1903 Kent became an assistant to the painter Abbot Henderson Thayer (1849–1921) in Dublin, New Hampshire, where he would spend the summers and the winter holidays. Kent was employed as a copyist to preserve stages of Thayer's painting on secondary canvasses. The older artist quickly took note of Kent's talents and encouraged him to pursue his own work, stating: "Go off and paint for yourself, and let me see what you can do."[11] It was here that Kent undertook his first important solo foray into the countryside, on a cloudless day, setting up his canvas in a pasture that afforded a view of Mt. Monadnock "in all its isolated splendor above the pines."[12] Kent's description of the endeavor points up characteristics that would be reiterated in many of his subsequent landscape paintings:

> I tried . . . by all the means that mere pigment afforded and by every expedient of composition to recreate the mountain in its majesty, the forest in its infinitude; and, above all, the sunlight of that day. I tried, through due apportionment of atmosphere, to give each plane—the foreground, the pines, the distant mountain and the sky—its place.[13]

It was during a subsequent visit to New Hampshire that Kent seems to have realized the startling quality that the presence of snow lent to such scenes. On a winter camping trip with Thayer's son, Gerald, the two young men crawled out from their hut after a lengthy snowstorm. Kent describes the experience:

> [W]e emerged into a world so spectacularly beautiful that for a long time we could only gaze at it in awed and speechless wonder. In the prevailing stillness the whole land and every branch and twig lay blanketed in snow; and

---

11. Kent, *It's Me O Lord*, 99.
12. Kent, *It's Me O Lord*, 99.
13. Kent, *It's Me O Lord*, 99.

on it shone the golden light of the nearly setting sun—the orange and golden light and the long shadows, blue as the zenith.[14]

The urge to capture these interplays of radiant winter sunlight—or, alternatively, moonlight and starlight—upon snow-covered, mountainous landscapes would remain with Kent for the rest of his life.

In the end, rather than serving as assistant to Abbott Thayer, Kent became a friend of the family. His regular visits to New Hampshire provided him with much more than just a new landscape to paint. The Thayer household impressed him deeply; with a fireplace as its only source of heat, the simplicity of the home was contrasted by the powerful political and literary intellectual ferment that seethed within. Here, Kent found inspiration in the writings of the anarchist Prince Kropotkin and the anonymous Icelandic author of *Njal's Saga*, which was then more commonly referred to as *The Saga of Burnt Nyal*. The saga is a tragic medieval tale of human interactions and machinations at the turn of the first millennium, the time at which Christianity first came to the tiny island republic. Kent said of this remarkable story: "*Burnt Nyal* opened the gate upon that highway to the North which led at last to Greenland and Alaska."[15]

The first public exhibition of Kent's paintings took place in 1904 in New York. He sold two works: *Dublin Pond* and *Mount Monadnock*. After a brief stint as an architectural draftsman, he headed to Monhegan Island, Maine. This environment exhilarated him greatly and provided further elements to capture in his landscape paintings: surging water and barren, rocky cliffs. His time on the island was another defining moment:

> Truly I loved that little world, Monhegan. Small, sea-girt island that it was, a seeming floating speck in the infinitude of sea and sky, one was as though driven to seek refuge from the impendent cosmic immensity in a closer

---

14. Kent, *It's Me O Lord*, 102.
15. Kent, *It's Me O Lord*, 110.

relationship to people and to every living thing. I came to know each individual flower and bright colored mushroom and toadstool that grew beside the woodland paths.... I won't say that I loved the rocks; I just respected them.[16]

In 1906 Kent built a house on the island by hand, and another for his mother the following year. He lived on Monhegan through the summer of 1910. Much later in life, he would return again to stay and paint there, even re-purchasing his original house (which had become severely dilapidated) in the 1950s. The island's contours seem to have made a permanent impact upon his visual consciousness: scenes that he would paint in subsequent years in Newfoundland, Alaska, Greenland, and Tierra del Fuego frequently reveal similar compositional elements.

In the fall of 1910 Kent began the first of his excursions farther north, visiting Newfoundland. This experience resulted in series of paintings that take everyday events (heading out to fish at sea) and tragedies (death at sea) and elevate them to a level that is both realistic and mythic in its atmosphere. Other paintings from this period provide images of sun-worship and human revelry in the natural world.

Over the next two decades, Kent would alternate between living and working in New York City and traveling to stay in remote locations. While in the city, Kent fulfilled varied commissions for commercial illustrations, as well as architectural and advertising work. When he was able to travel, he would retreat far away from any urban environment. Kent would ensconce himself in a place where he could paint his dramatic surroundings, keeping illustrated journals of his experiences. These trips included a yearlong visit to Brigus, Newfoundland, in 1914–15, which resulted in a cycle of paintings exhibited in New York in 1917.

Kent's fascination with the literature of Iceland had grown over the preceding years, and turned into a voracious appetite. This instilled an urge to visit the land that had spawned these stories:

---

16. Kent, *It's Me O Lord*, 138.

"The North Wind," illustration from "Wilderness: A Journal of Quiet Adventure in Alaska," 1920.

The Njal Saga... had introduced me to the whole Homeric literature of the tiny medieval republic of the Far North. And these books, fairly "slipping out of my fingers"... as I read them, had contributed to the urge which had sent us all to Newfoundland. Now, read and re-read many times they impelled me, in the winter of 1917, with an almost nostalgic urge toward Iceland. Yet our own entry into the war ... closed the Atlantic to us. . . . turning my eyes to the American continent, I fixed my hopes upon the mountainous West.[17]

Zarathustra's Companion

The following year Kent found the financial resources to embark upon his western journey. He was accompanied on the trip by his eldest son, eight-year-old Rockwell III. Traveling first by train and then by a series of boats, they finally reached their destination of Fox Island in Resurrection Bay, Alaska. Here they lived for two-thirds of a year in a one-room log cabin together with a "lonely old Swede," L. M. Olson.

As usual, Kent kept a diary. His account of the time spent on the island, accompanied by a bold series of drawings, was published in 1920 as *Wilderness: A Journal of Quiet Adventure in Alaska*. Kent describes their arrival in dramatic and even epic tones:

> We came to this land, a boy and a man, entirely on a dreamer's search; having had a vision of a Northern Paradise, we came to find it.... Doubt never crossed our minds. To sail uncharted waters and follow virgin shores—what a life for men! As the new coast unfolds itself, the imagination leaps into full vision of the human drama that is there immanent. The grandeur of the ocean cliff is terrible with the threat of shipwreck. To that high ledge the wave may lift you; there, where that storm-dwarfed spruce has found a hold for half a century, you could perhaps cling. A hundred times a day you think of death or of escaping it by might and courage.[18]

Wilderness contains nearly fifty black-and-white illustrations by Kent. Many of these are allegorical and symbolic in nature and express a quasi-mystical side of his personality. Kent also produced a number of paintings during his stay on Fox Island,

---

17. Kent, *It's Me O Lord*, 324.
18. Kent, *Wilderness*, 1–2.

which in Richard West's view possess a "far more vigorous, optimistic, even heroic tone" than much of his preceding work.[19] This is evident even in a serene landscape such as *Blue and Gold (Resurrection Bay, Alaska)* in which the sky emanates—and the sea reflects—powerful horizontal bars of almost metallic light. The regal, radiant glow is triumphant, and the snow-covered mountain range across the center of the panel is subdued by comparison.[20]

At the outset of his journal Kent describes the provisions they brought to the island in detail, even providing a list of every book he had packed. This is telling, and reveals much about his interests. Among other volumes, the list includes: Snorri Sturluson's collection of Old Icelandic poems of gods and heroes known as the *Prose Edda*; Hans Christian Andersen's *Fairy Tales*; books by and about the English painter, poet, and mystic William Blake; *The Iliad* and *The Odyssey*; Goethe's *Wilhelm Meister's Apprenticeship*, Fridtjof Nansen's *In Northern Mists*, and Friedrich Nietzsche's *Thus Spoke Zarathustra*.[21]

The diary entries by Kent that make up the text of *Wilderness* alternate between descriptions of the climate, everyday chores and activities on the island, ruminations on his son's development and the relationship between father and son, descriptions of Olson or stories related by Olson, reactions to whatever book Kent had just been reading, and occasional philosophical and near-mystical reveries.

The first full-page illustration in the book is captioned with a quote from the philosopher Friedrich Nietzsche (1844–1900): "Zarathustra himself led the ugliest man by the hand, in order to show him his night-world and the great round moon and the silvery waterfalls nigh unto his cave."[22] The drawing depicts a statuesque naked man leading another up onto a ridge, while grasping outward toward the stars and a moon—glowing more like a sun—which rises up from between two mountain peaks.

---

19. West, *"An Enkindled Eye,"* 20.
20. See color plate in West, *"An Enkindled Eye,"* 66.
21. Kent, *Wilderness*, 15.
22. Kent, *Wilderness*, 3.

"Sunrise," illustration from "Wilderness: A Journal of Quiet Adventure in Alaska," 1920.

A waterfall pours down on the right side. Similar visual motifs of the central radiating orb, or of a strong vertical form with a cascading stream of water or stardust on its right side, would often turn up later in Kent's book ornaments, illustrations, and bookplates. Other images in *Wilderness* that radiate an overtly Nietzschean sensibility include *Sunrise, Superman, Weltschmerz, Victory, Zarathustra and His Playmates, The Imperishable, The Star-Lighter*, and a series of illustrations concerning "The Mad Hermit." One also finds less easily categorized illustrations in *Wilderness*, too, although many of them would likewise sit well amid the pages of Nietzsche's "anti-Bible."

It is well evident that Kent's enthusiasm for Nietzsche ran high during his island stay. Speaking of Nietzsche's *Thus Spoke Zarathustra*, he exclaims at one point: "What a book to illustrate!"[23] Kent's biographer, David Traxel, reports that the artist had a gold band on his fountain pen which he later had engraved with Nietzsche's dictum "Schreibe mit Blut: und du wirst

23. Kent, *Wilderness*, 168.

erfahren, daß Blut Geist ist" (Write with blood, and you will learn that blood is spirit).[24] Kent was passionately engaged with Nietzsche's *Zarathustra*, and carried on an internal debate in his head with the philosopher's ideas. His reaction at one point is revealing of his own egoistic tendencies:

> The translator of it says that Zarathustra is such a being as Nietzsche himself would have liked to be,—in other words his ideal man. It seems to me that the ideal of a man *is* the real man. You *are* that which in your soul you choose to be; your most beautiful and cherished vision is yourself. . . . My chief criticism of Zarathustra is his taste for propaganda. Why, after all, concern himself with the mob. In picturing his hero as a teacher has not Nietzsche been tricked away from a true ideal to an historical one? Of necessity the great *selfish* figures of all time have gone down to oblivion. It's the will of human society that only the benefactors of mankind shall be cherished in memory. A pure ideal is to be the thing yourself, concerning yourself no bit with proving it. And if the onward path of mankind seems to go another way than yours—proud soul, let it.[25]

Kent's Alaska drawings are split roughly between mundane images and those of a mythical-allegorical sort. Some pictures straightforwardly depict familiar activities of sawing and hauling wood, sleeping in a rowboat, or life inside the cabin, while others feature a heroic or godlike figure, naked and inhabiting a mountainous landscape in solitude. Flying or winged beings also appear in images like *Victory* or *The North Wind*. As the latter title indicates, such a being can represent Boreas, the Greek god of the north wind. These hovering figures become a recurring motif in Kent's later illustrations, taking on different nuances. Frequently they are female and angelic in their qualities. After his visits to Greenland they appear garbed in traditional Greenlandic clothing,

---

24. Traxel, *An American Saga*, 109.
25. Kent, *Wilderness*, 168.

and represent the peaceful guardian spirits of that island.[26]

Images of the local terrain in Resurrection Bay starkly depict the geographical features that had come to enchant Kent. Mountains, often blanketed in snow, provide a jagged backdrop, which is then contrasted by a flat expanse of water, or land, in the foreground. In the center of the composition is a closer body of land that directly meets the water. This is usually a bulky island—à la Monhegan—with a long and imposing strip of rock cliffs. Compositional elements of the landscape that might have been familiar from Maine or Newfoundland were now augmented in Alaska by monumental glaciers and the shimmering light that comes with greater altitudes and higher latitudes. The features that would typify a great number of Rockwell Kent's paintings were now in place. He would later remark about himself and his consistency: "Kent's art points north. And whether, as some say, this is a sign of his limitations, of his inability to 'grow,' or of mere steadfastness in a true belief, only time, measured it is probable by vast social changes, can give a final verdict."[27]

Heaven in Greenland

Upon returning to New York, Kent had two successful exhibits of his recent works that had arisen from his experience in Alaska. He moved to a farm in Vermont where a "heightened perception of the mysterious undercurrents that bind man and nature can be seen in a series of paintings begun there in 1921."[28] Unlike most of his other landscapes, these works prominently depict wildlife in the form of deer, hawks, and other creatures.

The following spring Kent traveled to Tierra del Fuego, South America. Amid his various activities there he made sketches (some of which served as studies for later paintings) of the dramatic and mountainous landscape that shared similar dramatic characteristics with Kent's beloved North. In the middle of the 1920s Kent took trips to Europe, including a stay in Ireland on the rocky

26. See, e.g., *Rockwell Kent: An Anthology of His Works*, 74.
27. Kent, *It's Me O Lord*, 477.
28. West, *"An Enkindled Eye,"* 21.

AN ILLUSTRATION OF GREENLAND FROM "N BY E," 1930.

northwest coast of Donegal. His autobiography recounts his pleasures in finding the strong communal ties that existed among the countryside's impoverished residents, who were nevertheless rich in generosity and hospitality. Experiences of this sort affirmed his faith in socialism.

In January of 1928, Kent had a visit from his friend Arthur Allen who mentioned that his son was planning a trip to Greenland in Allen's 33-foot cutter sailboat, the *Direction*. Kent immediately asked if he could come along, and it was soon agreed that he would. The opportunity was a dream come true for the artist, who recalled:

> From my first reading of the Njal Saga twenty years before, on through every saga in translation I could lay my hands upon, through all that was recorded of the discovery and settlement of Greenland, of Leif's discovery of America and of Karlsefni's brave attempt to settle here, how I had hoped to someday, somehow, see the hallowed lands of those heroic people![29]

29. Kent, *It's Me O Lord*, 439.

ROCKWELL KENT IN GREENLAND, EARLY 1930S. ROCKWELL KENT COLLECTION.

Kent's Greenland voyage thus took place in the following summer of 1929. He and his companions set sail from Nova Scotia, and the bulk of the journey went smoothly. Their arrival turned out to be one of high drama, however, as the *Direction* was wrecked and destroyed in a fjord on Greenland's coast. The small crew successfully made it to land—Kent was even able to salvage his painting supplies—where they stayed for a few months. Kent's account of the adventure was published in 1930 as an illustrated volume entitled *N by E*. It became one of his most popular books.

As is evident from passages in *N by E*, Kent often had Vikings in mind when he first spent time in Greenland. He later found an opportunity to illustrate a bit of his fascination for the Viking colonization of Greenland when he produced a frontispiece for the "Explorer's Club" deluxe edition of the Icelandic-Canadian adventurer Vilhjalmur Stefansson's book *Unsolved Mysteries of the Arctic*. Entitled "Greenland Settlers Looking for a Ship from Iceland," it depicts two determined figures staring easterly off to sea from a wind-blown, rocky cliff.

ROCKWELL KENT AND ARCTIC EXPLORER VILHJALMUR STEFANSSON AT ASGAARD, 1940S. ROCKWELL KENT COLLECTION.

When Kent finally sailed from Godthåb, Greenland, for Denmark in the early fall, there were two other noteworthy passengers aboard the vessel: the famous Greenland explorers Knud Rasmussen and Peter Freuchen. Kent struck up friendships with the men, who both admired his work. In turn, the two explorers became welcome aids to Kent and would facilitate opportunities for him to return to Greenland. This was a goal upon which the artist had already set his sights:

It is proverbial that those who have tasted of life in the

Far North become possessed by it. My own short visit to Greenland in 1929 had filled me with a longing to return and spend a winter there; to see and to experience the Far North at its spectacular "worst"; to know the people and, as far as could be, share their way of life.[30]

On the recommendation of Rasmussen, Kent chose Igdlorssuit on Unknown Island, off the west coast of Greenland, for his next visit. When he first arrived there in 1931, he built a cottage and enlisted a local woman, "Salamina," as his "*kifak* or housekeeper in all that, in a bachelor's home in Greenland, the term implies."[31] In Kent's 1935 book *Salamina*, and his *Greenland Journal* from the same period,[32] he sketches—in words and images—a vivid portrait of his time among the local people, and especially the native women. In addition to his ink drawings of maps, portraits, and details from local life, Kent also dedicated much of his time to painting on canvas with the landscape as his subject matter. He learned to use a dog sledge and would load up his canvas and supplies to head across the snow in search of formidable mountains, outcrops, or icebergs. Sometimes he traveled alone and on other occasions with a group of hunters. The result was a large body of work that captures the otherworldliness of the glacial landscape and the surrounding islands. Of such scenes he said, "The beauty of those Northern winter days is more remote and passionless, more nearly absolute, than any other beauty I know. Blue sky, white world, and the golden light of the sun to tune the whiteness to the sun-illumined blue."[33]

---

30. Kent, *It's Me O Lord*, 452.
31. Kent, *It's Me O Lord*, 454. Incidentally, "Salamina" is not likely to be the woman's real name, but rather a play on "My Sally," which is in turn a reference to Kent's beloved mother Sara's nickname. Kent also called his American wife "Sally." Cf. Fridolf Johnson's comments in *Rockwell Kent: An Anthology of His Works*, 64.
32. This was not published until 1962, however. It is dedicated to Salamina's memory and contains the entirety of Kent's original journal, whereas the earlier book *Salamina* is a collection of excerpts. See Rockwell Kent, *Greenland Journal*.
33. Traxel, *An American Saga*, 169.

Kent fell in love with the Greenlanders—and not just the women. He delighted in what seemed to him an enlightened manner of living that was a welcome antithesis to the commercialized, capitalist-driven lifestyles of the United States. He admired the older ways of tribal thinking that still played a role in the community of Igdlorssuit, and customs of behavior—particularly concerning sexuality—that offered a stark contrast to the Christian morality of the West. Kent would later give lectures on his time in Greenland and spoke of the natives' "improvidence and poverty and happiness; of their great goodness and rare badness; and how they were, in all their qualities of mind and heart, just like ourselves. Only—in many ways that count—more civilized."[34] At the same time, however, Greenland was a place quite removed from the concerns of modern civilization. Nietzsche had proclaimed that it is "better to live amid ice than among modern virtues and other south-winds,"[35] and for Kent, Greenland was so detached from urban social decorum that he could even refer to it as "heaven."[36]

Kent's Prometheanism

Rockwell Kent's evolutionism and socialism did not, in the end, preclude a certain mystical sensibility that finds expression in his images and writings. Kent's spirituality, if it can be so described, was atheistic and heroic-realist. It arose out of the individual's interaction with the natural world—preferably one-on-one in an environment that was extreme and uncompromising. Kent's outlook was thoroughly distinct from the technocratic glorification of science and labor that marks so much of materialistic socialist thought. Kent was aware that viewers of his work noticed these sentiments, though he would downplay such notions: "people have been inclined to find a mystic quality [in my work] that is so obviously at variance with my own proclaimed belief in

---

34. Kent, *It's Me O Lord*, 476.
35. "Lieber im Eise leben als unter modernen Tugenden und andren Südwinden!" (*Der Antichrist*, §1).
36. Kent, *It's Me O Lord*, 478.

realism, and my fundamental disbelief in Deity."[37]

Undoubtedly, Kent viewed the landscapes of the Arctic, and of the other remote places he had visited in earlier years, as a kind of primordial testing ground for higher forces. They reduced man to his essence—or even excluded him altogether.[38] These locations were worthy of awe. Despite Kent's atheism, he clearly thought in terms of allegories and symbolic associations. He envisioned mankind as engaged in a kind of religious mission, a struggle to develop human knowledge and improve the world according to higher, artistic ideals. He would even invoke the name of God in his conversations and writings. As he was wont to point out, however, he did so in his own idiosyncratic, vitalistic but atheistic way:

> God had become to me the symbol of the life force of our world and universe; a name for the immense unknown. Imponderable, yet immanent in man, in beasts and birds and bugs, in trees and flowers and toadstools, in the earth, sun, moon and stars. It—I choose the impersonal pronoun as alone consistent with my faith—It was to me a force as un-moral as such manifestations of itself as storms or earthquakes, and for that very reason greatly to be feared. It was as un-moral and impersonal and splendid as its sunset's light on land and sea—and for that reason to be reverenced. I feared and reverenced God. In fear and reverence I painted. That mood forbids defining art as self-expression.[39]

On the cover of a catalog for a retrospective exhibit of his works at the Wildenstein Galleries, Kent placed the following quote from St. Augustine: "And the people went there and admired the high mountains, the wide wastes of the sea and the mighty down-

---

37. Kent, *It's Me O Lord*, 423.
38. Kent occasionally included human elements (hunters, dog sledge teams, etc.) in his winter landscape paintings, but when they do appear they are often small and almost insignificant in terms of the overall composition.
39. Kent, *It's Me O Lord*, 138.

ward rushing streams, and the ocean, and the course of the stars, and forgot themselves." He then explained his artistic intent: "That these paintings may convey to those who see them some of the elation of self-forgetfulness is all they are meant to do."[40]

Kent's impulses vacillate between such a proclaimed "self-forgetfulness" and a very pronounced humanistic self-assertiveness. The humanistic sentiments were not unique to Kent, of course. They find a kinship, or precedent, in other artists and thinkers who notably influenced him, whether Nietzsche with his doctrine of the *Übermensch* or the biologist and "monist" philosopher Ernst Haeckel (1834–1919), with whom Kent had also identified at a young age.[41]

Kent's belief in himself, which was essentially a belief in the sovereign power of the gifted individual, stands in contrast to his sympathies for the common man and the oppressed masses.[42] And although he frequently lent his support to collective movements and efforts—and sometimes paid a dear price for doing so—in his own life Kent seems to have been perpetually drawn toward solitude. It was there, alone in remote and difficult environs, that he felt most inspired to create his art. These were the places that stirred his Promethean sensibility most fully:

> Everywhere...I have had the excitements of certain little risks that I have run, the enthusiasm of being where nature was immense, where skies were clear at night, where lands were virginal. I have stood in spots where I have known that I was the first white man who had ever seen that country, that I was the supreme consciousness that came to it. I have liked the thought that maybe there was no existence but in consciousness, and that I was in a sense the creator of that place. And because I have been alone so much and have been moved by what I have seen, I have

---

40. Kent, *It's Me O Lord*, 424.
41. Kent, *It's Me O Lord*, 50.
42. Kent shares quite a few traits with the writer Jack London, who was also a socialist and Alaskan adventurer. During at least one period in his life, Kent corresponded with London. See Kent, *It's Me O Lord*, 323.

had to paint it and write about it.⁴³

Friedrich Nietzsche's famous opening lines in *The Antichrist* would have undoubtedly appealed to Kent: "Let us look one another in the face. We are Hyperboreans—we know full well how far removed we live."⁴⁴ In 1926, a few years before he had encountered Nietzsche's writings, Kent wrote of his travels in County Donegal, Ireland:

> There is a deeply satisfying finality about land's end. Gone is that everlasting urge the inland traveler feels to journey on and on; there are no further peaks to beckon you; you have attained the absolute. We now sought only to refine that absolute: *land's* end we'd reached, but there were people there; if only we could find a little house beyond mankind.⁴⁵

Given the opportunity to work in such locations, far away from mankind, Kent could best tap into his artistic reservoirs. This enabled him to create images that he could then transport back to civilization for the edification of his fellow man.

Illustrator of the Heroic

Heroic Germanic literature inspired Rockwell Kent to visit locations in the Far North. At one point Kent had apparently hoped to take a journey that was specifically inspired by saga literature, but like his earlier plan to visit Iceland, it was not to be: an "opportunity to follow the course of Leif Ericson by sailing on a small boat from Denmark to America was off because of personality differences with a wealthy promoter."⁴⁶ Nevertheless, Kent's interests in this literary realm would lead him to illustrate the

---

43. Kent in *Rockwell Kent: An Anthology of His Works*, 79.
44. "Sehen wir uns ins Gesicht. Wir sind Hyperboreer,—wir wissen gut genug, wie abseits wir leben" (*Der Antichrist*, §1).
45. Kent, *It's Me O Lord*, 416.
46. Barry Tharaud, Afterword to *Beowulf* (1990), 174.

BEOWULF WITH GRENDEL'S ARM. ILLUSTRATION FROM "BEOWULF," 1932.

Old English poem *Beowulf* as well as one of the Icelandic family sagas: *The Saga of Gisli, Son of Sour*. The latter project was even executed while Kent was in Greenland for his third and final visit in 1934–35.[47]

The *Beowulf* edition was issued in a deluxe oversized format

47. Kent, *It's Me O Lord*, 481.

in 1932 and features eight lithographs by Kent. One of these depicts Beowulf as a triumphant naked fighter who has just torn the monster Grendel's arm from his body. In the original poem, the battle scene in the epic takes place at night while the warriors are at rest, sleeping in Hrothgar's hall. Beowulf lies in wait for Grendel and, although he fights barehanded, he is surely clothed in armor. Kent's depiction of the warrior as naked may have had personal significance. Kent makes occasional reference to his own nudist practices in his memoirs and they also find expression in some of his paintings. Of his time with his first wife and children he wrote: "Long before 'nudism'—that *reductio ad absurdum* of hygienic common sense—became a cult—we practiced it as, living in rare seclusion, we were both privileged and by the heat inclined to do."[48] A work from 1914–15 entitled *Nude Family in a Landscape* probably depicts Kent's own family. Kent's 1909 painting *Men and Mountains* depicts a group of nude men outdoors, on a plateau before a mountain range. While some engage in a kind of sun-worship, two of the others are wrestling.

Given his own heroic sensibility, the idea that Kent might depict a legendary hero like Beowulf somewhat after his own image is not hard to imagine. This tendency is even more pronounced in Kent's edition of *The Saga of Gisli*, a succinct classic of the medieval Icelandic saga genre. It relates the life and death of the doomed Viking farmer Gisli, outlawed and hunted down by feuding fellow countrymen. Kent, whose own combative nature was legendary, found more here than merely an appealing story set on a mountainous and glacier-decked Arctic island. In the protagonist of Gisli—a noble farmer and gifted artist who is persecuted by lesser men—he saw a very familiar face: if one compares Kent's 1934 self-portrait, *Das Ding an sich*, or photographs of the artist in Greenland, to his depiction of the saga hero, it is clear that he put quite a bit of himself into Gisli.[49]

Such heroic and grandiose imagery was not limited to Kent's

---

48. Kent, *It's Me O Lord*, 378.
49. For the self-portrait, see *Rockwell Kent: An Anthology of His Works*, 211; the illustrations in *The Saga of Gisli*. 49 (reproduced in the present article), 75, and 101.

GISLI ON HIS WAY TO SLAY THORGRIM. ILLUSTRATION FROM "THE SAGA OF GISLI," 1936.

illustrations of medieval texts. As Jake Wien notes in *Rockwell Kent: The Mythic and the Modern* (a volume that includes much of Kent's commercial work that was done for advertising and other commissions):

> Pagan deities and mythic figures symbolic of cosmic forces frequently appear in Kent's painted murals and in the advertisements he created. His was a secular vision that acknowledged America's diverse spiritual beliefs and

THORDIS HOLDING GISLI'S SWORD. ILLUSTRATION FROM "THE SAGA OF GISLI," 1936.

a waning religiosity. The result is an imaginative commingling of gods with goods and the spirit of eternity with the impulses of the moment.[50]

Here again we see Kent's consistent tendency to take his personal, almost mythic visions—which were often a product of his own physical engagement with the "cosmic forces" of the North

50. Wien, *Rockwell Kent*, 109.

together with his life-long fascination for its ancient literature—and give them a new place in the everyday world of the modern man.

The Farm of the Gods

Already as a youth Kent had broken irrevocably with Christianity. He looked askance at organized religion and once provocatively remarked, "If the devil himself engages in good work I'll join him. And, let me tell you, I will make no secret of it."[51] Above all, he was a humanist and pragmatist. For these reasons he could hardly have believed in the Old Norse gods, but he nevertheless felt a certain romantic kinship with them. This was surely inspired by his beloved pagan heroes in the Icelandic sagas. In 1927 Kent bought a large piece of farm property in the Adirondack Mountains of New York. It was only natural that such a grand plot of land should be given a name. Kent explained the reasoning for his choice as follows:

> The famed historian and poet of medieval Iceland, Snorri Sturluson, in describing the world as he knew or imagined it to be, speaks of the center of the world, and tells us that "even as the land there is lovelier and better in every way than in other places, so also were the sons of men there most favored with godly gifts: wisdom, and strength of body, beauty, and all manner of knowledge." He then tells of how the gods, who were called the Aesir, came to live there, they and their kindred, and "made for themselves in the middle of the world a city which is called *Asgaard*." It was, as we know, for such a site that Frances and I had sought; and having found it, we had built thereon our house and studio and barns, our "city," and, like the Aesir, called it *Asgaard*.[52]

In his biography of Kent entitled *An American Saga*, David Traxel describes the farm as follows:

51. Quoted in Traxel, *An American Saga*, 175.
52. Kent, *It's Me O Lord*, 447.

It lay far north of the Adirondack Mountains, just outside the small village of Au Sable Forks. The heart of the farm was an unusually level pasture of just over one hundred acres, with another two hundred acres of pine woods, hills and meadows. The edge of the property dropped steeply to the Au Sable River. Far off to the west stood the rugged form of Whiteface Mountain, while other blue peaks ranged the horizon.

... Ever since his early reading of the Icelandic sagas, the Vikings had symbolized adventure, exploration, fearlessness. They too were farmers and they had conceived of paradise as a giant, glorious farm. In their honor Rockwell named his place Asgaard, "The Farm of the Gods," which he had painted in letters several feet high, across the face of his barn.[53]

Kent nurtured a deep attachment to the farm. For several decades he managed to run Asgaard as a modest commercial dairy that sold milk and cream locally, but he was ultimately forced to abandon the venture in 1948. This came in the wake of controversy set off by Kent's political activism on behalf of the American Labor Party.

Although Kent would often travel to distant corners of the globe, the house and its fields always remained a refuge for him and his family. In addition to the constant work necessitated by the property itself, at Asgaard Kent would paint, entertain guests, and write. He involved himself in local politics. As he grew older, he traveled less and contented himself with painting the views from his fields (in particular, one which looked out upon Whiteface mountain) throughout the changing seasons.

In the spring of 1969, Kent's house at Asgaard was hit by a lightning strike that could be seen for miles around. The fire this set off was devastating: it entirely destroyed the house, various artworks, artifacts which Kent had collected from his travels around the world, and a library of around 10,000 books. One small consolation lay in the fact that about 50,000 pages of letters and

---

53. Traxel, *An American Saga*, 156, 159.

ROCKWELL KENT IN HIS STUDIO AT ASGAARD. © 1930 WORLD WIDE PHOTOS. ROCKWELL KENT COLLECTION.

manuscripts, which had already been consigned to the Archives of American Art, miraculously survived the conflagration more-or-less intact.[54] After the tragedy, Kent's wife Sally remarked that the "[n]ext day, as though in penitence for the deed, the heavens laid a funeral pall of snow upon the blackened ruin."[55]

If it hadn't been for this unfortunate turn of events, Kent's farmhouse and property would probably be a museum to the artist today. Access to his library and personal collection would have allowed for a clearer picture of all the elements that came together in Kent's orientation toward the Far North. A careful scrutiny of Kent's voluminous correspondence, which did survive the fire, would surely provide much further evidence. Nevertheless, as the present essay has shown, the reverberations of Kent's "northern impulse" rippled continually throughout his

54. See Garrett McCoy, "The Rockwell Kent Papers."
55. Quoted in *Rockwell Kent: An Anthology of His Works*, 76.

life, his philosophical musings, and his artistic work. Like the magnetic needle of a compass, Rockwell Kent was drawn in a single direction, and one that perfectly suited his vital, creative temperament. To return a final time to the words of Nietzsche, it was through this lonely Hyperborean yearning that Kent "discovered the happiness," for he "knew the path . . . the way out of whole millennia of labyrinth."[56] All else was sirocco.

Bibliography

Beowulf. Illustrated by Rockwell Kent. Verse translation by William Ellery Leonard. New York: Random House, 1932.

Beowulf. With reproductions of illustrations by Rockwell Kent. Edited and translated by Barry Tharaud. Niwot, CO: University Press of Colorado, 1990.

Ehrlich, Gretel. *This Cold Heaven: Seven Seasons in Greenland.* New York: Pantheon, 2001.

Kent, Rockwell. *Wilderness: A Journal of Quiet Adventure in Alaska.* New York: G. P. Putnam's Sons, 1920.

———. *N by E.* New York: N.Y. Literary Guild, 1930.

———. *Salamina.* New York: Harcourt, Brace & Co., 1935.

———. *This Is My Own.* New York: Duell, Sloan and Pearce, 1940.

———. *It's Me O Lord: The Autobiography of Rockwell Kent.* New York: Dodd, Mead & Co., 1955.

———. *Greenland Journal.* New York: Oblensky, 1962.

———. *Rockwell Kent: An Anthology of His Works.* Edited by Fridolf Johnson. New York: Knopf, 1982.

McCoy, Garrett. "The Rockwell Kent Papers." *Archives of American Art Journal* 12: II (January 1972): 1–9.

Nietzsche, Friedrich. *Der Antichrist.* Written in 1888; first published posthumously in 1894. Digital critical edition (eKGWB) at: www.nietzschesource.org

The Saga of Gisli, Son of Sour. Illustrated by Rockwell Kent. Translated by Ralph B. Allen. New York: Harcourt, Brace & Co.,

---

56. "Wir haben das Glück entdeckt, wir wissen den Weg, wir fanden den Ausgang aus ganzen Jahrtausenden des Labyrinths."(*Der Antichrist*, §1).

1936.

Stefansson, Vilhjalmur. *Unsolved Mysteries of the Arctic*. Deluxe edition for the Explorers Club. New York: Macmillan, 1938.

Traxel, David. *An American Saga: The Life and Times of Rockwell Kent*. New York: Harper and Row, 1980.

West, Richard V., with contributions by Fridolf Johnson and Dan Burne Jones. *"An Enkindled Eye": The Paintings of Rockwell Kent*. Exhibition catalog. Santa Barbara: Santa Barbara Museum of Art, 1985.

Wien, Jake Milgram. *Rockwell Kent: The Mythic and the Modern*. New York: Hudson Hills, 2005.

All of the Rockwell Kent photographs, illustrations, and artwork reproduced here are courtesy of the Plattsburgh State Art Museum, State University of New York, USA, Rockwell Kent Collection, Bequest of Sally Kent Gorton. All rights reserved. Special thanks to curator Cecilia Esposito for her helpful assistance.

THE MAIN BARN AT ASGAARD, NOW A MILKING AND CHEESE-MAKING FACILITY.

Appendix:
"Northward to the northern limits of the mountains" Rockwell Kent's Asgaard

Although he was often driven toward travel and adventure, Rockwell Kent's most beloved place was his property in Au Sable Forks, New York, which he named Asgaard. Here he made his home for over forty years. Although his attempts to turn Asgaard into a small commercial dairy farm were ultimately unsuccessful, the location served as fertile ground for his artistic work. He never tired of painting pictures of the property and its majestic views of the surrounding Adirondack Mountains. In a chapter entitled "Trail's End" in his memoir *This Is My Own*, Kent recalls his first visit to the location:

> A mile uphill, and we turned north again—turned north and stopped. And there, westward and heavenward to the high ridge of Whiteface [mountain], northward to the northern limits of the mountains, southward to their highest peaks, was spread the full half-circle panorama of the Adirondacks. It was as though we had never seen the mountains before.[57]

57. Kent, *This Is My Own*, 48.

LETTERING ORIGINALLY DONE BY KENT, WHO ALSO CONSTRUCTED THE WOODEN STAR ORNAMENT.

Shortly after buying the property in 1927, Kent designed and built a family house there. This was followed by other structures, such as modest guesthouse which was named "Valhalla." Crucial to Kent's own creative and commercial work was the wooden studio for himself in a secluded spot in the forest, a few minutes' walk from the main house. The interior of the building had a simple workshop foyer for carpentry (where Kent made his own canvas frames, easels, and the like) and a high-ceilinged central studio with large windows to receive the northern light.

After Rockwell Kent's death in 1971, his wife Sally remarried but continued to live at the farm for many years (she died in 2000). In the late 1980s, the property was bought by its current owners, who have rediscovered and carefully nurtured the original spirit of the place. Asgaard reopened in 2003 as a working livestock farm and dairy, specializing in European-style goat cheeses and high-quality meats.

Many of the buildings have been renovated and various touches from Kent's hand have been reinstated in their former places, including painted motifs and woodworking. Most remarkably, Kent's studio has been kept true to its original form. His

A VIEW OF THE ADIRONDACK MOUNTAINS FROM ASGAARD.

original woodstove still stands to one side of the room. The racks are full of his old canvas frames, and some of his art supplies can still be found on the shelves and tables. The light fixtures and even their bulbs (still functional) date back to his tenure there. A faint vestige of his spirit hovers about the place.

Rockwell Kent and Sally Kent Gorton are buried at Asgaard. The epitaph on his simple gravestone reads "This Is My Own." The phrase served as the title of one of Kent's autobiographies, and derives from Sir Walter Scott's *The Lay of the Last Minstrel*:

> Breathes there a man, with soul so dead,
> Who never to himself hath said,
> This is my own, my native land!
> Whose heart hath ne'er within him burned
> As home his footsteps he hath turned
> From wandering on a foreign strand![58]

---

58. Walter Scott, *The Lay of the Last Minstrel*, canto 6, stanza 1.

Top row (left to right): The original silos behind the main barn; a wooden sign carved by Kent for the guesthouse.

Center row: Kent's studio in the woods, southern entrance; remnants of Kent's paintbrushes and supplies.

Bottom row: The foyer for woodworking; Kent's woodstove, frame rack, and cot; the main studio with its northern windows.

All Asgaard Farm photos were taken in May 2014 by Michael Moynihan.

FERAL HOUSE

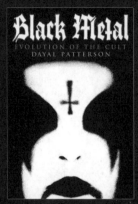

Black Metal: Evolution of the Cult

Epic 500+ page tome explores the history of Black Metal, featuring interviews and rare images from the most integral bands, photographers and hangers-on in the genre.
$27.95

Financial Vipers of Venice

Alchemical Money, Magical Physics, and Banking in the Middle Ages and Renaissance, by the author of Babylon's Banksters.
$19.95

Morris Graves: His Houses, His Gardens

Stories and photographs of the homes of Morris Graves, a leading figure in Northwest Art, and one of the most important American artists of the 20th century.
$45.00

Hashish

This illustrated novel is presented as a "pictoral opera" of love, hashish, and tragedy, and contains the first known depiction of hashish hallucinations.
$65.00

PROCESS

www.feralhouse.com   www.processmediainc.com

The Mead of Inspiration

Christian Rätsch

> "You must furnish for the Æsir
> ale-feasts without fail!"
> —from the Eddic poem *Hymiskviða*[1]

Today at many outdoor markets and Christmas fairs in Germany, mead is sold at the honey-makers' stands. It is a thick, sticky, and honey-sweet liquid. The mead drunk by our ancestors certainly had nothing in common with this curious stuff, just as our ancestors' beer had little to do with the modern variety. With beer and mead, the adjunct ingredients were far more important than the basic fermented components such as honey, grain, bread, and malt. The Germanic peoples made use of various brewing techniques and produced differently tasting and differently active brewed drinks that are described in ancient and modern literature as mead, honey wine, or beer. By definition, mead is produced from honey and water through the application of yeast, and beer is produced from malt or bread and water and yeast. However, drinks were often brewed from honey and malt that are referred to variously in the literature as mead, beer, or even honey beer. Both mead and beer contain 2%–5% alcohol. In order to preserve these drinks, or to brew them with good flavor or a more strongly intoxicating effect, different adjunct ingredients were added. These were most often herbs with antiseptic, aromatic, or psychoactive qualities.

In the history of brewing, there are probably no plants we currently recognize as psychoactive that *haven't* been added to beer at some particular time or place. The ancient Egyptians brewed a mandrake beer; the Indians spiked their corn beer (*chicha*) with coca leaves, datura seeds, and morning glory seeds; in the Orient beer was improved with hashish and opium; and

---

1. Translation from Ursula Dronke, *The Poetic Edda, vol. 3: Mythological Poems* (Oxford: Oxford University Press, 2011), 67.

in Siberia dried fly agaric mushrooms (*Amanita muscaria*) were crumbled into the beer. The ancient Gauls brewed beer from darnel,[2] and in the Middle Ages, thin beers were spiced with cinnamon, nutmeg, and cardamom. The addition of hops to beer is an invention of Christian monks. The brethren of the monastery were not to be stimulated by beer additives with aphrodisiac effects; to the contrary, they should be sedated by the hops. The heathen mead of inspiration was no simple beer or simple mead, but must have been a psychoactive drink whose intoxicating components would have had a stimulating effect on creativity. We know of various Indo-European traditions in which plant preparations served as sources of inspiration for the singers and poets: the soma of the Aryans, the *bhang* of the Brahmans, the mushroom wine of Dionysus. But how was the Germanic mead of poetry brewed? Which plants, which "spices" or "bitter herbs," did the Germanic peoples know and make use of?

The Drinks of the Gods, Spirits, and Men

In the Eddic poem *Alvíssmál*, the god Thor questions the dwarf Alviss (whose name means "all-wise") about the names for the drinks of the different beings. The all-knowing dwarf answers:

> *Ql heitir með mǫnnum, en með ásom biórr,*
> *kalla be veig vanir*
> *hreina lǫg iǫtnar, en í helio miǫð,*
> *kalla sumbl Suttungs synir.*

('Ale' among men, 'Beer' the gods among,
In the world of the Wanes 'The Foaming';

---

2. [The German name for darnel (*Lolium temulentum*) is *Taumel-Lolch*, meaning "reeling ryegrass," and its botanical and common names in various languages refer to its intoxicating quality (*temulentum*, for example, is Latin for "drunken"). Another common name in English is poison darnel. It is now believed that the grass itself is not poisonous, but that such effects were caused by the ergot fungus which sometimes infected it. Such ergot infections, and resulting cases of ergotism, are the suspected cause of medieval phenomena such as Saint Anthony's Fire. —*Trans.*]

'Bright Draught' with giants, 'Mead' with
dwellers in Hel,
'The Feast-Draught' with Suttung's sons.)[3]

Alviss also lists the main ingredients from which these drinks are brewed:

Bygg heitir með mǫnnum, en barr með goðum
kalla vǫxt vanir
æti iǫtnar, álfar lagastaf,
kalla í helio hnipinn

("Men call it 'Grain,' and 'Corn' the gods,
'Growth' in the world of the Wanes;
'The Eaten' by the giants, 'Drink-Stuff' by the elves,
In Hel 'The Slender Stem.')[4]

Unfortunately these descriptions are too meager to allow for a satisfactory interpretation. *Bygg* and *barr* are names for barley, *æti* ("The Eaten") could be a bread grain like rye, *hnipinn* ("The Slender Stem") might be oats, but could also be darnel. *Vǫxt* ("Growth") and *lagastaf* ("Drink-Stuff") are unknowable. It is even more difficult to interpret the names of the beverages "ale," "beer," and *sumbl*, "Feast Draught." Some of the designations also seem contradictory: for example, if the drink in Hel is mead, then the fermented basis of the drink should be honey and not a "Slender Stem" grain.

According to Nordic tradition, *öl*, also called *alu*, is a sweet, strong mead which serves as the "drink of the gods" and which the battle-slain warriors and heroes drink in Valhalla. "The company of men are made sleepy by the ale," it says in the *Háttatal* in Snorri's *Prose Edda*.[5] But elsewhere wine is expressly

---

3. *Alvíssmál*, st. 34. Translation slightly modified from Henry Adams Bellows, *The Poetic Edda*, 193.
4. *Alvíssmál*, st. 32. Translation slightly modified from Bellows, *The Poetic Edda*, 193.
5. Snorri Sturluson, *Edda*, trans. Richard Faulkes, 182.

ODIN/WOTAN ON HIS EIGHT-LEGGED HORSE SLEIPNIR. IN HIS HAND HE HOLDS A DRINKING HORN OR A CUP—PROBABLY FILLED WITH THE POETIC MEAD, THE MEAD OF INSPIRATION. DETAIL FROM THE TJÄNGVIDE PICTURE STONE, GOTLAND, EIGHTH CENTURY.

named as Odin's drink: "yet on wine alone, glorious in weapons, Odin always lives"[6] (*Grímnismál* 19). Should then the southern Germanic Wotan be seen as identical with Dionysus/Bacchus? With the adoption of wine-producing agriculture in southern Germanic regions, for example in the Rhineland, the Roman god Liber (an aspect of Bacchus) was identified with Wotan. Wine was exported to the Far North. It is because this intoxicating drink was especially rare and expensive in Scandinavia and Iceland that the drink was associated with Odin, the most important god (cf. the kenning *valkjósanda vín*, literally the "chooser-of-the-slain's wine" = Odin's wine). It was also the case that the valkyries handed out wine to the guests in Valhalla. According to a skaldic poem, Odin is the "Guardian of Beer" (*Yggs öl* = "Odin's ale").

The mead of inspiration was not the drink of Odin/Wotan

---

6. Translation slightly modified from Ursula Dronke, *The Poetic Edda*, vol. 3, 116.

per se or even of the gods (the Æsir and Vanir) in general, but instead derived from the giants who had possession of intoxicating drinks, according to the *Alvíssmál*.[7] The skaldic mead of the *Prose Edda* was brewed from the blood of Kvasir, whence also comes its name "Kvasir's Blood." The wise Kvasir was created from the spittle of the Æsir and Vanir. The mead, "whoever drinks from which becomes a poet or a scholar," was brewed by two dwarves from Kvasir's blood (possibly a plant sap?) mixed with honey. The name Kvasir has parallels in the Russian *kvas* and Norwegian *kvase*, both of which are slightly alcoholic drinks made from bread.

Some similar beverages are made by fermenting milk. The idea of intoxicating milk also turns up in the mythos of the Einherjar warriors; they live in Valhalla and drink "clear mead" from the udder of the goat Heidrun, whose name literally means "the one possessing a great secret." The goat nourishes itself from the leaves of the divine tree Larad, fermenting the leaves so to speak and producing a never-dwindling drink.[8]

In the best skaldic fashion, poetry itself is called "Kvasir's Blood," "Dwarve's Drink" or "Dwarve's Fill." The mead of the skalds that was originally prepared by the dwarves from Kvasir's blood came into the possession of the giant Suttung. Thus the mead is also called "Suttung's mead" and "Hnitbiorg's Liquid." Odin cunningly steals the mead, which is contained in three vessels (named Óðrœrir, Boðn, and Són), which he drinks from, assumes the form of an eagle (in other words he shamanically transforms himself), and flies off.[9] Arriving in Asgard, Odin "sent some of the mead out backwards, and this was disregarded. Anyone took it that wanted it, and is what we call the 'rhymester's share.' But Odin gave Suttung's mead to the Æsir and to those people who were skilled at composing poetry. Thus we call

---

7. See Renate Doht, *Der Rauschtrank im germanischen Mythos* (Vienna: Halosar, 1974), and A. G. van Hamel, "The Mastering of the Mead," in *Studia Germanica tillägnade Ernst Albin Kock den 6 november 1934* (Lund: Gleerup, 1934), 76–85.
8. See the Eddic poem *Grímnismál*.
9. See Horst Kirchner, "Odin im Adlergewand," in H. Gehrts and G. Lademann-Priemer, eds. *Schamanentum und Zaubermärchen* (Kassel: Röth, 1986), 42–47.

poetry 'Odin's booty' and 'find,' and his 'drink' and his 'gift' and the 'Æsir's drink.'"[10] But Odin must have also given the recipe for the skaldic mead to humans, otherwise they would not be able to brew it on earth, to continue to enjoy it and be able to rhapsodize poetically.

But what was the mead of inspiration? What was it made from? The historian Siegfried Fischer-Fabian, an authority on Germany, claimed that the Germanic peoples made use of a psychedelic drug similar to LSD:

> Mead is ascribed the power of providing inspiration to humans and opening the gateway for them to the supernatural world. To a certain degree it was thus the source of wisdom and of artistic awakening. The intoxicating effect was perceived as a transference of divine power to the human being. This is a description that brings to mind certain drugs of our own day such as LSD, with which one can "take a trip" or go on a journey. It is possible that the ancient Germanic peoples achieved a similar euphoria-laden, aroused state of the cerebral cortex and other parts of the central nervous system, that they became high, since they mixed their mead with various mysterious herbs.[11]

Mead is an alcoholic drink brewed from water, honey, other additives ("bitter herbs"), and wild or cultivated yeast (*Sacchamoryces cerevinae*). Traditional mead is normally weak in alcohol (approximately 2% to 5%) and not particularly sweet because the sugar in the honey is completely fermented into alcohol. The mead that is popular today is typically a sweet, sticky drink with about 14% alcohol; it is brewed via fermentation of a saturated honey solution. In the old literature there is rarely any differentiation made between mead and beer. This is because in earlier times honey was often mixed and brewed with malt. Mead was probably already being made in the Stone Age.

---

10. Snorri Sturluson, *Edda*, trans. Richard Faulkes, 64. Punctuation slightly modified.
11. Siegfried Fischer-Fabian, *Die ersten Deutschen* (Munich: Knaur, 1975), 196.

There is evidence for it in many parts of the world and it was known to the Indo-European peoples. Mead was sacred in all the ancient heathen cultures and was used as a libation and for collective ritual intoxication.[12]

In antiquity mead was used medicinally, as Dioscorides explains:

> *Vinum melitites* [honey wine; Greek *oinos melitites*] is given in long-lasting fevers to those who have a weak stomach because it gently loosens the bowels, induces urine, and purges the stomach. It is good for arthritis, kidney disease, and those who have a weak head. It is useful for women to drink with water as it has a fragrant smell and is nourishing.[13]

For the Germanic peoples, mead was seen as the "divine drink" and the source of poetic and prophetic enthusiasm or inspiration. The honey drink was sacred in particular to the gods Odin/Wotan and Balder. In the Germanic cultural realm, mead was improved in flavor through the addition of herbs such as meadowsweet or "mead wort" (*Filipendula ultmaria* [L.] Maxim., syn. *Spiraea filipendula* L.) or the juice from wild apples. Mead was also given aromatic character with spices, elder flowers, and linden blossoms. As a result, a particular drink would gain certain effects that corresponded to its additives.

The most important component of a magical drink is certainly not the alcohol. Alcohol is little more than a preservative and solvent. Along with the aforementioned Germanic myth of the theft of the mead, we also find the story of the theft of the psychedelic soma plant, which represents the essential active ingredient of a sacred drink ("O juice that is adorned with all poetic thoughts," *Rigveda*, IX, 86, 24). There has never been a

---

12. See Adam Maurizio, *Geschichte der gegorene Getränke* (Berlin and Hamburg: Paul Parey, 1933).
13. From bk. V, ch. 15 of Dioscorides, *De Materia Medica: Being an Herbal with Many Other Medicinal Materials Written in Greek in the First Century of the Common Era*, trans. T. A. Osbaldeston (Johannesburg: IBIDIS Press, 2000), 751.

definite botanical classification of the soma plant, however, and a similar uncertainty exists regarding the secret additives to mead, which are only vaguely referred to as "bitter herbs." By taking an ethnopharmocological approach, however, we can reconstruct an array of intoxicating drinks that correlate very well with the effects of mead as described in the Eddas. The fact that psychedelic or visionary states were known is evident from the Old Icelandic term *glámsýni* ("hallucination"), which appears in the sagas.[14]

Ultimately the question of exactly which magical plants were in the drink is not so important, since the intoxicating experiences are essentially similar. There is probably no single precise recipe that was handed down or remained in continual use, since there were many possible recipes. Certainly the history of drug use shows that some drugs were favored for use as sources of literary inspiration. Opium was one of the most important sources of inspiration for Islamic poetry and for the literature of European Romanticism. Cannabis preparations (hashish, ganja, *charas, bhang*) were among the inspirational sources for the poets of the Vedas, and for the tales of *One Thousand and One Nights*, as well as for many poets of the nineteenth century. Both opium and hashish can be classified as typical "poet's drugs." Up to now, there is hardly anything known about the use of fly agaric mushrooms, henbane, and meadowsweet as inspirational sources. For creative people, *all* sorts of stimuli or stimulants are certainly perceived as sources of inspiration and ecstasy. Even today we can imagine that the magical drinks were brewed in iron cauldrons. Witches, too, brewed their mysterious potions in cauldrons. The motif of the brewing kettle can be traced far back into the Germano-Celtic period. Archeological findings have shown that the Celts and Germanic peoples brewed their magical drinks, their beer and their mead, in special kettles that were often decorated with mythological scenes. One example of this is the famous Gundestrup cauldron, which could be of either

---

14. Wolf von Unwerth, *Untersuchungen über Totenkult und Odinnverehrung bei Nordgermanen und Lappen* (Hildesheim: Olms, 1977 [reprint of 1911 edition]), 173.

The Mead of Inspiration

BEER BREWED FROM MALT, HONEY, WATER, AND HENBANE TAKES ON A REDDISH COLOR. INTERESTINGLY, THE HEXENBIER ("WITCHES' BEER") MENTIONED IN MANY EARLY MODERN GERMAN SOURCES IS DESCRIBED AS "RED."

Celtic or Germanic manufacture.[15]

The brewing procedure was presumably simple. One took germinated grain (malt) or fermented breads, boiled them together with the desired additives, and then left them in the kettle for fermentation. From brewing residues that have been found, it is apparent that the Germanic peoples already possessed cultivated, top-fermenting beer yeast. The kettle was protected with *Donnerkeile* ("Thunder-Stones," the German name for belemnites), stones which are sacred to the hard-drinking thunder god.

Henbane and Pilsner

On April 2 in the year 921, the Muslim Ibn Fadlan was sent to the north by the caliph of Baghdad in order to further the expansion of Islam. In the area of Bohlgar on the Volga river the mission encountered the Rus, a group of Germanic Varangians (Vikings). Ibn Fadlan was a good observer and described in detail

---

15. See Ruth and Vincent Megaw, *Celtic Art* (London: Thames and Hudson, 1989).

the funerary ceremony for a chieftain, which entailed cremation on a "ship of the dead." For the occasion a special beer (called *nabīd* in Fadlan's report) was brewed, "which they drink until the day when his female slave will kill herself and be burned with her master. They stupefy themselves by drinking this *nabīd* night and day; sometimes one of them dies cup in hand."[16]

Hans-Peter Hasenfratz comments on this passage as follows:

> The excessive enjoyment of an intoxicating beverage (beer), often in tandem with the funerary rite, can be seen here as a solidarity ritual: it puts those who remain among the living into a kind of transcendent, paranormal state. This is the same state in which the deceased himself now seems to exist, whereby the funerary rite can be accepted as a "following into death."[17]

The activity described here seems to concern a shamanic accompaniment or guiding of the soul into the world of the dead. This description fits perfectly with the action of henbane (in German, *Bilsenkraut*) beer, which takes on a reddish color. Drunk in smaller amounts, a beer brewed with henbane is intoxicating; in medium amounts it has an aphrodisiac effect. Henbane beer—the "true pilsener"[18]—is the only drink that makes one thirstier the more one drinks, because the alkaloids cause a dryness in the mouth. In higher amounts, henbane beer leads to delirious, "stultified" states, confusion, loss of memory, and wild, seemingly senseless behavior. Overdoses of henbane can be deadly as a result of respiratory paralysis. The toxicology literature is full of such cases.[19]

---

16. Quoted in Hans-Peter Hasenfratz, *Barbarian Rites: The Spiritual World of the Vikings and the Germanic Tribes*, trans. Michael Moynihan (Rochester, Vt.: Inner Traditions, 2011), 11.
17. Hasenfratz, *Barbarian Rites*, 12.
18. [The German word for henbane, *Bilsen-kraut*, "*Bilzen*-plant," is assumed by some ethnobotanists to be at the root of the town name Pilsen (Plzeň, now in the Czech Republic); in the days before hops were used, the earlier "pilsner" beer presumably contained henbane additives, whence its name. — Trans.]
19. See, for example, Louis Lewin, *Gifte und Vergiftungen: Lehrbuch der*

Ibn Fadlan further describes how this same beer is given to a female slave before her ritual suicide, and what effects it has on her:

> The men came with shields and sticks. She was given a cup of *nabīd*; she sang at taking it and drank. . . . Then she was given another cup; she took it and sang for a long time while the old woman incited her to drink up and go into the pavilion, where her master lay. I saw that she was distracted; she wanted to enter the pavilion but put her head between it and the boat. Then the old woman seized her head and made her enter the pavilion, and she entered with the servant girl. . . . Then six men went into the pavilion and each had intercourse with the girl.[20]

All parts of the henbane plant contain the hallucinogenic alkaloids scopolamine and hyoscamine. Both the tiny black seeds and the dried leaves are suitable for brewing beer.

Germanic Drinking Rituals

Rituals are the key to understanding the inner constitution of human society.
—Diane von Weltzien[21]

In May in regions of northern Germany, the "Maibock" beers are brewed and imbibed in quantity—often to the point of unconsciousness. In the fall, the "Märzen" beer is tapped; the Oktoberfest lets loose outdoors, leaving a swath of drunken people in its wake. In Scandinavia, the Yule beer is tossed back to the point of collapse. These popular amusements trace back to older drinking rituals of the Germanic peoples. In the spring (which later became Easter), the aphrodisiacal bock beer was brewed for the goat sacrifice [*Bocksopfer*] and drunk in honor of the fertility gods and goddesses. In the fall, the harvest beer was collectively enjoyed at the harvest festival to honor the earth

---

Toxicologie, 6th ed. (Heidelberg: Haug, 1992), 811–14.
20. Quoted in Hasenfratz, *Barbarian Rites*, 16.
21. *Die Welt der Rituale* (Munich: Goldmann, 1994), 9.

deities. At the winter solstice (the holy nights), homage was paid with the Yule beer to the ancestors (the dead who stood under the protection of Wotan/Odin).

The ancient Germanic peoples were widely renowned for their drinking customs, their drinking feasts, and their drinking horns. As far back as the first century C.E., Tacitus wrote:

> To drink away the day and night disgraces no one. Brawls are frequent, as is normal among the intoxicated, and seldom end in mere abuse, but more often in slaughter and bloodshed. But the mutual settlement of feuds, the forging of marriage bonds, the adoption of leaders, even peace and war are often discussed at their feasts, as though at no other time is the mind more amenable to straightforward thoughts or quicker to burn with great ones.[22]

All the sources point to the fact that the enjoyment of beer, mead, or similar brewed drinks was associated with social and shamanistic rituals. People gathered for beer and drink sacrifices, they made use of special ritual drinking vessels, and they came into contact with gods and ancestors. In the early seventh century in the region of Lake Constance, the missionary Columbanus encountered the heathen Alemanni (a southern Germanic people) who were gathered around a large beer vat, which they collectively sacrificed in honor of their god Wodan.[23] The *Heimskringla*, Snorri Sturluson's royal history, relates of the heathen Yule fest in the north:

> The sacrificial beaker was to be borne around the fire, and he who made the feast and was chieftain, was to bless the beaker as well as all the sacrificial meat. Óthin's toast was to be drunk first—that was for victory and power to the king—then Njorth's and Frey's, for good harvests and for peace.[24]

22. From ch. 22 of Tacitus, *Germania*, trans. J. B. Rives (Oxford: Oxford University Press, 1999), 86.
23. *Vita Columbani*, ch. 53.
24. From ch. 14 of Snorri Sturluson, *Heimskringla: History of the Kings of*

Marsh Rosemary

Marsh rosemary (*Rhododendron tomentosum*, syn. *Ledum palustre* L.), belongs to the Ericaceae or heather family. Its German common names include *Sumpfporst*, *Grutkraut* ("gruit plant"), *Kienporst, Kienrost, Tannenporst* (from *tan*, "fire"), and it is known in English by the common names marsh rosemary, marsh Labrador tea, northern Labrador tea, and wild rosemary. In earlier times, widely differing plants were referred to by the names *Sumpfporst* or *Ledum*.[25]

The aromatic marsh rosemary or wild rosemary grows in the alpine regions, in northern Europe, in northern Asia, and in North America. For beer brewing, the fresh or dried plant was added to the mash or suspended in the brewing vat.

The flowering tops of marsh rosemary contain Ledum oil, which has a strongly intoxicating effect, and the entire plant contains an essential oil (0.5% to 1% in the leaves) that primarily consists of ledol (*ledum camphor*). In higher doses this can lead to cramps, furor, and frenzy. The Viking bands and berserkers likely made use of these qualities for their magical rituals, for animal transformations, and for the berserker rage. The Vikings brewed a strongly intoxicating beer (*porst* beer, *grut*, or gruit beer) with this psychoactive, aromatic additive.

Marsh rosemary is mainly used as an incense and healing plant, and potentially even as a shamanic entheogen.

The shamans of Buryatia in Siberia inhale large amounts of the smoke of *Rhododendron tomentosum* in their rituals. The shamans of the Tungus—from whose language the word "shaman" originates—and the neighboring Gilyak people mainly use marsh rosemary, along with juniper, as a ritual and trance-inducing incense. They inhale the smoke in deep breaths to fall into the shamanic state of consciousness. Sometimes, in addition to inhaling the smoke, the root of the plant was also chewed. This incense is also prized among the shamans of the

---

Norway, trans. Lee M. Hollander (Austin: University of Texas Press, 1964), 107.
25. See the *Kräuter-Buch* of Jacobus Theodorus Tabernaemontanus from 1731.

THE BLOSSOMING MARSH ROSEMARY (RHODODENDRON TOMENTOSUM, SYN. LEDUM PALUSTRE) IS AN EVERGREEN AROMATIC PLANT CLOSELY RELATED TO THE ALPENROSE (RHODODENDRON FERRUGINEUM L.) AND THE HAIRY ALPENROSE (RHODODENDRON HIRSUTUM L.). THIS EURASIAN PLANT IS DISTRIBUTED FROM NORTHERN EUROPE TO THE ALPS. IT IS ALSO PRESENT IN THE NORTHERN UKRAINE AND IN ALL OF NORTHERN ASIA TO JAPAN. IT ONLY GROWS IN RAISED AND TRANSITIONAL BOGS.

Ainu, the indigenous people of northern Japan.

In the Nordic countries, marsh rosemary is used for treating pertussis on account of its narcotic effects; it is taken internally or inhaled as a medicinal incense. The Slavs (Poles) and Sámi also use marsh rosemary as an incense for all ailments of the lungs.

Although marsh rosemary was employed as a healing plant in Europe, for it was most significant as an intoxicating beer additive (for *Grutbier* or "gruit beer") and ritual plant. Marsh rosemary, along with henbane, was the most important psychoactive additive for the Germanic beers of the sort that were brewed before the *Reinheitsgebot* (German beer-purity law) of 1516. Since the oil from marsh rosemary has the ability to stimulate aggressive behavior, it has been asserted that the Viking berserkers used the popular "porst beer" to put themselves into the proverbial "berserker rage."[26]

26. See W. Sanderman, "Beserkerwut durch Sumpfporst-Bier," *Brauwelt* 120

BREWING SCANDINAVIAN GRUIT BEER. (WOODCUT FROM OLAUS MAGNUS, "HISTORIA DE GENTIBUS SEPTENTRIONALIBUS," SIXTEENTH CENTURY.)

Many writers still make the claim that the berserkers used fly agaric mushrooms (*amanita muscaria*) to put themselves into their battle ecstasy. But fly agaric mushrooms are presumably not suited for this since they rather have a calming, opium-like effect that is conducive to dreaming or listening to music.

Marsh Rosemary, Gale, and Gruit Beer

The aromatic plant marsh rosemary has been added as a flavoring to beer since early times. In Sweden in the Viking Age, beer was brewed with marsh rosemary, sometimes mixed with the aromatic sweet gale (*Myrica gale*). In Nordic and medieval literature, this beer has been called "gruit beer" since the fifth century. It was brewed for feasts and ceremonial occasions and always consumed down to the dregs.

In the Scandinavian sources for beer and beer brewing, gruit beer is repeatedly mentioned as a cause of berserker rage. At gruit-beer feasts, things frequently erupted into nasty quarreling.

(1980): 1870–72, and Christian Rätsch, *Urbock: Bier jenseits von Hopfen und Malz* (Aarau: AT Verlag, 1996).

THE DEADLY AFTERMATH OF A NORWEGIAN PEASANT DUEL OF THE SORT THAT WOULD HAVE BEEN FUELED BY GRUIT BEER. ENGRAVING OF A WORK BY THE NINETEENTH-CENTURY NORWEGIAN PAINTER ADOLPH TIDEMAND.

The strife that arose frequently degenerated into bloodshed. In certain regions of Småland [Sweden], the two combatants strapped themselves together with a belt, from which neither could escape until one of them was done in by a knife wound. Women were therefore obliged to bring along winding-sheets if they accompanied their husbands to drinking feasts.[27]

Gale also turns up under the name *Rausch* ("intoxicant") in the old German herbals. But this name was also understood as referring mostly to the bog bilberry (*Vaccinium uliginosum*) and its intoxicating effects.

Hildegard of Bingen was familiar with the gale bush. She wrote: "If someone wishes to make beer, he should cook the leaves and fruits of this tree with the beer, and it will be healthful

---

27. Sandermann, "Beserkerwut," 1870.

and not harm the one drinking it."[28]

(Translated by Michael Moynihan)

Addendum:

Henbane Beer [makes approximately six gallons]

malt extract for a 6 gal. batch of beer
2 lbs. [900g] honey (forest honey if possible, such as spruce or fir honey)
1/6 oz. [5g] gale or another type of *myrica* (this ingredient can also be left out)
1½ oz. [40g] dried henbane (herbage of *Hyoscamus niger*)
top-fermenting yeast
6 gal. [23 liters] water

First boil the henbane and gale (if used) in 2 pints of the water (to ensure the requisite sterility). Leave the henbane in the water until it has cooled down. In a clean, sterile, and appropriately sized brewing vessel add the malt extract along with a half-gallon of the water, heated, and the honey. Stir until the ingredients are thoroughly dissolved. Add the henbane water together with the herbage. Stir thoroughly. Add cold water to make a total of approximately 6 gallons of liquid. Pitch the yeast into the mixture and cover. In order for the top-fermenting yeast to work properly, the wort should be allowed to stand in a warm location (68°–78° Fahrenheit). Fermentation will begin slowly because the tropane alkaloids will initially inhibit the yeast. The primary fermentation will last four to five days, after which the secondary fermentation will begin. The yeast will slowly settle and form a layer at the bottom of the vessel. The beer can now be siphoned into bottles. A small amount of priming sugar can be added to each bottle to promote an additional after-fermentation and

---

28. *Physica* III, 42.

carbonation. Henbane beer tastes best if it is stored in a cool location, such as a cellar, for two to three months before drinking.

[NB: For basic information on the proper equipment and procedures to be followed in brewing a beer recipe like the above, see a standard manual such as Charlie Papazian's *The Complete Joy of Homebrewing*.]

The (Nine) Doors of Perception: Ralph Metzner on the Sixties, Psychedelic Shamanism, and the Northern Tradition

Carl Abrahamsson and Joshua Buckley

By now it might almost be counted among the founding myths of Western popular culture: a buttoned-down Harvard psychologist named Timothy Leary takes magic mushrooms in the ancient Olmec city of Cuernavaca, flips his proverbial wig, and returns to the university to preach the psychedelic gospel. Leary would famously declare that he had learned more about human consciousness during his five-hour mushroom experience than "in the preceding fifteen years of studying and doing research in psychology." A term coined by Aldous Huxley and the English psychiatrist Humphrey Osmond, the word *psychedelic* is a compound of the Greek words *psyche* ("mind") and *delos* ("clear, visible") and thus, its etymological sense is that of "mind-revealing" or of something "manifesting in the mind." For a psychologist like Leary, who was determined to plumb the depths of human consciousness, what could be more appealing? Back at Harvard, Leary and Richard Alpert founded the Psilocybin Project and the Concord Prison Experiment (in which prisoners were dosed with psilocybin and taken on guided trips navigated by Leary and his associates). Alpert would also notoriously "turn on" one of his undergraduate students, explicitly defying the administration's directives. Ralph Metzner was an aspiring young scholar with an Oxford degree when he started working—and tripping—with Leary and Alpert, and he would eventually become a full-fledged colleague. He was there when the duo left Harvard (Alpert had been fired, thanks largely to the efforts of future holistic health guru Andrew Weil), and he would follow them from Zihuatanejo in Mexico to the fabled Millbrook estate in upstate New York. Leary himself ultimately landed in California, where the Jefferson Airplane and the Grateful Dead would show an entire generation what life could look (and sound) like through the psychedelic prism. The world would never be the same again.

It's almost a cliché to say that the sixties ended badly—that the neon dream of chemical utopias and permanently expanded consciousness lead instead to burnout, addiction, and the grisly media spectacle of the Tate-LaBianca murders. And it's also only partially true. While Leary may have been naïve about the darker aspects of the many-headed hydra he was unleashing, there can be no doubt that psychedelics opened up whole new vistas of possibility, allowing people to see beyond the narrow, workaday conformism of their parents. Just as Richard Alpert would travel to India and reinvent himself as Baba Ram Dass, millions of Americans would discover Zen Buddhism and Vedanta, begin practicing yoga, and start to explore long-forgotten European pagan traditions. Even excepting overtly psychedelic painters like Alex Grey, much of the genuinely engaging art and music produced over the last fifty years has had psychedelic roots. Rebel scientists like (the recently deceased) Alexander Shulgin continued their research on the outer fringes of the entheogenic frontier, while writers like Daniel Pinchbeck have mapped out their own experiences with alternate perceptual realities. Well-to-do doctors and lawyers now routinely pack themselves off to Peru on ayahuasca retreats, hoping for the kind of meaningful spiritual transformation that the churches have failed to deliver. These days, marijuana carries about as much social stigma as your grandfather's Manhattan, and it will undoubtedly be fully legalized over the next few decades.

Like many of his contemporaries in the first wave of serious psychedelic exploration, Ralph Metzner has continued his work with altered states of consciousness. Now a psychotherapist and Professor Emeritus of psychology at the California Institute of Integral Studies, Metzner has written numerous books and articles on MDMA, psilocybe mushrooms, and ayahuasca. As a physician, he utilizes the technical apparatus of both the Eastern and Western esoteric traditions in his psychotherapy practice, and his research has delved deeply into the I Ching, the Tarot, alchemy, and yoga. But Metzner—who was born in Germany and often gives lectures and workshops in German-speaking countries—also feels a powerful personal connection to the myths and traditions of the North. This should come as no surprise. As a healer, Metzner's role model is the shaman, who journeys to the realm of ancestral spirits in order to recover their wisdom. His spirit ally is the ultimate proto-shaman himself: Odin. Who better to accompany the true psychedelic wanderer into the outer reaches of inner space?

Metzner has documented his unique perspective on Germanic cosmology in *The Well of Remembrance: Rediscovering the Earth Wisdom Myths of Northern Europe* (Shambhala, 1994), which has just been republished in a sumptuous new German edition as *Der Brunnen der Erinnerung* (Arun Verlag). Moreover, Metzner recently took a retrospective look at his career (along with his old friend Baba Ram Dass) in *Birth of a Psychedelic Culture: Conversations about Leary, the Harvard Experiments, Millbrook and the Sixties* (Synergetic Press, 2010). The first part of the interview that follows was conducted by Carl Abrahamsson at the Swedish Museum of National Antiquities in Stockholm, and delves into this broader historical context, while the second half, conducted over the Internet by Joshua Buckley, deals specifically with Metzner's personal approach to Germanic myth. Those interested in Metzner's current projects are encouraged to contact the Green Earth Foundation: www.greenearthfound.org

(Introduction by Joshua Buckley)

Part I

When you talk about personal illuminations, regardless of how they're achieved, my experience is that once people have reached a state of illumination, most of them seem to want to retract to a normal state of mind and life in general. What was it that spurred you on or inspired you to move ahead and just keep going in your quest?

My interest in transformations of consciousness started when I was at Harvard, with Leary and Alpert. It has just continued from that time. At first, I thought psychedelics could be useful as an adjunct to something, like psychotherapy. But it quickly expanded beyond that. Leary felt that and I did too. The area of art and religion attracted us. It went quite a bit beyond psychotherapy as we saw it. We also saw challenges in how we should understand it. How should one understand a psychedelic experience? We didn't really get anywhere with Freud. At that time at Harvard there was only psychoanalysis and behaviorism. Neither had anything to say about altered states of consciousness at all. Jung had a bit more to say and he was more interested in Eastern mysticism. The question was "An expanded state of consciousness, and then what? What do we do with it?" I felt like tuning in to the shamanic tradition. The concept of "set and setting" became important. The intention was to find out what could be done; it was a very experimental attitude. I could see that tools for a spiritual path could be used or misused. Or perhaps used only recreationally. I'm not opposed to that, but it is a different thing.

My interest is in the knowledge and understanding that can be gained from expanded states of consciousness. States of consciousness can be contracted also, as they are in concentration. The expanded ones are more interesting for enhancing healing and creativity. How do you build them and turn them into a lasting condition? Say, if someone is depressed, they don't want to just be un-depressed for a little while. How can you hang on to a state of mind that's lasting and get to the bottom of

RALPH METZNER. PHOTO BY CARL ABRAHAMSSON.

personal problems, for instance? How to integrate such states? I wrote a book called *The Unfolding Self*, which I based on twelve classical metaphors that appear in different spiritual traditions over and over—processes of transformation, such as from a dark state to an enlightened state, the idea of death and rebirth, taking a shamanic journey, etc.—using myths, following the lead of C. G. Jung and Joseph Campbell in bringing out the psychological meanings of those myths. These are basic themes that exist everywhere. Life is like a journey of self-discovery, of aspiration, and the altered states are like a journey too. The shamans don't talk about altered states of consciousness; they say: "I'm going on a journey. The beat of the drum is my horse or my bird."

Quite often, they go for a purpose, say of healing. The intention of shamanic travel is usually healing and envisioning, not making predictions—that's a common misunderstanding—but rather divination. I call it shamanic divination or alchemical divination. I see alchemy and yoga as the Western and Eastern descendants of shamanism. They are symbolic technologies of transformation involving methods such as psychoactive plants and fungi, drumming and fasting, as well as spiritual understanding. The basic idea is healing on all levels, physical and emotional. Healing negative experiences from childhood. Envisioning or divination is looking ahead into the future. That's where I see that psychology can expand. Psychotherapy doesn't really acknowledge that one can predict, but every day people predict all the time. But envisioning isn't prediction, it's more like looking into probabilities and seeking guidance. It's not just curiosity. Almost all the indigenous people have an active interest in the future.

In most forms of divination, you're in your ordinary waking state and use divination tools like the runes, the I-Ching, or tarot cards. But the core process is a question-and-answer process. "How can I heal this painful thing? How will this or that turn out?" Back in the old days, people would go see a *Völva* [Germanic seeress] and ask for advice or vision, for answers. Those people had high standing and were active professionals. They would go into an altered state with their questions that would then serve as a key for where to look. "Will this battle turn out okay?" If the *Völva* wouldn't say yes, then the people backed off. It was accepted as a normal practice. It's just our general worldview now that says we can't possibly anticipate things like that. But we do it all the time.

In English, there are two words that are interesting in this regard. One is "forethought" and one is "foresight." But they're hardly used anymore. If you look up "divination" in a dictionary it's defined as "prediction of the future making use of supernatural means." Wait a minute! It's not supernatural and it's not about predicting either. It's about guidance. Should I do this or should I not do this? When the Native American Indians would go on a vision quest, it was all about their life. Big questions. What am I going to do with my life? They prayed, fasted, and perhaps were granted a vision. Or like with Black Elk, who had visions for his entire people. When you have a vision, you should not neglect it. You should express it, tell it, and make it real. If you don't, it can make you sick—or it's even worse, if you go against it.

Isn't that what essentially happened after the sixties? People thought it was a wonderful thing, but then they let it slide for the most part.

I don't really see it that way. I don't think the sixties faded away at all. We recently had a gathering in Sonoma in California where we asked the question, "Whatever happened to the sixties?" People were a bit amazed because we found out that the actual spirit was very much alive. What I think happened was that the states of consciousness that people got into triggered a cascading wave that changed the culture and the society. I'm not saying all those people took psychedelic drugs, but the general quality of the change of society was comparable to an expanded state of consciousness.

Six or seven social change movements started in the sixties. One was the environmental movement. Another one was the civil rights movement. People could understand that the environment was in danger and they could see Southern policemen

METZNER, LEARY, AND THE SWEDISH MODEL NENA AT THE TAJ MAHAL, 1964. PHOTO FROM "BIRTH OF A PSYCHEDELIC CULTURE," COURTESY OF SYNERGETIC PRESS.

beat up Black people. The Vietnam War was another important factor. People started asking questions in a new way, I think. Many of the hippies became organic farmers and applied their psychedelic experiences to environmentalism. When you expand consciousness you become aware of things you weren't aware of before. Also, when the women's liberation movement started, they called their meetings "consciousness raising." The sexual revolution was important, too. The Pill was invented and made contraception much easier. In all of those movements people were saying, "Let's not take for granted all of what we've been taught." A person who has taken LSD can never look at the world in the same way again. The old way of looking at the world is no longer working. Leary said "turn on, tune in, and drop out," but he was very much an Irish trickster. He didn't mind making people confused, so they would think for themselves. He himself didn't drop out and it wasn't his intention that everyone should. But he wanted people to think about it.

Why do you think that all of these movements coincided at the same time?

It's interesting, but I don't really know. Perhaps there are cosmic or planetary factors involved. I've been looking at cultural collective transformations and historical trends and I've certainly speculated about it. The hard work now is for people who inherited the expanded visions to try and integrate them, to make everything real. That's true of any kind of visionary process. If a young person gets a vision, they want to hang on to it. But later, they may need specific training and schooling to get there, to make it happen and to make it real. There were a series of cultural changes. I'm a student of Gurdjieff and interested in stages of development. I can see the end of the Second World War as especially interesting, with the making and exploding of the first atom bomb and the discovery of LSD basically happening at the same time. It's almost as if someone was saying: "Wait a minute, we have to give them something to change their minds..."

The minute fragmentation of the atom vis-à-vis a very big holistic worldview?

Einstein said that the atom bomb has changed everything except our way of thinking about the world. LSD may not change the world, but for those who take it, it definitely changes the way we think about the world. Anyway, something happened back then. The whole story of that is so fascinating in terms of synchronicity. (Albert) Hofmann had already synthesized LSD some five years before. And then he says that he "accidentally" absorbed some in 1943. Wait a minute. Here's a Swiss chemist—a guy like that wouldn't accidentally absorb anything! It's amazing that a chemical can affect your consciousness in such a way. He didn't really know about that then; he had no idea. He was a chemist, not a psychologist. He had his magical bicycle ride and started understanding. He realized the trip had taken him to the same place he'd been as a child, to his nature-mystical experiences as a child. He felt in touch with everything and realized there must be something in the substance that activated this. That was a major starting point.

Then in the fifties, Gordon Wasson researched the cultures of indigenous people and the mushroom cults. He wrote an article about it in *Life* magazine, which had something like five million readers. Ancient visionary mushrooms, with pictures of this mushroom woman handing this Wall Street banker some mushrooms—in *Life* magazine! Suddenly people became interested in these old cults and their practices with entheogens. In the sixties, our Harvard project was a bunch of people talking to psychologists, psychiatrists, doctors, and ministers about how we should handle LSD. At the same time, people like Ken Kesey were more artistic and hedonistic, and they were giving psychedelics to thousands of people at the same time, at concerts and gatherings. That shocked us. We were trying to keep everything clinical and controlled in a way, and these people were just going crazy.

At the time, did you feel that people like the Merry Pranksters were detracting from your scientific work?

No, not really. It was a phenomenon. What could we do? It just happened and we were all amazed. Later on, the professionals in the field blamed Leary for the fact that the government wouldn't allow LSD to be used clinically in research. But first of all, we weren't the people who were giving out LSD at these mass events. And secondly, I think Leary became a scapegoat for everyone. The government didn't want this kind of research anyway, so Leary's actions and comments were just perfect for them. But it wasn't Leary in himself that got the experiments banned.

In retrospect I don't think we failed with our experiments.

Psychedelic Sessions Poster. Image from "Birth of a Psychedelic Culture," courtesy of Synergetic Press.

On the contrary, I think we succeeded within what was possible. Our mission was never to make LSD legal; it was to get people to use it. We got people thinking about it and they're still thinking about it—and people are still taking it, too. And taking it seriously. They're being healed and they're having visions and they're getting a deeper understanding. Research is still going on, whether it's in the government labs or not. Whatever people want to do, they will continue to do. As soon as a substance is discovered, people will try to figure out what to do with it, whether it's legal or not.

It's interesting to note that the "war on drugs" and the "war on terrorism" use the same rhetoric. It doesn't have to do with drugs or terrorism, but rather with instilling fear. The war on drugs isn't working on people who are using drugs. They're obviously not afraid of drugs, plus of course they don't believe the government either. It's not addressed to them. The people who use drugs don't care. It's rather addressed to the people who don't know about drugs and who vote. Middle-class people who are afraid and suddenly want to make everything triple-illegal. The war on terrorism is the same thing. It's the government terrorizing the population with fear of "terrorists" so that they'll vote for more police and more control.

Don't you see changes happening in a good way too? In the UK, both ecstasy and marijuana were downgraded recently.

Sure, many European countries are moving in a much more sensible direction. They seem to accept that people want to take substances like that and instead focus on harm reduction and information. In America, more effort is put into draconian measures. A lot of good things are happening in the world, but people don't hear about them. The media are all part of the empire, they're just purveyors of the official lies. But even in America good things are happening.

One thing is that more people give birth at home and more people choose to die at home. They're taking both of those basic processes life back to themselves. It's not an illness to give birth; it doesn't deserve to be medically treated. People are also questioning the prolonging of vegetative states. What is the point? I think more and more people will try to take responsibility for their own health. People will say: "I don't care what you say. It's my life and I do what I want with it."

A lot of the problems we have today stem from the anthropocentric point of view. If we adopt a more holistic worldview, however, couldn't one say that essentially it is human beings that are the problem? One could even play Devil's Advocate, and ask whether or not the Earth would be better off if humanity ceased to exist altogether.

I think it's a false dichotomy. Earth First! was radical and said "no compromise in the defense of Mother Earth." The politically active people have to make compromises all the time, even in order to have access to politicians and legislators. It's a valid position not to want to make any compromises. It's a matter of making humans equal to the rest of nature, not putting humans down. I think a worldview transition is going on and it's being worked out in different areas. It has to do with systems of interconnectedness, but it's not a reversal of hierarchies for its own sake, like "Earth first and humans second." Everything is interrelated and interconnected in complex ways. You have to look at how the effects work out. You have to think systemically. I like the work of Thomas Berry and others who espouse a "systems view" of regarding the biosphere and respecting all its interconnected eco-systems. Everything is interconnected in visible and invisible ways, which you can study and learn to understand.

That's another great advantage of psychedelic use: you become aware of the notion that everything is interconnected.

Diversity on a biological level is protection against degradation. Cultural diversity, like biological diversity, is key to sustaining vital survival knowledge. Ecosystems must have diversity. On a higher level, too, the universe is extremely, unbelievably diverse. And theologically speaking, it's important. For us, it's been "one God, lawgiver, rule-maker." But we have a whole variety of deities of many different kinds and I think people are beginning to honor that more. Who are we to say that someone else's god is no good or doesn't exist?

On an individual level, it's like psychic multiplicity: each individual is a multiplicity of parts that are interconnected. It's also the same in a family, with different parts that are related and communicate and work together. Relations are not an optional add-on for an individual. It's logically impossible to be an individual without relations. Think about it: you cannot be a human being without a father and a mother—both are essential relations. All the other things we are, the roles we play—brother, sister, friend, boss, employee, writer, publisher, journalist—involve relations with others, whether with humans, animals, the environment, communities, and so forth.

At this point, would you say that you're more of a utopian or a dystopian?

I don't think I'm either, or perhaps I'm a little bit of both. There are so many levels to everything. I'm not saying that to be diplomatic, but what we need is an open-minded system. Things are far too bad and it's far too late to be pessimistic or passive. I go with the Buddha and support anything that brings more consciousness. You have to deal with real problems and also be attentive to illusions and self-deception. A starving child in Sudan may not need empathy as much as food. It's better to give food than teach him to meditate. But right now I'm sitting here trying to do what I can in this situation. There's no point in taking on a responsibility yourself for what is really a collective responsibility—whether of a family or a society.

I was born in Germany as a German national, and I went through a period where I felt personally responsible for the Holocaust, personally responsible for the murder of millions. Until I was able to expand my consciousness and realized that I couldn't go on feeling like that anymore. It doesn't help anyone. That doesn't mean I don't care. It's just a mistaken thinking. It doesn't mean I don't have compassion. Nothing human is strange to me. If I were born a Palestinian, I might have become a suicide bomber—what do I know? It's very much about how you grow up. Consciousness and life are two values that matter to me and that inform the way that I work and what I teach.

Speaking of that kind of Buddhist approach, you integrated the Buddhist Bardo concept early on at Harvard. How was that looked upon by the Buddhist community?

As far as I know, everything was okay. There's a great book called *Zig Zag Zen* that talks about that merging of psychedelics and Buddhism. Charles Tart, a psychologist, sent out a series of questions to Buddhist practitioners and teachers. Those who had psychedelic experiences talked about their experiences as spiritual beginnings. It gave them experiences of the possibilities of expanding consciousness that you're aiming for when you're doing meditation. The psychedelic experience tells you what's possible. It might even be a great motivation to be able to meditate for months or even years—an inspiration, even.

But isn't that overestimating the value of the psychedelic experience in a way? If you look at it through order structures and you have to go through years of work and initiations and training—can one experience really replace that? That criticism was there already in the sixties, the question of whether a chemical illumination can be spiritually valid.

I don't think that was the message, though—I think one should look at it as a preview, a vision. In the end, it can differ a lot from various kinds of spiritual experiences. In Zen, they're striving for a kind of ultimate simplicity. According to them, there's a danger in spiritual structures too that the ego might get in the way, that you look at developments as spiritual achievements. Tibetan Buddhism is more shamanic and very much a cultivation of the visionary experiences. I think psychedelics are tools and it's great if you can integrate them into your spiritual path. If you take them only for recreational purposes, it can be okay but it's not going to make any contributions to your spiritual path.

Do you know Mark McCloud in San Francisco, who curates his own LSD art museum, the Institute of Illegal Images? He mentioned to me that in a way he regretted all those initial trips before he took what he called "the big dipper," the one that really changed his way of thinking. But perhaps that wouldn't have happened unless he'd taken those first trips.

For me it was more the other way around. The impact of my first trip had long-term consequences. It's harder for me to resonate with people who take LSD now, because of the drug association. Back then, it was very much set and setting and an emotional and psychological experiment into the unknown. People nowadays usually see it as three letters and a trip that unfortunately becomes associated with some kind of stigmatized underworld. But people have always wanted to exchange states of consciousness and drugs have always been one way of doing that.

On my first trip, I listened to that Leary LP (*The Psychedelic Experience: A Manual Based on the Tibetan Book of the Dead*, Broadside Records, 1966), and there's a section where Leary's going "Ralph, Ralph, where are you Ralph. . ." Now I know: you're right here!

That's right. He's playing the role of the guide and I'm in the role of the voyager. . .

Part II

You seem to have adopted Marija Gimbutas's view of the Indo-Europeans as the villains of prehistory—bellicose, patriarchal land-grabbers who violently subjugated the settled, matriarchal cults of "Old Europe." Yet you emphasize the reconciliation between these tendencies in the myth of Kvasir. This seems to be an important component of mythology for you, the *coincidentia oppositorum*, the point at which these historical or metaphysical antagonisms are overcome.

In my book *Green Psychology*, in the chapter on "Sky Gods and Earth Deities," I wrote that "during the hundreds, even thousands of years of cultural interaction there was undoubtedly not only conquest, assimilation and superimposition of an alien religion, but also intermarriage of peoples, a blending and combining of religious and mythic images." Gimbutas's concept of *hybrid mythologies* provides a kind of corrective lens with which many previously obscure and incomprehensible features of European mythology can be understood. So I don't see the Indo-Europeans as the "villains of pre-history"—they were invaders who became settlers, and their social customs and belief systems over time were hybridized with that of the indigenous Europeans. And the descendants of those intermingling peoples are the multi-ethnic Anglo-Saxon cultures that dominate the Western world today and have spread around the globe—still obsessed with militarism and the quest for knowledge and power (which is not to deny or diminish their considerable achievements in science, technology, and the arts).

In that same chapter, I discuss three mythic themes that arose out of that millennia-long hybridization of cultures, not only in Nordic, but also in Greek and Irish mythology. One theme was *Myths Justifying Invasion and Domination:* The story of Gullveig, the golden sorceress, who belongs with the Vanir, is an example of this in the *Edda*. Gullveig supposedly "provokes" the Æsir into attacking her and the other Vanir. One of the earliest examples of a rape-justification story: "she must have been asking for it." The second theme I discuss is *Myths of Resistance and Retaliation:* the indigenous inhabitants and their gods fight back against the invaders and their gods, and tell their own stories. An example of this theme in Nordic mythology is the story of the Vanir rejecting the emissaries sent by the Æsir, by decapitating Mimir, one of the emissaries, and sending his head back. Speaking to this mythic metaphor, I wrote "the decapitation of Mimir, the memory holder, can be seen as a metaphor for the forgetting of evolutionary wisdom, consequent upon disrespect for the old nature divinities." The third mythic theme is *Myths of Compromise and Reconciliation,* of which the story of the Eleusinian Mysteries is an outstanding example, and also the story of the generation of the wise and kind Kvasir, and his subsequent metamorphosis into a drink that inspires creativity.

Your personal embrace of Odin in his role as psychopomp seems like a natural one, considering your lifelong work with altered and expanded states of consciousness. But isn't Odin also a figure known for treachery and double-dealing? While your own work focuses on the potential for healing inherent in consciousness expansion, do you think the Odin archetype can express the fact that these experiences can

also be fraught with danger?

The deity Odin/Wodan in Nordic/Germanic myth has three roles: he is the god of the warriors, especially the dedicated *berserkers*, who were fanatically devoted to their liege lords and believed they would ascend to Valhalla after dying in battle; he is also the guiding spirit of the knowledge-seeking magicians, who knew how to read the runes, the secret language of Nature; and he was the god of the poets, the skalds, who were also the storytellers. In *The Well of Remembrance*, I say that I'm not at all related to Odin as warrior, but I've received inspiration from that archetype-spirit in the other two areas. As for his dualism, yes, he has good sides and not-so-good sides—like all deities, male and female, in other ancient mythologies, and for that matter, like all human beings in actuality, ancient and modern. The polytheistic, shamanistic worldview of ancient civilizations and indigenous people worldwide accommodates a large diversity of types of beings at various levels of evolutionary development. It is only in the monotheistic religions that there tends to develop an obsessive concern with good and evil, judgment, sin, and the like. Because you have this huge dilemma of a supposedly all-powerful and all-knowing God, who permits terrible evil to occur in the world.

The "Well of Remembrance" you describe in your book sounds very much like Jung's collective unconscious. One controversial element of Jung's system is the extent to which this could also be seen as a racial unconscious. I find the idea that one would resonate more with the myths and archetypes of one's own ancestors relatively unproblematic. Yet it certainly contradicts the liberal, Rousseauian view of human nature, the idea that each of us enters the world as a blank slate.

The "collective unconscious" is an abstract concept, whereas the "well of memory" is a mytho-poetic image—other than that, yes, there is some overlap of meaning. Pre-literate cultures in general,

The (Nine) Doors of Perception

RAM DASS AND RALPH METZNER, CALIFORNIA INSTITUTE OF INTEGRAL STUDIES, 1989. PHOTO FROM "BIRTH OF A PSYCHEDELIC CULTURE," COURTESY OF SYNERGETIC PRESS.

dependent on oral tradition for the transmission of knowledge, rely more on images and symbols rather than abstractions. That said, the Jungian concept of a personal and a collective unconscious was developed further by later Jungian writers to include an intermediate layer of "cultural unconscious"—those images and stories we share with all members of our religious or cultural group, and the collective unconscious being those shared with all humans. In *Green Psychology*, I suggest that the pan-human, cross-cultural collective unconscious is the human species level of (un)consciousness; and beyond that there are layers of (un)consciousness shared with all animals, with all living beings and Earth herself, and with the universe beyond ("cosmic consciousness").

As to whether we have preferential access, so to speak, to the collective memory of our own genetic (racial) ancestors—the evidence doesn't seem to support it. I got started on research and writing *The Well of Remembrance* by a vivid dream of communicating with one of the gigantic stone heads of the ancient Olmec culture found in Mexico—yet I have absolutely no genetic connection with Meso-American people, don't even speak Spanish, and at the time had no knowledge or even interest in the pre-Hispanic cultures. Another example: a North American man living in California, took ayahuasca, the South American visionary vine medicine, and had a vision of an Egyptian lion-headed goddess and her rituals—which he had no prior knowledge of, and only later was able to confirm the name and other details. So, it appears that through the well of remembrance we can access evolutionary memories and also soul memories of other human lifetimes.

The recent work of scholars like Andrei Znamenski has questioned whether the concept of shamanism is meaningful in and of itself, or whether it has served more as a vehicle for Westerners to project their own fantasies and spiritual aspirations onto more traditional, non-Western societies. Part of what you find attractive about ancient Germanic culture is its shamanistic aspects, especially to the extent that they might help modern Europeans meaningfully reconnect with nature. Do you see pagan Germanic or Celtic cultures as fundamentally shamanic? What does shamanism mean for you?

I got interested in Germanic mythology after becoming acquainted in an experiential way with shamanic practices of otherworld journeys through the work of Michael Harner. Like other observers who have gone beyond a purely academic, scholarly approach, I found the imagery of shamanic journeys throughout Germanic (and other ancient mythologies). In fact, even at the time of writing *The Well of Remembrance*, I did not fully appreciate the extent to which the unknown poets of the Eddas put coded references to shamanic divination practices into their writings. For example, there are three divinatory memory practices implicit in lines referring to Mimir's well (in addition to the fact that *Mimir* means "memory"): one is to drink from the well; another is to look into the well, analogous to looking into a crystal ball; and a third is to immerse oneself completely in the well—becoming completely absorbed in the experience.

How have you integrated your work with Germanic and other European mythology into your therapeutic practice? How do you feel about more direct attempts to revive these mythologies, as in reconstructionist pagan groups?

I use the term *divination* to include therapy and healing, which are always concerned with the past for diagnosis and causes; and also to include visioning and guidance-seeking, which are concerned with probable and possible futures. So I include the three practices associated with the Well, mentioned above, in my work with individuals and groups—particularly when delving into the depths of memory. I also work with the imagery of the World Tree—each individual has a tree which is symbolic of the development of that individual life from seed to fully grown. I describe this imagery in a chapter in my book *The Unfolding Self*, and use it as a divination guide for people to explore their history and potentials, and do drawings that represent their individuation process.

I don't have much to do with the various neopagan movements that reconstruct some of the culture-specific rituals and symbols, though I don't have anything against it. I do invoke spirits of nature—animals, plants, minerals, the four directions—as well as ancestral and other guiding spirits and deities, prior to ceremonies, as is done in shamanic journey work in all cultures—with each individual practitioner developing relationships with spirits with which they have an affinity.

In Norbert Mayer's essay that appears in *The Well of Remembrance*, he makes reference (p. 145) to a so-called Academy of New Berserkers, which Christian Rätsch and presumably yourself have also participated in. Would you care to say anything more about this group, its activities, and any insights these meetings may have facilitated?

This Academy of New Berserkers was founded in Munich, Germany by Norbert Mayer and friends. I was elected an *Ehrenmitglied* (honorary member) but have not participated in any of their gatherings, due to geographical distance.

Along with your writings and workshops that are rooted in aspects of Germanic mythology and *The Well of Remembrance*, you have also worked extensively with the symbolism and psycho-spiritual templates that can be seen as underlying the alchemical process. Do these two areas overlap, and if so, in what ways? Carl Jung also wrote extensively on alchemy—has his work been influential on your own in this regard?

I've written a lot about alchemy: in my 1998 book *The Unfolding Self*, I quote from alchemical philosophers and compare their descriptions of alchemical processes with the descriptions by contemporary people of their psychedelic visions. Jung and his followers have done the same comparison of alchemical texts with dreams, which led Jung to conclude that alchemical symbolism provided the objective language of the psyche that he was looking for. He saw it as a counterpart to the objective language of science, which ignored the psychic and spiritual aspects of human beings completely and focused exclusively on the material. In Part I of my 2008 book *The Expansion of Consciousness*, I give a very brief history of alchemy—pointing out how C. G. Jung was responsible for rehabilitating the reputation of alchemy in psychology and philosophy, and how another Swiss, chemist Albert Hofmann, with his discovery and correct recognition of LSD, identified the missing link between spirit and matter known as "the philosophers' stone."

I've come to see shamanism, alchemy, and yoga as the three main traditional teachings and practices of transformation, at every level—physical, emotional, mental, and spiritual. Shamanism is the oldest, dating back to paleolithic times, with yoga and alchemy being the Eastern and Western extensions and developments of those teachings. In my teaching and therapy work, as described in the 2009 book *Alchemical Divination*, I use elements from all three traditions.

One thing I find especially interesting in your book is that you take the *Völuspá* seriously as a series of prophecies. The Ragnarök anticipates large-scale ecological disasters, followed by the rebirth of a "new, green Earth." This seems to take us full-circle, back to the world of Gimbutas's Old Europe. Can you expand on this?

One of the interesting things about prophetic visions like those of the *Völuspá* is that they are non-specific as to the exact timing. They describe events, not dates. This is true of dreams as well—we may dream a scene from the future as well as the past, and won't necessarily know until the time comes. Some of the scenes in the *Völuspá* could apply to the environmental devastation wreaked by modern technology since the industrial revolution, and certainly to the disastrous world wars of the twentieth century. The wars and environmental catastrophes of the present time can be seen as even further manifestations of those visions of world destruction. In the Ragnarök, the gods named as surviving are Baldur and Hödur, sons of Odin and of Thor, both Æsir. We don't really know what happened with the main Vanir deities, Freyr and Freyja, in the Ragnarök—except we know Freyr couldn't fight because he'd given up his sword to woo the giantess he wanted to marry. He wanted to "make love, not war."

The Ragnarök tells of a struggle of gods and men against monstrous natural catastrophes (floods, fires, earthquakes, volcanic eruption, and the like) in which many gods and humans are defeated—and eventually "a new green Earth arises." A new generation of gods and humans starts the process of civilization all over again. That kind of almost total civilizational catastrophe has happened before—as born witness by the legends of Atlantis—and may yet happen again. And the Earth will certainly endure and regenerate itself, in time. What human populations and cultures will survive and how many—remains to be seen.

BLUTLEUCHTE

by **Gerhard Hallstatt**
Foreword *by* Joscelyn Godwyn

A compendium of all AORTA and AHNSTERN booklets dating from 1.994-1.999:

LUCIFER RISING | KONNERSREUTH | NIGHT OF THE STIGMATA
ANUBIS | SCHWARZKOGLER | KARL MARIA WILIGUT | KATHARSIS
CASTEL DEL MONTE | CORNELIU CODREANU | THE BLUE LIGHT
MONTSÉGUR | Z'EV | STORM SONGS | BLUTLEUCHTE | LEONORA
ANGIZIA | FIDUS | MITHRAS | BLOOD AXIS | OSKOREI
VIKTOR SCHAUBERGER | LUCIFER RISING II | BAPTISM OF FIRE
HIDDEN WORLD | HEIDNAT | BROWN MAGIC
FIELD OF FORCE | FEATHERED DREAMS | ANDREAS EPP

324-page hardbound book with 2-color print and 16-page photo section. $40 ppd US/$50 ppd World.

WWW.AJNABOUND.COM   AJNA   POBOX 1523, JVILLE, OR. 97530

Finding the Lost Voice of our Germanic Ancestors: An Interview with Benjamin Bagby

Joshua Buckley

"Early Music" is usually defined as music originating prior to the end of the Baroque period in 1750. As most compositions written before the eighteenth century were under-prescriptive, one of the central issues for early music performers is the open-ended nature of historical interpretation. For performers of medieval music, or music written earlier than 1300, the problem is even thornier. As Benjamin Bagby has written: "We sometimes may know how this music was performed, but we will never know how it sounded." This is why the quality and style of early music (and especially medieval music) can vary so dramatically. Performances tend to oscillate between dry academicism (many early music performers are more qualified as professors than musicians), and what Bagby calls "drums and fun" (think: Renaissance Fairs, the Society for Creative Anachronism, and pointy shoes). While Bagby has lamented the fact that medieval music has yet to embrace the kind of rigorous discipline one finds in other genres, his own work has been a remarkable exception. Since forming the medieval music ensemble Sequentia with the late Barbara Thornton in 1977, Bagby has continued to develop as a researcher and scholar, a teacher, and performer. He has thoughtfully dissected and carefully reassembled the concept of historically informed performance. And perhaps most importantly, his ability to balance scholarship with passionate personal engagement has earned Sequentia its reputation as the most famous medieval music group in the world.

Among the many projects that fill out Sequentia's sprawling discography, the group has performed some of the earliest songs ever written in the English language (*English Songs of the Middle Ages*, 1988), explored early Spanish music (on the *Vox Iberica* trilogy, 1992), and recorded a sampling of monophonic narrative songs by the Tyrolean poet Oswald von Wolkenstein. Perhaps Sequentia's most well known project, however, has been the ensemble's ambitious attempt to record the complete works of Hildegard von Bingen. Fortuitously or not, this coincided with a more general revival of interest in Hildegard, at least among the (semi-)educated public. Whether New Agers intrigued by the mystical abbess's holistic approach to healing and herbalism, or feminists looking for a medieval female voice, this surge of enthusiasm transformed Sequentia's 1994 album *Canticles of Ecstasy* into a most unlikely pop-culture phenomenon. Among other honors, the album sold over a million copies, and captured a Grammy nomination for best choral recording. Yet another outlet for Bagby's scholarly and artistic pursuits since the mid-1980s has been the "Lost Songs" project. Enlisting the support of philologists and other academics to navigate the obscure and often opaque manuscripts that comprise their sources, Sequentia has explored texts like the Old Saxon *Heliand* and the Old High German *Muspilli*. For 1999's *Edda: Myths from Medieval Iceland*, Bagby spent his research residencies in Iceland poring over archival recordings of traditional Icelandic *rímur* singers, as well as studying the complicated metrics used to compose the *Edda* with the philologist Heimir Pálsson. The purpose of this painstaking research: to construct a "modal language" (a concoction Bagby has likened to a "modal mead") with which to bring the poetry back to life. This attempt to balance creativity and authenticity extends to Bagby's instrumentation as well. For the *Edda* performances Sequentia utilized a harp modeled after an original found in a seventh-century Allemanic gravesite, as well as a small, swan-bone flute. The latest incarnation of the Lost Songs series will see Bagby and crew tackling the songs and canticles of the Carolingian Empire, in a project tantalizingly titled "Frankish Phantoms."

But with the exception of Sequentia's Hildegard recordings (whose popularity Bagby still views with some ambivalence), it is Bagby's monumental Beowulf performances that have done the most to cement his wide critical acclaim. The San Francisco Chronicle wrote of a recent performance: "Bagby's imaginative re-creation of the Anglo-Saxon epic poem . . . is a double tour-de-force of scholarly excavation and artistic dynamism." Inspired by a meeting with the Anglo-Saxonist Thomas Cable (author of *The Meter and Melody of Beowulf*), Bagby began performing selections from Beowulf as part of his work with Sequentia in the mid-1980s. With the untimely passing of Barbara Thornton in 1998, Bagby's focus on the project intensified. Guided by theories of oral epic gleaned from scholars like Milman Parry and Albert B. Lord, Bagby has now memorized 1062 lines of the poem, relying primarily on his own musical accompaniment as a mnemonic device. For Bagby, this attempt to recapture the mindset of an Anglo-Saxon *scop* has been a welcome antidote to the conventions of conservatory tradition. A 2007 *Beowulf* DVD release (filmed by the Swedish director Stellan Olsson) attests to his ability to captivate everyone from high school students to the most jaded of New York theater goers.

So why, dear reader, is all of this so important?

Bagby himself has provided us with an insight into his own artistic motivations, as well as the historical context for his music in the essay "Searching for the Lost Voice of My Germanic Ancestors (or, Is it still possible for us to enjoy ancient songs about Sigurd the Dragon-Slayer, Brynhild the Valkyrie, and Attila the Hun?)." "There is one thing we must never forget," Bagby writes, "During this entire period, all of these people—in their huts, their fields, their boats, on horseback, around their cooking fires, their pagan shrines, and even in their Christian monasteries—were singing, listening to song, myth, instrumental music, and long sung tales of their ancestors' deeds, real and imagined." Thanks to the vision and dedication of Benjamin Bagby and Sequentia, we, too, can savor the depths and texture of this resonant and inspiring musical heritage.

Beowulf performance in December, 2011 at the Hochschule für Musik, Basel, Switzerland. Photo by Susanna Drescher.

Tell us about your formative years as a musician. I read somewhere that you were first exposed to medieval music when you were sixteen, and formed an ensemble with other students around the same time. What do you think it was in your own personal and musical background that made you receptive to this kind of music?

I had a perfectly normal musical upbringing for the circumstances of my childhood and my environment, with classical music always considered an important part of education. At home there was also a lot of jazz being listened to, and in fact my older brother was a professional jazz musician. My schools were extremely arts-friendly, the level of music performance was unusually high, and I participated in very fine vocal ensembles, musical stage productions (as well as non-musical stage drama) and instruction in music theory and history. I spent all of my time in the high school music building, practicing, studying and devouring scores with like-minded nerds. My summers were spent studying and listening to music, both classical and contemporary. While visiting a summer music academy when I was sixteen, I heard, quite by chance, a concert of medieval music given by the New York Pro Musica, and it utterly transfixed me. I have no idea why it did so—but there was the raw adolescent nerve and there was the music which struck it. Something clicked. It started a long process of searching and enjoyment which has never ceased. Back at school, I immediately started my first ensemble, rounding up some fellow high-school students and plunging in headlong with absolutely no idea of what we were doing—kind of an early music garage band—learning everything the hard way. I'm basically still doing that today.

Later, as a voice major at Oberlin Conservatory I was called upon to jump through all the usual hoops of classical vocal study, but my interest in early music, especially medieval music, continued to grow. By my third year I was already working for one semester as an assistant for the New York Pro Musica, and during my last year at school, and also in the summer, I was singing with that ensemble on a professional basis. Immediately following graduation (with both a music degree and a degree in German), I left for Europe on a Charles Watson Foundation Fellowship year, the stated purpose of which was to study the state of medieval song performance in Europe, and to learn about related song types in the Middle East. This blissful *Wanderjahr* led me all over the map, with one important stop at a summer course given in Istria (now Croatia) by the German singer Andrea von Ramm, where I hoped to study troubadour song performance. There, I entered a new world and met a number of people who were to remain friends for a long time. And that's where I also met Barbara Thornton. Although I frequently visit North America for concerts and teaching, I have lived in Europe since that time.

What was the state of medieval music when you and Barbara Thornton formed Sequentia in 1977, and how has it changed since then?

There was actually a lot going on in the 1970s; in fact, sometimes I have the feeling that there is a much less of a dynamic, energized feeling today surrounding medieval music performance than back then, when absolutely everything was new and being discovered seemingly for the first time. The early music scene was certainly exciting (it was, after all, the 1970s), but then I was young and easily impressed, and in fact when I listen now to the recordings from those days which I admired, I realize that the standards of musical perfection were laughable as compared with today's. So probably I'm perceiving the past in a golden haze which actually did not exist at that time—and I do remember feeling impatient, dissatisfied, and wanting to change the world. Well, who hasn't been twenty-three and felt like that? The point I want to make is that the feeling in those times was one of immense freedom and limitless possibility.

Our first real mentors in this field were Thomas Binkley and Andrea von Ramm (*Studio der frühen Musik*), who taught in Basel at the Schola Cantorum Basiliensis. The Schola had started a medieval music diploma program in the early 1970s, unique in the world, which attracted a large number of foreign students interested in the work of the Studio, a highly successful ensemble which had relocated to Basel from Munich. Their recordings in the late 1960s and early 1970s caused an enormous stir, and they were far ahead of other ensembles in the dynamic, coherent, and intellectual way they presented medieval music in performance. Once at the Schola Cantorum as professors, they began incorporating their students into their recordings on the EMI/Reflexe and Telefunken "Das alte Werk" labels, and this was a powerful stimulation for motivated young performers. As teachers they were always demanding, fascinating, hypercritical, and often merciless and cynical (think *House*), truly not creatures from academia but from the real world of performance, and this was appealing to young and ambitious students. Although they could also be fun and inspiring, they were often chaotic, and sometimes arrogant, difficult, and contradictory, which made studying with them an education in diplomacy, survival, and patience. Sometimes they taught by negative example, and sometimes they taught by showing us how to teach ourselves. We were lucky to have not only the immense resources of the libraries in Basel at our disposal (in pre-Internet days, this was essential), but to have other expert Schola teachers in medieval notation, history, counterpoint, and instruments, and to find ourselves in a group with other students who were equally motivated and curious.

Today, there are several layers of performance orthodoxy in place which did not exist then, and so we felt uninhibited to experiment, which we freely did. The audience for medieval music was younger, less experienced but more passionate, and actually larger than it is today. On the negative side: we performers had great difficulty accessing sources—in spite of the fabulous musicological libraries in Basel, the old microfilms were not always easy to read, and it might take weeks to locate and see one manuscript which one can find online in twenty seconds today. When we weren't rehearsing, we were camped out in the library.

You seem ambivalent about how the conventions of classical chamber music and the conservatory have shaped how medieval music is performed and taught, and how different

this must be from when the music was part of a living tradition. This seems to be a real source of creative tension in your work.

The main modern convention which is contrary to something we might call a "medieval way" is the slavish veneration we have for written sources, for the primacy of "the score." Medieval musicians generally lived in a series of interlocking oral traditions and had memory skills which we can hardly imagine. The cult of the genius composer was in its infancy in the fourteenth century, and most medieval musical works were created—and later written down—anonymously. But this is only one aspect of how we study music today, especially music of the past.

Although the last forty years have witnessed an expansion of the number of music schools which teach early music performance, the spectrum of repertoires and styles in music before, say, Beethoven, is simply too large to offer instruction in all types and genres of historical music. Early music, once thought to be a limited body of uninspiring works (which a music-history professor of mine once referred to collectively as "pre-music"), is in fact an overwhelmingly varied complex of repertoires. And the traditional classical music conservatory is inevitably evolving into the role of "specialist" school (offering instruction in a period of music which encompasses roughly 250 years), whereas an early music program must contend with at least a thousand years of documented musical creation. The trend is clear: along with jazz, world music, and electronic music, most professional music schools today offer a course of study in something called early music, which in most cases means an intensive course in Baroque music performance. But in the environment of early music study, the medieval period—and for that matter, the Renaissance—is still largely neglected.

Orality in musical transmission can be a fertile ground for creative tension, but this is not what music schools are generally interested in pursuing in the training of young musicians. The basic course of study in all early music schools remains focused on the traditional model for performers: the technical mastery of an instrument or voice, the learning of the canon of pieces most performed, the acquisition of a sense of appropriate style and ornamentation, the chance to work in ensembles with expert coaches, advanced master classes with famous performers, and finally, competitions. We can hardly expect students of Baroque music to be interested in a world where music was transmitted orally, where rhetoric and ancient languages are as important as music, where improvisational skills are valued more than sight-reading. It's messy, time-consuming, and difficult to evaluate with traditional exams and juries.

A dedicated school for medieval music would need to approach this type of study very differently. I have always dreamed of starting a school which pursues these essential aspects of musical study, but it remains a dream and I am the first to admit that there is simply not a critical mass of students—especially paying students—who would be interested, nor is there solid employment waiting for such students when they finish their diplomas. Without a doubt, the big energy field now in early music performance is the Baroque—and for singers, especially, Baroque opera—where there is a solid career to be built and a decent living to be earned. We lack enough passionately interested and gifted candidates for serious, full-time institutional programs in medieval music performance, and this situation guarantees that the general level of performance skill will continue to remain generally low. Expectations remain correspondingly low, and as a result medieval music performance does not enjoy the competitive ascending spiral of excellence which the Baroque music scene has so brilliantly created. Luckily, there are some wonderful exceptions to this state of affairs, but they remain exceptions.

Can you speak a little bit about the idea of "historically informed performance?" Obviously, this seems to be the main problem for anyone dealing with early music to unravel.

The idea of *HIP* was developed about a generation ago when we all realized how mortified and neurotic we felt to be talking about "authenticity." That self-satisfied word is long-since taboo (and yet I continue to use it liberally in a completely different sense: the authenticity of musical communication). There is a general consensus that we simply cannot know "how music sounded then" or "what the composer intended" and these ceased to be criteria in our performances as long as we remained "informed." We know a lot about how music was performed, but until a time machine is invented we'll never know how it sounded. It's like any difficult relationship: we agree to cohabit with the past and not give in to despair about those "truths" we cannot know, and in return we enthusiastically pretend to represent that past to our listeners. After a while, as performance conventions settle in and are accepted, the whole awkward mess starts to feel like a cozy world of oral tradition which we can inhabit in good faith and which seems good, sounds good, and therefore must be valid. The younger generations of early-music performers are much more relaxed and cool about these things. But this is a long and complex story—read Richard Taruskin's essays from the 1990s and you will see how this idea was once densely and passionately argued.

Were you surprised when *Canticles of Ecstasy* achieved the kind of popularity that it did? There seemed to be a huge crossover audience, especially from New Age listeners who might not ordinarily be exposed to such serious material. What do you think was going on there, and were you aware at the time of the burgeoning popular interest in Hildegard of Bingen as a visionary spiritual figure?

Yes, we were surprised, but not entirely delighted. Putting this phenomenon in context, we should recall that at roughly the same time (circa 1993) a rather bland Gregorian chant recording of the Benedictine monks of St. Domingo de Silos, repackaged and aggressively marketed as *CHANT*, was hugely popular. This runaway bestseller CD was sold largely to young people who had neither an interest in nor any knowledge of Gregorian chant or medieval music, but were charmed by the calming effect of this dreamy, "spiritual" mode of performance as they sought to "chill" after too much techno music and too much ecstasy (the drug). The image of the chanting monk in his hooded habit became in and of itself an image of mystery and coolness, and with clever marketing the record labels brought out more and more of such "product" until the bubble burst. During that period of several years, every record label reissued whatever old or new chant recordings they could get their hands on and gave them a new look (usually monks in hoods) and title (something with the word CHANT). We were also victims of this phenomenon: one of our recordings was re-issued with a new look, without our knowledge, under the new title *Chill to the Chant*. In the eyes of the serious music world, we were sometimes considered sell-outs, as if this had been our greedy plan all along.

Our Hildegard recording, which was actually a serious musical effort unrelated to this phenomenon, fell into the turbulent *CHANT* maelstrom by default and was cleverly exploited by our record company at the time, BMG Classics. It was a golden disc in France, and I was recently told it sold more than 1.5 million copies worldwide. Of course some of the interest was genuine and centered around Hildegard as a composer and historical figure, but more often we were criticized by the Hildegard purists and even the press for having participated in the gross commercial feeding frenzy around *CHANT*. There were also pop and world-music versions of Hildegard's works on the market, and our work was sometimes lumped together with them—all very painful at the time. The positive aspect of all this was that the record label, which made a lot of money and was in an optimistic mood, signed a multi-CD contract with Sequentia which allowed us to embark on the project to record Hildegard's complete works, a project which will be finished in 2013 (long after that contract had lapsed). The real interest in Hildegard reached its climax in 1998, the 900th anniversary of her birth, but there were so many releases of her music in that year alone that the market was saturated and nothing much has happened since.

The entertainment industry functions most efficiently in the exploitation of such huge bubbles of youth-oriented marketing, whether those bubbles are filled with heart-warming fantasy worlds, adorable wizards, sexy young vampires, soft-core pornography, or hooded monks chanting in the monastery.

Now I want to talk mainly about the "Lost Songs" project, as this is of particular interest to our readers. The scope of the project is really impressive—it seems to be an outlet not just for you as a performer, but for your work as a scholar as well. You have also involved specialists from a number of other fields to help in piecing these productions together. From a personal standpoint, how do you assess whether you've "succeeded" with realizing your vision in a project like this?

I feel I have succeeded every time we give a performance and the listeners can make the connection that these undeniably ancient songs are a deep and visceral part of their own cultural identity and not merely "historical entertainment" or "charming old songs." These texts—and hopefully their performances—can provide us with small portals through which we perceive the very people our ancestors were and which we are still capable of understanding. The connection is palpable: listeners are often surprised by the immediacy and honesty of medieval texts, set to music in songs which were created without a success agenda. The oldest texts are still with us for a good reason: they mark us and inhabit the deepest zones of the archaic and sometimes dark world which children instinctively know. If my project can help to being these scattered and fragmentary lost songs and their images back to life for ninety minutes or so, inhabited by the human voice and performed in front of an actual physical audience which is truly and actively listening, then my vision has been realized and it is a thrilling success. But my ambitions are tempered by the knowledge that today's larger cultural world has different values, a short attention span, and favors performances which are fun, bright, short, accessible, harmless and even a bit ironic. So I have learned to measure and enjoy our successes in very small quantities. I always preferred the little treehouse I built myself to a visit to Disneyland.

With *Beowulf*, you have said that you were trying to put your vocal performance in the service of the storytelling, which goes against your conservatory training and the idea that vocal usage should be standardized. How has that approach developed over the last fifteen years?

Perhaps I'm not the one to judge my own development, but I feel as if I have gained a huge amount of freedom in the way I use my voice in that language (Old English), and I also feel I am able to do more with less. Maybe this is just the illusion which comes with advancing age: that is, older singers finally feel they "know" how to sing but can no longer "do" it. My approach was formed when I was in my thirties and I have been working on it ever since—it's an ongoing story. I will increasingly have to develop strategies for remaining vocally viable as I get older and try to delay the ultimate victory of gravity over everything. And hopefully I will know when the time has come to stop.

In *Orality and Literacy*, Walter Ong wrote about the shift from oral culture to literate culture, and the changes this would have effected in people's consciousness. Is this something you have thought about in terms of your own experiences working with oral epic, and particularly in the incredible undertaking of memorizing *Beowulf*? This is something most of us moderns have completely lost the capacity for. Is a deliberate attempt to regain such skills of memory something inherently worthwhile?

The memorization of *Beowulf* was indeed a huge effort and I'm sure an Anglo-Saxon *scop*, were he to observe me, would laugh himself silly at how hard I had to work for something so gloriously simple and easy. But the act of memorizing Beowulf was already a big mistake on my part: instead I should have learned to speak/sing Old English so perfectly, and mastered the art of extemporaneous alliterative poetry so completely, that I could "re-tell" the Beowulf story in my own words at every performance, sticking mostly to the known formulae but also adding my own ideas and elaborations, changing things to fit the mood of the audience or my own mood, perhaps even changing the story. *THAT* would be a totally honest performance in the style of the *scops*. What I'm doing is still not much better than a very carefully studied formal re-enactment. Perhaps the next generation of modern *scops* will take the art of this kind of performance to the next level. The tiny oral tradition which is me will probably die with me—I have no apprentices, nor would I expect any talented young person in today's world to be so foolish as to attempt such a thing.

Listening to your *Beowulf* performance in a modern concert hall is clearly a very different setting than the one in which a traditional storyteller might have originally performed the piece, both for you and for the audience. Do you think this is a disadvantage? In a perfect world, how would you want an audience to experience the text?

One of the hard realities of early music is that we can approximate the historical performance but we cannot begin to approximate its audience. In a perfect world, I would perform *Beowulf* for a small gathering of people who are also able to move around quietly, get a drink, or dream a bit. But they would also know the text, intimately, in advance of the performance, in the same way a child knows the bedtime story you are about to read for the fiftieth time. The story itself is known, but the telling of it—again and again—is essential to the listeners and connects them to their first experiences of hearing it. We tend to forget that night was utterly dark in pre-industrial Europe, and extremely long in the winter, especially in the North. People did not live with the amount of bright light, noise, and distraction that we consider normal (a medieval intellectual, visiting any of us today and observing our daily lives and the machines which surround us, would have no doubt that we are all living in hell).

A story lasting four to five hours (such as *Beowulf*) would be a comforting entertainment for the listener, and would not be measured in units of time. In such a storytelling environment, life slows down, the mind wanders, and the story's images become almost real (alcoholic beverages can help here); the *scop's* gift was to make use of this intimate surrounding to weave a magic spell with the others in the same space. Storytelling was essential for identity and survival. A tribe without a *scop* and his stories was a tribe without memory, without heritage, without history, and therefore without respect. Each retelling of an old story reinforced what Doris Lessing famously called *SOWF* (= Sense of We Feeling). No matter where I perform today I can't hope to play that original role, but in performing I hope to conjure it for a few moments. It's a brief glimpse of what we have lost in becoming who we are today.

I used to fantasize that some enlightened concert presenter would build a small Anglo-Saxon mead hall where epics and other intimate repertoires could be performed, but then I realized that by the time such a hall would be in compliance with today's fire rules, access codes, signage and proper lighting for emergencies, smoke alarms, etc., the whole place would have been turned into something else, basically a modern hall wearing a fake medieval costume. Frankly, I would now prefer a neutral space where people could listen in comfort, without distraction, and don't feel self-conscious. I don't wear a costume, so why should I put one on my performance space?

However, I feel strongly that cinema could create the most genuine experience of epic poetry in performance. I have long thought about that, and was deeply inspired by the example of Im Kwon-taek's film *Chunhyang* (2000), which brilliantly combines Korean Pansori epic performance with cinematic storytelling techniques. But there is probably no producer in the world who would accept to go there, especially not after the dismal series of *Beowulf* films we've been subjected to in the past years. It's probably a good thing that my *Beowulf* performance remains relatively far beneath the general cultural radar.

Can you talk a little bit about the technique of "modal language" you've utilized in setting epic sources like the Eddas and *Beowulf* to music?

This is something which I cannot describe effectively in writing and it would require a long, hands-on workshop to explain. Basically stated, my work involves absorbing a large amount of musical material and distilling its modal essence into recognizable modal units, and then using these units, like components of a tiny language, to tell stories, forming the larger shapes on pre-existing medieval metrical forms and structures. The process is, by definition, highly intuitive and personal. Another musician might try the same process with the same material and come up with very different results from mine.

For the *Edda* project, you worked extensively in Iceland studying *rímur* in the Árni Magnússon Institute. How were you able to adapt certain structural elements of that tradition to your own reconstructions? Have you had any contact with, or exposure to, the modern exponents of the *rímur* tradition such as Steindor Andersen and the Kvæðamannafélagið Iðunn (the Iðunn Society of traditional *rímur* singers)?

The structural and modal elements of some (by no means all) *rímur* melodies informed my work with the Eddic texts. As in the previous question, I cannot accurately explain how I went about doing this, but it involved interiorizing a large amount of modal/gestural material from that repertoire, and sometimes actual melodies (the obviously archaic ones), and using this material in turn to re-imagine the roots of its modality and generate new models fitted to the subtle metrical structures of the medieval texts. I enjoy listening to today's *rímur* singers, but in no way do I try to copy their art—I am looking for a way of vocalizing a text which may have pre-dated *rímur* by many hundreds of years.

Sequentia worked with Ping Chong to stage *The Rheingold Curse* as a full dramatic performance. What do you think of the idea of scholars like Bertha Phillpotts (and more recently, Terry Gunnell) that the Eddic material is actually connected to ancient Scandinavian drama?

STILL FROM PING CHONG'S PRODUCTION OF "EDDA: VIKING TALES OF LUST, REVENGE AND FAMILY."

I completely agree with Terry Gunnell that many of these texts were "re-enacted" in some way, but that doesn't necessarily locate the performers on the stage of a theater (a place where we would expect to experience "drama"). These may have been ritualistic, or even informal re-enactments, possibly for a very few onlookers (notice I also avoid the word "audience"). Since source material is so scarce and fragmentary, we may never be able to answer this question. The Ping Chong staging was modern and sought mostly to capture a particular archaic feeling which the texts awakened in Ping. We performed it frequently in 2001–2002 but it was very expensive to produce and to transport the set. Since 2002 we perform the same program with only a very simple series of positions and scene shifts, so that all of the focus is on the text and on the performer who is speaking/singing. I feel this brings us closer to the kind of *scop*-like performance situation which Terry was describing.

With *Fragments for the End of Time* you have (at least in

the live-performance version) juxtaposed both Christian texts and those with a secular or pre-Christian perspective. This is evident in *Beowulf* as well, and scholars have endlessly debated whether the poem is more Christian or pagan in character. Another Sequentia program is *The Monk Sings the Pagan*, which will feature classical authors set to the music of the tenth to twelfth centuries. Historians used to characterize the early Middle Ages as a period of "dual faith," when Europe was no longer heathen, yet not entirely Christian, either. Are these grey areas of friction and/or syncretism something that interests you?

Yes, the confrontation (or accommodation) of differing belief systems fascinates me. Even today, in some Christian churches I sometimes have the feeling that the Old Gods are only thinly disguised. In the program concept for *The Monk Sings the Pagan*, I am mostly interested in pursuing the ways in which pagan themes penetrated the Christian monastic milieu and cathedral schools as a result of the monks' desire to study Latin grammar. The venerable old (pagan) texts were sometimes doctrinally awkward (or downright naughty) but they were uncontested as a means for learning to speak and write in Latin beautifully and clearly. Despite all of the propaganda surrounding the Renaissance as a time of reconnection with classical antiquity, the fact is that classical authors were valued and studied throughout the so-called "Dark Ages." Clerics managed to ignore the pagan origins of the texts and accept them for their brilliance and their craft. And the fact that so many texts from antiquity survive in medieval manuscripts with musical notation attests to their elevated status in the clerical world. Texts by Homer, Virgil, Horace, Terence, and others were sung by Christian clerics and monks, well into the twelfth century.

As a second question with regard to *Fragments for the End of Time*: What compelled you to collect these varied texts on a single performance and recording? Do these apocalyptic texts speak to a modern audience in some way that other

doctrinal Christian texts might not?

The genesis of this program was a discussion between myself and my colleague Norbert Rodenkirchen, in the old Sequentia hangout Cafe Central in Cologne. We were examining the fragmentary Old High German text called *Muspilli*, which is Christian but mentions an absolutely pagan/Germanic word (*muspilli*) in connection with the end of time, conflagration, annihilation of the world, and Last Judgment. It's linked to the Old Norse Ragnarök and the pagan gods in their final battle with the race of giants. Suddenly, the relationships began to branch out, showing how the early Christian world in northern Europe was interconnected with the older beliefs. I don't know if these texts speak to modern audiences at all, but they speak to me, even though they are filled with stern and moralistic ideas of sin and judgment, punishment and salvation. They speak to the timeless fear of all humans: that life on this planet will simply cease to exist (which is a certainty, although hopefully a distant one)—we want the feeling that someone powerful and wise, somewhere, is in charge of things and that our demise will not be random, anonymous, and devoid of significance. Modern audiences are always struck by the harsh and unsentimental tone of these medieval texts, in which nowhere is to be found a sweet and forgiving Jesus or a mild Virgin Mary, but only images of destruction and accountability: prophets, Antichrist, a dragon, terrifying angels blowing horns, dead bodies rising from the earth, widespread sickness, violent warfare, random death, firestorms, the moon and stars falling down, the mountains leveled, the seas and rivers dried out, utter darkness as the sun is extinguished, and then—a court date with the most terrifying judge. In the mind of each individual listener, pagan or Christian, we would expect to find the world's most sophisticated special-effects department, hard at work creating a horrible vision which, somehow, is shared by all.

One of your latest projects is *Frankish Phantoms*—I am especially excited about your rendering of the *Hildebrandslied*! As these are also "lost songs" whose melodies have been

forgotten, I am curious how you and the Cambridge musicologist Sam Barrett have been approaching the manuscripts? For example, can you talk about the degree to which the literal plot line or drama of the words themselves informs how you interpret them musically and vocally?

I have worked with Sam Barrett mostly on those Latin-texted songs for which we have some neumed sources, several of which are performed in our program. However, other pieces (such as the *Hildebrandslied*) are found in sources without neumes, so that I must create the musical version based on similar criteria to other epics I have performed, such as *Beowulf*. As in *Beowulf*, I never make use of musical notation in my work but only deal with the text, the instrument, my voice and my memory. In such cases, it is the tuning of the harp which provides a "matrix" of tones from which I can work. I am never thinking of "melodies" or trying to create them, but I am working with the different registers which this particular tuning yields: most potently a series of sounding perfect fourths, one below and one above. In the course of learning this story, I naturally fell into the rhythms and registers of the dialogue between father and son, the whole crux of the story and tragedy. (The story: father and son, separated for thirty years, meet in single combat as warrior-champions in front of their respective armies. During their initial exchange of formal words, the father, Hildebrand, realizes that he is facing his long-lost son, Hadubrand, in combat and must either kill him or be killed by him. His attempt to explain the situation and hand over a peace offering is rebuffed by the hotheaded and suspicious younger man—who basically calls Hildebrand a "tricky old Hun"—and so the old warrior laments cruel fate, rousing himself to the deadly encounter. The fragment breaks off as the shields begin to splinter under their blows.) But there is also the role of the storyteller, who advances the description and sets the scene. Therefore, I needed the instrument to provide me with three distinct registers and modes for the three functions I must fulfill as a performer. A fairly small and stable amount of modal material—provided by the six strings of the harp—is used by the singer to tell a wide-ranging story, sometimes spoken, sometimes sung, sometimes a little of each.

For *Frankish Phantoms* you will be using songs in Latin as well as Germanic and Romance dialects; your *Beowulf* performance is rendered in the original Old English. You have expended a huge amount of effort in mastering the cadences and pronunciation of these languages as they might have actually been spoken. Why is it so important to work with these texts in their original dialects? Would your reconstructions even be conceivable if the material was translated?

I believe very strongly that text is music. Each language has its own "music"—its own inflections, cadences, modes. If we translate a given text into another language, the music of that text would also change. My reconstructions would be utterly ridiculous if the language were not the original one. I would have no problem with hearing someone performing all of these pieces in modern English translations (or German, or Spanish, or Mandarin), but then I would expect to hear radically different musical versions, to hear different instruments employed, to hear a different approach to time and rhythm, color and pitch-level. The performance would necessarily become a "composition," setting a contemporary text inspired by an ancient source. This type of music making has a venerable tradition in European Classical music, but this is not where I am interested in going with my own work. My work is and isn't "composition;" in fact, it isn't really early music either (I find myself in that category by tradition and by default) and so my work belongs absolutely nowhere in today's accepted modes of creative endeavor. I think of myself as sitting between the chairs.

When you started Sequentia in the seventies, there was a burgeoning interest in medieval culture, both in academia and as a pop-culture phenomenon, with the counter-culture and so forth. Nowadays it seems that much of this interest

SEQUENTIA MEMBERS BENJAMIN BAGBY, NORBERT RODENKIRCHEN, AND WOLODYMYR SMISHKEWYCH. PHOTO BY JAN GATES.

has waned from an overtly counter-cultural perspective, although in some ways the Middle Ages are more popular than ever (albeit through a Tolkien/fantasy lens). What do you see as the future for medieval music, both as an area of scholarly interest, and as something non-specialist listeners can relate to? And by the same token, how concerned are you with the reception of your own work by scholars and popular audiences?

In the scholarly field, I believe we are already seeing historical medieval musicology move out of its specialized corner and beginning to interact more dynamically with other disciplines, with less narrow focus on manuscript sources and more on the interaction of the sources with performance, orality, social context, and liturgy. In any case, the number of surviving manuscripts, although huge, is actually finite, and almost all of the important musical sources from the period of the ninth to the fourteenth centuries have been studied in detail. Non-specialist listeners would generally not find the scholarly literature enjoyable or interesting to read, and of course the field becomes increasingly more specialized as the zones of study become more clearly and narrowly defined. On the other hand, generalized studies about medieval music—which have always been with us since Gustave Reese's post-World War II *Music in the Middle Ages* —are no longer an attractive prospect for publishers. Students today are still using textbooks from the 1970s and the critical mass of students interested in studying medieval music is not sufficient for a flourishing textbook market to exist. At best, the Middle Ages merit a few chapters in a general history of music. Historical musicology is no longer the dominant force it was fifty years ago, and in academia it is being slowly eclipsed by areas of study which respond to an expressed need for a more "relevant" course of study: ethnomusicology, analysis, composition, technology, gender studies, queer studies, semiology, etc. Medieval manuscripts lacking pictures are generally not considered "sexy."

There is a reflection of this tendency in the arena of performance as well, as sources of medieval music increasingly serve as platforms for new genres of entertainment only loosely related to the Middle Ages. The buzzword has long been "crossover" and the motivation is to prove that medieval music is not austere, difficult, or boring, but rather "rich and varied" (a PR phrase which should be retired). In fulfillment of this need, we increasingly find concerts which seek to sell the audience an image of the Middle Ages as a time filled with people who are comfortingly "just like us" only they wear silly costumes—and of course we see this reflected in Hollywood films, Medieval Fayres, and the entire spectrum of fantasy entertainment and the SCA re-enactment and role-playing scene. The innate strangeness of our own culture's deep past has been tempered by what we would like to believe (well, who doesn't experience history in this way?), and by the need we have to enter fantasy realms which explain everything very clearly, which offer us a simpler version of ourselves which we find more attractive, more human, even more heroic.

"Rich and varied" has become an imperative. Performers of medieval music are increasingly including in their concerts other types of music as well, especially new music written for medieval ensembles and also traditional music which makes use of similar vocal or instrumental sounds. The boundaries of identity are less and less clear as we become more focused on interesting sounds and not so much on historical repertoires, texts, languages, styles, and functions (for example: liturgical music no longer has functional meaning for most people today). As this type of concert experience becomes the status quo and role model for young performers, we will probably see the emergence of new genres of programming which we could call "medieval-inspired." In our increasingly entertainment-oriented society, in the world of short attention spans and a musical "shuffle mode" in which anything can be combined with anything else, the honest confrontation with musical genres from our own deeper past is probably going to become a rarity. But these are cycles:

What has been will be again, what has been done will be done again; there is nothing new under the sun. (Ecclesiastes 1:9)

I'm not overly concerned about the reception of our work by scholars, but I'm always pleased when a scholar likes (in the non-Facebook sense of the word) what we do. We try to bear in mind that scholars are, by their training, highly critical observers and will always object to something or other. And some scholars may even enjoy our music per se without necessarily agreeing with the way it's produced. In the best cases, it provokes a dialogue and one can always learn something from that. As for the popular audience: we rarely come into contact with this segment of the concert-going public, since we normally appear in rather special venues which are either marked out as an early music zone or are closely associated with a dedicated festival, or (in North America) a university or (in Europe) a historical place—church, chapel, castle hall, or other medieval performing space. The larger, popular audience will always gravitate towards a genre of medieval music which is known in my circles as "drums and fun" (see above), and there is plenty of that to go around. In the end it's a relatively big tent, in which there is room for everyone, and we treasure our little corner of it while it still exists.

I try to keep foremost in our work the honesty of the texts themselves, the deep integrity of the human voice as a vehicle of communication, the power of language, rhetoric and mode, allowing the direct presentation of this music to the listeners, without distractions. It's a fulfilling life's work.

The New Old Ways: An Interview with Cult of Youth's Sean Ragon

Joshua Buckley

Music genres can be hard to navigate, especially for the uninitiated. Therefore, it's probably not unreasonable to wonder if even the most self-serious music journalists know what they're talking about when they prattle on about *post*-punk, *post*-industrial, or *post*-rock music, as if an album or a song can be defined strictly in terms of what it is *not*. Yet these are precisely the dilemmas one encounters in trying to categorize a record like *Love Will Prevail*, the latest offering from Sean Ragon's Brooklyn-based Cult of Youth. Ragon's own background is firmly rooted in punk, and that spirit comes across in almost every aspect of his work, from the driving earnestness of the music, to Ragon's seemingly indomitable work ethic. But Ragon's much wider range of musical interests is apparent in how he curates his music label, Blind Prophet. Blind Prophet's releases range from postpunk to folk, to synth-pop to techno-industrial. Ragon also owns Heaven Street Records, a venue that showcases his connoisseurship with offbeat and eclectic music, and the shop has firmed up its reputation as one of the premier independent record stores on the East Coast. Critical accolades have also been forthcoming for Cult of Youth. The band has been featured in outlets like *The Quietus* and even *MTV Hive*, and their latest album garnered an overwhelmingly positive review on that barometer of indie-music credibility, *Pitchfork*.

Yet one aspect of Ragon's music that seems to trip-up reviewers is its strong connection to neofolk, a genre that is itself notoriously difficult to define—which is not to say that no one has tried. One of the more ambitious attempts was Stéphane François' 2007 article in the *Journal for the Study of Radicalism*, "The Euro-Pagan Scene: Between Paganism and Radical Right." While François' approach was wrong-headed in many regards (not the least of which was the absurdity of trying to pack the many groups and subcultures he considers into one coherent narrative—especially one with a cohesive political outlook), François was closer to the mark in suggesting that the only real common denominator might be the recurrence of certain motifs. This is certainly evident in Ragon's work, and it is a context that is largely lost on outsiders. A student of the runes who has expressed his admiration for the work of Edred Thorsson, Ragon's interest in European paganism, magic, and ancient cultures dates back to his early childhood. Cult of Youth has also shared a stage with artists more familiar to neofolk audiences like Boyd Rice and Death in June. Along with tour-mates Iceage, whose own tangential connections to neofolk have confounded critics (and led to predictable political denunciations), Cult of Youth may be the first neofolk crossover act. Ragon's own personal statement of punk-traditionalism (how's that for ambiguity?) might be inferred from the song "New Old Ways": "And the new old ways (the old ways, never change the new ways) / For the old ways (the new ways, never change the old ways) . . . To defy their logic / And to step outside / Is the only way to reclaim."

So what does Cult of Youth actually sound like? Since recording his first 7" as a one-off solo project, Ragon has worked with a revolving cast of other musicians; most recently, he has added three permanent members: bassist Jasper McGandy, drummer Cory Flanigan, and Christian Flanders on electric guitar and keyboards. *Love Will Prevail* also features backing vocals by Beverly Hames which, combined with cascading horns and the sharp, staccato percussion the group is known for, helps to flesh out Ragon's compositions into their fullest form yet. The most distinctive aspect of CoY's sound, however, is how Ragon handles his guitar. Despite seldom plugging in, he hammers at it with raw, punk rock abandon, and his vocals have a similarly aggressive edge. He shouts and sputters occasionally, but mostly declaims his lyrics in a sharp, authoritarian bark. The vocal style is reminiscent of a lot of neofolk artists, but it's also a characteristic of bands like Crass—and lest we forget, both Death in June and Sol Invictus (those venerable godfathers of the neofolk sound) arose from the ashes of the early English punk band, Crisis.

The last thing I want to do, however, is imply that Cult of

Youth are making music that is overly derivative of their predecessors. Whatever their influences, and however you choose to define their sound, Cult of Youth's music has an expansiveness that points beyond these things to something more intangible, an oddly compelling convergence of introspection and intensity. It's music that is thoughtful, spiritual (in the best pagan sense of the word), and maybe just a little bit dangerous.

The postpunk label gets applied rather indiscriminately to a lot of music that doesn't seem to have much of anything else in common. What elements of punk have carried over into all these other genres? Is it an attitude or just a general approach to things?

Postpunk can be a very misleading term. It implies some kind of response to punk. However, many bands that could be considered postpunk have roots that stretch back before punk (such as Pere Ubu, for example). Postpunk has more to do with the rise of the independent label and the rise of the independent distribution network. It came from a combination of bands such as The Desperate Bicycles or Scritti Politti self-releasing records and independent shops and distributors like Rough Trade opening doors for different forms of music to reach a wider audience. Postpunk was really just an outlet for an experimental form of stripped down rock that grew up in the same cultural climate as the first wave of punk (teenagers reacting against the AOR and progressive rock environment of the mid-seventies). Over time the more interesting bands of the genre got cloned (it happened to punk too) and there you have it—postpunk was born!

It's also worth noting that the so-called golden year of punk was 1977 (yes, to some it was 1982), whereas the golden year of postpunk is generally considered to be 1978. These bands all existed at the same time.

Your label Blind Prophet has released a lot of really eclectic independent music. What is it that makes you interested enough to work with any one particular artist? Do you see

the bands represented on your label as having some kind of common ground?

The common ground is that I need to feel some kind of personal connection with the artists. It's actually something that can cause a bit of difficulty from a business perspective since the majority of people buy music along strict genre lines (and there's absolutely nothing wrong with that). Thankfully, through doing the record store I have developed relationships with most of the major distributors for the different genres that the label covers. It leaves me in a unique position where I have the ability to follow my heart and take chances.

You definitely have that DIY ethos that's associated with punk—you run your own label, you built your record store from the ground up, and you even designed the studio where *Love Will Prevail* was recorded. I've often felt like people hide behind the DIY idea as an excuse for putting out a shoddy product. In your case, though, it seems to come from a real sense of inner discipline and conviction.

Thank you. My DIY ethos has never come from anywhere other than it has always been the easiest, best, and sometimes the only available way to get what I want without compromising my integrity or values. I always strive to make the best possible product that I am capable of. Had different resources been available, there is a good chance I would have chosen different paths to similar results. I am a hard worker, and I do whatever it takes to accomplish the things I choose to accomplish.

Although I had some construction experience in my past (I worked as a house painter/plasterer for five years) I had to teach myself carpentry to build my studio. I remember going over to my friend Ryan's apartment when I first set out and saying "I'm in over my head—do you have any idea how to build a floating soundproof floor?" His roommate Lou explained the whole thing the best he could in about ten or fifteen minutes, and drew me a crude sketch on a piece of paper. A week or two later I had built

CULT OF YOUTH IN JOSHUA TREE STATE PARK IN SOUTHEASTERN CALIFORNIA. PHOTO BY BEVERLY HAMES.

my first soundproof floor. From there on, I just learned the next part one step at a time. I now have a beautiful studio with hardwood floors and a glass window that looks into the live room.

There is absolutely nothing in this world that you cannot accomplish if you are disciplined and willing to put in the work. Society teaches you to reach a place of comfort and to settle down and breed. That is not all there is to life. As humans we need to continue to grow and keep our minds, bodies, and spirits active (even if only for the sake of raising our own children properly).

One thing I really like about Cult of Youth is that both the lyrics and the way the music is played has such a sense of urgency and sincerity. I think some people find that almost threatening—they're so acclimated to irony and hipster detachment.

I really just don't know how else to be. I take the things that I do very seriously because in many cases I've had to do them in the face of opposition. When Cult of Youth first started (as a home recording project in my bedroom) there was absolutely no viable outlet for the type of music that I was doing in New York (or America in general, for that matter) besides increasingly stagnant genre ghettos.

I honestly believe that when we first started taking off and going on tour in America (and we did it a lot) that we were doing something important and perhaps even groundbreaking. By getting in a van and hitting the road like a punk band we increased awareness of our culture and made contacts and tour routes that other like-minded bands began to use. I am still in contact with just about everyone that booked those early shows, and in many cases we still use the same people. Thankfully, there is so much more to be discovered, and every time we go back out we make new friends and discover new and exciting pockets of culture in the most unexpected of places.

Ironic culture is the only logical end result of the first generation that came of age online. I come to this conclusion for two reasons. First off, up until the late nineties the only way to find out about music or counterculture was through actual people. You needed an older friend to show you bands, or to go to a shop and talk to the person working there. You needed to seek out old 'zines and old books, and through this process you developed a respect for the jewels of information that you would come across. With unlimited access to all information about all things 24/7 (in the privacy of your own room, no less) came a detachment and a lack of hands on experience. It created the first ever generation of people that felt a sense of entitlement to information and it developed a worldview where the universe was evaluated based on how it entertained or serviced the needs of the voyeur. This led to a lack of respect for the traditions of cultures and subcultures.

Secondly, you had the first generation that grew up in public. The rise of social media had stark and devastating consequences in terms of childhood development. All teenagers do awkward and embarrassing things. I was fortunate enough to grow up in a time where I could do those things in relative privacy. When everything is up for criticism and everything is up for evaluation it can be difficult to put something real and honest out there. Many people did things that were intentionally ironic, sarcastic, of low quality, or just plain dumb so that if anyone criticized them the response could be "I know it's stupid, that's the point". There has been a backlash against this way of thinking as the next generation is now coming of age, so it appears that ironic culture is on the decline (for now).

There's obviously a strong neofolk influence in what you're doing, although I think that that context is lost on a lot of music journalists. The neofolk scene tends to be very insular and self-referential, but you reach a much wider audience. Iceage seems to have the same problem. Presenting this kind of material to people who don't have that background seems like it opens you up to a whole array of misunderstandings.

There have been some minor misunderstandings, but never anything major. I have always been up front about everything that I've ever been involved in and I've never backed down from talking about anything openly and honestly. Cult of Youth has never been a shock value band, and I have never promoted anything or used any symbols that I'm not prepared to stand behind 100%. I know my history, and I'm always happy to talk about it.

To me it's a cop out when people refuse to talk about their cultural or symbolic choices. Many people get in over their head with symbols that they don't understand, and when they're confronted by other people who also don't understand the symbols (such as leftist *antifa* groups) they have nothing to offer so they hide behind the old "we're not a political band" mantra. It makes all of us appear ignorant when those of us fortunate enough to have a platform cannot even articulate the beauty of our own religious and spiritual symbols.

You've been pretty open about the fact that you've had problems with drugs and alcohol in the past, and that you've been involved with various recovery programs. How do you feel that those experiences have shaped your outlook and approach to things now?

When I was younger I felt isolated and out of sorts with the world around me. Like many who came before me I turned to drugs and alcohol. As time went on and I got older certain habits became worse and eventually hard drugs entered the picture. My life became terrifying and I was set to destroy everything and everyone that was close to me.

The only way for me to get past this and make positive life changes was for me to get completely sober from everything (including alcohol). I was clean for a period of around three years, and for the first time in my life I took an honest look in the mirror without fear and without holding anything back. If this hadn't happened there is a very good chance that I would be dead or in jail right now.

That being said, I don't need to escape from my life anymore because it is better than I could have ever dreamed. I am able to drink recreationally and do so without the fear of things going back to where they were. This is only possible because when I was sober I did the work. Sobriety doesn't solve your problems, but it does put you in a position where you *can* solve your problems.

You've said that you were attracted to European paganism and magic from the time you were a kid. Were you still pursuing this when you were involved in the punk scene? I've always felt like punk was pretty cynical when it comes to these subjects. A lot of punks have absorbed that typical leftist / materialist attitude about anything related to magic or religion.

I have never changed anything I've been interested in for anyone or anything. I did keep a lot of things to myself as a teenager,

SEAN RAGON AT HOME IN BROOKLYN. PHOTO BY TAYLOR BRODE.

but that was partially because I didn't think anyone else would really care about most of my interests. Yeah, the guys growing up busted my balls a lot, but I'm from Boston—that's what people do there. I don't recall getting it any worse than anyone else!

The punk scene at large is a complex and constantly changing organism. While it's true that the rise of Profane Existence–style punk in the early nineties replaced the esoteric paganism of early crust outfits like Amebix with the reactionary politics of the new breed of bands, there has always been room for those with an old school perspective. My record store is active in the local punk scene here in New York. Although here and there I'll get cock-eyed glances from people who don't understand quite where I'm coming from, the general attitude is an appreciation for the fact that I run a completely DIY business that services my community in a hands-on and direct way.

New York seems to have had a bit of an "occult revival" over the last few years; Catland Books in Bushwick (which is also where Heaven Street is located) have tapped into that. Do you feel like more people are looking into paganism and esotericism now in a way that's more serious than in the past?

I hope so. There hasn't been a widespread and radical spiritual revolution in popular culture for a very long time (the last one I can think of is Psychic TV/TOPY in the eighties). That being said, it's easy to get lost in a cultural bubble and forget about the rest of the world. I've created a life for myself where most days I don't even have to interact with people that are not deep into counter-culture. It's important not to lose focus and think that the world is on your wavelength when you are surrounded by co-conspirators twenty-four hours a day. There is still work to be done!

How do you feel about reconstructionist pagan religions like Ásatrú? Would you ever get involved with something like that, or is your work with the runes and other aspects of these traditions strictly a solitary pursuit?

I have nothing but respect for Ásatrú. Many of the books that have deepened my understanding of the runes and European religious symbolism have been Ásatrú-related publications. That being said, I have always been a bit of an outsider and I've spent much of my life being cynical of groups and organized religions. I understand that the heart of European spirituality is the community, and that I would gain a depth of understanding through participation that I wouldn't be able to get otherwise. Perhaps some healthy exploration is in my future!

One of the appealing aspects of CoY's music is that your

lyrics can be interpreted on so many different levels. A song like "New Old Ways," for example, seems like it could be about transformation in a personal, spiritual, or even a more political sense. Is that open-ended quality something you try to cultivate when you're writing an album? There's also a strong contrast between the ambiguity of a lot of the lyrics and the forcefulness of the delivery.

The lyrics of Cult of Youth are a direct gateway to my subconscious. The creative process is full of surprises, and if I were to tell you that I wrote lyrics with a premeditated purpose, for the most part it would be inaccurate. In fact, through reflecting on my own lyrics I have gained a deeper understanding of the self.

The subconscious communicates with the conscious mind through symbols, and this is why my lyrics are so rife with symbolism. The symbols represent ideas, but by thinking about these ideas in non-direct ways we are able to focus on them without the circular (and often negative) thought process of the so-called reptilian portion of the human mind. The forceful delivery (especially so live) is a magickal process intended to charge these ideas which are representative of my true will as dictated by my deepest and innermost subconscious. It can be looked at as a form of reverse sigilization.

You've played live with a pretty wide range of other artists, and I'm sure that this has exposed you to audiences with a variety of different expectations. What are some of the more memorable reactions people have had to your music?

On our last European tour we had a show booked in Glasgow, Scotland. Unfortunately for us, the venue that we were booked at shut down a month or two prior and we didn't find out until the very last minute. We were stuck without a show, but somehow managed to jump on as the opening act for another band that was playing that night. We thought it might be a cool show until we got there. Apparently the lead singer was some well-to-do young socialite who was dating Anthony Kedis of the Red Hot

Chili Peppers. Her whole backing band had face paint and ironic Indian feathers in their hair. Anthony Kedis must have dumped her or something because she was crying and having a temper tantrum like a baby, screaming at everyone, and slamming doors backstage.

Needless to say, the audience that came to see her did *not* like us.

We had these girls that we were staying with that Jasper and Christian had met on tour with their previous band (The Hunt). I guess one of them saw some guy standing in the back of the room while we played looking absolutely terrified with his hands over his ears. She went up to him and said "That's my friend's band." This guy, who was expecting a mellow evening of singer-songwriters, told her: "It's too loud!" She straight up slapped him in the face. After the set, she dragged him over to us and made him apologize for being disrespectful. It should come as no surprise that we had a great time once we left the show. Those girls really knew how to party.

There are fairly elaborate videos for several of your songs. How involved were you in producing the videos? Is film a medium you're drawn to? Are there movies that have been a significant source of inspiration?

To be honest, my taste in film is terribly lowbrow. I like movies where everything blows up and naked girls run around. I also enjoy romantic comedies and the most vulgar of giallo flicks. The majority of art films bore me to death. I feigned interest for most of my life, but I'm too old for that now. I like what I like.

That being said, I am fortunate enough to be friends with some incredibly talented filmmakers. I am drawn to the idea of using film as a form of ritual and I have had incredible experiences during the filmmaking process. My philosophy for this area of the band has always been: "hand over the keys to someone you trust, and do what they say."

A distinctive aspect of neofolk seems to be an interest in

history, both in terms of ancient cultures and with the more recent political upheavals that have defined the modern world. Is that something you've had a chance to indulge in when you've been on tour overseas? Do you try to get out and visit many sacred and/or historic sites? Are these things that are meaningful for you?

Tour is not a vacation, and it is not the time for sightseeing. I would love to one day travel to Europe without the burden of performing music and be able to explore and experience that side of things. The last time that we went to Europe (which was for an entire month), we only had one actual day off the entire trip. Thankfully, it was in Athens, Greece and we spent a day getting lost in a vibrant city surrounded by the remnants of an ancient civilization. We all had such a remarkable time that afternoon. Sometimes when I daydream I close my eyes and I can feel myself back there. It hurts when I open them up and I'm back in New York City in the freezing cold.

A few years back I took a trip with my fiancé to southern Mexico. We slept in a hut in the jungle, rented a car, and spent our days driving around and exploring the pyramids and ruins of the Mayan people. Although the better known sites were catered towards tourists and roped off, we found that if we drove around to small towns we were able to find lesser known sites where we could actually climb inside and get to experience these sacred places first hand. The native peoples of Mexico were very advanced (both spiritually and technologically) and this trip left a deep and lasting impression on me.

You took a break from recording to do this interview. What can we expect from the next release? How has your vision for the band changed since you started playing as Cult of Youth?

That's a tough one, since I never really know how to describe my own work. I'm definitely trying some new things on this record. I recently had my first experiences recording with human bones

"From this point on, it's a bonus and I'm living the good life." Photo by Sebastian Mlynarski.

as the source material. I have always loved bands like Zero Kama and Metgumbnerbone and there are plans to incorporate those elements on the new record. On the complete opposite end of the spectrum, there are also songs that are influenced more by bands like The Stooges or The MC5. There are some acoustic songs, and (of course) some songs that just sound like classic Cult of Youth.

I spent a lot of time the past year in the studio recording and mixing other bands and being involved in different creative processes. I even got a chance to work with Genesis P-Orridge on a few projects (which was a dream come true). I took it all in and rethought my own methods. The past year has really been a year of growth for me, and I can't shake the feeling that the next record will somehow be important.

Do you draw many influences from books that you've read?

Unfortunately, I don't get to spend as much time reading as I would like. It is the curse of being self-employed—there's never a day off, and there's always something else to do.

The last book that I read that left a lasting and thought provoking impression was *Qabalah, Qliphoth and Goetic Magic* by Thomas Karlsson. It caused me to rethink everything I thought I knew about Goetic magic, the Qabalah, and Luciferianism and inspired me to think that they might even hold a place in my personal magical practice (something I never imagined possible). The opening line of the new record is actually inspired by a meditation I did while deeply engrossed in this book.

I'm also dying to read the book about Ye Ye girls that Feral House just put out. Most likely by the time this sees print I will have!

Clearly, your personal taste in music is pretty adventurous. Tell me some things you've been listening to that might surprise our readers.

I have recently rediscovered my passion for spiritual jazz. I urge all readers that have a passion for Eurocentric ritual music to experience the works of Pharaoh Sanders or Alice Coltrane. The purpose of this music is an Afrocentric spiritual enlightenment and it fuses the more avant-garde disciplines of jazz with influences from pre-Christian African tribal and ritual music. This to me is not far off from the music of, say, Waldteufel for example. It's coming from a different perspective, but it's touching upon the same thing.

It's easy to criticize punk's political pretensions, but one thing I think a lot of people picked up from that is the idea that music can still be a catalyst for change. I know that for me, there were things I took from these subcultures when I was thirteen or fourteen years old, that have stayed with me to this day. Is that sense of idealism still something that keeps you motivated?

Music was the first thing that opened up the world to me. It provided me with opportunities and experiences that put me in a place where I am able to live a life better than anything I could have possibly imagined. I am an idealistic person, and being involved in music in a hands-on and direct way is something that keeps me honest, keeps me young, and keeps me motivated.

I've reached an age where a lot of the people I've been friends with over the years have started dying. I've had to take a long hard look at myself, accept my mortality and know that I could be next. I don't have any regrets, and I know that I have done things that have left an impression on the world I inhabit. It's the knowledge that there might not be a tomorrow that motivates me every single day from the moment I wake up to the moment I go to bed. I've already accomplished more than I ever dreamed was possible. From this point on, it's a bonus and I'm living the good life.

Reviews: Music

Kūlgrinda—*Ugnies Apeigos: The Rite of Fire* (Dangus); *Perkūno Giesmės: Hymns to Perkūnas the Thundergod* (Dangus); *Prūsų Giesmės: Prussian Chants* (self-released); *Giesmės Saulei: Hymns to the Sun* (self-released); *Giesmės Valdovui Gediminui: Hymns for King Gediminas* (self-released)

The *kūlgrinda* are hidden stone pathways that extend through the marshes, swamps, and waterways of Lithuania, connecting villages and farms. They were used over the centuries to escape invaders—locals knew where these sunken trails were and could move around undetected as needed. The heathen ritual music group Kūlgrinda takes its name from these secret roads, and the chanted hymns they sing to ancient Baltic gods evoke an archaic and enduring landscape.

Kūlgrinda was founded in 1990 by Inija Trinkūnienė and Jonas Jaunius Trinkūnas, who have long stood at the center of the Baltic heathen revival. The group forms an integral part of the spiritual organization Romuva, "the Lithuanian expression of Baltic faith," by leading rituals and performing ceremonies. In addition to being the founder of Romuva, Jonas Trinkūnas (28 February 1939–20 January 2014) was a philologist, song-collector, and folklorist. Romuva is also the name of the most important Prussian temple, which was destroyed by crusaders in the thirteenth century. In Lithuania, Romuva is a popular and vital religion. Its adherents fully embrace and enjoy the modern world while standing firmly in their roots, learning old songs and dances, ancient poems, and traditional martial arts. For Romuva practitioners, as for other heathens, ritual, life, music, and friends and family are all connected.

Similarly, there is no clear separation between Jonas Trinkūnas, Romuva, and Kūlgrinda. Trinkūnas's personal collection of ancient songs forms the backbone of both Kūlgrinda's repertoire as well as providing a framework for the rites of Romuva. This is because Kūlgrinda typically leads ceremonies in the Romuva

THREE OF THE MEMBERS OF KULGRINDA. PHOTO BY ANNABEL LEE.

tradition for weddings, baby-naming rites, the solstices, and other holidays. The group also performs for musical concerts and cultural events, both inside and outside of Lithuania (they have twice made trips to the United States).

Musically, Kūlgrinda's sound is centered around mesmerizing voices that are strong and unaffected. The Trinkunai family are the primary singers and musicians. The daughters Vėtra, Žemyna, and Rimgailė Trinkūnaitė sing and play the *kanklės*, a traditional Lithuanian zither. The different tonal qualities of the voices and the hypnotic chanting create an atmosphere fit for summoning the gods. The repertoire comes from a deep wellspring, as Jonas Trinkūnas once noted:

> We know many things, because our relatives are the trees, grass, birds, animals. They hide nothing from us. The forest is our home. We know thousands of songs. These are hymns for our gods and goddesses, for our ancestors, parents, brothers and sisters. We sing as the birds sing. We were taught this by our parents. As the forests rustle, so

Reviews: Music

KULGRINDA AT THE 2011 MJR FESTIVAL. PHOTO BY ANNABEL LEE.

the kanklės play and horns sound."[1]

In January of 2014, Jonas Trinkūnas passed on to the realm of the spirits and ancestors. His influence on Lithuanian heathen and popular culture today is immeasurable; many generations have benefited from his great knowledge and spiritual generosity. He was the Krivis, the high priest of Romuva, and he dedicated his life to studying the folk traditions of the Prussians, Lithuanians, and the Baltic region. He worked in the government for the Ministry of Culture as the Director of Ethnic Culture in Lithuania, following glasnost and the advances made by the Reform Movement of Lithuania (Lietuvos Persitvarkymo Sąjūdis). Although his primary focus was always Romuva, his commitment to a heathen revival transcended national borders and he also served as the chairman of the World Congress of Ethnic Religions.

Kūlgrinda also stands at the center of a wider Baltic heathen revival. Among other contributions, every year they open and

1. *Baltic Religion Today* (Vilnius: Romuva, 2011), 35.

close the annual cultural festival called Mėnuo Juodaragis (MJR), which has taken place in the Lithuanian countryside for more than fifteen years. The promoters of the MJR festival also run the Dangus record label, which has released several of Kūlgrinda's CDs.

Each year nearly 5,000 visitors—young people, families, and older folks—attend the MJR festival. Most camp out in tents, often sharing food and drink. An open-minded idea of what constitutes contemporary Baltic culture prevails. There are craftspeople and musicians from all over Europe, but mostly the Baltic area. The festivities consist of rituals, games, films, lectures and demonstrations, and the festival showcases many types of music, from electronic to heavy metal, along with a great variety of traditional folk groups. The majority of the bands sing in their mother tongues, and most have heathen inclinations. The festival is full of energy and excitement, and yet peaceful. Every year the organizers invite a few bands from outside of the Baltic region, and once in a while even from outside of Europe and Russia. In 2011, Michael Moynihan and I were lucky enough to be invited to play as Blood Axis. On our first evening there, the night before the festival began, we were brought to a Romuva ceremony intended for the festival workers. It was interesting to note how familiar the ceremony was, reminding us of other heathen rituals we've attended around the states and in Europe. The next day at a public opening ceremony, Kūlgrinda sang, chanted, and led their processional dances around a fire altar and an oak tree. Romuva ceremonies of this sort bookended the festival, making the entire weekend into a single ritual, with a meaning felt beyond the sheer pleasure of the music and friendship.

After the festival, we returned to the capital city Vilnius with our new friends and attended the large after-party held for the volunteers, workers, and organizers of the MJR festival. This took place at a huge, crowded alehouse and several music groups gave impromptu performances on a small stage. Michael and I were invited to play for the crowd, which was surprised to hear us doing traditional Irish acoustic folk music. Later that evening we met Inija Trinkūnienė backstage. When she realized that we

Images from the 2011 MJR Festival in Lithuania. All photos by Annabel Lee and Michael Moynihan.

Top row (left to right): The Lithuanian group Ugniavijas in concert; a female festivalgoer.

Center row: the MJR festival banner; Handmade balto-slavic jewelry, based on traditional designs; Iberian "Ur-Folk" group Arnica performing under a sacred oak.

Bottom row: Artisans' Assistant; Rantaturis, a youth ensemble from the Zarasai region of Lithuania.

played Irish music she called her husband Jonas, who decided to take a taxi down to the club to hear us instead of going to bed. After he arrived, we got our instruments out again and played privately for him and his family in the corner of the room behind a curtain. He was clearly charmed, and once we had played a few tunes, he asked his wife and daughters to sing for us. To sit in the midst of their voices was an experience of power that is still hard to describe. It was a special night we will always remember.

What follows is a short overview of most of Kulgrinda's music releases. All of the recordings come with descriptions of the rituals, and the lyrics of the songs are provided in both Lithuanian and English:

Ugnies Apeigos: The Rite of Fire documents a ritual that Kūlgrinda regularly conducts. It is performed by a large ensemble of twenty-one singers, including musicians who play the kanklės and the violin. Inija is the primary female voice, and hers rings out in contrast to the low rumble of Jonas Trinkunas, who also plays a single drum of variable timbre. Most of the rest of the singers are between the ages of seventeen and twenty-five, and their young voices lend a bold joy to the songs. According to the CD liner notes, *The Rite of Fire* is based on "family and holiday traditions. . . . During the ritual, glorification of the Fire is accompanied by ancient songs and stories about the meaning of the sacred fire in the traditions of Lithuanians and Balts." The rite begins with Kūlgrinda's main hymn, "A poplar stood by the roadside" (many of these traditional songs lack formal titles and are simply known by their first line). This is a Baltic *daina*, a type of traditional song sung at the winter and summer solstices and dedicated to the sun. The ringing *kanklės* sets the tone of the ceremony and is soon joined by violin and voices, which recount the story of the World Tree.

As is the case in most, if not all, heathen religious traditions, trees hold a place of particular honor among Baltic pagans. Some of these beliefs can be seen reflected in a Lithuanian prayer (collected in 1938, but with much earlier origins) that swoons over trees:

> That I may love and respect my mother, father and old people.
> That I may plant oaks, junipers, wormwoods and silverweed for their rest in cemeteries...
> That I may not fell a single tree without holy need; that I may not step on a blooming field; that I may always plant trees....
> The Gods look with grace upon those who plant trees along roads, in homesteads, at holy places, at crossroads, and by houses. If you wed, plant a wedding tree. If a child is born, plant a tree. If someone beloved dies, plant a tree for the Vele [spirit of the dead].
> At all holidays, during all important events, visit trees. Prayers will attain holiness through trees of thanks.[2]

Another remarkable piece on this recording is "Dūno River," which is a type of song unique to the Baltic region and called a *sutartinė*. These polyphonic choral chants often have choruses with rhyming words of no known meaning. This one is sung by the women, whose voices are smooth, rhythmical, and lead to unexpected harmonies. Another *sutartinė* begins with the line "I rolled the wheel" and is dedicated to the sun. It features a pretty female solo voice and a choir that responds in a chanted echo.

A cheerful and bright hymn is offered to Žemyna, the Earth goddess. As Jonas Trinkūnas explains, "Žemyna is the mother of all. In the morning and evening she is greeted as a mother... The earth is also mother of the dead."[3] This is followed by a traditional solstice song from southern Lithuania which is sung by Kulgrinda in a round. There is also a jolly little ode to hemp.

Perkūno Giesmės: Hymns to Perkūnas was released in 2003. The god of thunder Perkūnas is the most prominent god in the Lithuanian heathen pantheon. The recording features men's voices and drums on this collection of traditional Lithuanian and Old Prussian songs to the ancient thunder god and the oak. Of

---

2. From the Romuva website: www.romuva.lt/en.
3. *Baltic Religion Today*, 16.

this god, Jonas Trinkūnas writes: "his symbol is the swastika ... and his home is the oak tree ... one can communicate with Perkūnas through prayers to fire, oak trees, hills, through song and dance."[4] Perkūnas is celebrated on three major occasions: February 2nd; June 23rd (the summer solstice called Rasos or Kupolinės); and again on September 21st, the autumnal equinox. There are nineteen performers on this masculine recording. Jonas Trinkūnas is the main soloist.

Prūsų Giesmės: Prussian Hymns came out in 2005. The cover features an illustration of the three main Prussian gods in gold on a prussian blue background. This is an entire album of songs in the ancient language of Old Prussian (which died out in the early Modern period), one of Jonas Trinkūnas's special areas of research. As the liner notes explain:

> The Prussian nation belongs to the family of Western Balts ... they had their own religion, which was called 'Druvis.' They did not want to accept Christianity, which was being imposed on them since the tenth century. In 1230 the Knights Templar launched a cruel and bloody religious war on the Prussians ... in 1283 they were conquered and converted ... but Christianity only became strong when the Prussians were assimilated into German culture.

These songs were outlawed over the centuries and the conquerors even destroyed the traditional drums. Most of the chants on this recording come from the archives of the early nineteenth-century collectors Ludwig Rhesa and Christian Bartsch. In 1809 Rhesa wrote: "Tell us: what crime did this nation commit, which wasn't looking for gold or conquests, but only worshipped their own gods in a quiet shadow of the forest? Why did you go armored in steel to their land to seize their fields, to destroy their temples and their homes?"

The recording begins with wolves howling and a beautifully stark and earnest woman's voice. The songs that follow include

---

5. *Baltic Religion Today*, 15.

bagpipes, drums, and the powerful voices of Kūlgrinda. A particularly mournful bagpipe instrumental is called "Daudas." There are powerful chanting solos by Inija Trinkūnienė on "Sat our goddess in the middle of a manor under a linden tree." She also leads a graceful song to Žemyna, the earth goddess, daughter of mother Sun and father Moon. On another song to Perkūnas, Jonas Trinkūnas calls out with his voice and drum: "Our greatest, our Thunder . . . Unite us, strengthen us."

Giesmės Saulei: Hymns to the Sun was released in 2007. Saulei is the most important goddess in Lithuanian mythology. With its solemn hymns, this is the most hypnotic Kūlgrinda recording. It includes instructions on how and when to perform many of the songs. The sun rises to a greeting of drums and bagpipes and the chanting of "rise, rise, mother sun!" and continues on her path, accompanied by further prayers and songs. The liner notes state: "These hymns have ancient origins. They are related to the Vedic and Homeric hymns to the sun." The opening instrumental music initially evokes the sort of archaic sounds that might have been once heard across Europe and into the East, but with the introduction of voices the aural landscape shifts back to the Baltic. The "great mother sun," whose name in Lithuanian is Saulei, is one of the oldest European deities. For this album, Kūlgrinda collected Baltic hymns that are typically sung at dawn and dusk, and especially during the important rye harvest. The twelve songs carry the sun through its cycles, with the drum serving as a primary element of this rhythm-based recording.

Giesmės Valdovui Gediminui: Hymns for King Gediminas came out in 2009. This famed and heroic ruler was born in 1275 and reigned as Grand Duke of Lithuania from 1315/16–1341, the year of his death. Music was said to be an important feature of his court, and would have likely included folk songs, *sutartinės*, and instrumentals. Kūlgrinda has sought to recreate this royal medieval atmosphere using *sutartinės* from southeastern Lithuania and other pieces written in the Lithuanian folkloric tradition. Most of the songs are in Old Prussian, with a woman's bittersweet chanting that resonates together with the tender tones of the *kanklės*. The bagpipe, drums, and violin fill out the archaic atmosphere. King Gediminas founded the city of Vilnius after being told to do so by a wolf in a prophetic dream.

A more recent Kūlgrinda recording is *Giesmės Žemynai: Hymns to Žemyna the Earth Goddess,* which was created in collaboration with the Lithuanian avant-garde composer Donis in 2013. I have only been able to hear an excerpt from it. The atmosphere of the hymns is sometimes jubilant, sometimes mournful, but they always have the ring of prayer and the spiritual blessings of a primordial heritage. Donis's electronic music provides a superb backdrop for the hypnotic chanting of Kūlgrinda. The instrumentation here is more complex, but the immediacy of the performance is undiminished.

Kūlgrinda is at home performing at folk festivals, rock concerts, rituals, weddings, and many other varied events. The group continues to nurture the old traditions while living thoroughly in the modern world, adapting the ancient ways to keep them alive, useful and relevant. In addition to being a music ensemble, they are bearers of heathen ritual tradition. Their recordings are highly recommended.

For more information on Kūlgrinda, one may consult the band's website as well as the many performance clips to be found on YouTube. The Romuva website is also relevant. The Trinkunai family has branched out and Vėtra Trinkūnaitė currently lives in Dublin, where she is pursuing a solo career in folk music as a singer and *kanklės* player (www.vetramusic.com). For an analysis of the wider context of this music, see also the article "Paganism-Inspired Folk Music, Folk Music-Inspired Paganism and New Cultural Fusions in Lithuania and Latvia" by Michael F. Strmiska in *Handbook of New Religions and Cultural Productions,* edited by Carole M. Cusack and Alex Norman (Leiden: Brill 2012), pp. 349–98.

—Annabel Lee

Fire + Ice—*Fractured Man* (Fremdheit / Tesco)

It has now been nearly twelve years since the last Fire + Ice CD was released, and there was some question whether or not Ian Read would return to the studio at all. In the interim, Read has not stopped singing entirely, appearing on albums by groups like Forseti, Sonne Hagal, and the Italian outfit Albireon. He has also performed traditional English folk music as part of Figg's Academy, most notably at the Wave-Gotik-Treffen in Leipzig in 2008. This is how Read's career as a performer got it's start: he notably contributed his distinctive vocal style to now classic albums by Current 93 (*Swastikas for Noddy*, 1988) and Death in June (*Brown Book*, 1987) and was a member of Tony Wakeford's group Sol Invictus during what was, in my opinion, that ensemble's most interesting creative period. The reason for Fire + Ice's long absences, however, has less to do with a deficient work ethic than it does with Read's commitment to other projects. Or, as he explains it: "Music is [only] one way I pass on the Tradition." Read has spent considerable time pursuing his scholarly interests in ancient Germanic and English history and linguistics, writing (Read was the publisher of the magazine *Rûna*, which has sadly ceased production), and martial arts (Figg's Academy is named for James Figg, the father of modern boxing, and arguably the first in the lineage of heavyweight boxing champions). Read's last album served as his master work for Stephen Flowers's initiatory organization the Rune-Gild, and Read devotes considerable time to his responsibilities within the Gild as well as his own Eormensyl Hall in London.

But the last year or so has seen Read refocusing on his music, and Fire + Ice has played shows throughout Europe, from Paris to Copenhagen. Moreover, Read was a headliner at the 2013 *Stella Natura* music festival in northern California. The release of *Fractured Man* coincides with this renewed burst of energy, and the album is just as potent an offering as anything that's preceded it. Some listeners might find Read's at times tremulous vocals an acquired taste, but I find his style well suited to a storyteller or *scop*, and that is exactly what he is. Fire + Ice's music is of

IAN READ VISITS THE TRUNDHOLM SUN CHARIOT AT THE LANDESMUSEUM FÜR VORGESCHICHTE IN HALLE, GERMANY. PHOTO BY UWE NOLTE.

course largely concerned with themes derived from Germanic culture and other aspects of the European heroic tradition, and this can also be a mixed bag. In the wrong hands, the material can devolve into Tolkien-esque hokiness (with apologies to Tolkien himself) or, conversely, pretentious totalitarian bombast. Read is someone who has truly internalized these traditions, however, and he invokes them in a way that reveals the intimate nature of his engagement. It is the heartfelt quality of his singing, and the mix of erudition and poetic inspiration that characterizes his songwriting, that sets his own work apart from other musicians who have tried less successfully to navigate this terrain.

Fractured Man features performers from several of the groups Read has worked with over the years, including Douglas P. (Death in June), the German neofolk group Sonne Hagal, *TYR* editor Michael Moynihan, and Annabel Lee (Blood Axis). The album also includes a cover of the track "Mr. Wednesday" by the group The Lykes of Yew, as well as lyrics borrowed from poets like Rudyard Kipling and Rolf Schiller, the latter of which Read recites in the original German ("Nimm"). Another track, "Verloschen" was composed in German by Read himself. The remainder of the album consists of lyrics penned and sung by

Read, each skillfully woven into a dense, multi-instrumental tapestry which complements—but seldom distracts from—his voice. Consistent with his role in the Rune-Gild, which emphasizes the Odinic path and embraces the dangers that that kind of commitment entails, there are elements of foreboding and existential angst in these songs that are unmistakable. As stated above, Read is a man who takes his religious vocation seriously, and he has put in the work to prove his dedication. That these efforts have crystallized into the artistic vision one finds on an album like *Fractured Man* is ample evidence that he has hardly labored in vain.

—Joshua Buckley

Wolves in the Throne Room—*Celestial Lineage* (Southern Lord)

Like most people, I first became aware of black metal via the sensationalistic media coverage of the events in Norway that transpired in the early 1990s—which there is no real reason to rehash at any length here. To put some perspective on how long it's been, Varg Vikernes has now completed his prison sentence for murdering Øystein Aarseth and burning medieval churches, and has resumed his career releasing Burzum albums. There is still plenty of black metal coming out of Norway besides Burzum, of course, but the scene has since become far more geographically diffuse (black metal was never an exclusively Scandinavian affair, after all). More interestingly, the music and culture affiliated with the genre has continued to develop in a myriad of different directions. Purists will argue endlessly about what constitutes "true" black metal, or what the real meaning of the movement is, but these are debates I have very little stake in. In the interest of full disclosure, I will preface what follows by saying that I am not really a fan of black metal *music* at all, especially in its "purest" form. While most black metal records I've listened to contain moments where the cacophony builds into something of an almost transcendent quality, I can seldom listen to one of these albums in its entirety. The aspects of black metal I do find relevant are its intersections with other types of music (from traditional to classical to post-industrial) and its embrace of so much intriguing thematic material. Many music critics seem to have come to similar conclusions and—much to the annoyance of black metallers themselves—it is now quite possible to speak of "post"-black metal music. If you listen to any of the older, "truer" albums that started the whole thing in the first place, it's still hard to fathom how so much genuinely thoughtful and creative art could have originated from such sonically inauspicious (at least to my ears) beginnings.

Wolves in the Throne Room's Aaron Weaver has provided one possible answer in his assertion (in a 2011 interview) that what differentiates black metal from, say, hardcore punk, is its implicit spirituality. This may seem strange to outsiders who simply (and quite logically) associate the scene's over-the-top Satanism with the nihilism of bored and volatile teenagers. A deeper look, however, reveals the ways in which this antinomian outlook does contain genuine religious elements. Much of the bleakness inherent in black metal aesthetics has a decidedly mystical aspect, often tied to a reverential attitude towards nature, especially in its dark, primeval aspects. Many black metallers have parlayed this sensibility into serious explorations of paganism and cultural nationalism, and if they gravitate away from black metal itself it is often to pursue traditional or neo-medieval styles of music. Furthermore, black metal's occult and pagan trappings have propelled many of the movement's adherents to pursue these subjects in more depth, and a handful of the young academics entering university-based esoteric studies programs can trace their own intellectual origins to the scene. Brothers Aaron and Nathan Weaver are clearly not lacking in smarts (or crossover appeal), and this can in part account for the fact that the Wolves have turned up in such unlikely places as the review section of the *New York Times* and a spot on National Public Radio's *All Songs Considered*.

First off, consider Wolves in the Throne Room's music. While the Weavers have said that they don't consider their work to be black metal at all, the distinction would probably be lost on anyone who's not a dyed-in-the-wool fan. The "blast beats" and screeching buzz-saw vocals that characterize the genre are here in ample supply, and will probably present the biggest stumbling block for potential new listeners. Nevertheless, there are also strong similarities to post-rock groups like Sigur Rós, Explosions in the Sky, or Godspeed You Black Emperor, with elements of noise and huge, undulating guitars that give the group's sound an oceanic, almost meditative feel. Furthermore, the Wolves have adopted high-end production standards (also eschewed by purists) and utilize a full stable of guest musicians, contributing string arrangements, harp, synthesizers, a mellotron and organ. The fifth track (entitled "Woodland Cathedral") is probably the album's most adventurous departure, and the piece that prompted the interest of NPR. Written as a hymn, the song features vocals by Jessika Kenney, who also appeared on the group's last album, *Two Hunters*. Kenney is a professional musician who teaches at the Cornish College of the Arts in Seattle, and is better known as a performer of Persian vocal music and *sindhenan* (Javanese classical singing)—in other words, not exactly your typical headbanger. Thematically, *Celestial Lineage* was conceived as the third installment in a trilogy (the first two parts being *Black Cascade* and the aforementioned *Two Hunters*) and the band intended it to complement the series' earthy qualities with what the Weavers describe as an "astral vibe." To be sure, listening to the soaring vastness of the band's nocturnal anthems, I am reminded of Rudolf Steiner's declaration that "every night man grows out into the cosmos... Whilst we sleep the starry heavens become our world, just as the Earth is our world while we are awake." If that sounds like a bit of a stretch (after all, we are talking about a heavy metal record), try listening to a track like "Thuja Magus Imperium" (the album's opener, and possibly its strongest offering) and see if you, too, aren't overcome with similar flights of grandiosity.

    The musical trajectory that seems to be leading Wolves in the Throne Room away from the conventions of European black metal is indicative of a larger trend of subcultural amalgamation. Black metal has always had a nature-mystical aspect, but in the Weavers' hands this has led to a more politicized engagement with the environmental movement. The group has been associated with Earth First!, and has moved to an old farmstead on the outskirts of Olympia, Washington where the band members spend their time working on their gardens and striving for ecologically sustainable self-sufficiency. They have distanced themselves from any kind of Satanism in favor of more positive expressions of heathenry, and this is evident in the group's lyrics. They have also been criticized for abandoning black metal's stereotypical uniform in favor of jeans and flannel shirts, which is of course a lot more appropriate than leather and corpse paint for hiking around the Cascade Mountains. In many ways, this is a uniquely West Coast phenomenon, well represented by the crowds that gathered annually at the Stella Natura festival in California. Blending elements of extreme heavy metal, neofolk, crust punk, and a neo-hippie sensibility, it has all the makings of a pagan counter-culture that is significantly more interesting than the sum of its parts.

—Joshua Buckley

Blood Ceremony—*The Eldritch Dark* (Metal Blade)

Retro heavy metal bands, especially those that try to out-Sabbath Black Sabbath, have become a virtual genre unto themselves. One could be forgiven, then, for thinking that Blood Ceremony is just another novelty act, especially given the many reviewers who have described the group as a cross between Black Sabbath and Jethro Tull. This is not to say that the comparison isn't apt. Blood Ceremony play doomy folk-rock with a heavy slab of nostalgia for the late sixties, early seventies sound, but also for the nascent occulture that was just beginning to seep out from the murkier depths of the psychedelic underground. *Dark Shadows* was on the television, and the *Man, Myth and Magic* book series was popularizing forgotten Victorian magicians and non-Western traditions like Vodoun and Santería. In the hands of latter-day warlocks like Alex Sanders, the witchcraft revival still had a whiff of danger about it, and the sight of a nubile young witch dancing sky-clad in the moonlight could still excite a healthy dose of frisson. For me, the most compelling thing about Blood Ceremony is how they've been able to bottle this heady atmosphere, allowing it to ferment into something that transcends the spirit of the original. Blood Ceremony's nostalgia may be for something that never quite existed (at least not like this—which is kind of how nostalgia works, anyway). But it should have.

The Eldritch Dark is the band's third outing, after 2008's self-titled debut and 2011's *Living with the Ancients*. The group's label describes their music as "flute-tinged witch rock," and the characterization is particularly accurate here. In fact, the folkier elements have really come to the fore on this release, though the rollicking pace should keep any discerning headbanger satisfied, and there is hardly a dearth of axe-slinging heaviness. This is courtesy of guitarist Sean Kennedy, who also writes most of the tracks. But lead vocalist (and flautist) Alia O'Brian is undeniably the group's central personality, bringing considerable charisma to both Blood Ceremony's recorded output and their flawless live performances (the group have toured with doom metal stalwarts Electric Wizard as well as genre-defying avant-metal pioneers, Ghost B.C.). Equal parts Maddy Prior and Joan Jett, O'Brian is utterly convincing as a rock'n'roll priestess of Pan or Diana; when she belts out that "black magic has risen in Witchwood" on the album's opener, you know right away that it's a place you want to visit.

"Goodbye Gemini" follows, with perhaps the disc's most accessible cut, a radio-friendly number with a surprisingly pop sensibility. The record continues with "Lord Summerisle," a strictly folk-rock salute to Christopher Lee's unforgettable pagan antihero. "Ballad of the Weird Sisters" features the welcome addition of fiddle, courtesy of guest-musician Ben Plotnick, as O'Brian recounts: "My friend and I we had great thirst, we drank our cups bone dry / But stranger yet was the drink's effect, 'it's witchery' I cried / Eye of newt and mandrake root, the devil's foot in brine / A fever-dream took hold of me, souls danced before my eyes." This is followed by the title track, then the hard driving "Drawing Down the Moon," and finally, the instrumental "Faunus." The album concludes with "The Magician," which conjures up the ghost of Oliver Haddo, W. Somerset Maugham's not-so-thinly disguised literary homage to Aleister Crowley.

As a concept band, Blood Ceremony works, because the concept is such a good one. I have often imagined that Gerald Gardner would be utterly disappointed with the embarrassing, watered-down spectacle that modern witchcraft has become. Blood Ceremony's "witch rock," on the other hand—with its potent brew of mystery, sexiness, attitude (and fun)—might be the perfect auditory rejoinder. "Come ye to the Sabbat, Hecate drawn from lunar womb / Our witch cult unites you, as you're drawing down the moon." Blessed be.

—Joshua Buckley

Hexvessel—*No Holier Temple* (Svart)

Matthew "Kvohst" McNerney is a British singer/songwriter with an extensive background in the European music scene. His resumé includes stints with metal bands like Code and Dødheimsgard, not to mention the more down-tempo goth/death rock outfit Beastmilk. While all of McNerney's projects have played liberally with audience expectations, Hexvessel's endearing mix of prog rock and acid folk betrays only the scantest traces of McNerney's origins in more "extreme" styles of music. Hexvessel sources its sound in the historical bedrock of groups like Comus and King Crimson, and McNerney himself has aligned his work here with modern Finnish (Finland is McNerney's adopted homeland) psychedelic bands like Pharaoh Overlord, Circle, and Jääportit. And while McNerney's other projects might revel in the dark aesthetics characteristic of the subcultures out of which they emerge, Hexvessel—by and large—looks to the proverbial light in the forest, cultivating a vibe built on vitalistic affirmation. In fact, this sense of playfulness and the group's seeming affability is one of its most outstanding features. That Hexvessel's music seems to be delivered with a smile, rather than the predictably dour sneer of so many of their contemporaries, might be reason enough to give them a listen.

The songs on *No Holier Temple* are built around fairly conventional folk and rock structures, with occasional jazz meanderings and some understated prog-rock shapeshifting. As represented on this album at least, the group are an octet, and strings, piano, mandolins and accordions are only a few of the instruments that augment Hexvessel's primarily guitar-driven songwriting. Emblazoned with quotes from John Muir and (Earth First! founder) Dave Foreman, the record's packaging alludes to McNerney's ecological sensibilities, which merge here with a sort of non-localized pagan pantheism, or panentheism. This is evident on the inaugural track "Heaven and Earth Magic," which serves as an invocation to the woodland spirits that are present pretty much throughout the rest of the album. McNerney calls on these beings with a nomenclature that cuts across more culturally specific traditions. They are the "green lord," the "corn king," the "stone man," and the "cloaked king of light." "Dues to the Dolman" continues the earth-magical theme with its poetic ode to the Neolithic monuments that litter the European landscape, or (as Hexvessel describes them) "abandoned churches within the great church." In interviews, McNerney is reticent about his own religious practices, but he has clearly found ways to engage ritually with his gods. His political commitments are also more than just fodder for his songwriting. In 2012, Hexvessel participated in the campaign organized around controversial Finnish ecologist Pentti Linkola's eightieth birthday, and the group are strong supporters of Linkola's Luonnonperintösäätiö (The Finnish Natural Heritage Foundation).

The last track on the record, "Your Head is Reeling" is a cover of a song by Ultimate Spinach from 1967, while quotes from Hermann Hesse in the liner notes are likely a nod to the counter-culture of an even earlier era. Like many of the groups I have reviewed in these pages, Hexvessel may well point the way to a new cultural alternative, tentatively taking shape within the ruins of Western consumer society. That their music is good enough to carry it all beyond the fringe is borne out by the critical accolades the project has received. In 2013 Hexvessel were invited to play at the SXSW music festival in Austin, Texas and *No Holier Temple* was nominated for the Critic's Choice Award at the Finnish Grammy Awards. For a musical outsider and dedicated psychonaut like McNerney, this kind of mainstream commercial recognition might be the strangest trip of all.

—Joshua Buckley

Steeleye Span, in collaboration with Terry Pratchett—*Wintersmith* (Park Records)

Terry Pratchett has written a large number of novels which, despite their humorous edge, also contain many interesting ideas about magic. He is a longtime friend of the scholar Jacqueline Simpson and clearly knows much about folklore. The famous English magician Dusty Miller opined that Pratchett's books about the witches of Lancre are the best information available on the subject of English witchcraft, and in the main I agree with this view.

Thus, a collaboration between Steeleye Span and Pratchett seems on the face of it to be an interesting marriage, and this definitely proves to be the case with this album. On the sleeve notes Pratchett writes, "When I was an adolescent young man, my mate Dante put me between two huge speakers and turned everything up to eleven . . . And that was my first experience of Steeleye Span."

Wintersmith is one of Pratchett's novels and his ideas run right through the lyrics of this CD that bears the same name. Furthermore, Steeleye Span are in great form and their rock-folk style has lost none of its steam after more than four decades of live performances and numerous album releases. That being said, some of the songs are of a more sedate nature, when this suits the mood.

I haven't heard any of the last few albums from Steeleye Span but reviewers of this new release mostly agree that they were somewhat in decline until *Wintersmith*, which has been well received in the main. The band's original singer, Maddy Prior, is well represented on *Wintersmith*, and some of the songs are sung by male members of the band, as well as guest singer Bob Johnson. Kathryn Tickell guests on Northumbrian pipes and John Spiers on melodeon (that's a button–keyed accordion). Terry Pratchett himself also has a spoken part to play.

There isn't a bad song or tune on the CD, and the band are in top form. Each song's lyrics are contained in a booklet and have an introduction which explains something about the song. My favourite at the moment is "The Making of a Man," which enumerates the chemical constitution of the human body in a most clever way, and leads to a conclusion the cynical amongst us may not be too surprised about. American readers (and others of a republican bent) will enjoy "The Wee Free Men," with its declaration: "No King, no Queen, no Master, We'll not be fooled again."

—Ian Read

Lasher Keen—*Wither* (self-released)

A few years back, I had the good fortune of witnessing a Lasher Keen performance at a small venue in Portland, Oregon at the behest of a long-time friend. Having never heard of them and not knowing what to expect, I was taken aback by their musical prowess, humor, and the ability to create an atmosphere that was both invigorating and engaging. Naturally, I was eager to acquire *Wither*, their newest release at the time.

Released in 2009 in a stunning digipak format by Verdandi Design (a company owned by Arrowyn Craban Lauer of *Hex Magazine* fame), *Wither* is testament to what I had heard live—raw, emotive, and jagged instrumentation with dual-vocals to match. The sound can be sparse at times, but it only serves to buoy the material. However, thanks to a high-quality analog recording, nearly every nuance of every instrument can be heard and nothing gets buried in the mix. And, make no mistake; there are a ton of instruments on this recording including cello, tin

LASHER KEEN, CIRCA 2013: BLUEBIRD SHEETS, DYLAN SHEETS AND THE LATE BROUGHTY COLE. PHOTO BY SIMON WELLER PHOTOGRAPHY.

whistle, and mandolin to name a few. Dylan Sheets's rugged guitar playing and Sage Arias's bass and banjo provide the framework for most of the tracks, sculpting traditional song structures into the psychedelic and avant-garde realm. Just the same, Dylan's and Bluebird's vocals are prescient in nearly every song, echoing that indefinable juncture of the natural world and the spiritual realm that should appeal to anyone with a pantheistic or heathen worldview.

Highlights include "Dead Valley Living Stream," which boasts a very memorable acoustic melody and a resolve at the end which can only be described as uplifting and gratifying. One particularly compelling verse proclaims, "Wail like the wind, and moan like the moon, cry like a crow. Burn like a moth, drawn to the flames, hissing a curse when a candlelight wanes." "Animal" is the most memorable and compelling track, bolstered by Gaia's vocal refrain and could be an anthem of sorts, given the lyric: "I'll be a fish at the bottom of the sea, but I won't rejoin the human race in all its wretchedry." "Every Curse Lifted" and "Altes Vogelherz" feature some rousing bodhrán.

A fitting contribution from fellow-travelers Waldteufel and the great Alfred Hitchcock (guess which track) round out a unique and worthwhile listening experience for those who appreciate folk in its many guises, be it traditional, psychedelic, or even old Appalachian. Highly enjoyable!

—Aaron Garland

Agalloch—*WhiteDivisionGrey* (Dammerung Arts)

Released in 2011, *WhiteDivisionGrey* is a two-CD compilation of two earlier Agalloch EPs, *The White* (2008) and *The Grey* (2004). Both EPs had limited pressings, and were released as a duo of sorts to showcase the band's musical variety. That said, Agalloch is generally considered a metal band, but this release contains almost no metal, instead delving into ambient soundscapes, acoustic folk, and grating drones of electronic noise. Nearly all of the material is instrumental, and showcases the band's ability to compose melodies that are repetitive yet hypnotic, upbeat yet melancholic.

The White EP contains eight tracks of remarkable and memorable acoustic songs in the traditional/folk vein, interspersed with pepperings of electric guitar, pounding percussion (courtesy of Markus Wolff), background voices, and piano. There are no lyrics, save John Haughm's reading of "Birch Tree Poem" by A. S. J. Tessimond, but with song titles such as "Panthiest" and "Sowilo Rune" (not to mention dialogue excerpts from *The Wicker Man*), the message comes through loud and clear!

Conversely, *The Grey* EP devotes itself to longer tracks and a much more experimental side of Agalloch. Opening track, "The Lodge (Dismantled)," is lengthy and musically dense with repetitive guitar riffs, bass, and drums that reach a frenzy, only to dissolve moments later into a maelstrom of noise and feedback. Agalloch pull this approach off really well, without sounding boring or tedious. "Odal" continues in much the same vein with repetitive gritty drones and soundscapes. "Nur.Noch.Asche" and "Dunkelgrauestille" feature some remixing from Gerhard Hallstatt of Allerseelen, whose presence on these tracks is unmistakable. "A Desolation Song" rounds out the EP in fine form with ringing orchestration that resembles a soundtrack piece more than a song.

Overall, *WhiteDivisionGrey* is probably not the most accessible Agalloch release, and newcomers may find their full-length LPs serve as a better introduction to a band that is musically enigmatic, talented, and still evolving. The two-CD set comes in digipak format with a handsome gatefold booklet and an embossed bind rune on the front jacket.

—Aaron Garland

Ironwood—*Storm Over Sea* (self-released)

Ironwood hail from Sydney, Australia circa 2006, and *Storm Over Sea* is their second offering—and what an offering it is! Inspired by a quote from Friedrich Nietzsche regarding the volatile yet tranquil nature of the ocean, Ironwood proffers a concept album of sorts based on the mesmerizing and unflinching nature of the waters that grace their shores. In the process, they have managed to successfully combine the often disparate genres of neofolk, progressive, and extreme metal into a cohesive whole. It can be a bit overwhelming, but the immaculate production and incredible and varied musicianship more than make up for it. Most of the material goes well beyond the verse/chorus/verse structure that you would expect from most metal, underground or otherwise.

"Hail Sign" begins with an ominous piano intro that slowly builds with sinister guitar riffs and then suddenly launches into black metal fury with "Infinite Sea." This is easily one of the standout tracks on the CD as it showcases Ironwood's penchant for blast beats, memorable mid-tempo riffs, and acoustic inter-

IRONWOOD LINE-UP FOR "STORM OVER SEA": PHIL BROWN, HENRY LAUER, DAN NAHUM, MATTHEW RAYMOND. PHOTO COURTESY OF HENRY LAUER.

ludes. What's more, a variety of vocal styles (including singing, screaming, and chanting) are incorporated with the sonic assault and restraint. A particularly memorable verse concedes, "Ocean wide dissolve my fear, Sun and stars guide me / Gave myself to mystery, To find she's always owned me." "Arctic Tern" is also notable for its somber and solo acoustic rendering courtesy of Henry Lauer, accompanied by the background roar and din of the sea. "Weather the Storm" is the centerpiece, with more musical variety and dexterity than one could hope for on a recording, much less a single track! Perhaps the most memorable riff is also the simplest—the two-chord refrain during the chorus, which is irresistible. "A Bond to Sever" successfully reflects upon the trials and tribulations of the ocean, as uttered in the verse, "My heart sings songs sullied by fire and frost, Of happiness and inextricable loss / My eyes stare emblazoned with pride-fettered fear, At shrouded horizons, their source insincere." Once more, the musical accompaniment consists of technical guitar soloing, intricate drumming, and upbeat melodies and time signatures that change at the drop of a hat. I would venture to say that Ironwood's musical forays accurately reflect the nature of the sea in its ebb and flow of violence and unceasing calm. "When It's All Over," the final track, features some unexpected and welcome piano amidst the roar and meshes quite well for the album's coda.

Overall, *Storm Over Sea* is an ambitious and mature release that is sure to challenge both metal and neofolk fans alike.

What's more, Ironwood's music demonstrates quite well that both genres aren't mutually exclusive, and can complement one another if executed with skill, integrity, and intelligent musicianship. Recommended.

—Aaron Garland

Reviews: Books

The Path of Cinnabar: An Intellectual Autobiography by Julius Evola. Translated by Sergio Knipe, edited with notes by John B. Morgan. Hardcover, 285 pages with index. Integral Tradition Publishing, 2009. ISBN 978-1-907166-03-7.

Julius Evola e la tentazione razzista: L'inganno del pangermanesimo in Italia ["Julius Evola and the Racist Temptation: The Lure of Pan-Germanism in Italy"] by Dana Lloyd Thomas. Softcover, 264 pages with bibliography and index. Mesagne, Brindisi: Giordano editore, 2006. ISBN 88-88456-33-3.

At last there is an English translation of *Il Cammino del Cinabro*, Julius Evola's "intellectual autobiography." Sergio Knipe, the translator, hits just the right balance between the Ciceronian periods of the original Italian and a readable English style: one that is inevitably old-fashioned and none the worse for that. I can imagine Evola's voice behind it, earnest and authoritative but attentive to its audience. John B. Morgan's annotations are an education in themselves. Evola drops many names, and whether they are famous or not, Morgan tells us who they were and how they fit in. Some of them must have taken considerable digging. An Appendix of eight interviews with Evola from the post-*Cinnabar* years rounds out the work and gives some of his final thoughts about his life and work.

I would urge anyone interested in Evola to read this, and if they have not yet read anything of his, to begin here. He describes the intentions and contents of all his major books, and from there you can decide where to go next. Just one word of advice: unless you are a historian of philosophy, skip the third chapter, on "The Speculative Period of Magical Idealism and the Theory of the Absolute Individual." Its pace, tone, and content are so much heavier than the rest of the book that you may be deterred from reading further.

JULIUS EVOLA IN HIS LATER YEARS.

This is no ordinary biography. Evola skims over his early years with not a single reminiscence of his parents and ancestors, his family home, school, teachers, friends, and childhood activities. Given the natural curiosity that many readers may feel, this silence implicitly tells them to mind their own business and pay no attention to the lowest level of the individual—a level scarcely visible from the heights now attained. Anyone disappointed by this lack of biographical details should remember that this is not a banal autobiography, but the chronicle of a journey on the Cinnabar Path. Perhaps Evola took pleasure in the thought that no one could explain his development as the result of infantile traumas and early influences.

Rather than summarize the contents, I shall compare Evola's autobiography to that of Carl Gustav Jung, and then to the non-autobiography of René Guénon: two contemporaries of equal importance to anyone trying to make sense of the modern world. In the "Memories, Dreams, Reflections" that Jung dictated to his disciple Aniela Jaffé, he also plays down the external events of his life, saying almost nothing about his activities, travels, friends, lovers, and involvement with the history of his times. All that, as he explains, has lost its importance or even vanished from memory, whereas the interior experiences (childhood visions and dreams, religious traumas of adolescence, psychical events) were the *prima materia* of his professional work. Perhaps this difference between autobiographies that both spurn the everyday level explains the roots of Evola's aversion to Jung and "depth psychology," which otherwise seems hard to understand. These two had so much in common, beginning with their interest in Oriental wisdom. Jung held a seminar on yoga and wrote prefaces to the *Secret of the Golden Flower*, the *Tibetan Book of the Dead*, and the *Tibetan Book of the Great Liberation*. In the esoteric field he was involved with Gnosticism (*Seven Sermons to the Dead*; *Aion*), with theories of cosmic cycles (*Aion* again), and of course with alchemy (*Psychology and Alchemy*; *Mysterium conjunctionis*). Jung knew the whole theosophic tradition, from Meister Eckhart and the medieval Rhenish mystics, through Böhme and Gerard Dorn, to the *Naturphilosophen* of the Romantic era. He used this as the basis for an esoteric interpretation of Christianity (*Psychology and Religions*; *An Answer to Job*), while entrusting his wife Emma Jung to explain the myth and mystery of the Grail. He also wrote on the phenomenon of National Socialism (*Wotan*; *After the Catastrophe*) not only to condemn but to comprehend it, which won him the unjust reputation of a Nazi sympathizer. As a young physician he took a position against the over-credulous world of Spiritualism and Theosophy, while admitting that psychical phenomena were real. Jung always considered himself, or at least wanted to be considered, a scientist, but the universe that he explored stretched far beyond the physical one.

For all this coincidence of interests and, in part, of methods, the "personal equations" of Jung and Evola were worlds apart. It was Evola, I think, who coined this phrase, so expressive of his own attitude to psychology: an "equation" being a fixed datum whose why and wherefore there was no point in analyzing. Evola's autobiography makes it clear that he situates these not in childhood but in prenatal existence. In the first chapter of *The Path of Cinnabar* he sketches, as though with a few brush strokes, the two dispositions that seemed to characterize his nature: first, an impulse to transcendence, then the *kshatriya* or warrior nature. How fitting is the first image of the book: "it would evidently be easier, for the purpose of bombing a city, to employ an individual possessed with destructive inclinations rather than a person of a humanitarian, philanthropic bent" (p. 6).

Needless to say, Jung had no such warrior disposition, which is not to say that he lacked courage. As for transcendence, it was only after middle age that Jung recognized its centrality, with the concept of the Self (the higher I) and the sense of its unity with the *unus mundus* (unified cosmos). Reflecting his own experience, the Jungian system of individuation only reaches the Self after the integration of the Shadow (the negative and rejected part of the personality, consequently projected onto others) and the Anima or Animus (the contrasexual part of the psyche, often projected onto the love object). It seems significant that Jung, at the beginning of his career, adopted willy-nilly the sexual theory of his master Freud, then abnegated it in obedience to the distant pull of transcendence, whereas Evola began tumultuously with his affirmation of the Absolute Individual, and only in later life turned to write a *Metaphysics of Sex*. It is not a matter of the superiority of one or the other personal equation, but rather a complementarity of the two for the education and salvation of the West. On the one hand, an exemplary life for those involved with the world of the psyche; on the other, a path for those who feel at least potentially detached from it. The history of the Western Esoteric Tradition will have to take account of both of them.

The rejection of banal autobiography, evident in Jung and more marked in Evola, reaches an extreme in the case of the Traditionalist philosopher René Guénon, another mediator of Oriental wisdom to the West. Guénon wanted to be perceived as the impersonal and authoritative voice of Tradition: he never wrote a word of biography. Nor was he involved with politics, but unlike Evola he did marry (twice), and to women who were hardly his intellectual equals. Guénon and the Traditionalists who follow him held psychology in contempt. They would have rather written about sport than descended to this lowly level of the human being! From the point of view of Jungian psychology, such people are sadly unindividuated and oblivious to their projections. From the Evolian point of view it would be more a case of a different personal equation, perhaps one that combined a sense of transcendence with the inflexible character of a Brahmin. There is another psychological difference: like most Brahmins, Guénon was religious by nature, hence his well-known insistence on the necessity to accompany any esoteric path with the practice of an exoteric religion. Although in later life, Evola became more open to the potential validity of the symbols and rites of the Catholic Church, there would be no question of participating. The Church could not claim that at the point of death he had crawled to the foot of the cross! Nor would Evola have dreamed of following Guénon into Islam—a tradition which he almost completely ignored, perhaps due to his ignorance of Sufism (Henry Corbin not yet having arrived on the scene). In any case, for Evola all the Oriental traditions were already corrupted by the cultural and colonialist influence of the West.

In some respects, Guénon's work fits within a particularly French tradition (using the word in a narrower sense), exemplified by his youthful formation in the shadows of Papus and Saint-Yves d'Alveydre, and, further back, of Eliphas Lévi and Fabre d'Olivet. This tradition contains a strong dose of Christianized Kabbalah; a mysticism not far distant from the popular faith in apparitions of the Virgin (Lourdes, La Salette, and so on); a Francocentric apocalypticism (Hiéron du Val d'Or; myth of the Grande Monarque); and a passion for symbols and their interpretation, which holds Freemasonry in high esteem. Not one of these influences was felt by the young Evola. In their place he had access to a tradition to which Guénon was totally, perhaps deliberately, oblivious: that of German philosophy rooted in Protestant soil (Herder, Schopenhauer, Hegel, Schelling, and Fichte). One can't imagine Guénon in his late work finding Nietzsche "more relevant than ever," as Evola did in *Ride the Tiger*; nor seeing in 1930s Germany any hope for the future of Europe.

Guénon had the good fortune to avoid any involvement with war. He was not called up in 1914 for reasons of health, so he passed the war years as a student, then teacher in France and Algeria. When the Second World War broke out, he had already emigrated to Egypt and was protected by the British allies. His circumstances saved him from having to make any political choices. He was anti-democratic on principle, seeing the optimal social structure in the traditional system of the four castes but not being surprised by its collapse, along with other traditional structures, in the final stage of the "reign of quantity" into which modern civilization had fallen. One imagines that Guénon continued to write for the benefit of the few surviving "Brahmins," with no illusions about the end of a world that "never can be anything but the end of an illusion" (epilogue of *The Reign of Quantity*). Ideally, the Brahmin regards this illusion as a cosmic game in which he, in his innermost being, is not implicated. He does not deign to answer the question: If the manifested universe is *Maya* or illusion, why should a world exist, rather than not? In his most metaphysical works (*The Symbolism of the Cross; The Multiple States of the Being*), Guénon draws the inevitable consequence, privileging Non-Being over Being. To the Kshatriya, the question has more urgency, as for Prince Arjuna on the battlefield which, in the *Bhagavad Gita*, symbolizes the universe. Why is there existence, with its polarities and oppositions, conflict and inevitable suffering? Evola could answer that even in his twenties: it is because the I, the Absolute Individual, has willed it. Guénon's metaphysics lacks the sense of this I. The last and best destiny of man, as he explains it from the Vedanta, is the supra-individual state. Here is the fundamental difference between the two, which a detached observer, not hesitating to privilege psychology over metaphysics, might dare to explain through another difference of personal equation.

Turning to the Western Esoteric Tradition, Evola's major contribution was the work of the Gruppo di Ur and its publication as *Introduction to Magic as Science of the Self*.[1] Before this, the liter-

---

1. The first of three volumes is published as *Introduction to Magic: Rituals and Practical Techniques for the Magus*, tr. Guido Stucco, ed. Michael Moynihan

ature on magic was an exasperating mixture of mystifications and incompatible theories, often intended only to vaunt the wisdom of some so-called Magus. A rare exception was the teachings of the Hermetic Brotherhood of Luxor, used by many Theosophists and probably known to the Ur Group. Another was the work of Giuliano Kremmerz, which was certainly known and used by them. In his own essays in *Ur* and *Krur*, Evola took on the task of de-mythologizing magic, changing it for ever, separating it from faith and religions, and treating it as a science. Intentionally or otherwise, he followed the example of Blavatsky's Theosophy in rejecting both religion and materialistic science, investigating the latent potencies of man with the aid of the wisdom writings of the whole world, but free from nineteenth-century moralism such as warped Blavatsky's attitude to Tantra.

Evola was free not only from that largely sexual moralism, but also from the twentieth-century moralism in which the taboo is not against sex but against discrimination between different human types. To bomb the citadel of political correctness (to adapt the words already quoted), it doesn't take "a person of a humanitarian, philanthropic bent." A keen awareness of diverse human types was at the basis of Evola's thought, rooted in his sense of himself as a man apart from the great majority of humanity and liberated from the Christian hypocrisy concerning the equality of all in the eyes of God. Evola was the philanthropist of the differentiated *anthropos*, for whom his work is an inestimable gift. For the rest of humanity, he seems to have recommended an eventual return to a traditional social order in which each finds himself in a position suited to his "race" of body, soul, and spirit: an unfashionable but far from misanthropic hope.

At the time of writing this autobiography, Evola did not anticipate the attention that his brief career as a painter would attract. The canvases and water colors that he gave away fetch high prices today. When summarizing his period of artistic creativity he only grants it a cathartic intention, pressing the modernist tendency to dissolution to the limit of insignificance in the quest of something transcendent in words or colors. Perhaps he was

---

(Rochester, Vt.: Inner Traditions, 2001).

not sufficiently interested in modern art to see his work in its true context, which was not that of Dadaism or Futurism but of the abstract painters, especially Russian (Kandinsky, Malevich, Mondrian) who were devoted, at least for a while, to the "spiritual in art." What remains in Evola's early work after ninety years is not the provocative side that dominated their original exhibitions in the 1920s (some of them would be *entartete Kunst*, "degenerate art," by National Socialist standards), but more the sense of the long hours spent in their creation, the atmosphere of solitary, concentrated work during which the young searcher used this technique to penetrate his own state of soul, and to go beyond it. Sometimes what he discovered was dark and sad, the muddy colors relieved by a fierce orange; the transcendence, if such there was, that of impersonal forces unfriendly to humanity. At other times he could fill a canvas with a seductive lightness (e.g., *Five O'clock Tea*, 1916–17, now in the Brescia Museum of Art, which anticipates Roberto Matta) that would have earned him a career as fashionable abstract artist. His stylistic range went through realism, mannerism, symbolism, abstraction in various styles (geometric, scenographic, industrial *à la* Fernand Léger), displaying a talent not so much painterly (he never troubled to learn drawing) as omnivorous and self-confident. In this artistic work, which was far from being the only fruit of the years 1916–21, Evola first showed his genius for rapidly mastering a subject and making something unique and lasting out of the encounter. He would do the same with idealist philosophy, the Grail legend, mountain-climbing (scoring some Alpine "firsts"), alchemy, Taoism, Theravada Buddhism; and this is to say nothing of his abilities as a journalist and translator, nor of the erudition that made this drop-out engineer the equal of many professors.

The creative impulse persisted after Evola had discarded all forms of expression except expository prose. During the "speculative period" he took a mythological view of the world and its history which he first expressed in *Pagan Imperialism*, and then—after the encounter with the mythologizing theories of Bachofen, Guénon, and Herman Wirth—on the broader canvas of *Revolt Against the Modern World*. There is no historical justification for the version of human prehistory that begins in Hyperborea and Atlantis, but that does not detract from the essential theme of the work: the overturning of the modern myth of progress. For this "myth" in the commonplace sense of "untruth," Evola substituted a myth in the true sense: a story that conceals truth of a higher order. Behind the myth of Hyperborea or Thule, which Wirth tried to prove with material evidence of prehistoric culture in the circumpolar regions, there lies the myth of a humanity "centered" spiritually and conscious of its unmoving "pole," which is not unrelated to the concept of the Absolute Individual. The story of Atlantis, quite apart from any question of its existence, mythologizes a humanity that offended the gods through an excess of materialism and pride, and suffered the consequences. Perhaps it once happened; perhaps it will happen again. More important still is the myth developed after Bachofen: that of the two civilizations, one solar, Uranic-virile, Olympian, and the other lunar, chthonic, matriarchal. The geographic substratum of this myth is just as dubious as that of the contrast between an active West and a passive East, for which Evola criticized Guénon. Nonetheless, after reading *Revolt* these myths stick in the memory, serving not so much for understanding history as for intuitions about the "races" of soul and spirit.

The choice of title, *The Path of Cinnabar*, deserves a last word of comment. Cinnabar, sulfur of mercury (HgS), is a red mineral compound found in nature, from which the ancients extracted mercury through distillation. By recombining mercury with sulfur one obtains a new cinnabar with the impressive and symbolic color of the *rubedo*, final stage of the alchemical work. The title phrase does not come from Western or Arab alchemy, but from the Chinese alchemical tradition, in which the passage from one cinnabar to the other represents the path of liberation. (See H. T. Hansen, preface to *The Hermetic Tradition*, Rochester, VT.: Inner Traditions, 1995, p. xii.)

I turn now to Dana Lloyd Thomas's work, which can only be read in Italian, and hence merits a summary rather than a commentary. It is the fruit of many years' involvement with Italy, with esoteric studies, and especially with the journal *Politica Romana*. No English speaker knows better the "Hermetic politics" of the peninsular, nor has a better command of its sources. The two things that put this book ahead of most Evolian studies are Thomas's diligence in seeking out the hundreds of articles written by Evola for the popular press, and his discoveries in the National Archives of Washington, London, and Berlin concerning Evola's political activities in the 1930s and 1940s.

Evola's attitude to race, as presented in his autobiography, seems to have been far different from that of the Nazis', in that he privileged the "races" of the spirit and soul over the biological race. Thomas's investigation shows that this is a comforting but misleading notion. What we read in Evola's books is quite far removed from the polemical and often crude racism of his journalism, while his involvement with the Nazis went much deeper than his admirers would like to think. As is proper in a scholarly study (though uncommon in this field), Thomas does not moralize. He lets the facts and documents speak for themselves, weaving them into a fascinating story of friendships and enmities, plots and rumors of plots, sycophancy and betrayal.

Disillusion begins with the Reghini affair. Arturo Reghini was a neo-Pythagorean philosopher, high-grade Freemason, Evola's initiator into esoteric circles, and his doorway to the concept of the Integral Tradition. Together they founded the "Ur Group" and published its remarkable essays on magic "as science of the self." Differences arose between the leaders; Evola displaced Reghini and broke with him, but that was not the end. By this time (1929), Reghini had already been silenced as the Fascist regime clamped down on Freemasonry. Evola then denounced him in the newspaper *Roma Fascista*, accusing him of still being active in the Grand Orient lodge, and recommending that he take some "island air," a euphemism for prison. Reghini was never arrested, but put on the blacklist and subjected to years of police snooping (p. 55).

Another episode is surprising in view of Evola's well-known Kshatriya nature. He had served in World War I as a young officer of artillery, though he never saw battle. In 1930 he published in his paper *La Torre* a scurrilous attack on another officer, who challenged him to a duel. Evola refused. Although dueling was officially prohibited, it was still regarded in military circles as a proper way to settle differences, and to refuse a challenge was conduct unbecoming to an officer. For this and for his defiance of an order to cease his publication, Evola was stripped of his rank (p. 64). Now if he volunteered, he would have to enter the army as a private. The demotion also barred him from working as a war correspondent (p. 62) or joining the Fascist Party, to which he applied in 1939. His last appeal for reinstatement as an officer was turned down in 1943 (p. 207).

Thomas, like his *Politica Romana* colleague Piero Fenili (who writes the Foreword), is ready to acknowledge Evola's mastery of esoteric traditions and the great service he has done them, especially in Italy. Perhaps because Evola has become the center of a posthumous cult, as well as out of a scholar's concern that the truth not be suppressed, their writing about him is largely critical. It is not of the shrill "antifascist" type, but a careful sifting of what in Evola's work enlightens the reader, and what derives from his less admirable traits. Among these is his lifelong anti-Semitism.

The Nazis' obsession with Jews puzzled the Italians. They could understand the resistance to Jewish economic monopolies, but the German idea of a "super-race" threatened by Jewish blood was alien to them (p. 100). Evola took pains to educate his countrymen. He had believed at least since the mid-1920s in a Jewish-Masonic conspiracy against "traditional" Europe. The French Revolution had been their master stroke; the Risorgimento, sacred to Italians, not much better. The *Protocols of the Elders of Sion*, to which he later wrote an approving Introduction, laid bare their methods (p. 104). No wonder that he felt more at home north of the Alps. In fact, as Thomas shows through many pages of evidence and analysis, Evola's political activity was driven by a mystical Pan-Germanism.

Of Evola's central work Thomas writes: "*Rivolta contra il mondo moderno* was not conceived as a pure and simple political tract, but rather as the attempt to create a new 'mythology of politics,' founded on a *völkisch*-derived interpretation of Western and Italian history" (pp. 85–86). The myth, indebted to Theosophy as well as to Herman Wirth, described the tough Nordic-Aryan race with its primordial spiritual tradition, driven from its Arctic stronghold to seek a new *Lebensraum*. There it encountered the inferior races with their orgiastic cults of the Great Mother and their decadent habits. This is exactly how Evola pictured his native Italy: as a land with a minority of superior, masculine types who shared the Nordic heritage of their German neighbors, then the Italy of "mandolins and canzonets," even of "Mediterranean monkeys" (p. 170), sentimental and devoid of tradition. Moreover, in case we should think of *Rivolta* as a corrective to Rosenberg's biological anti-Semitism, Thomas reproduces the dedication in the copy that Evola gave to the Nazi ideologue (noticed by H. T. Hakl in the Staatsbibliothek, Munich): "This book, which has as its central theme the defense of the Nordic-Aryan idea, cannot be more justly dedicated to anyone than to the courageous author of *The Myth of the Twentieth Century*. To Mr. Alfred Rosenberg, most devotedly, J. Evola" (p. 102).

Thomas writes that Evola's studies of race theory, presented as objective and historical, served two purposes: they made racism a respectable area of study, and all the examples he gave came to the same conclusion, affirming the superiority of the "Nordic race" that was effectively equated with the Germans—with all the political consequences (p. 128). But this was not just talk. As war loomed, Mussolini was pressured by his allies to adopt Nazi racial laws. By this time Evola was moving not among Anthroposophists and magicians, but among the strongest supporters of such policies. In 1941 he complained that Italy's racial laws were not strict enough. For an Italian not to be classified as "of Hebrew race," it was sufficient not to have a Jewish parent, whereas in Germany, racial purity was defined through the third generation. Evola cites the Mendelian law of heredity, warning that the influence of, say, one Jewish grandparent may be latent, but "no less dangerous and real for that, especially if one considers the element of 'character' and the spiritual element of race, beyond the purely anthropological one" (pp. 140, 193–94).

On reading this and other quotes from Evola's journalism, it appears that his much-vaunted "soul race" and "spiritual race" were, after all, subservient to physical heredity.

We also learn that Evola, always contemptuous of bourgeois life, accepted a job in the Fascist bureaucracy. From 1941–1943 he drew a salary of 2,000 lire a month from the Race Office. He continued to travel to Germany, where he had found a new patron in Rosenberg's rival Heinrich Himmler, and a new ideal in the SS with its *Ordensburgen* (Castles of the Order). Although elements in the Fascist regime continually hindered him, understandably regarding him as a loose cannon, Mussolini overrode them. He allowed Evola a long leash because of his usefulness as a link with Nazism (p. 173).

Mussolini himself had often despaired of the task of forging a properly Fascist state out of the human material available to him. This was perhaps why he was drawn to Evola's racial theories as an explanation of the problem (pp. 188, 199). Evola, in his new office, described the ideal "Aryan-Roman" type: "He is not necessarily blond and blue-eyed; he should be long-limbed though he may be mesocephalic and, in certain cases, of short stature; but he will still show the same harmonic proportions of members as the Nordic man, and by the outlines of his high forehead, his more or less curved nose, his accentuated jaw, he will give the identical impression of an active and vigilant type, ready to attack" (p. 197). Thomas remarks drily that the postwar increase in stature and longevity of Italians arrived without any contribution from racial ideology (p.199n).

As Evola's critics realized, dividing Italians from one another on racial lines was a foolish policy for a nation at war (pp. 222, 241). In the reorganization of government following Mussolini's deposition, Evola was dropped from the Race Office. Under German occupation he became, in effect, an agent of the *Sicherheitsdienst* (SD), the German secret service. By his own account, it was as a researcher into historical and cultural matters, but as Thomas says, it is hard to imagine a merely "cultural" collaboration with an organization dedicated to rooting out "Judeo-Masonic" subversion (pp. 231, 233).

Thomas concludes by bringing the reader's attention back to the real theme of the book: "When in *Rivolta contro il mondo moderno* Evola launches the fascinating but instrumental myth of a historical and political causality that goes from ancient Atlantis, through a Germano-Catholic Middle Ages, to flower in the Nazi *Ordensburgen*, he ends up formulating a justification for the pretended superiority of the Nordic race, and consequently for the expansionist politics of Pan-Germanism" (p. 250). What begins as an archival study of one man's activities becomes the story of Italy's seduction by Germany, and of why this affair was never quite consummated.

None of this redounds to Evola's credit. To use his own terms, his "soul-race" was blighted with a Manichean outlook and a lack of human sympathy. Yet his "spiritual race" was of another order, as witness his insights into magic, alchemy, Buddhism, and Taoism. His revolt against modernity is couched in mythic terms that we may well discard, but the critique remains intact. The late works will always be an inspiration to those destined to stand as "men among the ruins" or to "ride the tiger." Now that we know the worst about Evola, we should ponder on how it could cohabit with the best of him, and on what that means for all aspirants to transcendence.

—Joscelyn Godwin

***How the World Is Made: The Story of Creation According to Sacred Geometry* by John Michell, with Allan Brown. Hardcover, 272 pages with 231 illustrations. Rochester, VT: Inner Traditions; London: Thames & Hudson, 2009. ISBN 978-1-59477-324-2.**

John Michell's last book, published shortly after he died on April 24, 2009, is a fitting capstone to his life's work. It is a very beautiful book, with hundreds of colored illustrations of the patterns he was designing and painting during his later years. Michell never pretended to be an artist but was a meticulous draughtsman, plotting his geometrical figures and illuminating them with watercolors. In time they became so complex as to tax even his patience and skill, and that is where Allan Brown comes in as co-creator of this book. The hard-edged perfection of his medium—computer graphics—might well jar with the reproductions of Michell's handiwork. But the triumph of the book is that Brown has textured and softened his diagrams so that one can scarcely tell which ones are his, and which are not. There is also a unity to the color palette that gives the book a distinct visual style.

Some of Michell's own designs, like the emblem books of the late Renaissance, combine a symbolic image with a pithy verse. As readers of his book *Euphonics* will recall, Michell is a good rhymester (not, thank goodness, a "poet"). Here is his comment on a magnificent design of two pentacles, one light and one dark blue, and ten little figures in bright red and orange that spin off from them:

> Two pentacles (five-pointed stars) agreed to intertwine.
> They did it in the natural way that pentacles combine.
> Their children were five pairs of twins, not all of them identical.
> That's just the way it happens when you're breeding from a pentacle (p. 187).

Geometrical figures like pentacles or heptagons are alive to Michell because they are the cells of a living and intelligent cosmos. The diagrams often suggest cellular or crystalline formations, which are some of the ways that the cosmic intelligence makes itself perceptible. As for those who don't believe that there's any intelligence there, that is their loss. Michell writes: "One thing we do know, not just from the ancient philosophers but from common observation, is that the world is reflexive and responds to however we choose or are taught to imagine it" (p. 2). To imagine the world as geometrical might seem as sterile as the fantasies of scientific materialism, but to Michell this is not so. On the contrary, it leads to "that constantly, ever-recurring picture of the world which has many names and symbols—the

JOHN MICHELL AT GLASTONBURY TOR. PHOTO COURTESY OF THE MICHELL FAMILY ARCHIVE.

perennial philosophy, the cosmic canon, divine law, the heavenly city, the garden of paradise, the philosopher's stone, the holy grail" (p. 6).

How the World is Made develops all these metaphors. The Perennial Philosophy, though prehistoric in its origins, comes to our culture through Plato, who disclosed the numerical and geometrical archetypes on which the physical world is modeled. The Cosmic Canon begins with the ratio of the earth's diameter to that of the moon, and, by dividing their combined radii by 5040 (1×2×3×4×5×6×7), creates the measure of distance that we know as the English mile. Divine Law is evident in the unalterable facts of geometry, beginning with the circle (image of heaven) and the square (image of earth). However, as soon as these are drawn, they involve teasingly irrational ratios such as π and $\sqrt{2}$, which remind us that "what we have is merely the best possible universe, a material copy of the transcendental reality in which alone can be found pure reason or pure anything" (p. 39).

Early in his career, Michell interpreted the Heavenly City of the Book of Revelation as the clue to a diagram uniting circle and square, earth and moon, sevenfold and twelve-fold geometry. The Garden of Paradise, which comes at the other end of the Bible, is based instead on fivefold geometry, that being the number of growth and reproduction. Some of the book's most beautiful figures are developed from this, like the "Garden of Allah" and the "Garden of Cyrus" (pp. 200–01). Unlike Perennialists in the Guénon-Schuon line, to whom religious revelation is the important thing, Michell puts the geometrical revelation first. Christianity, Islam, and Zoroastrianism, to which these diagrams pay tribute, are authenticated by geometry, not the other way round.

The Philosopher's Stone, according to a famous emblem by Michael Maier (analyzed on p. 50), is achieved by constructing a circle and a square of virtually the same area. This may not seem very exciting, but it involves the union of opposites that is at the core of alchemy, and of Michell's creationist vision. Last of this list, the Holy Grail is the legacy of the gods who periodically appear and rule over us. So long as we follow their prescriptions, their measures and their music, all goes well. "But entropy is always at work and human nature is weak. Eventually the order established by the gods becomes diluted and the enchantment that held it is broken. That is when progress begins, the march of civilization and the rise towards the great state of Babylon—or, in Plato's allegory, doomed Atlantis" (pp. 153–54).

Ever since his first book on number and geometry, *The View Over Atlantis* (1969), Michell was certain that these studies could reverse the process by initiating a state of *nous*, a Greek word meaning "divine intelligence." When societies were ordered by a canon of number and measure, when earthly existence followed the cosmic pattern and harmony prevailed, this initiation was collective. The possibility still exists for the individual of "a spiritual rebirth, an entry into a new world, illuminated by *nous*. It is the same old world but seen with new eyes and recognized for what it really is, a divine paradise." And Michell reassures us: "That perception has been gained by many people, spontaneously" (p. 62).

Some people declare that they have come to this through contact with crop circles. As with UFOs, ridicule by journalists has deterred serious interest in the phenomenon, but Michell always paid close attention to it. Several illustrations in *How the*

World Is Made replicate crop circle designs and analyze their geometry. One of these shows the Crooked Soley circle of 2002, which wove a DNA-like pattern round a ring, "divided by 72 arcs into 1296 little sections, in 792 of which the crop was laid to the ground, while 504 clumps of wheat were left standing." The design appeared overnight, in an isolated spot that just happened to be overflown and photographed before it was harvested later in the day. Michell does not pretend to know how it was made, but admits that "beyond the technical mystery is the even greater one, the mystery of the mind and purpose behind this significant design" (p. 60), for these numbers are the essential ones of the earth-moon diagram.

Some readers may be familiar with the essays gathered as Michell's *Confessions of a Radical Traditionalist* (Dominion Press, 2005), which has one of his geometrical diagrams on the back cover. His mockery of Darwinism in that book caused some disquiet in America, where it seemed to play into the hands of Christian fundamentalists. The same may be said, by superficial critics, of the praise of Intelligent Design in this book. Of course Michell's standpoint is above what he calls "the fruitless battle between the rival dogmatists, religious and scientific, to establish a single, hard-and-fast explanation for the wonders of our existence" (p. 173). As for who or what is responsible for the design, "He is not the dogmatic, humanized God of religious creationism, and he is not encumbered with the literalism that evolutionists apply to their First Principle. We call him the Great Geometer, just for the sake our story. But without him and his wonderful Creation there would not be any story to tell" (p. 167). This kind of story is the personified vehicle for universal truths that we call a myth.

As in many mythologies, there is a humorous side to it, exemplified by the coupling pentacles in the verse quoted above. Michell's approach defies the solemnity of "sacred geometry" as usually purveyed. He writes: "Examples of wit—the highest form of humor—are constantly noticed by cosmologists and occur throughout studies of number and creative geometry" (p. 182). Wit in the prose, and beauty on the page, are the handmaidens of

PENTAGONAL HOUSE AND FAMILY BY JOHN MICHELL.

Michell's mathematical muse, and there are readers (whom I'm sure he would have encouraged) who find that quite sufficient without following the constructions or calculations.

Without denying Michell's originality, I can see a parallel between his work and that of Claude Bragdon, a Theosophical architect of the earlier twentieth century. Bragdon lacked the advantages of color printing and computer graphics, but he illustrated with his own expert hand works such as *Projective Ornament*, *The Frozen Fountain*, and *A Primer of Higher Space*. He too blended philosophical geometry with aesthetic values, showing how it could be a new and fertile source for motifs in the decorative arts. Similarly, I cannot look at Michell and Brown's illustrations without thinking of what splendid tiles, wallpapers, printed fabrics, quilts, and stained-glass windows could be made out of them. Only the Islamic world, denied representation, has fully exploited the decorative possibilities of geometry. If this is appreciated at all in our world, it is thanks to Keith Critchlow, the English architect and perennial philosopher to whom Michell dedicates this book.

The other body of work that impinges on Michell's is that of a loose grouping of cosmologists that includes John Martineau,

Robin Heath, and Ofmil C. Haynes. Much of their work has appeared in the eccentric, miniature format of "Wooden Books." It shows how the layout of the solar system and the patterns of planetary movements are symbolic through and through; how the cosmos is a web of coincidences so numerous and extraordinary as to beggar the imagination. What does one do with such data, or, come to that, with Michell's "New Jerusalem" diagram that takes the earth-moon system and the English mile as its basis? The implication is actually rather a stern one. Humanity can either realign itself with the true nature of things as revealed here, or it can continue with its mistaken imaginings, which reflect back as the cosmos it deserves.

—Joscelyn Godwin

The Golden Thread: The Ageless Wisdom of the Western Mystery Traditions by Joscelyn Godwin. Softcover, 200 pages with bibliography and index. Wheaton, IL: Quest Books, 2007. ISBN 978-0-8356-0860-2. Clothbound edition, Waterbury Center, VT: Dominion Press. ISBN 978-0-9712044-5-4.

Since the lamentable demise of the journal *Gnosis*, its devoted readers have found some comfort in a stream of books, amounting to a small industry, that have take up its mission of bringing the heritage of the hermetic tradition, especially the West's own traditions, to the modern world. Several of these have in fact been written by *Gnosis* editors and writers, such as Jay Kinney (*The Inner West*, as well as the foreword to the book now under review) and Richard Smoley (*Inner Christianity*) or indeed both (*Hidden Wisdom*, now in its second edition). One of the best of these illuminati has been Joscelyn Godwin, and it's no surprise that his new book, *The Golden Thread*, is also one of the best of the class.

Godwin acknowledges that these chapters had their origins in a series published in another sorely missed journal, the New York Open Center's *Lapis* (now revived online under Ralph White's editorship) and indeed I remember getting each issue and eagerly turning to the latest installment of Godwin's "Annals of the Invisible College." I was equally eager to revisit them, revised and under one cover, and they do not disappoint in their new incarnation. No one looking for a lucid yet detailed and accurate survey of the Western hermetic tradition need look any further.

Godwin starts his Preface with a clear statement of his method: since "the thread of esoteric wisdom in the Western world . . . is timeless, each stage is perpetually present." Therefore, each chapter "makes reference to some aspect of contemporary life" (p. xi).

Thus, a tripartite structure emerges from the concept of the Golden Thread itself: historical origin, real or imagined, and eventual loss, deliberate or not; rediscovery; and contemporary resonance. Godwin could start anywhere on this continuum, but he actually chooses to start his book at the second stage, rediscovery. We shall see that there may be more than a rhetorical reason for that.

Thus, his first chapter already finds us in Renaissance Italy, the court of the Medici, where Gemistos, a high official of the Byzantine Empire, brings news of "a 'primordial theology' (*prisca theologia*) [comprising a] 'perennial philosophy' (*philosophia perennis*), the wisdom common to Jews, Christians, and pagans" (p. 2). Gemistos also provides his Western European hosts with a handy list of scriptures, each attributed to an appropriately ancient author. Though most of these attributions are fanciful, and the works long ascribed to the later Platonic schools, Godwin will make use of these attributions to provide his historical framework.

Conveniently, Gemistos favored the Chaldean Oracles, allowing Godwin to move smoothly from history to doctrine. But first a little more history: though Gemistos attributed them to Zoroaster, they were actually composed in second-century Rome, by a family of magicians (hence, "Chaldeans") known as the Juliani. In the first of his contemporizing moves, Godwin compares them to today's popular "gurus," and the Oracles themselves to the channeled scriptures of the New Agers (p. 3–4).

We also meet what will be another recurrent theme: immortality. In the Chaldean case, this took the form of methods of "bodily transmutation" by which it "becomes indistinguishable from the subtle 'radiant body,'" a phenomenon Godwin acknowledges in the case of some saints, and even Tibetan adepts in our time (pp. 4–6). All these themes have their analogues in Islam, he notes, culminating in Suhrawardi's methods of developing a subtle body for exploring the *Mundus Imaginalis*.

While Gemistos thought that the Hermetic Tradition descended from the Egyptian god Thoth, Godwin's second chapter deals with the more historical subject of how the *Corpus Hermeticum* "restated the themes" of Egyptian wisdom for the "cosmopolitan Greek-speakers living under the Roman Empire" (p. 11). Hermes, as the Greeks named Thoth, taught esoteric but practical sciences, such as astrology, medicine, sympathetic magic and, most importantly, alchemy, by which men could regulate the cosmos and overcome "human limitations, such as the trauma of death." As an "essentially cosmological and practical teaching, rather than a theology" (p. 15), hermeticism offered "an ideal meeting place" for all religions, especially the quarrelsome Abrahamic faiths (pp. 11–13) On the other hand, Godwin is disturbed by another consequence of its practical outlook: "there is no guarantee of personal immortality." Since he admits that the construction of the subtle body to preserve the adept from the loss of personality in death is "obviously similar" to the Chaldean doctrine, it's hard to say why it only concerns him now.

On the contemporary front, hermeticism, unlike the comforting but bickering Abrahamic theologies, led to *useful* knowledge and disciplines whose exoteric forms are still with us, such as astronomy, chemistry and medicine. Spiritually, hermeticsm can be found wherever faiths meet in peace, as in Freemasonry, and even among non-materialistic versions of science, where "people become aware of the Divine Mind through the works of Nature" (p. 17).

Orpheus, while still mythological, is also more human, in fact a figure best known for his ability to charm. He, and the humans in his tradition, used what might be called the "numerate" arts, music and architecture, to enchant both landscapes and their people (p. 21). The Orphics also "humanized" the mysteries (what Nietzsche called the Greek "spiritualizing" of the Dionysian rites in *The Birth of Tragedy*) while also becoming the first *esoteric* religion. These populist reforms based on the idea that all are divine or have divinity within them, if only potentially, led the Orphics to soften "conditional immortality" into something available to all (pp. 22–25). In later versions of the myth Orpheus is so humanized as to become a tragic figure, and the god is transformed from a triumphant psychopomp to the dying and rising god familiar to many religions. Indeed, "some of the early Christians regarded Orpheus as a kind of pagan saint, even confusing his image with that of Jesus" (p. 24).

The Orphics also provide a more humanized version of the "Great Chain of Being" metaphor that has too often produced not harmonious society but brutal tyranny, especially in the twentieth century. The sages must not only know how to enchant their people, but have "their subjects' spiritual interests at heart." Godwin sees the need for this kind of "gentle persuasion," since the sorry state of modern society, especially as mirrored in, and produced by, modern arts, reflects a soul that is "not in good health." For how can modern men and women "enter the soul's domain with no songs to sing, no poetry to charm Pluto and Persephone?" (p. 28) One can imagine that those raised in the "culture" of rap would not see the need for charm at all, even on this side of the Styx.

We enter the historical period with a chapter entitled "Pythagoras and His School." The two-part title of this chapter is significant, because Pythagoras is as important as the founder of a distinctive type of mystery school as for his own achievements. In response to the mini–Dark Age that separated the prehistoric period from historical times, Pythagoras combined scientific learning from around the known world with the teachings of the Orphic Mysteries, creating the first philosophical school. Although the Mysteries were secret, they were open to all, took place over a few days, and did not "require the participation of the rational mind " (p. 36). "Orpheus' lyre . . . became in Pythagoras's hands a scientific instrument" (p. 31). Initiates remained silent for five years before they could ask a question, and attended endless lecture series from behind a curtain; this wisdom "could only be cultivated by those who were in love with it; anyone who did not would be unbearably bored" (p. 33).

Perhaps to balance this rigorous esotericism, Pythagoras introduced the doctrine of reincarnation, or more correctly, metempsychosis, which provides some comfort to Godwin's anxieties over "hard-won" immortality, although he wisely adds that "Perhaps there is no single, universal answer, because different souls may follow different destinies" (pp. 34–35). What Pythagoras bequeathed to the modern world was the use of the "sciences of number" to "hone the student's intelligence to a fine edge" with the goal, perhaps forgotten today, of "conscious and deliberate participation in the drama of life and death" (p. 37).

Chapter 5, which we might call "From Plato's Cave to Capitol Hill," finds us at last on firm and familiar historical ground. Godwin does a remarkable job in summarizing Platonism in just two or three pages; he seems to be so eager to get to his modern, in this case political, ruminations that he gives short shrift to immortality this time, leaving Platonism's development of the idea implicit. But the reader can be grateful, since Godwin has some perhaps wise, but certainly beautiful things to say. Returning to the Orphic theme of "gentle persuasion," he emphasizes the too-often overlooked point that the Guardians must love the people; as Godwin expresses it, each state of being, and thus each part of society that mirrors it, is a product of a higher state, which "loves it as its own child, and is loved in return," otherwise there is nothing but cruel tyranny (p. 42). As for today's tyrants, he finds them in "the special-interests lobbies, the military, legal, and medical industries, the bankers and speculators, the multinationals, etc." (p. 45).

In Chapter 6 politics comes to center stage, for the Romans were not interested in personal salvation, but in preserving the Republic, and ultimately, the Empire. Here Godwin brings in an idea that may be new to most readers, the "egregore" [Greek for "the watcher"]. In the enchanted world of the pagan, every living thing, including the State, has its own Spirit that must be cared for. Rather than anti-clerical skepticism, a critical look at Roman ritual suggests that the gods depend as much on ritual as the city depends on them. With the arrival of the Mystery religions from the East, this relationship was challenged, since sustaining the State became secondary to the initiate's pursuit of immortality. Compromise was possible (Mithraism, for example) but ultimately the Egregore had to transfer its loyalty to the new religion, and thus Christianity shed its world-denying "Christian" virtues and took on its imperial, Roman, form. It is indeed "a theory worthy of consideration by anyone who can admit that the universe is a very strange place, and that there is plenty of room in it for beings bigger than mankind." This will perhaps be the most interesting chapter yet for readers of *TYR*, due to its positive coverage of the small details of paganism and its conflict with the new religions.

In Chapter 7, the "Meddling God" calls home. Before Christianity hardened into its own empire, with its accompanying dogma, there was a vast range of Christian thought, much of it known now as Gnosticism. Godwin thinks that "it is time to dust off the Gnostic mythology and to reconsider it in a dispassionate frame of mind. There are two questions to be considered. The first is the epistemological one: does the human being have a potential for gnosis, and if so, how do we recognize it? ... The second question is the historical one of whether the human race may have undergone interference from outside in the distant past" (pp. 62–62). The latter question leads Godwin to gently consider some modern theories on the extra-terrestrial "origins of humanity."

Chapter 8 informs us that after taking care of the Gnostics, the Church then made sure that "The Dark Ages knew of no mystery schools such as had flourished in Antiquity." Nevertheless, "we can sometimes glimpse, like a golden thread half buried in the soil, the legacy of a Christian theosophic tradition that was very different from the mainstream." Most often, this took the form of "negative theology," especially in the work of Dionysius the Areopagite (who eluded the orthodox by being confused with a disciple of Paul) and the later contributions of John Scotus

Eriugena and Meister Eckhart. All, perhaps implicitly, call into question "the 'one way' mentality" of orthodoxy, which takes a tribal egregore (YHVH) and illicitly transposes it with The One of the philosophers and initiates.

Godwin suggests that:

> (T)he indescribable experiences of these mystics be taken as the best evidence we have of the central truth of monotheism: that there is one reality behind and beyond all things, to which the human being is mysteriously connected. But the sacred and revealed books, the contentious theologies, the laws, clergy, and qualified images of God seem to me proof positive of the central truth of polytheism: that there are many higher beings than us in the universe, some of whom enter into relations with mankind. Gods and goddesses, angels and daimons, spirits, egregores, or extraterrestrials...

He is right to conclude that "the matter is probably very complex and beyond our categories of thought" (p. 72).

But what cannot be thought, without error or without meddling and violence, may perhaps be built. Chapter 9 discusses the cathedrals, eighty built in the years between 1180 and 1270 in France alone, which were "a finely tuned vehicle for getting souls to heaven" as well as "one of the greatest adornments of civilization that the world has ever known." Among those achievements which derived from "the mathematics of sacred buildings," were the development of the science of acoustics and that of musical harmony ("number made audible"), "from which a clear line can be traced to the more familiar music, popular and classical alike, whose harmonic nature everyone takes for granted."

How could such monumental structures be built at all in this illiterate period? The "mason's secret" was that through training in The Art of Memory he could "construct an entire building in his imagination, so that once work began on the site he could give instructions at every point" (p. 85). Since these were sacred buildings, filled with myths and symbols, "the mental construction of temples and churches was inseparable from meditation on the meaning of those myths, while the intense effort of imagination could easily pass over into visionary experience." From the imaginary sea voyages of Irish monks, to Dante, to Swedenborg's angelic conversations, the Western esoteric tradition, in parallel with Sufism and the Kabala, "has always emphasized the use of the imagination as the primary way of access to higher worlds" (pp. 85–86).

Modern scholars, "typically unacquainted with the workings of the creative mind," recognize "no intermediary between fact and fiction [and] would call them hallucinations" (pp. 88–89). Yet Ignatius Loyola was able to adapt these methods into the most rigorous mode of education (or indoctrination) the West has known, while a later Jesuit, Athanasius Kircher, "pioneered the magic lantern and described the first moving light images" (p. 90). Sadly, all of this seems to have developed into a world where children are set down "in front of the television" rather than trained in exploring "the inner world of imagination" (p. 93)

It is such images that determine a culture, not "theology and faith in things unseen." While some may cherish the romantic dream that the Middle Ages represented a traditional society unified from top to bottom, or perhaps crushed under the weight of the Catholic Church as one prefers, history shows that by the fourteenth century cracks began to appear. Soon the superstitious fear of classical images wore off, and a growing fashion in secular arts began to favor classical subjects, and "Christian images were joined by a rival body of images . . . with which they lived in grudging compromise" (pp. 96–98). "No one could evade the influence of the new imaginal environment, and few would want to, for it opened the senses to the Eros of earthly beauty." This divided consciousness, unable to throw off one or the other, "Moses and Homer, Caesar and Christ," remains the "unsolved conundrum" of our Western culture to this day (pp. 101–2).

By now, Godwin's historical narrative has caught up with his rhetorical device, and we find ourselves in the Renaissance *per se*. Subsequent chapters will mostly look at concepts ("Religion

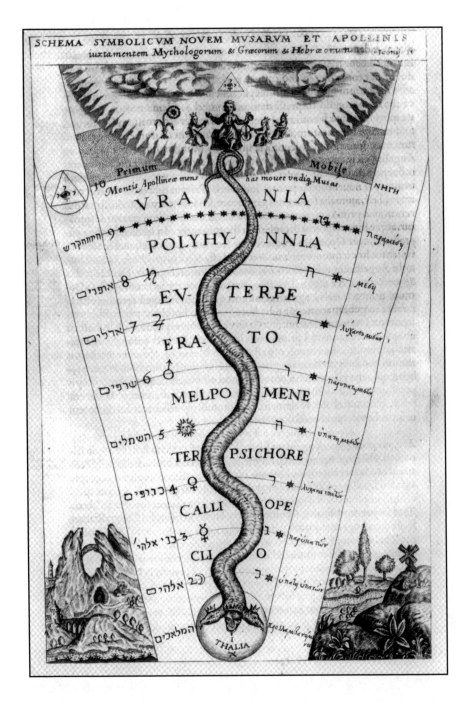

"Symbolic scheme of the nine Muses and Apollo, after the idea of the mythologers, the Greeks and the Hebrews" by Athanasius Kircher (1602–1680).

TYR: Myth—Culture—Tradition

of Art") or techniques ("Inner Alchemy") as they appear and subsequently develop in later history until their contemporary types or "anti-types" emerge today.

First up is the dilemma of the philosopher: "In every generation there have been a few people who did not believe so much as know some of the answers to the external questions of humanity." But what if these wise people find themselves in a society that has no use for them, or even views them with scorn or enmity, as during the sixteenth century's Wars of Religion? The dilemma is how to respond: work privately on oneself, perhaps with a small, secret group, or work to transform society? The Jesuits were the first to "take the bull by both horns"; they capitalized on their expertise in the training of the imagination by solidifying personal belief in the face of religious and scientific controversy, while using a host of imaginal techniques, from magic lanterns to applied sciences, to capture the imagination of the young for the Church. Another tack was taken by the Rosicrucians, a group of Lutheran friends who concocted a new, homemade myth of their own, capturing the imagination of a Europe exhausted from religious strife with the idea of a "secret fraternity of wise initiates who genuinely wish the best for humanity and toil behind the scenes to bring it about" (pp. 105–7). By "steering between the twin shallows of sectarian religion and scientism," they managed to avoid the sterile controversies that otherwise made up the so-called "Age of Enlightenment."

Alas, all these efforts have come to naught; the Jesuits have been frequently closed down and expelled from one country to another; modern day Rosicrucianism no longer seeks to change the world, but merely provides its members with "self-improvement through occultism," while by contrast the closely related Freemasons have abandoned hermeticism entirely and become no more than just another "fraternal organization" among the hundreds that thrive in the United States of Babbitt. Rather than benevolently ruling us, or toiling behind the throne, the philosopher kings have simply "packed their bags and left" (p. 112).

Chapter 13 draws an interesting parallel between the "inner" methods of Christian Theosophy and alchemy. Both are relatively "intellectual" appropriations of their very different imaginal worlds, Christian mythology and metallurgy, creating "an experiential path [which] addresses the intellect as well as the emotions" (p. 114). Their work has found modern exponents such as Basarab Nicolescu, who has explored the links between Böhme's cosmology and post-quantum physics, and the post-war "New Alchemists" who, after C. G. Jung, "revalidated alchemy for the educated public" as a psychological system, began to "work with physical substances but with an awareness of subtle forces . . . and the operator's effect on the material." The rest of us moderns who know nothing of such techniques of inner development are "only able to perceive and live in a normal, undeveloped world, which is the world known to [materialistic] science" (p. 116–20).

But these "esotericisms without a corresponding exotericism" were elite affairs; unlike Christianity at its best, there was nothing here for the common people, so ultimately the spiritual quest became literally unpopular, even among the church-going. The "subjectivity and interest in one's own inner processes and emotion" that is the esoteric path took up a new home: art, especially Romantic art (pp. 123–24). Godwin is a specialist in the occult nature of music, both traditional and modern, and has much of interest to say here: "To those able to suppress the verbal and visual associations, absolute music offers something akin to meditational states" (p. 129). About literature, he leans on Kathleen Raine's perhaps overly dramatic view that "the Muse of poetry today is virtually dormant," (not, one thinks, while Jeremy Reed is still alive and kicking), while Godwin asserts that the novel has remained a popular genre due to its resistance to the anti-romantic spirit of Modernism. Ultimately, though, the "religion of art" is no substitute, to say nothing of an advance, for a real, public religion: "But what is missing is the sense of the sacred, to say nothing of a community devoted to its members" (pp. 129–30).

The spiritual vacuum attracted another solution that was much more successful, and much more to Godwin's liking: "wise men from the East" (including some who spoke through a woman, H. P. Blavatsky) "who did not just radiate sanctity" but also had "supreme knowledge of the spiritual path and total, compassionate understanding of the disciple's predicament." Unlike the Rosicrucians and other pretenders to the role of philosopher-kings, these wise men had a "much stronger impact on the Western imagination," leaving an "indelible mark" on those of Godwin's generation (p. 139). After the exuberant and philosophically profound polytheism of Hinduism had made Abrahamic exclusivity seem quaint, three successive waves of Buddhism: ascetic Theravada; Zen, tinged with the Japanese aesthetic sense; and the colorful and dramatic Tibetan, showed in turn how perennial wisdom can both influence, and adapt to, a new ethnicity. But perhaps the net effect was rather negative, a diminished Christianity finally reduced to only one intellectually honest role: social welfare agency.

In his final chapter, Godwin looks around today, and finds that despite all these efforts, today "the Golden Thread has frayed into a myriad [of] fragments." "There is no central institution, no single curriculum, no diploma of authenticity" (pp. 143–45) Nevertheless, he is heartened by at least one new esoteric movement, as he sees it: Jungian depth psychology, which possesses wisdom of which "many an historic adept was unaware" (p. 145). Another heartening sign is the vague movement called the New Age, whose popularized versions of hermeticism can be seen as a kind of exoteric-esotericism, and whose most characteristic method, channeling, takes us right back to the Chaldean Oracles—a Golden Moebius Strip?

Thus Godwin is firmly in the optimistic camp, and sternly rejects the supposed "pessimism" of the Traditionalists, whose own version of the *prisca theologia*, born in modernity, dismissed Blavatsky, Jung, and the New Age as "pseudo-religions" and spiritual dead-ends. For Godwin, once-secret "knowledge has been put into our hands . . . together with the freedom to discuss and follow it without fear of being executed for heresy. Is this not cause for rejoicing?" And if the price, as it were, is the modern world, where from the initiatic point of view, the inmates are running the asylum? Then "so be it" (p. 149).

Godwin has certainly succeeded in the task he sets in his Preface: tracing "the thread of esoteric wisdom in the Western world . . . for the guidance and entertainment of others." Of course, no one could cover so much ground, even in so little space, without making some choices and assertions that might be questioned by some of those other seekers. Here are two issues that affect his overall presentation.

First, although Godwin is clearly knowledgeable about the Mystery Religions, neither here nor in his fuller treatments elsewhere (*Mystery Religions in the Ancient World*, for example) does he even acknowledge the work, from Gordon Wasson to Carl A. P. Ruck, Blaise Daniel Staples, Clark Heinrich, Michael A. Hoffman and others, including *TYR*'s own Christian Rätsch, which has documented the role of visionary plants in the Mysteries, and, through them, pervading entire cultures of the ancient world. Without having to accept any particular conclusions of theirs, such as specific and highly controversial plant identifications, Godwin would still have been less likely to assert that "we still don't know exactly what happened" in the Eleusian Mysteries, or that they "did not require the participation of the rational mind," unlike the Pythagorean schools (p. 36); nor would he be prone to easily assert that the Orphic mysteries were a mere "foretaste" of eternity, like the later Christian Eucharistic placebo, rather than a precise hermetic technique for producing the state itself.

This may also be the reason Godwin thinks that we can only participate "in a passive mode in the experience" by reading the accounts of the mystics themselves. He might even have been less pessimistic about the religion of art lacking "the sense of the sacred, to say nothing of a community devoted to its members," if he could have perceived the "golden thread" of entheogen-derived consciousness that leads from Eleusis to the modern heavy metal subcultures. This lack of what might be called the entheogenic dimension perhaps accounts for his short-changing Alan Watts as merely a purveyor of "a diluted form of Zen philosophy" (p. 138), when Watts was actually a brilliant and influential expositor of the psychedelic experience, as well one of the first to investigate the key component which Michael A. Hoffman has identified as "loss of cybernetic control and panic" (see Watts' essay "Zen and the Problem of Control").

While Godwin asserts that immortality is a "constant concern of esoteric teaching and practice" (p. 22), he himself seems constantly concerned with making sure everyone goes to heaven. This leads him, as we have seen, to imply an almost "progressive" teleology onto the historical sequence of this supposedly timeless wisdom, reminiscent of the old-time idea of a progression from polytheism to monotheism (which Godwin certainly is free of; quite boldly asserting that "Semitic monotheism was ... actually a retrograde step in almost every respect" [p. 70]).

This urge to democratize, as it were, immortality is a symptom of the second recurring issue: Godwin is an unabashed enthusiast for Renaissance, and indeed Enlightenment, forms of humanism and individualism. He follows the Traditionalists in their "revolt against the modern world" but only back to the Renaissance—no further. Both in structure and in content, the book takes the Renaissance for its axis, looking backward to find liberalizing reforms to praise, looking forward to delight in our supposed liberty. He constantly finds the bright side of this or that modern phenomenon, in ways that might be expressed as "traditionalists may be right in condemning this as a spiritual disaster, but look how much freedom we have to go along with it."

Godwin has had the intellectual honesty, worthy of another pagan enthusiast, Nietzsche, to address his disagreements with Evola and other traditionalists head-on in several places, even in the first issue of *TYR* itself ("Julius Evola: The Philosopher for an Age of the Titans"). Yet it may seem that nothing Godwin says here about "optimism" and "pessimism" refutes the Traditionalists' essential point, that although medieval society was an ossified structure that combined Roman legalism with an alien and fanatical monotheism, it was overturned in the name of precisely the worst elements it had nurtured in the West: individualism and egalitarianism.

Indeed, the book itself might lead one to that very conclusion: does it not show that each one of the modern movements Godwin has such hopes for, from the Rosicrucians and Freemasons to the

Theosophists and New Agers, have all failed in their larger goal of social reformation, and precisely by breaking up on the shoals of "freedom," "individuality," "democracy," "equality," and so on? Each has merely become one of the more colorful parts of the vast mosaic of secular modernity, which, far from reforming, they implicitly support by testifying to its liberty and tolerance. It is at least questionable whether the answer to the problems brought about by secular individualism can be found by adding more of the same, rather than in a new, perhaps more authentic, understanding of tradition. Godwin himself suggests such an approach in comments (reminiscent of Ken Wilber's distinction between hierarchy and holarchy) on the need for Platonic guardians who love as well as wisely rule.

A review is not the place to settle such issues, or even give them the attention they deserve. But equally they need not detract from the pleasure and instruction, and even occasional enlightenment, which Godwin again brings to the often obscure topic of the Western esoteric tradition.

—James J. O'Meara

Signs, Cures, and Witchery: German Appalachian Folklore by Gerald Milnes. Hardcover, 245 pages with illustrations, bibliography, and index. Knoxville: University of Tennessee Press, 2007. ISBN 978-1-57233-577-6.

Signs, Cures, and Witchery: Appalachian Cosmology and Belief. Video documentary produced by Gerald Milnes. Elkins, WV: Augusta Heritage Center of Davis and Elkins College, 2001.

Powwowing Among the Pennsylvania Dutch: A Traditional Medical Practice in the Modern World by David W. Kriebel. Hardcover, 295 pages with illustrations, bibliography, index, and appendices. University Park: Pennsylvania State University Press, 2007. ISBN 978-027103213-9.

There are three related resources of which the general readership of *TYR* should take note. These works—two books and a documentary film—are by no means "new," having been published between 2001 and 2007. But they are certainly not as well known by this community as they might be, or in fact, as they should be. Gerald Milnes's *Signs, Cures, and Witchery: German Appalachian Folklore*, along with its accompanying film of the same name, and David Kriebel's *Powwowing Among the Pennsylvania Dutch: A Traditional Medical Practice in the Modern World*, together provide a rare and insightful vision of the ways in which archaic traditions of belief and ritual practice persist, adapt, and even flourish in the contemporary world.

Signs, Cures, and Witchery offers an extensive exploration of modern German-Appalachian folk belief, ritual, and festival practice. Milnes argues for the profound and meaningful influence of German folk belief and practice on the emergent vernacular culture of Appalachia. While the presence of German immigrant communities in the region has been acknowledged by many folklorists or historians writing about the region since the early twentieth century, few have focused on them—preferring instead to emphasize the Anglo-Saxon or Anglo-Celtic origins of the people who settled these hills, and to characterize Appalachian folk culture largely in terms of survival and persistence of customs, beliefs, music and narrative from the north of England, Scotland, and Northern Ireland. Folklore luminaries like Vance Randolph assert that "most of the hillman's folk beliefs came with his ancestors from England or Scotland" (*Ozark Magic and Folklore*, 1964, p. 4). Historian David Hackett Fischer likewise maintains that 90% of those who settled the American backcountry hailed from "Ulster, the Scottish Lowlands, or the North of England" (*Albion's Seed: Four British Folkways in America*, 1989, p. 635). These prevailing narratives have led, it seems, to an assumption that Appalachian folk belief is mostly, if not entirely, Anglo-Celtic in origin. Where other ethnic and regional roots are present, they have largely been de-emphasized in relevant scholarship.

Milnes takes this idea to task in his twin works, arguing in both book and film for a significant German influence on

Appalachian culture—particularly with regard to its cosmologies, ritual practices, and beliefs about the supernatural. While other reviewers have noted some shortcomings in this work—notably the tendency to adopt an overly romantic, early twentieth-century attitude toward "the Folk" and their lore—the material the author has collected does seem to establish a rich trove of persistent tradition which can be demonstrably (if not exclusively) linked to German antecedents.[2] While the work draws some of its conclusions and connections from historical data and extant collections of folk tradition, the bulk of the text is focused on ethnographic data collected through field interviews with twentieth-century folks living in Pendleton County, West Virginia (which, Milnes maintains, has been called the "Dutchiest county in West Virginia"). Named informants tell their stories, describe their beliefs and practices, and reference traditions they learned from their immediate forebears. At every turn, traditional beliefs are rooted in the everyday circumstances of individual lives. In compiling this collection, Milnes provides some fascinating material that fills a notable lacuna in Southern Appalachian folklore studies.

Early chapters are largely concerned with establishing the vibrant presence of German immigrants in the region, with particular attention paid to some of the more mystical or radical religious communities who chose to settle in the hills or who, in passing, left their mark there. A subsequent chapter on "Astrology" includes details on the practice of "planting by signs" derived from seventeenth- and eighteenth-century German almanac traditions that continue to influence the horticultural and culinary practices of present-day hill folk. One should not, for example, make sauerkraut or pickle beans when the moon is

---

2. I should make clear Milnes is not attempting to argue the primacy of German influence on Appalachian culture. He subscribes "to the idea of Southern Appalachia being a distinct cultural region. Scots-Irish, German, and English immigrants, with far lesser numbers of Africans and Native Americans (among others) came together ... in a way that solidified a culture by way of necessity" (p. xii). Nor is he unaware of the substantial body of scholarship treating German-American folk culture elsewhere in the U.S. (notably in Pennsylvania).

in Pisces—"the sign of the feet"—lest the preserves take on the smell of sweaty feet! Other chapters, including those on "The Occult," "Folk Medicine," "Water Witching," and "Witch Balls, Conjuring, and Divination," offer a solid introduction to the diverse corners of Appalachian folk belief.

The most valuable parts of the text are those passages in which Milnes allows his interlocutors to speak for themselves. We hear directly from Dovey Lambert—an octogenarian healer who "doctors" for witchcraft—describing in detail the ritual procedures she uses to heal children and adults who have been attacked by occult means. Elder Johnny Arvin Dahmer ("in his ninth decade of life") recounts tale after tale of the supernatural healing—and harming—traditions that are a pervasive aspect of his everyday worldview, including reference to his family's "cure book": a handwritten compendium of occult lore kept by his family and augmented over the course of nearly a century. Several of the charms and cures from the Dahmer cure book are transcribed and analyzed in this work—including charms against evil spirits, against "wildfire" (*erysipelas*), and others to stop bleeding wounds. Sylvia O'Brien, another of Milnes's consultants, tells a fascinating story about the ability of witches to steal milk from their neighbors' cows by occult means—in particular by milking the handle of an axe. Milnes draws connections between O'Brien's narrative (and numerous others like it that he has collected) and Old World antecedents, including a woodcut from Geiler von Kaiserberg's sixteenth-century work *Die Emeis* depicting a witch milking an axe handle while her cauldron bubbles merrily nearby.

Each of these tradition-bearers—along with a number of others—appears in the associated documentary film. Their interviews and stories are juxtaposed with footage shot on location in Pendleton County, giving the viewer an intimate look at the regional landscape—at once harsh and verdant—that incubates and nurtures these traditional beliefs and practices. Of particular note are the interviews that include participants of several generations. While Milnes clearly concentrates on the "old-timers," there are at least two informants who attest to the persistence of these folk beliefs and practices in later generations as well.

The only real drawback to the video is the fact that the filmmakers seem, in places, to have succumbed to some of the more unfortunate trends established in the faddish "paranormal" documentaries of recent years. Significant interviews with Dovey Lambert, for example, are filmed and lit from a low angle giving the sequence in which she appears a flamboyantly lurid appearance, and making her descriptions of occult warfare and ritual practice seem a trifle hokey. This is very likely unintentional, as Milnes's tone when conversing with Lambert and other tradition-bearers in his written text is infinitely respectful and free from irony.

David W. Kriebel's *Powwowing among the Pennsylvania Dutch: A Traditional Medical Practice in the Modern World* offers a similarly ethnographically based exploration of what has become a largely hidden nexus of belief and practice in contemporary central and southeastern Pennsylvania. Kriebel spent roughly seven years in the field interviewing practitioners of *brauche* or *braucherei*: Pennsylvania German folk healing. This is a landmark work—thus far the most extensive book-length scholarly treatment of this elusive practice and the men and women who preserve it. Kriebel builds on the work of earlier researchers—most notably Don Yoder and Barbara Reimensnyder—but adds considerably to the database with his own substantial fieldwork efforts.

Kriebel introduces the fundamentals of powwowing and *Braucherei*, situating these beliefs and practices in both historical and cultural contexts in his second chapter "A Powwow Primer," which is as solid an overview of the practice as one could wish. Subsequent chapters offer in-depth analyses of the structure and performance of powwow healing ritual, revealing a consistent inner logic to these rites, helping the reader to grasp the fundamental sophistication of a healing practice that is too often glossed over as mindless superstition. He offers a three-fold scale for categorizing and describing powwow performances based upon increasing ritual complexity, providing the reader with a typology that can be used to identify commonalities in rituals that might initially seem highly idiosyncratic and individualized.

ILLUSTRATION FROM WALLACE NUTTING'S "PENNSYLVANIA BEAUTIFUL."

Kriebel's analyses dovetail nicely with the material in Milnes's work, and I would argue that, taken together, these form one of the best complementary introductions to a vernacular New World Germanic *Weltanschauung*.

Of particular interest are Kriebel's concluding chapters, in which he explores the future of the practice in the changing cultural landscapes of the twenty-first century. Addressing the question "is powwowing really in decline?" (citing the prevailing view of much prior scholarship and the opinions expressed by many of his consultants)—the author offers some compelling arguments to the contrary. He cites the increased cost of biomedical care, as well as the growing acceptance of "alternative" or even "New Age" (his term) therapies as influences that contribute to powwow's persistence, even among conservative communities like the Old Order Amish and the Mennonites. These "plain communities" (as Kriebel identifies them) often prefer medical treatments they perceive as less invasive than allopathic biomedicine, and will seek out "chiropractors and reflexologists . . . hydrotherapists, therapeutic touch practitioners" and, indeed, powwowers, whose healing methods are also seen as non-invasive (p. 217). (Although as he points out, some of the overtly occult components of powwow may create other tensions, particularly

MODERN HEX DESIGN BY HUNTER YODER. PHOTO COURTESY OF HUNTER YODER.

in communities like the Old Order Amish.)

Kriebel also wonders at the emergence of "a new form of powwower—the Neo-Pagan," and identifies the efforts of contemporary pagan author Silver Ravenwolf as an example of non–Christian, non–Pennsylvania German individuals attempting to adopt and adapt powwow practice in an alternate context. Although he acknowledges that Ravenwolf appears to have learned powwowing from a traditional resource (Braucher Preston Zerbe of Adams County), Kriebel is appropriately skeptical of her efforts to interpret and apply powwow outside of a traditional, Christian, Pennsylvania Dutch worldview. Kriebel does consider that this reinterpretation may be one vector for the survival of powwow's ritual patterns and processes, albeit in a radically re-interpreted form. It is unfortunate that at the time of his writing he was only familiar with Ravenwolf's work, and did not also explore the growing interest in powwow, *braucherei*, and hexcraft among members of the modern heathen movement—artists like Hunter Yoder, for example, or the practitioners of

Urglaawe[3]—whose interpretations and explorations of these arts may be equally radical, but which do attempt to situate them in a Pennsylvania German cultural and linguistic, yet not overtly Christian, context.

Kriebel does attest to a rising interest in traditional powwow among a younger generation of Pennsylvania Germans who are not part of revival movements like those described above. While the number of living powwowers may have lessened in the last century, the processes by which these practices are transmitted have not wholly disappeared. Kriebel cites several examples of younger folks who have undertaken traditional instruction from Powwowers in their families, or elsewhere in their communities, and who continue to practice in what is a more or less traditional form, a process he describes as a "retrenching" (p. 220) of powwow. He observes that his own research may have inadvertently reawakened interest in these healing arts, and he found himself on occasion acting as a "powwow broker"—providing the names and contact information for practitioners he had interviewed to potential clients or patients in need.

Taken together, these texts offer considerable insight into the processes by which forms and examples of vernacular culture persist through time and across geographical space. They further illustrate the ways in which traditions of belief and practice function in the daily lives of individuals who preserve and perform them. As windows into tradition-rich lives, these resources are invaluable to those of us who want to better understand the mechanisms by which cultural forms and examples persist and survive. The perspectives expressed in these works offer an important and, I would contend, a practical counterpoint to the more abstract philosophical arguments of many of the Traditionalist authors whose oeuvres are perhaps more familiar to readers of *TYR*. This, we might argue, is the other face of Tradition: hybrid, earthy, quotidian, more than a little messy—comprised of concrete expressions that emerge from an

---

3. *Die Urglaawe* ("The Original Faith" in Pennsylvania German) is a modern revival movement that describes itself as "A Heathen Path with a Deitsch Identity" (www.urglaawe.org).

intricate network of real human needs, fears, and desires. And such expressions are no less sophisticated for being concrete. When the men and women interviewed in these resources speak of "blood-stopping Bible verses," "sign cures," or "doctoring for witches," they articulate complex and nuanced understandings of the relations that exist (or that believers feel should exist) between human, natural, and supernatural worlds. The beliefs that comprise Pennsylvania German *braucherei* and Appalachian folk magic offer vital ways of knowing and understanding one's place in these worlds, and the associated practices offer those who preserve them traditional tools to help with the daily struggles of life beset with illness, jealousy, anxiety, and hardship. We can learn much from exploring these traditions, including much about the workings of Tradition itself.

—Stephen C. Wehmeyer

***The Pagan Religions of the Ancient British Isles: Their Nature and Legacy* by Ronald Hutton. Hardcover, 397 pages with notes, additional source material, and index. Oxford: Blackwell, 1991. ISBN 0-631-17288-2.**

Ronald Hutton is known to Oxford dons and neopagans alike as an authority on the folk traditions of the British Isles. *The Pagan Religions of the Ancient British Isles* is a representative example of his rigorous scholarship and strict adherence to the facts; originally published over twenty years ago, it has lost none of its relevance. Hutton undertakes a survey of our knowledge concerning the beliefs and practices of the pre-Christian peoples of the British Isles, their echoes after Christianization, and the many misconceptions surrounding these topics. Hutton carefully examines the archeological and historical record to give us a nuanced discussion of how much—or how little—is truly understood about the religious beliefs of the various "pagan" societies that have made the British Isles their home over the course of millennia: pre-Celtic Stone Age peoples, Celts, hybrid Romano-Celtic cultures, and Anglo-Saxons.

Reviews: Books

Kit's Coty House, a Neolithic chambered long barrow in the county of Kent. Nineteenth-century steel engraving by E. Penstone.

Hutton begins with an analysis of cave art. The evidence presented provides only the foggiest picture about the religious beliefs of the Paleolithic and Mesolithic British, as there are a variety of interpretations about the meaning of cave art, which includes intriguing abstract forms along with depictions of human and animal forms. Whether they are depictions of life, myth, or magic remains a riddle. Hutton cites the suggestion made by Dr. Steven Mithen in the article "To Hunt or to Paint: Animals and Art in the Upper Paleolithic," which stated that the animal figures were actually used to teach hunters to identify different types of game. The meaning of cave art is an open question, as is the nature of prehistoric religion. Mesolithic culture may well have contained mysteries in the religious sense, but it certainly offers them in the secular one.

The Neolithic era provides scholars with a bit more solid evidence to work with, in the form of various tomb structures made from stone. Much of what we can infer about the nature of Neolithic religion comes from these monuments, some of which pre-date the Levantine Goddess cult. Hutton discusses the various types of tombs—including barrows, dolmens, and passage graves—along with various subtypes, perhaps to a depth that may be daunting to the casual student of archeology. In addition to being resting places for the dead, the tombs were also spacious enough to accommodate rituals. We find evidence of ritual activity with potsherds, remains of pigs, and ashes. Moreover, pieces of skeleton indicate that the human remains also played a role in these rites. There is evidence of cremation in some tombs, yet in others there are complete bones, often mixed together from several skeletons. In some tombs the bones of men and women are separated, in others they are mixed. However, we do not know much about the people interred in the tombs other than their ages and sexes. Only a small proportion of the population was interred, and whether they were chosen because they were members of a ruling family, for religious purposes, for their talents in life, or for some other unknown reason, is an area open to speculation. We can surmise a few things about the nature of their society, which was becoming more agrarian, with large-scale animal husbandry prevalent by the mid-Neolithic. This was also a time of warfare, as evidenced by the stone fortifications dated to 3800 B.C.E. at Carn Brea. Citing the book *Women in Prehistory* by Margaret Ehrenberg, Hutton surmises that the bellicose nature of Neolithic Britain indicates a more socially stratified society than the one portrayed by advocates of a Neolithic matriarchy. Yet he acknowledges that we can only theorize about the social and political nature of Neolithic Britain.

Still lingering is the question of what role the rituals in the tombs played. The nature of the religion also remains a mystery; the idea of Neolithic Goddess cult stretching from the Levant to England has been debunked in Peter Ucko's monograph *Anthropomorphic Figurines of Predynastic Egypt and Neolithic Crete* and Andrew Fleming's article "The Myth of the Mother Goddess" published in the journal *World Archaeology*. The archaeological record in England provides a few leads. There are two statuettes that are possibly Neolithic. One, from the Somerset Levels, dates from around 3800 B.C.E. and it may depict a hermaphroditic figure. However we cannot tell whether it was merely a toy or a ritual artifact. The other one is a chalk statuette depicting a female, found alongside chalk spheres and chalk phalli in flint mines in Grimes Graves, Norfolk. This is thought to be an example of sympathetic magic designed to restore the wealth of a flint mine that had been depleted. The chalk statuette may be a goddess. However, we do not know whether she was one of many gods or a universal deity. The fundamental ambiguity of the archeological record is something that the discerning reader should take from this book.

Continuing chronologically, Hutton proceeds to discuss new forms of architecture and the evidence of cultural changes in the mid-Neolithic era. The passage graves become more architecturally complex, as evidenced by the famed Irish site at Newgrange. A greater variety of motifs were carved into the stones, yet the purpose of this art—be it purely aesthetic or spiritual—still eludes us. With the changes in art and architecture there were also changes in the burial practices, which in turn indicate changes in culture. Hutton cites grave goods such as antler maces and boar tusks laid next to un-cremated adult males in the central chambers of barrows, which may testify to the elite status of the dead. Moreover, we see barrows where bodies were not mixed together, which may indicate a certain amount of individual privilege, or a change in the religious beliefs dealing with death. Furthermore, as Hutton makes clear, the evidence varies from location to location. In addition to the development of the tombs, we see the emergence of circles of megaliths, eventually culminating in the henges. We can, however, tell a few things about the nature of the religion from the archaeological record. He states that "we have strong but not conclusive evidence of a religion or religions in early Bronze Age Britain and Ireland, mediated by figures like tribal shamans and containing a cult of the sun and perhaps of the moon."

This begs the question: does the layout of these various monuments reflect astronomical patterns? Hutton takes a skeptical view of archeoastronomy. At Stonehenge astronomers can identify at least 112 different possible orientations, many of which are mutually exclusive in terms of a religious system. Yet Hutton admits that Aubrey Burl's suggestion that rings in Kerry and Cork were dedicated to lunar rites, while the wedge tombs of those areas were dedicated to solar ones, is a possibility. On the other hand, Hutton is less open to the ideas of more "alternative" scholars, like Nigel Pennick, Paul Devereux (who co-authored the book *Lines on the Landscape: Leys and Other Linear Enigmas*) and John Michell, the author of *The View Over Atlantis*, on the subject of the alignment of ancient monuments with "leys," a term coined by amateur historian Alfred Watkins for straight lines connecting monuments. The idea that ley lines were roads connecting various monuments (some of which didn't exist until medieval times) in some grand sacred geometrical arrangement doesn't appear realistic when these lines cross impassable terrain such as swamps and mountains. Even less credible is the idea that the leys are lines of magic energy, perhaps detectable with dowsing rods. Among the many flaws Hutton finds with these authors are attempts to impose ideology on archeology, as well as spurious etymologies, and over-generalizations about the nature of religion. Moreover, he notes attempts to ascribe the henges to the Celts when Celtic mythology explicitly states that they were built by pre-Celtic peoples. Indeed, the Iron Age inhabitants cleared out preexisting monuments to make room for their own settlements. This destruction compounds the archeological mysteries that scholars have to investigate, and so we must apply the utmost caution when making any judgments about the nature of Stone Age religion in the British Isles.

Hutton's treatment of the Celts is similarly rigorous. He addresses the problems in Celtic scholarship since its beginnings. The romantic Druidic revival spearhead by Edward Williams, who dubbed himself Iolo Morganwg, and culminating in the publication of the *Barddas*, is dismissed outright. Hutton's criticism of Caitlín Matthews's work, featured in books such as *The Elements of the Celtic Tradition*, is more nuanced. He praises her knowledge of the Irish and the Welsh, but faults her for overgeneralizing about the existence of a "Celtic World" from Ireland to Switzerland, and for utilizing non-academic mystical sources alongside more rigorous material. Ultimately, he believes she is attempting to create a modern religious movement with some historical Celtic elements. A work treated more harshly is Robert Graves' *The White Goddess*, which has been responsible for many popular misconceptions about Celtic religion. Graves' "Triple Goddess" concept of the maiden, the mother, and the crone is problematic, for example: although there are goddesses that come in threes in the mythology (such as the Irish war goddesses Morrigan, Badhbh, and Nemhain), they do not fit the pattern that Graves presents. His "Celtic Tree Calendar" is a blatant fabrication, as the Celtic holidays were the cross quarters, Lughnasadh, Beltine, Imbolc, and Samhain, and it appears that the early Welsh ignored Lughnasadh, Samhain, and Imbolc, so these holidays were not necessarily pan-Celtic. Graves later admitted that "it's a crazy book and I didn't mean to write it."

In addition to modern accounts of the Celts, classical texts receive a thorough inspection. The reports of Greeks and Romans are faulted for their ideological biases. In the case of Timaeus, the Celts are portrayed as noble savages; whereas in the writings of Julius Caesar they are portrayed as deserving of Roman conquest. The classic texts of the Celtic tradition from Ireland and Wales receive some criticism as well. The Welsh *Mabinogion*, committed to its final form in the late eleventh century, is filled with an assortment of tales of various provenances, some of which emerged from Egypt, China, or India, in addition to tales of Welsh origin. Hutton ultimately deems the tales of the *Mabinogion* to be "too far removed from their sources to be useful in reconstructing the original religion." The Irish texts are viewed as a stronger source, but we should be wary because they were written by Christian monks, who were educated in Greek and Latin classics, and those views may have influenced their work. Hutton cites the example of the Irish Tuatha Dé Danann as a pantheon that may have been constructed from various local deities peculiar to a certain tribe or region into something along the lines of a pan-Irish pantheon by the classically educated Christian scribes who recorded the tales.

Archeological evidence seems to support the idea of various localized cults and tribal deities like tutelary goddesses, rather than an overarching pan-Celtic religion with a pantheon in the style of the Greeks and Romans. However, this does not preclude the existence of pan-Celtic deities, such as Lugh, attested as Lugoves throughout the European continent. Out of the 375 known names for Celtic gods, 305 appear only once in the historical record, which lends further credence to the idea of very localized deities. The concept of the tribal tutelary goddess appears to play an important part in Celtic religion. For example, the Irish goddess Brighid may really be a tutelary goddess of Leinster—indeed, there might be up to twelve different local Irish variants of her. On the other hand, she could be a pan-Celtic deity known in Britain as Brigantia. It is also possible that Danu, the Mother Goddess of the Tuatha Dé Danann, was a tutelary goddess of Munster. In Ireland, sacred kings symbolically wed the tutelary goddess during their investiture. The sacred king served as the most important mediator between the human and the divine. In theory, the monarch could be deposed if his reign was plagued with misfortune such as defeat, sickness, or starvation. In Ireland, sacred taboos called *geisa* bound the king and to violate them would invite divine wrath. In addition to the king, the elites attested to in Greco-Roman sources are the druids, priests who tended to focus on philosophy and counsel; the *vates*, who practiced divination and sacrifice; and the bards, elite poets who often chronicled the great deeds and history of their rulers. The bardic tradition of court poetry continued into the seventeenth and eighteenth centuries in Ireland and Scotland, leaving us with some insight into the history of the tradition, with the bardic title being inherited among men from generation to generation. Also, it should be noted from the historical record that while only men were druids and kings, Celtic religion was not solely male-dominated, as women could be prophetesses, poets, or magicians.

Yet Celtic religion still remains enigmatic. The physical forms of the deities are mysteries. We only have one pre-Roman representation of a god from the British Isles, a coin depicting a bearded man with antlers and a crown with a wheel emblem on it. As to what system of ethics or morality these gods taught, we have nothing concrete. We know a few things about Celtic beliefs regarding the afterlife. From the early Irish and Welsh tales we know of a Celtic Otherworld, superior to the mortal world, which can be entered and exited by human heroes. In Irish legend, the House of Donn, a country of the dead, is a rather dreary place, much more unpleasant than the rather heavenly Otherworld. Some tales, such as the Irish story "The Wooing of Étaín" from *The Yellow Book of Lecan*, feature reincarnation. In addition to the stories regarding the nature of the Celtic afterlife, we do have evidence of religious rituals. Archeology has revealed a great deal of weaponry thrown into rivers, springs, and bogs. One interpretation is that these goods were deposited in the water along with the ashes of the deceased; indeed, this appears to have been the case at the beginning of the Iron Age. The Greek and Roman historians Strabo and Diodorus Siculus state that the Celtic Gallic tribes cast the spoils of war into pools as a ritual offering to their gods. Whether these gods were war deities, river deities, or their tutelary protectors is not known. As for human sacrifice, evidence can be found in propagandistic Roman literature, and the remains of bodies have been found placed under the ramparts of Iron Age forts like Maiden Castle, Hod Hill, and South Cadbury. Yet Hutton is skeptical of the commonly held belief that Celtic headhunting had a religious significance. In many ways we are left with more questions than answers as to the precise nature of Celtic religion.

In contrast to the lack of religious imagery in the Celtic archeological record, the Roman invaders left a wealth of stone artifacts and monuments. The Roman penchant for stonework leaves us with reliefs, sarcophagi, temples, and inscriptions. In addition, the Romans introduced writing. Thus we find written curses, where worshippers invoked the wrath of the divine upon their enemies, and votive tablets recording the desires of supplicants. Moreover, Roman literature, though not specifically Romano-British, is a rich source of knowledge about the religious customs of the empire. Evidence of syncretism between the faiths found throughout the empire abounds. New gods were imported and existing ones took on new personalities. A feature that modern mystics might appreciate about the Romans was the ability of any person to create a religion and have it approved by an act of the Senate as a legitimate cult. However, Roman tolerance had its limits. The druids were suppressed, largely for the political reasons of their resistance to Roman conquest. Hutton suggests that the assimilation of Celtic druids into Romano-British religion was a likely fate as well. Moreover, the practice of human sacrifice was outlawed in Roman jurisdictions (yet the presence of severed heads at several sites may indicate a continuation of the practice). Notwithstanding certain incidents of Roman heavy handedness towards the natives of the British Isles, there developed a rich Romano-British culture that contained elements from all over the empire.

The Romans introduced the mystery cults (focused on deities such as Mithras and Cybele), which were popular among soldiers and merchants. However, these had limited appeal to the general populace, who appear to have worshipped a variety of Celtic and Roman gods, often melding names and personalities. The Roman God Mars was well received by the Celts; indeed, Hutton states that there exist twenty-one known examples of Mars syncretized with local deities. The imported cult of the Matres, who were depicted as three females, became popular with Roman soldiers in Britain. Hutton speculates that the Celtic tutelary goddesses may have influenced these figures. However, he warns that the lack of specifically Romano-British historical sources makes this impossible to confirm. Furthermore, Celtic gods became identified with Roman ones, such as the conflation of Maponus with Apollo. On the other hand, there is evidence that Romans took to worshipping local Celtic deities such as Cocidius, Belatucadrus, and Coventina. To provide further evidence of cultural cross-pollination between the Celts and Romans, we see a marriage between the Roman Mercury and the Celtic goddess of abundance, Rosmerta, depicted on a stone in Gloucester. Yet there are gods we associate with the Romano-Celtic culture that were not worshiped in Roman Britain, such as Cernunnos, the horned god depicted on a carved pillar found in Paris and dated to the first century c.e. In addition to the multitude of pagan deities found in Romano-British culture, Christianity was also imported.

The Christianization of Britain was by no means uniform, nor was it primarily achieved by violence and oppression. Hutton's characterization of Christianization is well balanced and free of the ideological biases that prevailed in earlier accounts. In the nineteenth century and the first half of the twentieth century, historians portrayed the conversion of the Roman Empire to Christianity as a positive event in a violent, corrupt, and tyrannical Roman Empire. Hutton is careful to note that this view was generally foisted on the public by novelists and filmmakers, as the Christians of Rome were generally accepting of slavery, torture, and the harsh forms of punishment common in that era. In the latter half of the twentieth century, proponents of "alternative archeology" and believers in the cult of the Neolithic Mother Goddess (which is not necessarily historical) depicted the coming of Christianity to Roman Britain as the beginning of the repression of women, the destruction of the environment, and the censorship of art. Regarding the rights of women, the Romans were unambiguously patriarchal, while attitudes of the pagan Celts, whose gender norms we know much less about, are still an object of speculation. However, utilizing the research of Donnchadh Ó Corráin, Liam Breatnach, and Aidan Breen presented in *Peritia* and *Marriage in Ireland* in 1984 and 1985, we can infer from the early Medieval Irish law codes something about the rights of women in Celtic society. Like in the Roman law codes, Irish women could be property owners and they could initiate divorce. However, women were expected to be faithful to their husbands, whereas the husband could take multiple concubines. In addition to legal codes, literature provides a window into their society, but certain caveats must be taken into consideration when dealing with such texts. Though there are strong female characters in Celtic literature, there were also strong female characters, such as the Amazons, in the literature of the strictly patriarchal Greeks. It appears that women could be queens, although succession rights favored males. Furthermore, there are many misogynistic comments in the epic of Irish literature, the *Táin*, so it seems that women were not unequivocally respected, even in positions of authority. It appears that the coming of Christianity did not significantly alter the position of women in the British Isles, at least not immediately, but as the Middle Ages progressed the power of women declined. In regard to the environment, the Christian destruction of sacred groves is well attested. Nevertheless, wholesale environmental destruction occurred at the hands of the Iron Age Celts and pagan Romans as well, so Christianity doesn't seem to be a motivating factor in the destruction of the forest. The allegation of Christian censorship and outright destruction of pagan art and literature has some merit, as we have lost a great deal of texts containing pagan religious works, and numerous examples of art portraying pagan deities were destroyed. However, the Catholic Church did preserve a great deal of pagan literature; indeed, Hutton notes, it preserved most of what has come down to us.

The process of Christianization seems to have been generally peaceful. Once again there is evidence of syncretism. At Sulis Bath we find votive tablets (a pagan device) cast into the spring with Christian messages on them. We find that there were Christian burials with pagan-style grave goods. Christianization appears to have entailed a slow process of losing the pagan traditions. This seems to have largely been completed by the fifth century in Britain. In Ireland, the last known king to celebrate a marriage to the Celtic tutelary goddess died in 565, and it is likely that his children were Catholic. Furthermore, King Diarmait maintained friendly relations with the monastery of Clonmacnoise, so the relationship between Christians and Pagans at this time was not necessarily antagonistic.

Indeed, we see pagan and Christian cooperation for purely political reasons in the age of the Anglo-Saxon invasion as in the case of the pagan king Penda and his Christian ally Cadwallon. With the invasion of the Angles and the Saxons there was a partial reintroduction of paganism to Britain, this time in a Germanic form. It shares many deities in common with the religion of Scandinavia: Woden, the equivalent of Odin; Tiw, the equivalent of Tyr; Thunor, the equivalent of Thor; Frey; and Frigga. But there are also attestations of deities we do not find elsewhere, such as Hreda and Eostre. However, by this time paganism was not dominant, as members of the same dynasty, indeed the same court, could follow different religions. Christians and pagans freely intermingled during this time. We even see this in the most well-known Anglo-Saxon pagan burial site, Sutton Hoo, where Christian baptismal spoons are found among pagan grave goods. The fact that the pagans were surrounded by Christians ensured that the heyday of Anglo-Saxon paganism was short. The conversion of the powerful Anglo-Saxon King of Kent, Ethelbert, who married a Frankish Christian, accelerated the process. The conversion of the Anglo-Saxons was largely peaceful, excepting a few martyrs on both sides. But the conversion of the Anglo-Saxons was not the last hurrah of paganism in the British Isles, as the Viking invasions in the following centuries provided a fresh injection of Germanic religion. By the eleventh century, however, the Norsemen had accepted the new faith as well.

While the Christian faith appears to have achieved total dominance by the Middle Ages, a great deal of speculation about the "underground" survival of paganism has been made by people such as Gerald Gardner, Charles Godfrey Leland, and Margaret Murray, who authored *Witchcraft Today*; *Aradia, or The Gospel of the Witches*; and *The Witch Cult in Western Europe*, respectively. These topics, including claims that the witches of Medieval Europe practiced a preexisting British pagan religious tradition, are addressed by Hutton in this book. For a more thorough examination of the relationship between paganism and witchcraft, however, Hutton has written an equally authoritative volume, *The Triumph of the Moon: A History of Modern Pagan Witchcraft*. The historical evidence allows us to say fairly confidently that the victims of the medieval witch-hunts were not practitioners of a pre-Christian religion. Moreover, the records we have of the accused show that only a small minority were even practitioners of folk magic or anything that could be considered non-Christian. For the most part, the victims of the witch-hunts were people unpopular in their community who suffered at the hands of their neighbors, a situation compounded by the religious struggles against heresy and conflicts arising from the Protestant Reformation. The witches prosecuted were

THE BURNING OF BARTLE AT YORKSHIRE IN THE 1950S. DO CUSTOMS LIKE THESE ORIGINATE IN ANCIENT FERTILITY RITES, OR DO THEY HAVE A MORE RECENT PROVENANCE?

not part of any underground organizations, nor did they practice anything pagan in nature. For the most part they were innocent victims. The historical record does not support the witch-cult hypothesis, which claimed medieval witches practiced an organized pre-Christian religion.

In addition to explicit claims of pagan survival, it has also been asserted that various symbols, found in the art of the Medieval British Isles—such as the Green Man, the Sheela-na-Gig, and the Wild Man—represent relics of British pagan religion. In reality, none of them are images of pagan spirits. Even if they drew upon pagan imagery, they are products of a twelfth-century renaissance. The Green Man first appears chronologically in French Romanesque churches, his leafy visage associated by medieval authors with sins of the flesh, marking him as a lost or damned spirit, rather than a pagan deity added by British craftsmen out of affection. The Sheela-na-Gig figure has origins in Spain and is a representation of carnal sins as well. The Wild Man's origins date to pagan antiquity, but he is not a religious figure. Rather, he is the representation of barbarous peoples taken from Greek and Roman geographic and historical texts. But not all aspects of pagan religion were banished from popular consciousness. The tradition of rolling blazing wheels downhill at midsummer dates back to antiquity, as does the Beltaine tradition (which persisted into the nineteenth century) of building bonfires and driving cattle between them. The folklore of Ireland, with its fairies and banshees, derives a strong influence from pre-Christian Celtic mythology. In the folklore of Northern England, the characters of Jenny Greenteeth and Peg Prowler, who drown small children, can be seen as demonized incarnations of river goddesses such as Verbeia and Coventina. In the Mummers' plays of England, a character known as Humping Jack or Happy Jack appears with the accouterments of the Irish Celtic deity Daghda: a pan and a club. The worship of Daghda is not attested in England, so we must view this as an import and not a homegrown tradition. We can conclude that while paganism itself died out in the British Isles, it bequeathed a rich legacy of folklore, art, and literature. Indeed, *The Pagan Religions of the British Isles* could be seen as part of that rich inheritance as well.

Ronald Hutton's commanding examination of the archeological and historical record is marked by skepticism and a careful evaluation of the available evidence and competing theories. Moreover, he concedes in the preface to the paperback edition that ongoing or future investigation may overtake the evidence put forth in this work. He focuses heavily on the archeological evidence, and Hutton is careful not to impose any preconceived notions upon a complex past that resolutely defies the simplistic narratives of modern ideology.

—Anthony Harberton

The Forest Passage by Ernst Jünger. Softcover, 97 + xi pages. Candor, NY: Telos Press Publishing, 2013. ISBN: 978-0-914386-49-0.

Reading *The Forest Passage* requires some familiarity with Ernst Jünger's wider body of work, and especially with the development of certain *types*. These types are the key to Jünger's literary output as well as the focus of much of his theoretical writing. Moreover, Jünger did not invent his typology out of thin air. Throughout his long and protean life, he experienced the figures of the Soldier, the Worker, the Rebel, and the Anarch as the personifications of facets of his own historical epoch. There is a continuity between these types that also reflects the intellectual and historical trajectory of Jünger's personal development. As a keen observer of the plant and animal world (Jünger studied marine biology after the War, and was distinguished as an entomologist), it was probably second nature for him to construct a taxonomic structure for understanding the catastrophes he experienced at close quarters.

Not the least of these was the First World War, which Jünger chronicled in crystalline detail in the *Storm of Steel*. This remains one of the greatest war memoirs of all time, and Jünger's experience in the trenches gave rise to the figure of the Front Soldier. Like Pierre Drieu La Rochelle and other European intellectuals, Jünger's jarring immersion in modern mechanized warfare taught him, first and foremost, that the possibilities for individual heroism in more archaic forms of conflict were gone forever. There is nothing left of chivalry when facing down a machine gun nest or a barrage of chemical weapons. Instead, Jünger saw the war as the testing ground for a new, higher form of consciousness. In contrast to the calculating, liberal-bourgeois mentality (which is also the hallmark of Nietzsche's Last Man), the Front Soldier fights without fear of death or a personal stake in the outcome of battle. The goal for him is to forge a new bearing towards the world, one characterized by aristocratic detachment and iron resolve. Not only is this consistent with Jünger's anti-bourgeois, counter-Enlightenment sensibilities, it is necessitated by the technological worldview itself. This is similarly expressed in the figure of the Worker. The Worker carries the "heroic realist" disposition of the Front Soldier into the civilian world of skyscrapers and jet planes, hydroelectric dams and munitions factories. Here, Jünger is on similar footing as the Futurists, who also saw the emerging world of technology as

ERNST JÜNGER (1895–1998) WITH FRIEND.

the birthplace of a New Man, one who could sweep away the old liberal order and inaugurate a new one.

Unsurprisingly, Jünger's ideas during this period have caused many to describe him as a sort of proto-Fascist, and the charges are not unwarranted. However, although clearly a man of the Right, Jünger never threw in his lot with the Nazis, even though the regime tried desperately to woo him. In fact, the National Socialist period saw a decisive turn in Jünger's thinking. This is first evident in *On the Marble Cliffs*, a fantastical novella intended as a parable against all forms of totalitarianism. Despite being published in Germany in 1939, the book escaped censorship because of Jünger's reputation as a war hero and his Conservative Revolutionary credentials. Rather than ushering in a higher form of consciousness, the experience of totalitarianism convinced Jünger that the technological world had far more power to degrade and enslave human beings than to elevate them. Nor was this view tempered by the triumph of Western "democracies." These, too, are characterized by the same instrumental rationality that culminated in the death factories of Hitler and Stalin. Here, his critique dovetails with that of his friend Martin Heidegger, who saw the realization of the technological worldview in the reduction of human beings to *Bestand* ("standing reserve"—or, in the jargon of modern corporate America, "human resources").

Jünger's orientation remained geared toward achieving the higher consciousness he had envisioned for the Front Soldier and the Worker, only now the question becomes how one can secure the existential space that this true freedom requires. For the Rebel (and later the Anarch) conventional political activity is not an option. To illustrate this point, Jünger devotes considerable space to the implications of modern elections, and specifically to the man who votes "no." While Jünger reserves some admiration for the action of this hypothetical dissident, he emphasizes its ultimate futility. Far from threatening the established order, the very presence of the "no" vote only strengthens the establishment, first, by upholding the notion of free will and consensus upon which the system justifies its power, and second, by providing a semblance of resistance which the system can use to validate its continued expansion. Thus, the man who opposes the system by participating in its elections has "fallen into a trap." A more effective means of opposition is taking one's "no" out of the ballot box, for "there are other places where it can make things significantly more uncomfortable for these powers—on the white border of an electoral poster, for instance, on a public telephone book, or on the side of a bridge that thousands cross every day. A few words there, such as 'I said no,' would be far more effective." One should harbor no illusions that these petty vandalisms will topple the regime, but they may point the way forward for others trying to secure their own independence. Here, perhaps, Jünger anticipates the Situationists, or the ontological anarchism of Hakim Bey.

The Rebel must seek out the forest passage, a concept Jünger uses in both a literal and a metaphorical sense. The forest passage is a horizontal retreat from the Leviathan (Jünger's favored term for the modern state, which he borrows from Hobbes), but it is also "concealed in every individual." The man who takes the forest passage is like the ancient Icelander who has chosen outlawry, while the forest itself is a deliberate allusion to the Tacitean primeval wastes. This is the home of the uncorrupted and noble barbarian, who lives safely beyond the reaches of Empire. The forest, Jünger writes, is "the great theme of fairy tales, of sagas, of the sacred texts and mysteries." In contrast to the historical world of political terror, the forest represents "supra-temporal being." It is there that man confronts his innermost self, which is where the deepest founts of true freedom lie.

The Rebel can look to several allies as he sets out on the forest passage: these include the poet, the philosopher, and the theologian, and Jünger discusses each in its turn. Even more important, however, is the Rebel's encounter with the world of myth. Myth stands outside both the stream of historical necessity (Eliade's "terror of history"), and the instrumental rationality of the totalizing State. What the irrational world of myth can ultimately provide the Rebel, however, is a release from fear. By identifying himself with the non-contingent world of myth, the Rebel taps into that eternal part of himself that transcends time and death. The Leviathan can still destroy him, but in the absence of fear, that destruction has lost its meaning.

From this vantage point, the Rebel can launch various combat offensives, for—while the Rebel is distinct from the Front Soldier in many ways—he is nevertheless also a fighter. In linking sovereignty to the willingness for combat, Jünger recalls the old Germanic maxim (once enshrined in the Constitution of the United States) that the armed man is a free man. This willingness to fight cannot be subordinated to any narrow political ideology, however: it comes from that inner place of freedom that the Rebel encounters on the forest passage. This is the true homeland for which he fights, and he must rely on his own inner directives (guided by the higher realities of myth) to tell him when and where to take his stand. At this point, Jünger offers up a significant caveat. While the Rebel bears many superficial similarities to the criminal (and in the eyes of the system, he undoubtedly *is* a criminal) he is bound to a spiritual and ethical orientation, which the criminal (who is motivated solely by narcissism and self-interest) is not. Tactically, the Rebel "will make his moves where greater destruction can be effected with minor effort: at choke points; on vital arteries leading through difficult terrain; at locations distant from the bases." In invoking the principles of fourth-generation warfare (which military theorists did not begin to articulate until the late 1980s) Jünger proves his remarkable prescience. The modern Leviathan relies on hugely interconnected networks that can be disrupted quite effectively with little personal or financial expenditure (consider the massive threat of cyberwarfare). This explains the tremendous success of the insurgencies in Iraq and Afghanistan—which, in certain instances, the figure of the Rebel may be said to portend.

Like all of Jünger's formulations, the Rebel is a product of a certain historical moment: in this case, the early 1950s, when the struggle for sovereignty must have seemed like more of an open question than it does today. The Anarch, Jünger's later and final formulation, takes a more vertical route of retreat (although the forest passage remains open to him, as an occasional alternative), eschewing actual combat for a more rarified form of detachment. Like Heidegger, the Jünger of this later period concluded that the present age must be seen through to its exhaustion, so that another, more congenial manifestation of Being might arise. In this, his attitude resembles that of Julius Evola, who also awaited the dawn of a new age, albeit the one promised by Tradition. In Evola's definition (from *Ride the Tiger*), the "inner imperative" of this form of *apoliteia* is "to defend the world of being and dignity of him who feels himself belonging to a different humanity and recognizes the desert around himself." In our own era of managerial intervention into every aspect of private life, of constant surveillance, drone strikes, and the increasing criminalization of thought, this may be the only tenable form of resistance left.

This edition of *The Forest Passage* is part of a small resurgence of interest in Ernst Jünger in the English-speaking world. Telos Press (*Telos* is the leading American journal of critical theory) has also produced recent editions of Jünger's essay *On Pain* as well as *The Adventurous Heart*, a collection of short vignettes. These books are beautifully translated and packaged, and include immensely valuable introductions that provide both the necessary historical background, as well as elucidating Jünger's relevance on a host of contemporary issues. Jünger has also begun to attract attention in counter-cultural circles, where his early experiments with psychedelics (and the impact these experiences had on his writing) are finally being acknowledged. Jünger's reflections on LSD have appeared recently in the Swedish occultural journal *The Fenris Wolf* and an illustrated English-language edition of the psychedelic masterpiece *The Visit To Godenholm* is in preparation.

—Joshua Buckley

The Mystical State: Politics, Gnosis, and Emergent Cultures by Arthur Versluis. Softcover, 155 pages with notes and index. Minneapolis: New Cultures Press, 2011. ISBN: 978-1-59650-011-2.

Gnosis and *Gnosticism* are both loaded concepts that have always been hotly contested. The existentialist philosopher Hans Jonas defined Gnosticism in terms of its supposed "anti-cosmic dualism," while Eric Voegelin further muddied the waters by claiming that political movements like Marxism somehow represent an immanentizing form of gnosis, based on their conviction that a "heaven on earth" can be created in history. Both of these views were formulated before the translation and wide dissemination of the Nag Hammadi codices. Scholarly knowledge about Gnosticism has proliferated exponentially since then, but the appropriation of supposedly "gnostic" ideas by certain segments of the New Age has added yet another layer of confusion, at least to the public perception of what gnosis might actually mean.

Arthur Versluis is a professor of religious studies at Michigan State University, and is clearly deeply knowledgeable about Gnosticism as a concrete historical phenomenon (readers who want to pursue Gnosticism from this more scholarly perspective might turn to the works of Kurt Rudolph, for example). By contrast, *The Mystical State* is little concerned with a strictly empirical approach to the subject. That Versluis's "Gnosticism" includes largely rejected esoteric currents within Judaism (Kabbalism), Islam (Sufism), and Christianity (the theosophy of Jacob Böhme and others) suggests that for Versluis, "Gnosticism" in this context may be shorthand for Western esotericism in general. To be sure, the six fundamental characteristics of esotericism elucidated by Antoine Faivre—which include the theory of correspondences, the idea of living nature, the practice of concordances, and the use of imagination and meditation—dovetail rather nicely with what Versluis means by Gnosticism here. Gnostic ideas represent the shadow-side of Christian theology, the "excluded Other" whose rejection by heretic-hunters like Tertullian was a defining historical moment. If we accept the thesis of the "theological origins of modernity" (as Versluis clearly does, even suggesting that Enlightenment rationalism represented a "second rejection of gnosis"), than we can see how a reconsideration of Gnosticism might be a good starting point in ferreting out alternatives to modernity's more destructive aspects. Gnosticism (in Versluis's formulation) is characterized by the personal experience of transcendence, and an openness to the sacred. This contrasts with both the either/or dualism inherent to both monotheist theology, and the instrumental rationality that has devastated the world of living nature and reduced human beings to a mass.

So what, exactly, would a society based on Gnostic principles look like? This is a key question, since any attempt to reform a culture must first acknowledge its origins in the *cultus* (the fact that Western secular society has rejected any connection to the sacred suggests that it is, in fact, an *anti*-culture). Here, Versluis seems to channel the congenial conservatism of William Cobbett, a bona-fide radical traditionalist who could elicit praise from both Karl Marx and G. K. Chesterton (not to mention Cobbet's most prominent twentieth-century disciple, John Michell). First and foremost, Versluis's polis would be highly decentralized, consisting of a confederation of small-scale tribes, with an emphasis on local "town-culture." It would reject "gigantism" in favor of agrarianism, craft-culture (think Wendell Berry or the Southern Agrarians) and extended family relationships. It would strive to maintain an intimate, human scale, and it would emphasize an altruism that was not strictly anthropocentric. The purpose of this is twofold. Tremendous worth would be placed on the life of contemplation, and other functions of society (such as the economic sphere) would be subordinated to values more conducive to quiet reflection. Secondly, the world of being (and the transcendent world with which it is closely intertwined) would be allowed to simply *be*. Significantly, Versluis points out, this was precisely the meaning of the ancient *nemetons* (or sacred groves) of the Celts. What gave these sites their numinous power was the fact that they had been set aside from human intervention. The idea that open spaces might be the best place to encounter the divine fits comfortably with Versluis's embrace of the negative theology espoused by mystics like Meister Eckhart. The god of the mystics cannot be confined by the narrow doctrinal constraints of the Abrahamic religions (or, one might argue, the rigid formalism of Traditionalists like René Guénon). It is best encountered through inner experiences that are—by their very nature—inarticulable.

Versluis does manage to offer some practical guidance as to what a "mystical State" might look like, and does not entirely ignore the realities of issues like military defense and commerce. He is especially partial to the Swiss model, and spends some time considering the "political mystic" Niklaus von Flüe (or "Brother Klaus" as he is affectionately known), who remains the patron saint of the Swiss confederation. But a new culture must precede a new politics. Versluis devotes a chapter to the hippie movement as an example of an "emergent culture" with a decidedly Gnostic bent. Many of us have become accustomed to associating the hippies with the New Left, civil rights, and opposition to the war in Vietnam. However, if the all-pervasive narrative of "progress" is set aside, it probably makes more sense to regard the hippie phenomenon as a return of the "suppressed archaic." This is especially true of the communal movement, which embraced organic forms of social organization and attempted a large scale return to the land. The hippies rejected the materialist ethos of the modern West, and dropped out of the post-war rat race to pursue more fulfilling ways of life. Whereas the Beats had experimented with drug use mostly as a reaction against the bourgeois social mores of their parents, the hippies did so with more explicitly spiritual aspirations, and many of them would eventually find their way to Eastern philosophies, the Jesus movement, or even more adventurous religious experiments like the recently re-discovered and (for the moment at least) newly fashionable Process Church of the Final Judgment. In fact, the entire hippie culture could be seen in its best light as an anti-modern reaction against the de-sacralization of the world and, more importantly, an attempt (however clumsy) to articulate an alternative.

This is also Versluis's aim in writing *The Mystical State*, and while such an ambitious undertaking is probably bound to come up short, his efforts are admirable nonetheless. My main question for Versluis would be: why Gnosticism? If one really wants to invoke the "excluded other" supplanted by Christianity, why not turn to the indigenous pagan traditions of pre-Conversion Europe? Reconstructionist paganism broadly encompasses the values of localism, tolerance, respect for nature, family, and small-scale tribal democracy that Versluis favors. Its metaphysics are non-dualistic, and it leaves ample room for personal experiences of the divine. Furthermore, I would argue that Gnosticism in the ancient world found itself largely in the role of an oppositional sub-culture. Paganism, on the other hand, *was* the culture of our Indo-European ancestors, before "religion" had become a category distinct from other facets of life (including the political). As Stephen Flowers has often pointed out, we still live in a world that is steeped in that culture. For a modern American, there should be nothing profoundly alienating about embracing the religious beliefs of the Anglo-Saxon people (for example) when we speak an Anglo-Saxon language, and live in a society shaped by Anglo-Saxon social and political institutions. But I digress.

As a scholar of Western esotericism whose academic approach is a strictly empirical one, Versluis is to be commended for his willingness to explore esotericism as something other than a dry object of study, detached from any more meaningful context (although, obviously, this perspective has its place). *The Mystical State* is a bold, thoughtful meditation (or manifesto, even), that should open up fruitful new pathways for dialogue.

—Joshua Buckley

Blutleuchte by Gerhard Hallstatt. Introduction by Joscelyn Godwin. Hardcover, 321 pages. Jacksonville, OR: AJNA, 2010. ISBN: 0-9721820-3-9.

Aorta and *Ahnstern* were small-circulation, photocopied monographs, written and produced by Gerhard Hallstatt (under the pseudonym Kadmon) in the 1990s. At the time, they had the look and feel of *samizdat* literature, a mystique that has been largely lost as content like this has migrated online. Not only did these strange little tracts deal with obscure and often relatively impenetrable subject matter, but they were written from Gerhard's strikingly singular perspective. These are both adventures in intellectual exploration, as well as in the more literal sense, as Gerhard chronicles his exploits as a traveler, spelunker, psychonaut, and amateur shaman. Whether dealing with Surrealism, *völkish* social and religious movements, experimental music, or incongruous aspects of European folklore, the common thread seems to be the extremes people have gone to in the service of transcendence. In "Heidnat" (roughly, "heathen home"), Gerhard articulates his personal approach to folkish paganism. This provides considerable context for much of his other work, and is also one of the most congenial takes on the subject I have come across. While *Aorta* and *Ahnstern* always included English translations, these were generally a little obtuse; here, Gerhard's work is rendered into much more readable language, and the value of having every issue under one cover is considerable. A charming introduction by academic esotericist Joscelyn Godwin gives this collection an added air of legitimacy that the content richly deserves.

—Joshua Buckley

A Most Dangerous Book: Tacitus's Germania *from the Roman Empire to the Third Reich* by Christopher B. Krebs. Hardcover, 303 pages with notes and index. New York and London: Norton, 2011. ISBN: 978-0-393-06265-6.

"With the speed of those who know their days are numbered, the

SS charged up the pebble-and-sand covered driveway." So begins *A Most Dangerous Book*, setting a tone reminiscent of *Raiders of the Lost Ark* or *The Spear of Destiny*, as Himmler's henchmen make a fevered dash to get their blood-stained Aryan fingers on the Codex Aesinas, the fifteenth-century manuscript of Tacitus's *Germania*. Author Krebs claims that *A Most Dangerous Book* is an "intellectual epidemiology," as if the *Germania* were a noxious pathogen whose cure was the final surrender of Germany at the end of World War II. I would counter by coining a phrase: books don't kill people, people who read books—however idiosyncratically—kill people. Tacitus himself could have never anticipated the troublesome future of his slender little volume, and there is much speculation as to why it was written in the first place. The old saw is that Tacitus portrayed the ancient Germans as noble savages (although not *too* noble—they were also drunk, lazy, and addicted to gambling) to shame his Roman countrymen into reforming their decadent ways. Another theory is that he meant to lambast Domitian by pointing out that, despite the Emperor's self-congratulatory declarations (not the least of which involved taking the title *Germanicus*), there were clearly plenty of Germanic people who had *not* been subjugated by the Empire. The story of the *Germania's* recovery by Italian humanist manuscript hunters in the 1400s, with all of its attendant intrigue, could be the setting for an Umberto Eco novel. These same Italian humanists were the first to equate Tacitus's *Germanen* with contemporaneous Germans, though this was often only to show that these latter were "barbaric donkeys." Later interpretations were far more favorable, as German nationalists enlisted Tacitus in constructing a homogeneous national identity. This could take all sorts of peculiar forms. Annius of Viterbo identified the god Tuisto (who Annius calls "Tuysco") as a descendent of Noah, while Tacitus's reference to Germanic *barditus* ("songs") led to speculations about an ancient German class of "bards"—despite the fact that the words are linguistically unrelated. Mostly, of course, eighteenth- and nineteenth-century Germans celebrated Tacitus's descriptions of the *Germanen* as loyal, brave, and independent, while the Nazis (predictably) would latch onto the Tacitean notion of Germanic "purity." Krebs's story is a fascinating work of cultural history, although at times he seems to fall into the postmodern literary fashion of assuming that, because the text has been interpreted so many different ways, it must have no real meaning of its own. He takes a similar tack when it comes to the relationship between Tacitus's *Germanen* and the modern Germans. While Krebs is right that this identification can be problematic, it simply does not follow that there is no meaningful historical continuity between these ancient and modern populations. Archeology and other literary analogues have validated much of Tacitus's description, and it remains a valuable piece of history, however flawed—and regardless of how "dangerous" its implications might be.

—Joshua Buckley

Tree of Salvation: Yggdrasil and the Cross in the North by G. Ronald Murphy, S.J. Hardcover, 239 pages with bibliography and index. New York: Oxford University Press, 2013. ISBN: 978-0-19-994861-1.

Pope Gregory the Great famously advised the Abbot Mellitus to pursue an accomodationist strategy in converting the Anglo-Saxons. Pagan temples were to be re-purposed for Christian use, and less outrageous popular customs could be retained, "for surely it is impossible to efface all at once everything from their strong minds." To this day, European Christianity remains very much a hybrid religion, even after wave upon wave of joy-killing Protestant reforms. This has allowed northern Europeans to feel at home in Christianity, a process Fr. Murphy seems to very much approve of, and which also colored his classic earlier study of the *Heliand, The Saxon Savior.* Here, Murphy's theme is the culturally loaded symbolism of the cross, and how this became conflated with the world-tree Yggdrasil, whose branches sheltered Lif and Lifthrasir during the conflagrations of Ragnarök. In this sense, both "trees" can be said to have salvific aspects, and there is also a suggestion of continuity between the old world of paganism and the new one brought about by Christ's sacrifice and resurrection. In this sense, Murphy seems to have taken inspiration from certain Scholastic theologians, who salvaged the gods of Classical Antiquity by recasting them as part of an incomplete, pre-Christian revelation. Many of the chapters in *Tree of Salvation* could stand alone as self-contained essays. These range over the symbolism of medieval stave churches, to the use of tree trunks as coffins in burial mounds, to the Anglo-Saxon *Dream of the Rood*, to the symbolism of the Christmas Tree and wreath. Murphy is full of fresh and compelling ideas (his unique interpretation of the rune sequence in the elder futhark is sure to inspire controversy) and his obvious affinity for the "Germanicized" elements of Christianity gives his scholarship a highly personal cast. While there is certainly much truth in Murphy's account, my main complaint is epitomized by his discussion of the Skog tapestry, which depicts "three large figures walk (ing) away from the church." Murphy asks:

> Are Woden, Thor, and Frey spirits of the forest who are now returning to the woods whence they came? Next to Woden, there is a tree, looking rather like an evergreen. Is it Yggdrasil, the Awesome One's Horse? The three gods are leaving peacefully, and quite contentedly, in this artist's representation, perhaps because they are leaving Yggdrasil's temple in the hands of Christians and Christ, for whom they prepared the way by embodying ancient stories of wisdom, strength, and happiness—and by helping all to remember the deep roots of Mimir's old and hopeful story that salvation would come in the form of a tree. It did. And then they left, graciously leaving their stave house to Christ.

In many instances, the conversion of Europe was accomplished through fire and sword, leaving a trail of broken bodies in its wake. A world, and a way of seeing the world, was lost that can never be fully recovered. The idea that the indigenous gods of the North simply packed up and left "graciously," like satisfied

Reviews: Books

DETAIL FROM THE SKOG TAPESTRY, TWELFTH CENTURY, WHICH IS NOW HOUSED IN THE MUSEUM OF NATIONAL ANTIQUITIES IN STOCKHOLM.

guests at a dinner party (who hadn't planned on staying long, anyway), seems to me a rather unsatisfying—and disingenuous—attempt to re-write history.

—Joshua Buckley

Modern Pagan and Native Faith Movements in Central and Eastern Europe **edited by Kaarina Aitamurto and Scott Simpson. Hardcover, 358 pages with bibliography and index. Bristol, CT: Acumen Publishing Limited, 2013. ISBN: 978-1-84456-662-2.**

This is the second installment in the series "Studies in Contemporary and Historical Paganism." The collection is part of a wider push within academia to carve out a niche for "Pagan Studies" from the more established field of New Religious Movements (or, NRMs), chronicled by journals like *Nova Religio*. The reasons for this are sketched out in one of the articles here.

Reconstructionist pagan religions tend to have more broadly cultural aspects and are far more decentralized than most conventional NRMs. There is also the issue of continuity. Most pagans are wont to invoke a historical pedigree that sees their practices as anything but "new." Of course, these claims can be highly contestable (the *Book of Veles* is a good example), and the convergence of tradition and innovation in these movements is fertile ground for scholarly investigation.

For the lay reader (and I include myself in this category), much of the material in this anthology may prove a bit tedious, especially when the focus is on social scientific examinations of group dynamics, terminological classifications, or the way the groups under discussion use the Internet. One interesting approach (in an article by Piotr Wiench) is the use of post-colonialism (or subaltern studies) as a lens for interpreting neopaganism in Eastern and Central Europe. For most of these groups, a common point of reference is the period of Soviet rule, and Wiench sees the adoption of "native faith" as a counter-hegemonic strategy against foreign domination. Not surprisingly, the Christianization of the Slavic people is viewed as a historical precedent for this attack on ethnic sovereignty.

Politically, many of the groups described in these pages have a more conservative bent than their Western European and American counterparts, and are closer in spirit to the folkish adherents of Ásatrú than to more liberally inclined Wiccans. Consider the following statement of the value-system of Dievturi in Latvia:

> What is the highest value, the greatest benefit in this new morality? The human, Humanity, or God? Neither the first, nor the second or the third, but Folk! Folk is the highest value, benefit, and sanctity, Folk is the center of the world! Folk is above everything else! Folk in the first place.

This viewpoint was shaped largely by the Soviet experience, where any expression of folk culture could constitute an act of

LATVIAN PAGANS ASSOCIATED WITH THE DIEVTURA MOVEMENT.

political defiance. This is exemplified by the "singing revolution" in Estonia, which some readers may have encountered in the emotionally moving 2009 documentary film of the same name. The turbulent history of Eastern Europe brought confrontations with other forms of totalitarianism as well, and Scott Simpson describes the underground resistance group Wkra in Nazi-occupied Poland. "Under the leadership of Stefan 'Bolek' Potrzuski, the unit was reported to have had a shrine to Światowid in their secret forest lair and conducted group rites with toasts of mead around a wooden figure." Potrzuski was eventually tracked down by the Gestapo and shot, and many other dissident pagans would meet their fates at the hands of the Russians. Still others managed to emigrate, and continued nourishing their beliefs in such unlikely outposts as Toronto, Canada or rural Wisconsin, where the Dievsētā ("God's Homestead") was established in the 1970s, and still exists to this day.

There is considerable historical material here, tracing the development of neopaganism to Romanticism as well as the Slavophilic and more politically-oriented pan-Slavism inspired in part (like the *völkish* movement in Germany) by the writings of Herder. Ample space is given to the Romuva community in Lithuania, which has achieved more mainstream acceptance than most of the more obscure groups mentioned. Many of these, like those affiliated with Rodzimowierstwo in Poland, have accepted their minority status, viewing themselves as a vanguard dedicated to protecting the essence of true Polish-ness. Other chapters consider neopaganism in Hungary, the Czech Republic, Romania, the Ukraine, Bulgaria, and Slovenia. Essays on Armenia and the Mari El republic (the Mari are a non-Slavic, Finno-Ugric minority in the Russian federation) make for fascinating reading, as information about the pagan movements in these regions is almost wholly inaccessible in the English-speaking West. While the focus here is almost overwhelmingly on neopaganism as an ethno-nationalist expression, Maciej Witulski also examines the adoption of "imported" Celtic and Odinist beliefs in Poland.

Michael York (who is himself a leading exponent of Pagan Studies) has written extensively about paganism as a world religion, both highly diverse due to its localized nature, yet adhering to certain common principles. The collection under review suggests that, in this part of the world at least, reconstructionist paganism—in whatever guise one finds it— is a cultural phenomenon that is here to stay.

—Joshua Buckley

The Nordic Apocalypse: Approaches to* Vǫluspá *and Nordic Days of Judgement edited by Terry Gunnell and Annette Lassen. Hardcover, 238 pages with index. Turnhout, Belgium: Brepols Publishers, 2013. ISBN: 978-2-503-54182-2.

The *Vǫluspá* is found in the Codex Regius and Hauksbók manuscripts, which date from the thirteenth and fourteenth centuries. Additionally, twenty strophes of the poem appear in Snorri's *Gylfaginning*. The *Vǫluspá* is one of the most enigmatic of Eddic texts, but it is also one of the most important for unraveling the Old Norse cosmology and eschatology. The papers collected here are the result of a conference held in Iceland in 2008. A central question for the attendees was the extent to which the Ragnarök narrative in *Vǫluspá* has been Christianized. Does it represent a genuine heathen tradition, was it entirely a literary creation of the Christian Middle Ages, or (as is most likely the case) does it contain elements that would be familiar to both Christian and (hypothetical) pagan readers? All of these viewpoints are dealt with in a clear and concise fashion.

Hilda Ellis Davidson took the position that any similarities between the Ragnarök and Christian apocalyptic literature were due solely to "convergent individual imaginations." It will probably not tarnish her reputation to suggest that, in this regard at least, she may have been glossing over the issue. Kees Samplonius and Pétur Pétursson argue for a primarily Christian origin for the poem, and do a commendable job of itemizing its potentially Christian motifs. Of most interest is Samplonius' contention (based largely on etymology) that the figures of Surtr, Fenrir, and Loki (whose name Samplonius derives from "Lucifer") may originate almost entirely from a Christian background. Surtr is the bringer of "black fire," a motif Samplonius identifies in medieval accounts of the Christian Judgment Day, while the symbolic significance of Fenrir may be contained in a simile attributed to the English abbot Ælfric: "The wolf is the devil, which lies in ambush about God's church and watches how he may fordo the souls of Christian men with sins." In "Heathenism in *Vǫluspá*," on the other hand, John McKinnell argues for those elements of the poem that clearly have no Christian analogues, or are even antithetical to Christian doctrine. These can reliably be ascribed to pre-Christian origins. One particularly vexing passage in the *Vǫluspá* (which appears in the Hauksbók but not the Codex Regius) concerns *inn ríki*, who will appear after the final conflagration. *Inn ríki* is typically translated as "the mighty one," and there is a fairly broad consensus that this was a reference to the second coming of Christ. Even this is questionable, however. "Typology" was a common hermeneutic strategy in the Middle Ages. Typologists worked to harmonize elements of the Old and New Testaments, but also to tease Christian meanings out of ancient texts. This would account for much of Snorri's approach to the Eddic material (Samplonius even suggests that the entire point of recording the *Vǫluspá* was to demonstrate the "self destructive nature of paganism"). Yet while the idea that *inn ríki* is Christ seems fairly compelling, several of the authors here suggest that things might not be so simple. For one thing, the world reborn after Ragnarök is a *physical* world. For another, the gods Hœnir, Baldr, Höðr, and their offspring also seem to have survived, an idea scarcely consistent with monotheist theology. Furthermore, these gods (and presumably, *inn ríki* himself) come not to judge, but "to resume the innocent games their forefathers had previously played." Gro Steinsland argues that *inn ríki* may actually be a transformation of Heimdallr, a surmise she bases on the language used to describe this shadowy, un-named—but clearly significant—figure.

Other articles deal with the early scholarly reception of the *Vǫluspá*, its relation to oral tradition, and whether or not it was intended to be performed—this latter question is considered by co-editor Terry Gunnell, and will be familiar to readers of his well-known *The Origins of Drama in Scandinavia* (Brewer, 1995). Another issue is the *Vǫluspá's* relation to the Sibylline Oracles. The Sibylline books (some of which may date back as far as 800 B.C.E.) contained a series of prophecies that later Christian authors would see as foreshadowing the coming of Christ. In fact, certain enterprising missionaries doctored up Sibylline forgeries of their own to make the point a little more emphatically! The *Vǫluspá* is of course the prophecy of a *völva*, or female seeress, and does bear striking structural similarities to this type of literature. Whether or not it served a similar purpose, or whether it is (for the most part) an authentic repository of heathen lore, is a source of the kind of conjecture that gives this collection its special fascination.

—Joshua Buckley

Ancient Song Recovered: The Life and Music of Veljo Tormis by Mimi S. Daitz. Softcover, 368 pages. Hillsdale, NY: Pendragon Press, 2004. ISBN: 978-157647-009-1.

I first heard the music of the Estonian composer Veljo Tormis about fifteen years ago, when a good friend shared a tape of one of Tormis's best pieces—*Kalevala XVII Rune*—which is based on a song from the Finnish national epic. In the song, the heroic bard-magician Väinämöinen wakes the giant-witch Vipunen and acquires the magic spells that he needs to build a ship. Tormis chose two traditional Karelian folk melodies to describe the two characters as well as assigning instrumentation to each. While the five-string instrument the *kantele* symbolizes the bard Väinämöinen, Vipunen's arsenal of noise-makers includes a rattle, a buzz-bone, wooden bells, and shamanic drums. Over the course of nearly forty-two minutes, the choral piece unfolds a cyclical, repetitive, and dynamic—yet minimal—atmosphere that evokes ancient ritual while sounding thoroughly avant-garde and "modern." I came to think of Tormis as the "pagan" counterpart to his countryman, the more well-known Christian composer Arvo Pärt.

For those wishing to delve more deeply into Tormis's background and work, there is no better place than this book, first published in 2004. *Ancient Song Recovered* places Tormis's work and life into the context of the turbulent history of his tiny Baltic homeland, as well as providing in-depth examinations of some of his best-known works. The composer emerges as a reserved yet persistent man who early on became fascinated with folk song, making it his mission to breathe new life into the folk tradition by marrying it to more contemporary modes of musical expression. The accompanying CD of excerpts and short songs functions as an introduction to Tormis's *oeuvre*. Particularly fascinating is the inclusion of a rural field recording which is followed by the composer's adaptation of the song.

Most of his more than five hundred works are choral in nature, and are frequently based on *regilaul*, as Estonian traditional song is called. Many of the pieces are performed without accompaniment, although Tormis has written some more orchestrated works. It may have been the dance and theater background of his wife that persuaded him to tackle the ambitious ballet-meets-cantata *Eesti ballaadid* (Estonian Ballads), a work that features an orchestra, choir and soloists, folk instruments and also incorporates dance with its components of costume and stage design. In its scope and vision, the nearly two-hour opus seems to resemble Carl Orff's *Carmina Burana* as well as evoking ancient Greek theatre and elevating ritualistic folk-poetry to the stage.

In his famed 1972 essay "Folk Song and Us" (a full translation of which is included in Daitz's book) Tormis affirms both the aesthetic and ethical qualities of folksong as the embodiment of the living values of the people. He goes on say that "the foundations of the old national and popular art still exist today in the language and mentality of the folk. Related to this are many of the values which have endured to the present day—the people's cultural dignity, their internal equilibrium, identification with nature, their sense of generational continuity, and a great deal else which is now about to disintegrate due to multifaceted global phenomena (international tension, technical progress, pollution etc.)."

These prescient words carry even more weight today. Around the same time, Tormis composed *Curse Upon Iron* (*Raua reedmine*), a powerful evocation of the madness of the Cold War-era arms race. In the liner notes to the CD *Litany Of Thunder*, Tormis writes that he was inspired by shamanism: "in order to acquire power over a material or immaterial thing, one communicates knowledge to the object. Thus, the describing and explaining of the birth of iron to iron itself forms part of the shamanic process. The magical rite is performed to restrain the evil hiding inside iron." A real Koryak shaman's drum was used in the recording.

When he was asked in a 1990 interview if *he* would make a good shaman, Tormis was a bit evasive, stating that a modern shaman had told him that he is one, but that he lacked actual knowledge of charms, nor had he used *amanita muscaria*! Yet one could argue that his works as a whole have had a healing power on the Estonian soul, and this certainly could be considered a

VELJO TORMIS.
PHOTO BY TRIINU OJAMAA.

shamanic feat. His famous quote "I do not use folk song, it is folk song that uses me" certainly reinforces the impression that Tormis is the voice of these "forgotten peoples," as one of his song cycles is called.

One more recent development not covered in the book is Tormis's collaboration with an Estonian "pagan metal" band, Metsatöll. The band, which sings in Estonian and has incorporated ethnic instruments such as *kantele* and bagpipes into its furious sound, has received praise for reviving interest in Estonian folklore among young people. With the aid of an arranger and the Estonian National Male Choir, the band adapted Tormis's famed opus *Curse Upon Iron* for their 2007 album of the same name (available from the Westpark Music label). The package also includes a DVD with impressive live footage from a performance in an old castle.

—Markus Wolff

Deep Ancestors: Practicing the Religion of the Proto-Indo-Europeans by Ceiswr Serith. Softcover, 293 pages with one illustration, bibliography, no index. Tucson, AZ: ADF Publishing, 2009. ISBN 0-9765681-3-6.

The group of languages known as Indo-European (IE) is the most widely spoken today on earth, far more so than any other linguistic family. The very designation "Indo-European" is a reflection of this remarkable dispersion, as it was originally intended to describe the geographical expanse of ancient IE speakers. This area was once seen as stretching from the Indian subcontinent in the south to the Scandinavian limits of Europe in the north. The designation could have equally well described the east–west boundaries of the language group, but the recent discovery of incontrovertible evidence for the presence of ancient IE-speakers in the Tarim Basin of what is now China has changed all that.

These many and varied IE languages have a common prehistoric source in what linguists call Proto-Indo-European (PIE), a language that would have been spoken roughly 5,000 to 8,000 years ago. No textual evidence exists from this period, so the vocabulary and contours of PIE have had to be reconstructed, primarily using the scientific method of comparative historical linguistics. The ongoing reconstruction and understanding of the ancestor language has developed to a remarkable level over the past 150 years, and along with these linguistic insights have come many speculations and revelations regarding the culture of the original speakers of PIE: their economy, habitat, kinship system, legal and social customs, and fundamental religious ideas.

The religious practices of the archaic PIE culture evolved over millennia to become the various religious systems and paganisms of antiquity. These included the Zoroastrian and the Vedic; the Greek and Roman; the Celtic, Germanic, and Slavic varieties of cult and custom; and countless others, known and unknown. Reconstructing the most ancient PIE core that lies at the root of this process is therefore not only of interest to scholars of the history of religions and comparative mythology, but also to those

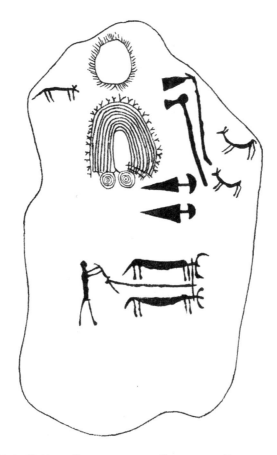

The Bagnolo Stela 2, found in Ceresolo-Bagnolo, Malegno commune, Brescia province, Lombardia, Northern Italy. The engravings may symbolize Indo-European tri-functionality: sun/sky, weapons, and agriculture.

who might feel a more direct and personal affinity with these spiritual ideas today.

Modern-day pagan reconstructions of pre-Christian European religious beliefs are, on one level, part of a "search for origins." In a thoroughly fragmented world such as we now inhabit, this impulse is understandable. Ideally, if the search is successful it leads to a reconnection with more ancient thought-ways, allowing for the re-expression of the latter in a meaningful way today, in the here and now. The secular, scientific scholarship into ancient European literatures and languages has naturally provided a wealth of material from which such reconstructions can draw. The same is true of the scholarship surrounding PIE myth and religion, although it also offers its own set of potential problems due to its extreme time-depth and entirely reconstructed nature.

Modern paganism encompasses a wide swath of approaches and neo-traditions, and the tendency in the last few decades has been one of increasing specialization and diversity. In general terms, this situation probably bears some similarity to the ancient world in Europe and elsewhere, where there existed a polytheistic plethora of cults that ranged widely according to ethnic ties, membership in particular social institutions, age and gender. But how much real resemblance these modern attempts may bear to actual ancient practices—let alone worldviews—is another question entirely.

Given the aforementioned trend toward specialization, it was only a matter of time before attempts would be made at re-establishing some form of PIE religion. This is no easy task, however, and it is one that could easily run aground before ever getting out of the harbor, so to speak. To even begin to discourse convincingly about this subject means to have an erudite knowledge of a number of ancient mythic and religious systems, each of which has its own cultural context, practices, and vocabulary. It also requires that one be able to fill in gaps where actual historical documentary evidence is lacking, in order to re-create a larger picture.

In writing *Deep Ancestors: Practicing the Religion of the Proto-Indo-Europeans*, Ceisiwr Serith (the pen name of David Fickett-Wilbar) has clearly done his homework. He is well-read in various branches of Indo-European studies—particularly the Celtic, Greco-Roman and Indo-Iranian—and the book has a fine bibliography attesting to this fact. He also has a good grasp of the linguistic issues involved, which is an area that is typically the province of academic specialists. As a complement to this book-learning, he is also an active member of the Celtic pagan community (*Deep Ancestors* is published by the Ár nDraíocht Féin, an American Druidic organization) and the author of a number of books aimed at a more general pagan audience (*A*

Book of Pagan Prayer; *A Pagan Ritual Prayer Book*; and *The Pagan Family*, which are far more interesting than their rather bland-sounding titles might suggest), and his emphasis on practice is based on years of actual experience. *Deep Ancestors* is undoubtedly a sincere effort and not an attempt to simply produce yet another eclectic spiritual current by selling a few books to susceptible New Agers, ever hungry for some as-yet-untasted new or old variety of ethereal "soul food."

Deep Ancestors consists of nineteen chapters and three appendices. (Unfortunately, the table of contents gives no titles for any of these, making it a rather useless list of page numbers.) The author explains his general approach in a short preface, where he also provides some important caveats. One is a recognition that his PIE religious reconstruction could be seen as eclectic, or even anachronistic or ahistorical, as it draws conclusions from sources that range immensely across time and space. To this, he responds:

> If anyone is uncomfortable with my use of "Proto-Indo-European," then perhaps they can simply replace it in their mind with "common Indo-European" each time they encounter it. Indeed, this might even result in a more compelling construction, since it will replace the question of why we should do what some ancient culture did with the recognition that what is included here is in fact that which those of us who come from an Indo-European culture hold in common (p. 2).

Even more importantly, he notes that the book is necessarily a work in progress rather than any kind of definitive statement: "As time goes by, new research will be done, new ideas and data presented, and old texts and archeology reinterpreted. This will require changes in the beliefs and practices of reconstructed Proto-Indo-European religion." Serith remarks that he had to alter or dispense with many of his own earlier ideas as new information came to light during his research. This was not a negative scenario, however, as the "changed vision was always more moving, more powerful, more meaningful than that which it replaced" (p. 3).

In terms of its focus, the book can be divided roughly into two parts: the first deals with mythological and ideological matters (which from an IE religious standpoint are inseparable), the second with ritual. The text begins with a brief history of the Indo-Europeans and their original social structure. This is followed by several well-wrought chapters on cosmogony and cosmology. One enduring cosmological conception is that of the tree and the well, which will be familiar to many for the form it takes in Germanic myth and religion. In its most ancient expression, however, Serith interprets the waters of the well as symbolizing chaos, which provides a necessary foil but also sustenance to the more orderly cosmos embodied by the tree. The inherent principle of divine order (both in the universe as well as in the individual) is exemplified in the concept of the *$\chi ártus$, a reconstructed term that shares its semantic root with words like "art," "rite," and "harmony." The same principle permeates noble values and ethics as well, and these are discussed at some length. They include Truth, Justice, Hospitality, Courage, Loyalty, Temperance, Excellence, Responsibility, Duty, Piety, Knowledge, and Love. Serith then presents the major reconstructed PIE deities, many of whom in fact form a divine family (just as they do in the later iterations, such as the Greek or Germanic pantheons). The descriptions of individual gods, goddesses, and other divine entities vary considerably in length, but overall this is a fascinating and worthwhile collection of comparative information.

The second major thrust of the book concerns ritual. This subject is touched upon throughout *Deep Ancestors*, but the latter dozen chapters handle it in great detail. Serith covers all the essential aspects of ritual here (sacred space and orientation, dress, equipment, symbolic substitutions, and so forth) with practical information that is underpinned by a wealth of mythic and comparative support. He also provides a complete set of rituals that he has developed and made use of over the years. These range from individual prayers to family and group rites, to seasonal festivals and social ceremonies. Many of these rituals are quite elaborate and involved.

The appendices consist of a short glossary of key terms; a guide to the pronunciation of PIE words (which for the purposes of this book are transcribed phonologically, as Serith explains clearly enough); brief instructions on making clarified butter (i.e., *ghee*), which is used in a number of ritual procedures; and instructions on how to lay out a rectangular area of sacred space for ritual purposes without resorting to external measuring equipment.

For neopagan readers who seek a deeper understanding of the roots of genuine European paganism and pre-Christian religion, this is a very useful book—and probably one that is far more accessible and easily understood than the underlying information would be if gleaned directly from the academic works whence much of it derives. For those readers who do not self-identify as practicing pagans it will hold much less attraction, and they might do better by investigating books like J. P. Mallory's *In Search of the Indo-Europeans*, Jaan Puhvel's *Comparative Mythology*, and Martin West's *Indo-European Poetry and Myth* if the general topic of IE religion is of historical and cultural interest.

Even for the first set of readers, however, I suspect that *Deep Ancestors* will still present some stumbling blocks. Primary among these is Serith's use of reconstructed PIE terms for deities and concepts throughout, along with whole sentences of (newly composed) ritual speech in the reconstructed language. While this might add an aura of mystery to what is being invoked and honored, it also moves things into a quasi-exotic realm that will seem very alien to many. The linguistic exoticism is pushed even further by the inclusion of laryngeals, a series of phonemes that disappeared at an early stage in the various IE branches (the long-dead language of Hittite being the rare exception to this rule). Serith points out, fairly enough, that these were part of the proto-language (a fact accepted by professional linguists, although the details of the actual sound of these phonemes is still a point of debate) and therefore it would be improper to ignore them. But by retaining laryngeals, one ends up with some quite strange-looking strings of consonants: take for example the word Serith gives for "living fire," *hng^wnios*. Another of the laryngeals, which is written as "H_2," in phonemic linguistic reconstructions of PIE, appears here as X. Despite its appearance, this is not in fact a capital X, but rather is supposed to represent the Greek letter chi used phonetically to stand for a /ch/ sound (as in the Scottish word loch). Thus the word which I reproduced as **xártus* above actually appears in the book simply as Xártus. (Serith does explain his methodology in an appendix.) Such peculiar effects are even more evident with whole phrases of ritual speech like "*Déiwonz spndntéi g^weg^wm-me!*" ("We have come to worship the gods!"). Serith's dedication and diligence in working out all this PIE is admirable on some level, but coming up with a powerful set of modern English equivalents might have better served the aims of his larger endeavor.

Unfortunately, in the first edition under review here, the book is somewhat hampered by its presentation. Some of the resulting limitations are merely cosmetic/aesthetic, such as the inelegant cover with its Helvetica titles and a dull illustration of an odd-looking (proto-?) horse (the Indo-Europeans are famed for their horsemanship, which was a major factor that abetted them in their vast expansion). The Helvetica font continues throughout the entire book itself. While the text is perfectly readable, it has the blandness of an old typescript. And in a volume filled with exotic and often unrecognizable terminology, the choice to dispense with any italicization is puzzling. Typographical errors crop up regularly, although they are of a minor sort. (Despite these and other flaws in the editing and presentation of *Deep Ancestors*, it should nevertheless be acknowledged that this book still stands above the average print-on-demand title that increasingly invades the book trade.)

This is an ambitious book. It may even be an overambitious one, as the author himself admits. I will be surprised, but also impressed, if his method of ritualizing in reconstructed PIE speech ever takes a widespread hold among modern-day practitioners. As a first step, however, *Deep Ancestors* is a significant achievement. It integrates and interprets Indo-European religious ideas and practices into a consequentially reassembled framework, and in doing so provides much food for thought and action.

—Michael Moynihan

ALU: An Advanced Guide to Operative Runology by Edred Thorsson. Softcover, 235 pages with illustrations, no index. San Francisco: Red Wheel/Weiser, 2012. ISBN 978-1-57863-526-9.

There is little doubt that Edred is the foremost living authority on esoteric runelore, as attested to by his prodigious output in the form of books, articles and also the spoken word (through his Radio Free Rûna and Woodharrow podcasts and elsewhere). This output is of the highest quality both in regards to academic rigour and esoteric insight—the former due to his doctorate and ongoing academic research and study; the latter as a consequence of four decades of tireless devotion to self-transformation.

Sadly, there is also little doubt that most esoteric books on the subject of the runic mysteries are at best unsatisfying and at worst an egregious waste of the trees that went into their making. Quite simply, we who live for the quest towards the Mystery (*Rûna*) as she shows herself in Northern Europe, would be seriously disadvantaged without this man's work. Enough said. *Futhark: A Handbook of Rune Magic* was Edred's first stab at a basic introduction to runelore and I would second his recommendation in *ALU* that one read *Futhark* before reading the present volume. One needs to learn to walk before running is attempted. However, and Edred would be the first to tell anyone this, the mysteries one is pointed towards in this book cannot be learnt without tremendous and lifelong dedication. A real mystery is not something that someone will not reveal to another. Rather, it is something no one can reveal to another, for the revealing comes about in each individual's being based on and building upon that individual's level of transformation.

To aid the reader in such a quest towards this transformation, *ALU* offers the following in Chapter One: a grounding in the

ANGLO-SAXON FINGER RING WITH RUNIC INSCRIPTION, EIGHTH–TENTH CENTURY.

basics, including a look at magic, history, origins (beginning with the Older Fuþark, followed by the Anglo-Frisian Fuþorc, the Younger Fuþark and an alphabet from the Middle Ages), some working formulas, the Runic Awakening, and the place of tradition. Chapter Two contains the lore and expands on the runic meanings for the traditional runes contained in earlier works, as well as providing commentaries for all of the runes in the extended Anglo-Frisian system. The third chapter, "A Theory of Operative Runology," in Edred's words, "represents a synthesis of the best academic, or scientific, theories of magic and practical theories of magic." Edred concludes that "magic is dependent upon a system of *communication* between the individual will of the magician and the elements of the universe which lie outside of, or apart from, the individual will." The Runes are a means for such communication.

"The Practice of Operative Runology," our next port of call, leads us into the practical realm and how to communicate with the universe with Runes and effect change by doing so. Edred's focus on the importance of the being of the operator is emphasized here because it overturns the popularly held belief, based on wishful thinking, that, if only the would-be *runer* could find the right formula, he could perform miracles. Of course, only a transformed and disciplined Self can perform acts that defy the usual order, and that is hard work. One must Be in order to Do. Careful attention to this chapter and, equally importantly, working with what it contains, will bring results within the right souls, as those of us who have struggled long and hard within the rigorous regimen of Edred's Rune-Gild know full well. This is our promise but one that all too often falls on deaf ears.

Chapter Five moves on to explaining and offering examples for the operation of workings that Edred calls "Runic Meta-Communication." The practical examples are titled "To Gain Good Luck," "Healing or Good Health," "To Influence Others" and "A Curse Formula." But there is much more here too. There are three appendices. In Appendix A, Edred explains his theory of "Runic Dyads" or how the runes pair up in meaning so that, for example, the first two runes refer to "zoological quadrupeds," and the second two "represent greater-than-human powers," and so on. Appendix B, "Triadic Rune-Names," offers three names and meanings for each of the runes and is a valuable tool. Appendix C, "Grail Mythos in Old English Runes," asks the reader to consider the coincidence (?) that three runes appended to this rune-row, namely those meaning "cup," "stone," and "spear," may be a reference to the Grail Mythos. The book has detailed endnotes, and a full bibliography.

One is never finished with studying this wisdom for it embraces all there is and I, for one, am happy as Larry whenever someone who is on the edge of the known offers us a part of the road map that he created and used to lead him to wherever he has managed to clamber. Our path will not, and could not, be the same as that which Edred has taken, but it does each of us good to deeply consider his thoughts on where his soul has led him.

—Ian Read

Available from Edda Publishing

Fredrik Söderberg: Haus CG Jung (2013)

Recent paintings based on impressions of Carl Gustav Jung's houses at Küsnacht and Bollingen. The architectural structures come to life and display the rich inner vistas of Jung's mythically multi-faceted mind. A visual interpretation of inner life. With an introduction by Gary Lachman.

Carl Abrahamsson: Mother, Have A Safe Trip (2013)

An occult sex thriller set in an international environment. Unearthed plans and designs stemming from radical inventor Nikola Tesla could solve the world's energy problems. These plans suddenly generate a vortex of interest from various powers. Thrown into this maelstrom of international intrigue is Victor Ritterstadt, a soul-searching magician with a mysterious and troubled past. From Berlin, over Macedonia and all the way to Nepal, Ritterstadt sets out on an inner quest. Espionage, love, UFOs, magick, telepathy, conspiracies, LSD and more in this shocking story of a world about to be changed forever.

Aleister Crowley: Snowdrops from a Curate's Garden (2013)

Edited with an introduction by Vere Chappell. Illustrated by Fredrik Söderberg. While at his Scottish retreat Boleskine in 1903, Aleister Crowley decided to amuse his wife Rose and their friends by writing pornography – one new section each day. He concocted a tale that managed to be marvelously creative and utterly repugnant at the same time. No taboo escaped unviolated... Includes 38 pages of exquisite and explicit Söderberg images.

The Fenris Wolf, issue no 6 (2013)

This issue contains material by Genesis Breyer P-Orridge, Michael Horowitz, Frater Achad, Timothy O'Neill, Anton LaVey, Freya Aswynn, Nema, Philip Farber, Kendell Geers, Sasha Chaitow, Shri Gurudev Mahendranath a.k.a. Dadaji, Derek Seagrief, Robert Taylor, Marita, Aki Cederberg, Renata Wieczorek, Gary Dickinson, Vera Nikolich, Robert Morgan, Henrik Bogdan, Alexander Nym, Sara George, Anders Lundgren and Carl Abrahamsson, on topics as diverse as occult London, Tantric quests, rune magic and neurology, Cannabis, LSD, entheogenic influences on culture, the Mega Golem, Aleister Crowley in China, Bogomil Gnostics, decadent French author Josephin Péladan, the birth and death horoscopes of the Great Beast 666, *Liber AL vel Legis*, the psychosexual surrealism of Hans Bellmer, healing, death, the extraterrestrial origins of language, Ernst Jünger's psychedelic approaches, recent Satanic cinema, the occult potential of contemporary physics, "Babalon" as a magical formula, the mystical art of Sulamith Wülfing and a never before published poem, *The Litany of Ra*, by Charles Stansfeld Jones a.k.a. Frater Achad. And more...

Hans Andersson: S/T (2013)

Found photographs, geometrical patterns, torn sheets, crayons and pencils merge in a poetic and low-key expression of a mind fascinated by the dynamic relationship between inner and outer worlds. With an introduction by Peter Cornell.

The Fenris Wolf, issue no 5 (2012)

This issue contains material by/on Jason Louv, Patrick Lundborg, Gary Lachman, Timothy O'Neill, Dianus del Bosco Sacro, David Griffin, Philip Farber, Aki Cederberg, Renata Wieczorek, Genesis Breyer P-Orridge, Ezra Pound, Gary Dickinson, Robert Podgurski, Stephen Ellis, Mel Lyman, Hiram Corso, Frater Nagasiva, Peter Grey, Vera Mladenovska Nikolich, Kevin Slaughter, Lionel Snell, Phanes Apollonius, Lana Krieg and Carl Abrahamsson, on topics as diverse as the psychedelic William Shakespeare, secret societies, Rosicrucians, Illuminati, neurological interpretations of magic, the esoteric gardens of Quinta da Regaleira in Portugal, Italian witchcraft, Pierre Molinier, Derek Jarman, the I Ching, Geomancy, the logic of evil and vice versa, Remy de Gourmont, Aleister Crowley, *Liber AL vel Legis*, Macedonian vampires, Satanism, Goethe's *Faust*, and the creation of a "mega Golem" within the context of developing a contemporary yet timeless terminology of magic.

Edward Bulwer Lytton: Vril, the Power of the Coming Race (2012)

Sir Edward Bulwer Lytton's cautionary tale of occult super-powers and advanced subterranean cultures has fascinated readers since 1871. Part early science-fiction, part educational tract, part occult romance, *Vril* keeps spellbinding readers thanks to its wide range of themes and emotions, as well as its thrilling sense of adventure. Illustrated by Christine Ödlund.

Fredrik Söderberg: Paintings 2008-2012 (2012)

This book presents a selection of Söderberg's paintings. It contains classic images from his exhibitions, spanning thematically over the Golden Dawn, Aleister Crowley, Austin Osman Spare, Franz von Bayros, sacred sites and much more. With an introduction by Carl Abrahamsson.

Here To Go 2012 (2012)

An anthology for/from the symposium *Here To Go*, held in Trondheim in October 2012. Contributors: Martin Palmer, Carl Abrahamsson, Andrew McKenzie, Genesis Breyer P-Orridge, Jesper Aagaard Petersen, Karen Nikgol, Kendell Geers and Gary Lachman.

Available from JD Holmes in the US/Pacific Rim (www.jdholmes.com)
and from Edda in Europe and the rest of the world (www.edda.se)

Edda Publishing, P.O. Box 8105, SE-104 20 Stockholm, Sweden. E-mail: edda@edda.se

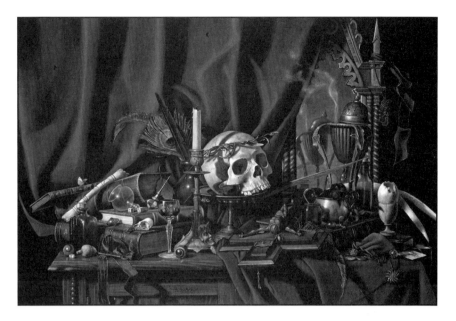

"Vanitas Vanitatum Omnia Vanitas" by Benjamin Vierling.

About the Cover Artist

Benjamin Vierling was born in 1974 and grew up in San Francisco and in the Sierra Nevada foothills in California. Yet while he is undoubtedly a contemporary artist, Vierling is anything but a *modern* artist. Vierling's paintings utilize the *mische* technique, in which egg tempera and oil based paints are combined to create a sense of realist naturalism, liberally infused with light and warmth. This can be seen in the works of old masters like Jan van Eyck and Albrecht Dürer, and in more recent artists like Ernst Fuchs and his student, the visionary painter Brigid Marlin. Invoking the stylistic heritage of the Brotherhood of St. Luke, the Pre-Raphaelites, and the Symbolists, Vierling's works are imbued with an unashamed romanticism that sits uneasily with the ironic detachment and fashionable political engagements of his peers. From his studio in St. Joseph's Cultural Center, a nineteenth-century convent and orphanage built during the California Gold Rush (which has also housed Tibetan monks), Vierling pursues his craft with indifference to the mainstream art establishment.

Nevertheless, Vierling is very much a working artist, and his paintings have appeared on numerous book and album covers. He collaborates regularly with Three Hands Press and Ouroboros Press, boutique esoteric publishers whose luxurious fine editions are the kind of thing even seasoned bibliophiles salivate over. One example is Daniel Schulke's *Veneficium: Magic, Witchcraft, and the Poison Path*, which features Vierling's painting *Sacred Heart*. Inspired by Baroque-era botanical images and Catholic mystical traditions, the piece exemplifies the convergence of form and spirit that is Vierling's forte. This is also evident in his pen and ink drawings, many of which channel the talismanic power of Renaissance alchemical illustrations.

Vierling's album art reflects his interest in the interplay of music and the visual arts, and he has fulfilled commissions for bands like Aosoth, Weapon, The Red King, and Fyrnask. His most ambitious (and famous) album cover to date, however, is the portrait of Joanna Newsom that graces her critically acclaimed 2006 album *Ys*. In an exhaustive article on Newsom that appeared in the magazine *Arthur*, Erik Davis described the painting as "luminescent, esoteric, and vividly detailed," the perfect visual complement to Newsom's oddly ethereal songwriting. Based on an initial sitting with Newson, as well as multiple photographic studies, Vierling spent months working to capture something more immediate and essential than a more literal likeness would have suggested. This is typical of Vierling's portraiture, and he has incorporated impressions of other friends and family members into many of his paintings. A recent solo exhibition at the Gage Academy of Art in Seattle featured his portrait of the graphic artist David V. D'Andrea, and his striking depiction of the Titan Cronus, grimly wielding his *harpē*, bears more than a passing resemblance to Vierling's long-time friend Tyler Davis, who helms the underground music label and publishing house, The Ajna Offensive.

Vierling's work has been included in a number of shows in galleries like Strychnin and Roq La Rue, which tend to specialize in pop surrealism (or what Robert Williams calls "lowbrow art"). However, as with Madeline von Foerster (whose work is frequently displayed with his), Vierling's oeuvre bears only a superficial similarity to the artists featured in *Juxtapoz* or *Hi Fructose*. While he certainly shares the emphasis on technical virtuosity (which the vogue for conceptualism has rendered passé), Vierling's themes have little in common with the often snarky tone of lowbrow art, with its roots in comic books, hot-rod culture, and tattooing. Like the classical European art produced under the patronage of the Church, Vierling's work is a vehicle for the expression of higher principles—albeit freed from the narrative constraints of Christianity.

The image on the cover of this issue of *TYR* is Benjamin Vierling's *Woman With Beast* (2009). The woman's plaintive expression and noble bearing begs more questions than it answers, while the boar she clutches in her alabaster hands has resonances in ancient European culture that span from Celtic iconography to the ship burial at Sutton Hoo. The painting also suggests a rapprochement between civilization and nature, and may be a call to another value espoused by Vierling (and us): the cultivation of wildness.

(Joshua Buckley)

Fine Handcrafted Botanicals & Aromatics

Magical Incense

Recels

Botanical Perfumes

Custom Blends

Germanic & Western Tradition

Made with Natural Resins Herbs, Oils Love & Intent

No Animal Products
No Synthetics

Organic & Wildcrafted Ingredients

INCENDIARY ARTS

WWW.INCENDIARY-ARTS.COM : NADINE@INCENDIARY-ARTS.COM

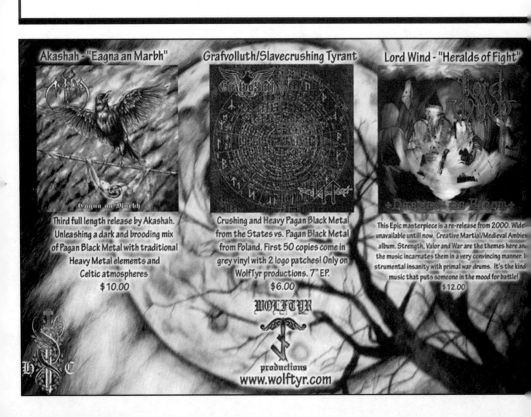

Akashah - "Eagna an Marbh"
Third full length release by Akashah. Unleashing a dark and brooding mix of Pagan Black Metal with traditional Heavy Metal elements and Celtic atmospheres
$10.00

Grafvolluth/Slavecrushing Tyrant
Crushing and Heavy Pagan Black Metal from the States vs. Pagan Black Metal from Poland. First 50 copies come in grey vinyl with 2 logo patches! Only on WolfTyr productions. 7" EP.
$6.00

Lord Wind - "Heralds of Fight"
This Epic masterpiece is a re-release from 2000. Wide unavailable until now. Creative Martial/Medieval Ambient album. Strength, Valor and War are the themes here and the music incarnates them in a very convincing manner. Instrumental insanity with primal war drums. It's the kind music that puts someone in the mood for battle!
$12.00

WOLFTYR productions
www.wolftyr.com

About the Editors

PHOTO BY CARL ABRAHAMSSON.

Michael Moynihan was born in 1969 in New England. He is an artist, musician, author, editor, and occasional winemaker and bookbinder. He has traveled and performed music on both coasts of the USA, in European countries ranging from Portugal to Russia, as well as in Japan. His award-winning non-fiction book *Lords of Chaos* (revised edition: Feral House, 2003), co-written with Didrik Søderlind, has received widespread interest and been translated into nine languages. He has written and edited numerous articles and has contributed to scholarly encyclopedias and topical anthologies. Recent work as a translator includes an annotated edition of *Die religiose Welt der Germanen: Ritual, Magie, Kult, Mythus* by Hans-Peter Hasenfratz, Ph.D., which has been published in English as *Barbarian Rites: The Spiritual World of the Vikings and the Germanic Tribes* (Inner Traditions, 2011). He most recently has collaborated on two volumes relating to the unsung pioneer of grotesque and occult imagery in photography, William Mortensen (1897–1965): as co-editor with Larry Lytle of *American Grotesque: The Life and Art of William Mortensen* and as author of the essay "Infernal Impact: *The Command to Look* as a Formula for Satanic Success" included in the new edition of William Mortensen, *The Command to Look: A Master Photographer's Method for Controlling the Human Gaze* (both books published by Feral House, 2014). With his wife Annabel Lee he also runs a small independent publishing venture, Dominion Press, which has produced works by Stephen Flowers, Hans Bellmer, John Michell, and Joscelyn Godwin in limited hardcover editions (www.dominionpress.net). Email: <dominionpress@comcast.net>

PHOTO BY LIBERTY BUCKLEY.

Joshua Buckley was born in 1974 in Sharon, Connecticut. He has contributed to a number of music-related and other counter-cultural magazines, in addition to pursuing his own publishing ventures. In 2009, he relocated from Atlanta, Georgia to South Carolina, where he lives with his wife Liberty, three daughters, and a variety of animals. He works for an Atlanta-based law firm and teaches Brazilian jiu-jitsu. Email: <elecampane@bellsouth.net>

About the Contributors

Carl Abrahamsson (b. 1966) is a writer, editor, and publisher based in Stockholm, Sweden. (www.carlabrahamsson.com)

Alain de Benoist was born on 11 December 1943. He lives in Paris, and is married with two children. He has studied law, philosophy, sociology, and the history of religions. A journalist and a writer, he is the editor of two journals: *Nouvelle École* (since 1968) and *Krisis* (since 1988). His main fields of interest include the history of ideas, political philosophy, classical philosophy, and archaeology. He has published more than fifty books and three thousand articles. He is also a regular contributor to many French and European publications, journals, and papers (including *Valeurs actuelles*, *Le spectacle du monde*, *Magazine-Hebdo*, *Le Figaro-Magazine*, in France, *Telos* in the United States, and *Junge Freiheit* in Germany). In 1978, he received the Grand Prix de l'Essai from the Academie Francaise for his book *Vu de droite: Anthologie critique des idées contemporaines* (Copernic, 1977). He has also been a regular contributor to the radio program *France-Culture* and has appeared in numerous television debates.

Collin Cleary, Ph.D. is an independent scholar living in Sandpoint, Idaho. He is one of the founders of *TYR*, the first volume of which he co-edited. Cleary is the author of *Summoning the Gods: Essays on Paganism in a God-Forsaken World* (San Francisco: Counter-Currents, 2011) and *What is a Rune? And Other Essays* (forthcoming from Counter-Currents). His essays have appeared in *TYR* and *Rûna*, and have been translated into French, Portuguese, Russian, and Swedish. He is a Master in the Rune-Gild.

Aaron Garland is originally from Atlanta, Georgia but was raised in Las Vegas, Nevada. He launched *Ohm Clock Magazine* in 1993, publishing five issues. The final *Ohm Clock* was released after he moved to Portland, Oregon in 1997. Garland pushed (or perhaps ignored) the limits of political correctness in the hyper-sensitive nineties, and has interviewed underground luminaries such as Robert Ward (*The Fifth Path*), Robert N. Taylor, and Trevor Brown. An interview with Aaron can be found in George Petros's book *Art That Kills*. Since then, he has sporadically contributed music and book reviews to *The Black Flame*, *Dagobert's Revenge*, and *Hex Magazine*. Aaron has accompanied the psychedelic-folk band Blood Axis as a bassist on three European tours in 1998, 2011, and 2013. In addition, he has appeared on a number of studio and live recordings with Blood Axis, In Gowan Ring, and Allerseelen, as well as playing live with Waldteufel. He currently resides in Washington state, and enjoys working in the medical field, spending time with his partner (Nadine Drisseq of Incendiary Arts), and exploring the prolific wilds of the Pacific Northwest.

Joscelyn Godwin is Professor of Music at Colgate University. His recent non-musical writings include *The Golden Thread: The Ageless Wisdom of the Western Mystery Traditions* (Quest Books/Dominion), *Athanasius Kircher's Theatre of the World* (Thames & Hudson/Inner Traditions), *Atlantis and the Cycles of Time* (Inner Traditions), and *The Forbidden Book: A Novel*, co-authored with Guido Mina di Sospiro (Disinformation/RedWheel Weiser).

Forthcoming is *Upstate Cauldron: Eccentric Spiritual Movements in Early New York State* (State University of NY Press). Someday he intends to translate Volumes II and III of the *Introduction to Magic as Science of the Self*, by Julius Evola and the Gruppo di Ur.

Jon Graham is a translator, writer, graphic artist, and editor who was born in 1954. His work has appeared most recently in *Hyperion* and *Abraxas*. His translations include works by André Breton, Hans Bellmer, Annie Le Brun, Alain de Benoist, Jean Markale, and Claude Lecouteux. He lives in Vermont.

Anthony Harberton is an independent scholar living in the northeastern United States.

Steve Harris teaches ancient Germanic languages and cultures at the University of Massachusetts, Amherst. He edits the journal *Old English Newsletter* and runs Old English Publications, LLC with his wife, Marian. They live with their two children in the foothills of the Berkshires.

Greg Johnson, Ph.D., is Editor-in-Chief of Counter-Currents Publishing. His translations from French include works by Maurice Bardèche, Robert Brasillach, Alain de Benoist, Guillaume Faye, Robert Steuckers, Dominique Venner, and Savitri Devi, among others.

Claude Lecouteux is a professor emeritus of the Sorbonne (Paris IV) where he held the chair of Germanic Civilization and Literature in the Middle Ages. He was also director of the academic journal *La grande Oreille, arts de l'oralité*. Only part of his proficient output has been translated into English; these books include *Phantom Armies of the Night*, *The Tradition of Household Spirits*, *The Book of Grimoires*, and *A Lapidary of Sacred Stones*. His book *The High Magic of Talismans & Amulets* was published in 2014. He lives outside Paris.

Annabel Lee, M.A., M.F.A., is an herbalist, musician, translator, and co-director of the independent publishing company Dominion Press. She has translated various works by Claudia Müller-Ebeling, Christian Rätsch, and Wolf-Dieter Storl. Her most recent translations include a collection of Albert Hofmann's essays, *LSD and the Divine Scientist* (Inner Traditions, 2013), and Ernst Jünger's psychedelic novella *The Visit to Godenholm* (forthcoming from Edda Publishing). Her translation of a major biography of Guido von List will be published in 2014. Her musical compositions can be heard on over fifteen recordings, including those of Alraune, Blood Axis, Knotwork, Fire + Ice, In Gowan Ring, and Waldteufel. She also teaches violin and plays Irish traditional music.

James J. O'Meara was born in the American Heartland, educated in Canada, and now lives in an abandoned glove factory in America's Rust Belt. From atop this crumbling remnant of America's industrial might, he broods with morose delectation over the inevitable reappearance of the hordes of youth known to history as the *Männerbünde*, or Wild Boys. His periodic bulletins on their activities appear on his blog, *Where the Wild Boys Are* (http://jamesjomeara.blogspot.com/), and at Counter-Currents.com. His writing has also appeared in *Aristokratia, Alexandria, FringeWare Review*, and *Judaic Book News*. A collection of his essays, *The Homo and the Negro*, was published by Counter-Currents in 2012, and they will bring out another, *The Eldritch Evola . . . & Others*, in 2014.

Nigel Pennick was born in Guildford, Surrey in southern England in 1946. Trained in biology, for fifteen years he was a researcher in algal taxonomy for a government institute. During this time, he published twenty-nine scientific research papers including descriptions of eight new species of marine algae and protozoa before moving on to become a writer and illustrator. He is the author of over forty books on European folk arts, landscape, customs, games, magical alphabets, and spiritual traditions.

Stephen Pollington has been writing on the subject of Anglo-Saxon history for more than two decades. His published work covers such topics as the military, the Old English language, art and material culture, burial mounds, the meadhall, and the herbal healing traditions. His most recent work (in collaboration with Paul Mortimer) deals with the enigmatic stone "sceptre" from Mound 1 at Sutton Hoo, which holds many secrets—revealed by minute examination of a museum-quality replica. His current projects include a review of the first thousand years of runic usage in northern Europe and an examination of the role of Woden in the rise of medieval kingship.

Christian Rätsch, Ph.D., is a world-renowned anthropologist and ethnopharmacologist. For more than thirty years he has researched the medicinal and ritual use of plants, and in particular the cultural usage of psychoactive plants in shamanism. His work has been featured in numerous scholarly publications and he provided extensive contributions to the revised edition of Richard Schultes's and Albert Hofmann's classic text *Plants of the Gods* (Inner Traditions). Books by Christian Rätsch that have appeared in English include *Plants of Love* (Ten Speed Press), *Marijuana Medicine* (Inner Traditions), and *Pagan Christmas* (Inner Traditions), and he is a coauthor, along with Claudia Müller-Ebeling and others, of *Shamanism and Tantra in the Himalayas* and *Witchcraft Medicine* (both published by Inner Traditions). He is also an author of the definitive *Encyclopedia of Psychoactive Plants* and (with Claudia Müller-Ebeling) the *Encyclopedia of Aphrodisiacs* (both also published by Inner Traditions).

Ian Read writes, composes, and sings with his band Fire + Ice. He is the former editor and producer of *Rûna*, a magazine "Exploring Northern European Myth, Mystery and Magic." As Drighten of the Rune-Gild in Europe, Ian teaches runes (mysteries) in the hope that something of the old knowledge will remain when this modern world finally collapses, and a new one is built on its ruins.

Stephen C. Wehmeyer, Ph.D., is a folklorist who specializes in the study of vernacular belief and ritual. A member of the American Folklore Society and the American Academy of Religion, his essays on material culture and ritual arts appear in *Western Folklore*, *Southern Quarterly*, and *African Arts and Social Identities* (among others). He lives in Vermont, where he teaches undergraduate college courses on Aesthetics, Contemporary American Religion, and The Hero Figure in the West. His most recent publication is "Playing Dead: The Northside Skull and Bone Gang" in the exhibition catalog *In Extremis: Death and Life in 21st-Century Haitian Art*, ed. Donald J. Cosentino (Los Angeles: Fowler Museum, 2013).

Markus Wolff is an artist, musician, translator and researcher living in Cascadia. He is currently working on a book about the German artist Fidus and the Life Reform Movement, to be published by Feral House in 2015. His translation of a Hanns Heinz Ewers short story will be published by Ajna Bound in 2014.

Dedication

Our greatest, our God
Our greatest, our Thunder
With your power, with your might
Unite us, strengthen us
Our greatest, our God
Our greatest, our Thunder
The powers of the Oak-tree,
The might of the Oak-tree
Unite us, strengthen us
Our greatest, our God
Our greatest, our Thunder
The brightness of the Fire, the power of the Fire
Unite us, strengthen us

—traditional Lithuanian *daina*

Jonas Jaunius Trinkūnas died on January 20, 2014. A folklorist, philologist, and ethnographer, Trinkūnas is probably best known as the *Krivis*, or high priest, of the Lithuanian heathen revival movement called Romuva.

Lithuanians were the last Europeans to practice an Indo-European pagan religion (Lithuania was officially converted to Christianity in 1387), and they resisted the incursions of Roman Catholic Crusaders until the late fourteenth and early fifteenth centuries. The Romantic period that took place in the nineteenth century saw a re-emergence of interest in these indigenous religious traditions, which had never completely died out.

Due to its unique history, Baltic folk culture is especially rife with evidence of pagan survivals. As in other parts of Europe, openly heathen religious groups began to appear in Lithuania at the beginning of the twentieth century. These efforts were quashed when the Soviet Union occupied Lithuania in 1940, and many Lithuanian heathens were removed to forced labor camps. Baltic paganism posed a dual threat to Stalinist orthodoxy: like Christianity, it represented a stumbling block to the

JONAS JAUNIUS TRINKUNAS: FEBRUARY 28, 1939–JANUARY 20, 2014.

official ideology of atheist materialism but, more importantly, it was a bold expression of Lithuanian ethnic identity.

Jonas Trinkūnas and his wife Inija Trinkūnienė founded the Vilnius Ethnological Ramuva in the 1960s, which worked diligently to document Lithuania's pre-Christian heritage of songs, rituals, and beliefs. In 1967 Trinkūnas helped organize the first Rasos (summer solstice) celebration in Kernavė, the medieval capital of the Grand Duchy. This celebration is recognized as a precursor to the "singing revolution" that fully flowered between 1987 and 1991, a broad cultural resistance movement that helped topple communist hegemony in the Baltic. Unsurprisingly, these overtly nationalist activities attracted the attention of the KGB; as a result, Trinkūnas was stripped of his position in the Philology Department at Vilnius University in 1973. With the loosening of Soviet control under glasnost, Trinkūnas was returned to a post in the University's Institute of Philosophy and Sociology, and he would eventually ascend to the leadership of the Ministry of Culture's Ethnic Culture Division.

During Trinkūnas's exile from academia, his ethno-nationalist interest in Lithuanian folklore deepened into genuine religious conviction. As the Soviet era drew to a close, Ramuva's attempts to revive Lithuanian folklore were bolstered by Romuva's more explicit focus on heathen religious reconstruction. In 1992, Romuva was recognized by the Lithuanian government as a "non-traditional religious community," and it remains an extremely active presence in Lithuania and amongst expatriate Lithuanians in Canada and the United States. Trinkūnas is also well known for his work with the ritualistic folk music ensemble Kūlgrinda. In 1998 he was appointed chairman of the World Congress of Ethnic Religions (re-named the European Congress of Ethnic Religions in 2010), a confederation of ethnic and traditional pagan organizations of Greek, Slavic, Baltic, and Germanic provenance. In 2013, the President of Lithuania awarded Trinkūnas the Order of the Lithuanian Grand Duke Gediminas, an honor bestowed for his dissident activities against the Soviet Union and for his tireless dedication to the preservation of Baltic folk culture.

Jonas Trinkūnas will be remembered by a wife, five daughters, and the entire Romuva community. His spirit will live on in all those who fight for the survival of older European folkways in this age of encroaching darkness. We respectfully dedicate this issue of *TYR* to his memory.

May the Eternal Flame burn through the ages; may the spirit of our ancestors protect us and may the gods and goddesses watch over us.

—Jonas Jaunius Trinkūnas